BLACK
FAMILIES
Second Edition

OTHER RECENT VOLUMES IN THE SAGE FOCUS EDITIONS

BLACK
FAMILIES
Second Edition

Edited by
Harriette Pipes McAdoo

SAGE PUBLICATIONS
The International Professional Publishers
Newbury Park   London   New Delhi

For information address:

SAGE Publications, Inc.
2455 Teller Road
Newbury Park, California 91320

SAGE Publications Ltd.
6 Bonhill Street
London EC2A 4PU
United Kingdom

SAGE Publications India Pvt. Ltd.
M-32 Market
Greater Kailash I
New Delhi 110 048 India

Printed in the United States of America

Library of Congress Cataloging-in-Publication Data

Black families.

   (Sage focus editions ; 41)
   Bibliography: p.
   1. Afro-American families.   I. McAdoo, Harriette
Pipes.
E185.86.B525   1988   305.8′96073   88-3251
ISBN 0-8039-3179-4
ISBN 0-8039-3180-8 (pbk.)

SEVENTH PRINTING, 1991

CONTENTS

PREFACE TO THE FIRST EDITION

The study of Black family life has been an area that has gone through periods of intense activity and then periods of quiescence. At one point it was possible to indicate the one expert in the field and later three or four, but the infusion of researchers has increased the production of research studies, books, and positions on the Black family. This increase in activity has been helpful for the field. It does make it more difficult when one is asked to make a definitive statement about "the Black family." The diversity of Black families, their value systems, and their lifestyles, make it impossible to be "the expert" on Black families. This is as it should be.

This book addresses some unresolved issues regarding Black families. No attempt was made in this volume to represent all sides of each issue, nor were all writings selected to promote any one prevailing view, interest group, or socio-political orientation. A careful reading of the chapters will reveal fundamental unresolved—and some probably unresolvable—differences in frames of reference of Black families represented by the authors.

This lack of consensus keeps the field of Black families lively, volatile, and continuously open to new interpretations as new and old data are incorporated by those writing in the field and those of us living it. The diversity of schools of thought is reflective of the diversities of Black life experiences and is reflected in the title of this book: Black Famil*ies* rather than *The Black Family*.

This diversity is also reflected in the manner in which the racial labels were handled in the various chapters. Conformity in usage is customary in an edited book, but the readers will note variations. The use of racial labels and whether or not to capitalize "black " and "white," during periods of flux, become more than just editorial style; they often become political statements or expressions of personal racial pride or individuality. The histories of our own life experiences, professional training, and ideological stances have affected all our perceptions of families. Conformity would have violated these expressions. Therefore, reflecting the diversity within the field of Black families, the decision was made to let each author decide whether Black, African-American, Afro-American, black, or Negro was to be used within their own chapter.

Some of the best thinkers on the American Black families were selected and asked to prepare chapters that would tie together the major issues, theories, and empirical findings in their area. These contributors were carefully selected from a variety of disciplines, regardless of their philosophical orientation, race, or agreement with my own biases.

This is the third in a series of books published by Sage Publications that began with La Frances Rodgers-Rose's *The Black Woman* and was followed by Lawrence Gary's *Black Men*. *Black Families* ties the male and female together into the family unit as they attempt to survive economically, develop their relationship in order to procreate and raise their children, and move as advocates for their children and families.

DEMYTHOLOGIZING BLACK FAMILIES

As interdisciplinary researchers we have been able to go beyond the negative stereotypical views that had been held as the position on Black families. Unfortunately the wider society has not made this journey, and many of us are continually called upon to speak against the negative images that are held about Black families—held by those who are often in the position to make policy and programmatic decisions that have a direct impact on the lives of Black families. Therefore some of our creative energies are continually channeled into reactionary activities when we would prefer to concentrate upon the more creative theoretical and empirical examinations of Black family life.

The demythologization of negative images about the Black family is an ongoing process that will probably continue for generations, for the ethnocentric concepts held by the mainstream social science literature about Black families will persist. The one main change that has occurred is that fewer writers are able to make blatant conjectures about Black families and remain unchallenged. Publishers and editors of professional journals, the "gate-keepers" of much of the literature on Blacks, have become more sensitized to these issues. While the process of putting myths to rest is essential, we must not truncate all of our efforts to achieve this one objective. This volume is a move to continue the examination of Black families on a conceptual level and to test some of the theories that have been brought forth on the families. It also was an effort to give a complete review within each chapter of the relevant works and to gather the most current facts and figures known about Black families.

DIVERSE CONCEPTUALIZATIONS

There have been major divisions within the field of Black family studies. The major disagreement has focused on whether or not Black families differ from non-Black families in any way other than the formers' greater level of poverty. One view has held that Black families are what they are simply because they are poor; if poverty was removed, then there would be a convergence of values and structure between all families. Another view is that poverty, plus the experience of slavery and Reconstruction, have left an indelible mark on families that has existed to the present. Still another view is that Black families are unique because of the remnants of African culture that have been maintained and have adapted to discrimination. These divisions found among Black scholars are now evolving into the "Africanist" and the "Empiricist" schools, with a growing personal polarity between the two.

The chapters that are included in this volume reflect both points of view and should move us closer to the answer to some of the age-old debates about the Afro-American family. The real "truth" will probably be found to be an amalgamation of all of these views.

There is no denying the soul-satisfying comfort that identification with a known ethnic lode of culture brings, whether it is retained directly from the old country or recreated in part within the new country. Too often the emotional pull of desiring a base of ethnic identification has caused many writers to go far beyond their data or knowledge to create cultural links that may be tenuous. While this performs a needed grounding in an emotional place of origin, it often is not based on a clear understanding of history.

The works of Herskovits (1941), Nobles (1976), Pipes (1951), Semaj (1980), Sudarkasa (1980), and Walker (1980) have contributed to the study in this direction. The link between African and American Black families has become more obvious as scholars have refined their analyses and as more writers join the effort with skills and expertise in cross-cultural analysis. The only danger in this is to avoid the romantic belief that a return to Africanism will somehow eradicate the problems that beset the contemporary Black family, such as plural marriages within a society that do not allow adequate support of even one average Black family. There may be few, if any, one-to-one direct carryovers, but the common patterns that have been found in non-Western families on the African continent, in the Caribbean, and in isolated areas of rural America would make it impossible not to acknowledge that there are some cultural continuities.

At the same time, one must support the view of those who feel that poverty and discrimination are the major factors impinging on Black families. It is a view that attempts to focus on the variables of Black family life in the here and now. Since we can only reconstruct what may have been retained from Africa or acquired during enslavement, emphasis should only be on what we can measure now. This pragmatic approach says that historians and those in literature will eventually be able to piece together more of the patterns that are now only speculation. Meanwhile we can focus on doing good descriptive studies and move into doing more theoretical pieces.

There is so much value that can and will result from the investigations of these two schools of emphasis that there is no need for antagonism between the two. Yet this tension may be the impetus that will generate even greater endeavors. Serious scholars will have to keep abreast of the dynamic debates and explorations that will come from the concentrations on cultural continuities and from the separate approaches.

KEY SCHOLARSHIP OF THE FIELD

This volume on Black families continues in the same vein as the work of DuBois in *The Negro American Family* (1967) and Robert Staples in his volume *The Black Family: Essays and Studies* (1971). In both of these editions the authors brought together what they felt reflected the best work done at that time on Black families. This volume will not give a historical portrayal of Black families but will concentrate on the contemporary family. The history of Black families has been succinctly presented elsewhere by noted writers and should be familiar to readers: DuBois (1967), Quarles (1964), Blassingame (1972), Lammermeier (1973), Bennett (1975), Gutman (1976), Pleck (1979), Haley (1976) and Drake (1980). In addition, there are large-scale studies with which the reader should also be familiar: Scanzoni (1971) and Heiss (1971), and the forthcoming work of James Jackson et al. at the University of Michigan Institute of Social Research.

Following the beginning made by DuBois, Frazier remains the undisputed leader in the social science study of Black families. While there is not total agreement with some of his analyses about family life, the clearness of his methodology, observations, and analyses, and the vacuum that existed before him, place him in a position that even his opponents have had to respect. The next wave of works was spearheaded by the key writers in the field: Billingsley with his *Black Families in White America* and Hill and his *Strengths of Black Families*. These were works that articulated the essence of where we were and where we hoped to go in the field. While not the only voices of that period, these two became the main spokesmen on Black families. Their theoretical and descriptive works provided a springboard for many of the writings on Black families during the 1960s and '70s.

SOURCE OF BLACK FAMILY RESEARCH DATA

There is one problem in highlighting the traditional leaders, for at the same time there were other scholars in different fields who were making similar observations but whose works were never picked up in the popular professional press. A review of many of the earlier Negro journals, newspapers, and writings in literature, anthropology, religion, education, and social organizations leads one to an awareness of the masses of beautifully documented works that exist scattered over the country and are therefore lost to scholars.

Even today dissertations are being written that are breaking new ground, but for a variety of reasons these findings are not being made known to others in the field. The doctoral and Master's dissertations that are found in the Howard University library, and materials in its Moreland Room, are probably the richest untapped source of information on Black life. Many of the works that were done on a Master's level in the first half of this century are far superior to doctoral dissertations that are now done in the major universities. This is the result of the striving for excellence and the Ivy League-trained professors who came to Howard, attracted by the caliber of minds on the campus and because of the racism that would not allow them positions on the non-Black campuses. They demanded and received a level of scholarship that would be difficult to replicate today with few exceptions.

Across the country are resources on Black family research that are being tapped only slightly: Atlanta and Fisk Universities are two others. Much of the archival work is being done at the larger universities that are able to provide resources that archivists, historians, and oral historians need. The Smithsonian has become another focal point during the present period.

The one continuing resource for data on Black family life has been the Black publications that are put out by professional organizations and a dedicated group of scholars *(Journal of Black Psychology, Black Scholar, Journal of Behavior and Social Scientist, The Western Journal of Black Studies)*. The problems are the costs and energy required to maintain these efforts, without the needed university or institutional support. Graduate students' works may not be exposed, and their professors are not familiar with them. These sources of data, in essence, have not been "validated" by the mainstream profession and thus are denied to graduate students, Black and white, who want to use them as their main theoretical bases. The lack of validation limits the use by students but frees writers and editors to take directions that are supportive of scholarly examination unhindered by acceptability of organized mainstream scholarship.

It would be myopic to indicate that only Black institutions and Black researchers are making inroads in advancing Black family studies. Several professional organizations have supported the efforts on scholarship on Black families. The National Council on Family Relations' *Journal of Marriage and the Family* took leadership with their Decade Reviews written by Robert Staples et al. and the groundbreaking special edition on Black families edited by Marie Peters. Black families had been so ignored in the major professional social science journals that this one edition significantly increased the number of articles published on Black families. The National Association of Social Workers has done likewise with their special edition, edited by June Hopps, on People of Color. Several other "special editions" have further disseminated the work on Black families.

While these target editions have made special contributions, it is unfortunate that Black family studies and papers are not regularly included in the ongoing editions of all major journals. For a variety of ethnocentric reasons, and lack of knowledge about the myriad of work done in this field, editors have not routinely included work on or by Blacks. This situation may be improved in the future with a more active participation of Blacks and other minorities in professional organizations and the professional publication processes. Meanwhile, the reality is that many social scientists do not value the diversity that is found in Black families, so the attitudes that are often encountered by Black researchers require that an active participation and support of the Black-oriented publication efforts must be continued. It will be necessary to continue actively giving energies on both fronts for the foreseeable future.

ROLES PLAYED BY PROFESSIONAL MEETINGS
IN BLACK FAMILY RESEARCH

The major professional organizations often are the validators of the field and control the academic and professional futures of young researchers and, indirectly, the funds for their research efforts. Therefore, a continuation of the integration of knowledge of Black family life is required to make it into the mainstream literature that will be available to all researchers. At the same time, the freedom to take unpopular positions and exploratory thrusts will not be allowed within mainstream journals. These efforts are only possible within journals or institutions that have gone beyond such debates as "Are Black families really a valid subject area?" "Are these really just polemic exercises?" "Are we giving too much emphasis to minorities?" "Can't we just focus on 'good research' and forget about all of this race business?"

There have been other points where the needed dialogue has become traditional. The annual meetings of the Association of Black Psychologists have become a rallying point for many researchers to expend and refresh their own concepts on Black families. The annual conferences that are held at the University of Louisville on Black families have become another point of excitement for those of us immersed in the field. Their selected themes each year have allowed attendees to become up-to-date on many unknown activities that are going on across the country. These meetings allow the "older" researchers in the field to come together and speak to each other, meet younger researchers, and return home to continue their concentration on families.

In past years symposia have been presented at the National Council on Family Relations by some of the contributors to this volume (Staples, Peters, Nobles, McAdoos, Hill, Johnson) on Black families. At each biennial meeting of the Society for Research on Child Development, contributors to this volume (Harrison, Peters, and the editor) have organized and presented information on the Black family and child. There has been a definite effort in these two organizations to bring together those who are doing work on the Black family and those who are working with Black children, for the problems and concerns with one will indirectly affect the other.

Similar efforts have continued over the years at other major professional meetings. Seminars have been organized by Peters and McAdoo at Groves Conference on Marriage and the Family for five years, which have brought together some of the key Black and other minority researchers to focus on one theme each year. The cross-fertilization that has grown out of these efforts has been widespread. These have allowed researchers and writers from all races to come together and share information. They have had some impact on those who are writing the textbooks to be used in college classrooms throughout the country and have brought together researchers for the first time from different disciplines who may never attend the same professional conferences. Similar efforts have been made by the contributors to this book and others at the American Educational Research Association, the National Association of Education for Young Children, American Sociological Association, and American Psychological Association. In addition, the Black and minority caucuses, sections, special interest groups, and other subdivisions of these professional organizations are contributing to the professional socialization of Black professionals and the dissemination of information on Black family life.

There was a period when a poor piece of research was heard and then quietly ignored, for a researcher who focused on Black families often came under so much attack from those in the profession that it was considered contrary to "the code" to also speak out against poor work (Welsing, 1970). We are no longer within the reactionary frame of reference when it was felt unwise to differ with the "leaders." We have to be able to give and receive criticisms within the field on any piece of research that is presented. Efforts at internal critiques have been found in the past six years among a small group of researchers who come together each year to present and to be critiqued in closed sessions at the Conference on Empirical Black Psychology. Papers have been presented and critiqued, and have become stronger as a result. This process supports younger researchers who feel they are unable to get this type of support at their diverse academic institutions and agencies.

In addition to the sometimes esoteric dialogues that are held at professional meetings, the real-world problems of families are continuing to be addressed by those in the community who are providing the leadership in the family advocacy organizations. At their seminars, annual meetings, during media briefings, and in publications, they are acting as watchdogs over the erosion of the Black family resources. They have made evaluations and designed programs and public education efforts in order to allow community persons and parents to take an effective active part in bettering the condition of their family life.

Organizations such as the Urban League, Children's Defense Fund, the National Black Child Development Institute, the NAACP, and the National Council of Negro Women are the major groups. Representatives from the key organizations have presented areas where efforts should be targeted and agendas that could be followed in each community.

PERSONAL REFLECTIONS

One of my special delights in this book was the in-depth study I was able to make of my father's book that led to the excerpt that is presented herein. I had quickly read the book for interest in high school and as an undergraduate, mostly looking for good references, so I felt I knew its contents. But it was only after going over the book repeatedly to select one of the sermons for this volume that I really had a chance to see all of the richness that was included in *Say Amen, Brother!* The Georgia sermons are a vivid reminder of the central role the rural "Black belt" churches played throughout the South. With the growing interest developing in oral history of the Black experience, several persons and major libraries have made copies of these now rare sermons, for mobility, education, and "sophistication" have gradually changed this sermon style, a direct link to the religious patterns found immediately after and probably during enslavement.

When I was a child, my parents, Bill Pipes and Anna Russell Pipes, would take me, their Victor recording machine, and a Brownie box camera down old dusty roads to the little churches to participate in the all-day church meetings, in order to make the recordings that are included in this chapter. I have vague memories of the recordings, and I grew up with the pictures and recordings of these sermons.

It is typical that children take their parents' works for granted and do not pay them the attention they deserve, since these books have always been around on our bookshelves. My oldest sons are having that experience now in college. They paid no attention to the stacks of papers and books all over the house as they grew up, until they were in a class and saw their parents' articles in a bibliography. They are amazed that anyone would bother to read them, let alone think that the papers that they had to eat around on the dining room table were worth their effort to read. They, as I pleasantly was, were surprised and delighted when they finally sat down and really began to understand what their parents had been doing all those years. This process was particularly poignant for me because my father died during the last stages of the production of this book.

Harriette Pipes McAdoo

REFERENCES

ASCHENBRENNER, J. (1973) "Extended families among Black Americans." Journal of Comparative Family Studies 4.

BENNETT, L. (1975) The Shaping of Black America. Chicago: Johnson.

BILLINGSLEY, A. (1968) Black Families in White America. Englewood Cliffs, NJ: Prentice-Hall.

BLASSINGAME, J. (1972) The Slave Community Plantation Life in the Ante-Bellum South. New York: Oxford University Press.

CLARKE, J. H. (1975) "The Black Family in historical perspective." Journal of Afro-American Issues 3, Nos. 3 & 4.

DRAKE, St. C. (1980) "Anthropology and the Black experience." Black Scholar 11, No. 7: 2-31.

DuBOIS, W. E. B. (1967) The Philadelphia Negro: A Social Study. New York: Schocken.

———— (1908) The Negro American Family. Cambridge: Massachusetts Institute of Technology.

FOGEL, R. and S. ENGERMAN (1974) Time on the Cross. Boston: Little, Brown.

FRAZIER, E. F. (1939) The Negro Family in the United States. Chicago: University of Chicago Press.

GURMAN, H. (1976) The Black Family in Slavery and Freedom, 1750-1925. New York: Pantheon.

HALEY, A. (1976) Roots: The Saga of an American Family. New York: Doubleday.

HEISS, J. (1971) The Case of the Black Family: A Sociological Inquiry. New York: Columbia University Press.

HERSKOVITS, M. J. (1941) The Myth of the Negro Past. New York: Harper.

HILL, R. H. (1972) The Strengths of Black Families. New York: Emerson-Hall.

LAMMERMEIER, P. J. (1974) "The urban Black family of the nineteenth century: A study of Black family structure in the Ohio Valley, 1850-1880." Journal of Marriage and the Family 35: 440-456.

NOBLES, W. (1976) "A formulative and empirical study of Black families." DHEW Publication (OCD-90-C-255). Washington, DC: Office of Child Development, Department of Health, Education and Welfare.

PIPES, W. H. (1951) Say Amen, Brother! New York: William-Frederick Press.

PLECK, E. H. (1979) Black Migration and Poverty: Boston 1865-1900. New York: Academic Press.

QUARLES, B. (1964) The Negro in the Making of America. New York: Collier Books.

SCANZONI, J. (1971) The Black Family in Modern Society. Boston: Allyn & Bacon.

SEMAJ, L. (1980) "Meaningful male/female relationships in a state of declining sex ratio." Black Books Bulletin 6.

SHIMKIN, D. B., G. J. LOUIE, and D. A. FRATE (1978) "The Black extended family: a basic rural institution and a mechanism of urban adaptation," in D. B. Shimkin, E. M. Shimkin, and D. A. Frate (eds.) The Extended Family in Black Cities. The Hague: Mouton.

STAPLES, R. [ed.] (1971) The Black Family: Essays and Studies. Belmont, CA: Wadsworth.

SUDARKASA, N. (1980) "African and Afro American family structure: A comparison." Black Scholar, Journal of Black Studies and Research 11, No. 8: 37-60.

WALKER, S. (1980) "African Gods in America: the Black religious continuum." Black Scholar, Journal of Black Studies and Research 11, No. 8: 25-36.

WELSING, F. (1970) The Cress Theory of Color Confrontation and Racism. Washington, DC: Welsing.

PREFACE TO THE SECOND EDITION

Significant changes have occurred in the lives of Black families across the nation during the past six years. Major policy changes at the Federal and local levels have truncated governmental programs that had contributed to the vulnerability of many of our families, and the occupational and educational avenues that are open for members of Black families. While some Blacks have benefited from earlier governmental programs of support and have been upwardly mobile, many others have fallen deeper into despair.

Governments have become more conservative and apparently less interested in supporting the striving toward stability and equality of family members of color. Verbal assertions of the need for economic self-sufficiency have run parallel to policy decisions that have limited the opportunities of families to remove themselves from dependency. The prevailing preference for white over Black has continued, has intensified, and has led to more overt demonstrations of structural and personal ethnocentricism and racism.

A decade that began with hope has not lived up to expectations. The need is even greater now to understand the economic situations, cultural patterns, and socialization practices of Black families. The African-American patterns of mutual support and coping strategies that were so effective in the past are more important now than ever. The authors of chapters in the second edition of Black Families have continued to make important contributions in their various fields. All the contributors have been actively living their own family lives, as can be seen by comparing their descriptions in the 1981 edition and this 1988 edition. We are all seven years older and, we hope, wiser. During this period babies have been born, marriages have ended, spouses have passed, children have graduated from college (three of mine from Howard), children have married, a Ph.D. degree was completed, tenure and professorships were earned, important awards were received, jobs have ended, and important professional positions have been assumed. These significant life changes are often reflected in the work of the authors.

Since the first edition was published, two of the contributors have died: my father, William Harrison Pipes, and one of my dearest friends, Marie Ferguson Peters. Both of them are dearly missed by me and by many of us.

This revised volume grew out of the need to bring the content current with ongoing research and literature, to reflect the demographic changes that have occurred in the past six years, and to expand the topics into newly relevant areas. Many of the classic chapters remain as they were. The new authors reflect the issues that have come to the forefront during the 1980s. Four new contributors have joined us: John Hope Franklin, Joyce Ladner, Julianne Malveaux, and Audrey Chapman. Their chapters have added special insights and depth to the volume. We welcome them to our collective effort. We hope that this Sage Focus Edition will contribute to greater understanding of the lives of Black families and the issues that must be addressed to successfully prepare us for the next generation of Black Families.

Harriette Pipes McAdoo

ACKNOWLEDGMENTS

The impetus for this volume originally came out of my frustration at not being able to find a book on Black families for my graduate classes at Howard University. I grew tired of teaching my family and child development courses from piles of reprints and library assignments. There were excellent individual works on Blacks, but they were all scattered around and difficult to assemble for a single course. I felt a strong need to assemble one volume of writings from the excellent scholars in the field that could be used for a survey course on Black families or as a supplement to family studies courses.

Many individuals were involved in the development of this volume. The authors of the chapters were the key contributors. For each topic, I invited the person whose work I most respected in that particular area. I was delighted that everyone who was asked was willing to take the time out of their crowded schedules to produce these chapters. The contributors themselves reflect diverse points of views and professional orientations, and I felt that this was appropriate to reflect the diversities of Black family lives. Attempts have been made to avoid stereotypical presentations of "The Black Family," a nonexistent entity.

The content of this book grew from my intense readings of the works of others over the years, presentations made at various professional conferences, lengthy discussions with my colleagues at Howard and around the country, and my own personal research and life experiences. Additional impetus came from participation in several professional organizations and meetings: the Groves Conference on Marriage and the Family; the National Council of Family Relations and its Ethnic Minorities Section; the National Association of Black Psychology; the Society of Research on Child Development; and the American Sociological Association. Our presentations, discussions, and interactions at these meetings have generated excitement about the field and have been supportive for those of us who often work in isolation.

Finally, the real impetus for writing about Black families grew from my own experiences of living within my own family of orientation, the Pipes family of Mississippi and the Russell family of Kentucky. My McAdoo family of procreation, composed of my husband John and our four children—Michael, John III, Julia, and David—has provided me with all the complexities, love, child-rearing traumas, support, and pride that could possibly be found in any family.

The first edition of Black Families received partial support from the Center for Minority Health of the National Institute of Mental Health and Columbia Research Systems, Inc. This second edition was supported by the McAdoo family and partially by a sabbatical leave from Howard University. Special thanks are given to Elsie Zdanis who typed the entire first edition and whose organizational skills were instrumental in the effort, even into this second edition. Other peers and friends, who remain anonymous, did blind reviews of the chapters and provided important feedback to all of us. Finally, thanks should be given to Mitch Allen of Sage Publications, whose patience was repeatedly tried as deadlines were missed during a rather traumatic year.

PART I

HISTORIC AND THEORETICAL CONCEPTUALIZATIONS OF AFRICAN-AMERICAN FAMILIES

We begin the discussion of the African American family with a overview of families within this country. As only he is able to do, John Hope Franklin presents a beautiful statement of the experiences of our families. He highlights the attempts of the enslaved men to be reunited with their wives and children when they had been sold away. The importance of the strong family tradition to the community of enslaved Africans is emphasized, as the families continued with two parents despite impoverishment.

Niara Sudarkasa's work on African and Afro-American family organization brings knowledge from an anthropological view and succinctly critiques, refutes, and sometimes supports the earlier works of Black and non-Black writers on the Black family. Sudarkasa gives an excellent overview of African family structure in an attempt to shed light on the forms and function of Black American family structure as developed within the context of slavery. The enslaved Africans were seen as placing consanguinity or biological kinship (by blood) over that kinship based on affinity (by law) or conjugality (by marriage). This emphasis is seen as the major difference between European and African families. This cultural-historical basis is the origin of Black family organizational differences, even when political and economic differences are held constant. In contrast to Gutman, Sudarkasa does not see the family structure as an adaptation to enslavement. She differs in part with Herskovits and supports Frazier in the formation of female-as-head domestic units that developed during slavery, an unknown permanent unit within western African culture. After enslavement, the extended family became the focus, not the households, with the kin networks having many of the features of the continental African extended family, built around the consanguine kin. Some of the corporate functions of lineages reemerged within the extended families.

The chapter by Wade Nobles focuses on the importance of the parent-child relationship and the need for the family to be geared to prepare the child for a unique type of existence in a hostile, racist societal environment. With a strong Afrocentric view, it gives a sound background for the scientific racism that formed the groundwork that allowed one group to receive preferential treatment over another. Nobles explores the changes that have occurred in social scientists' coverage of the Black family and the seminal work of Billingsley, Hill, and Staples. He uses the analogy of the centuries-long enslavement of Africans as an analogy to the existence of Blacks today. The supportive network of the extended family has been used to protect the child; and three domains are outlined that must receive attention if the children are to realize their potential: a sense of history, a strong sense of family, and a sense of the need and power of spiritual beliefs. It ties neatly into the chapters of Sudarkasa on the extended family and that by Pipes on the importance of religious participation. Nobles ends his chapter with the assertion that if the family is able to perform these responsibilities, then it is imperative that the state be supportive of the family. Nobles adds an element of spirituality that one does not often find in the family literature. He presents the cultural base but also supports the chapters by Hill and Edelman, on the importance of the parents operating within knowledge of the political system in providing for the children, but not at the expense of leaving the spiritual or cultural components of their lives to chance.

The Africanist versus culture of poverty debate is continued in the Pipes chapter. The amazing contrast about the Sudarkasa and Pipes chapters is that the works were done 40 years apart, yet they were addressing, in part, the same issues and arguments: the sources of Black American family and religious or cultural values. Although their fields of emphasis differ—one in anthropology and the other in speech and literature—their conclusions are the same. This shows one that we are still arguing the same arguments. More recent writers are not familiar with the writings that were done by the Negro intellectuals before the turn of the century and during the first half of this century. The fact that certain issues are still introduced in 30-year cycles reflects the importance of these issues to Black life and identity. The review of authors whose works are often unavailable today will add much to the present literature.

The analyses of the diverse concepts that are held on the Black family continue with the reflective analyses of Jualynne Dodson, in which she reviews the writers in the three major schools of thought: pathological or dysfunctional; cultural relativity; and social class as main determinant. For each school she gives an in-depth review of the major writers and the chief beliefs held by those in each school. This is presented within a historical context. This analysis is invaluable because it sets the stage for the chapters that follow: some were written by authors who represent one of the three identified schools of thought. She stresses the need for further empirical research before we are able to make a definitive statement about the cultural origins of Black family life. A schema is given within the reflective analyses of the minimum requirements needed to effectively evaluate the Black family.

Johnson effectively rounds out the discussion on diverse conceptualizations with her empirical study of the theoretical frameworks that have been presented in the sociology and social work journals with the widest circulation during the period 1965-1978. She first presents two conceptual frameworks on the value orientations reflected about the Black family, as presented by Walter Allen and Robert Staples, that are similar to those of Dodson's reflective analysis. Allen's three stages show the changes in orientation that the literature has taken as it has gone from a deviant view, to an equivalent view, and finally to a cultural relative view of the Black family and its function. Staples presented four trend stages that relate to the change in emphasis from looking at families as only victims of poverty, to pathological, to the reactionary stances of the 1960s, and finally to the emphasis on functionality of families, regardless of structure. In each is the clear value that one should put on the later stages, in preference for the earlier stages. Johnson took all the articles that related to the Black family from the ten journals and applied both typologies to each. This extremely useful analysis indicated that less than one percent of all empirical studies related to the Black family, and most of those were in special issues edited by Blacks or Black journals. Social work journals during that time were found to be surprisingly negligent in their coverage of Black families. Earlier articles tended to stress deviance and the later ones, especially those by Black researchers, tended to focus on Black uniqueness without the comparison with white family norms. Johnson lists each of the articles surveyed and provides a rating on each of the value orientations and the topics covered. This should be potentially useful for other researchers who would want to avoid those articles that have been rated as using the cultural deviant or pathological framework.

1

A HISTORICAL NOTE ON BLACK FAMILIES

JOHN HOPE FRANKLIN

The family is one of the strongest and most important traditions in the black community. How much of this tradition is an African survival and how much was developed in the New World is impossible to determine. It was doubtless some of both.

There is no question that early in their sojourn on this continent, enslaved Africans evinced their concern about the family unit. Their loyalty to the family defied the efforts of slave owners to promote a casual attitude among blacks toward this all-important institution. A great deal has been written about gentlemen slave owners who would not separate families, but the evidence clearly refutes this. "I think it is quite probable that this [runaway] . . . has succeeded in getting to his wife who was carried away last spring out of my neighborhood," one advertisement read. A Florida owner advertised for a 14-year-old who had escaped and was trying to reach Atlanta, where his mother was supposed to be. Another runaway was no doubt lurking in a certain vicinity near her children. Still another escapee was believed to be near Savannah, where he had a wife and children. Literally thousands of examples are known of slaves running away in search of members of their families. The attachment was real, and the warmth of their relationships persisted, despite their separation by the so-called gentlemen who claimed they never did such things.

The family was important to the slave community, if for no other reason than the lack of other institutions to which slaves could openly be committed.[1] In the quiet and intimacy of the family, slaves could provide the mutual support so necessary to withstand the abuses and cruelties of slavery. They married early and, if necessary, frequently—usually with the encouragement of the owner, especially if the prospects were bright for numerous offspring, which, of course, were additional capital for him.

Many slave men preferred to marry women from other plantations. As John Anderson put it, "I did not want to marry a girl belonging to my own place, because I knew I could not bear to see her ill-treated." Henry Bibb put it even more eloquently: "If my wife must be exposed to the insults and licentious passions of wicked slave drivers and overseers; if she must bear the stripes of the lash laid on by an unmerciful tyrant; if this is to be done with impunity, which is frequently done by slaveholders and their abettors, Heaven forbid that I should be compelled to witness the sight."

At the end of the Civil War, freedmen searched frantically for family members separated by slavery. Some wrote the Freedmen's Bureau seeking assistance in locating loved ones. One man who had fled to Pittsburgh in the antebellum period asked the Bureau in Greenville, South Carolina to help him find his parents. Some freedmen, not knowing where to turn or what to do, simply got on the road and began to search for their wives, husbands, or children. Some were successful; some were not. Some discovered that their mates had remarried, having given up hope of a reunion. In those early years following emancipation, nothing was more poignant than the sight of separated families attempting to reestablish their relationships. The institution of slavery had not destroyed the black family.

Since many slaves had been married by the mere consent or even suggestions of their owners, they sought at the end of the war to make their marriages legal and their children legitimate. In 1866, for example, 9,452 former slaves from 17 North Carolina counties registered their marriages by entering their names on the marriage records and paying the 25-cent fee. Herbert Gutman, who discovered the North Carolina records, tells us that many couples took the next step and participated in secular or religious marriage ceremonies. That this rural and illiterate population, fresh from slavery and living in the aftermath of a devastating war, could turn from their urgent activities and numerous anxieties to legitimatize their marriages, tells us something of the extent to which the sense of family was a part of the very fabric of the Afro-American community.

Family stability in the black community survived Reconstruction and was alive and well at the end of the nineteenth century. In the 1880s, most rural and urban southern blacks lived in husband- or father-present households and subfamilies. During those years, however, the number of women over 40 years of age heading father-absent households and subfamilies increased. In some instances the husband died. In others, he went away to work. The practice persisted, moreover, for young, single mothers to live with their parents or other adults, thus relieving them of the responsibility of heading a household. Gutman (1976) pointed out that in 1900 the kin-related household was the norm, and the size of the household had hardly changed since the end of Reconstruction. Long marriages continued to be common among rural and urban southern blacks, "and so was the attachment of parent to child."

It is remarkable that the great migration of blacks to the urban North during World War I and subsequent years did not adversely affect the stability of the black family to any significant degree. In Manhattan, for example, where the black population increased rapidly between 1905 and 1925, the black family remained intact, although it differed in characteristics from the southern rural and urban black families of a generation earlier. There were many foreign blacks—mostly West Indian—and understandably more boarders and lodgers than one saw in the South. Also, the simple nuclear household tended to decline in importance, while extended and augmented households increased in importance.

Surprisingly, with all these changes during these crucial years, no significant increase in male-absent households or subfamilies occurred. In 1925, for example, six of seven households had either a husband or father. As Herbert Gutman (1976) concluded in his *The Black Family in Slavery and Freedom,* "At all moments in time between 1880 and 1925—that is, from an adult generation born in slavery to an adult generation about to be devastated by the Great Depression of the 1930s and the modernization of southern agriculture afterward—the typical Afro-American family was lower-class in status and headed by two parents. This was so in the urban and rural South in 1880 and in 1900 and in New York City in 1905 and 1925. It was just as common among farm laborers, sharecroppers, tenants, and northern and southern urban unskilled laborers and service workers. It accompanied the southern blacks in the great migration to the North that has so reshaped the United States in the twentieth century."

The strong family tradition among blacks thus survived the slave system, then legal segregation, discrimination, and enforced poverty, and finally, they had to contend with racially hostile governmental and societal practices, policies, and attitudes. These forces ultimately weakened a family fabric that had for generations proved unusually resilient, even in the face of awesome adversity. Indeed, until the 1960s, a remarkable 75 percent of black families included both husband and wife. In 1983, *A Policy Framework for Racial Justice* concluded: "Since the 1960s, rapid urbanization, and especially ghettoization, has had a devastating impact on many black families. As large numbers of blacks migrated to large cities from rural areas, black males have often been unable to find work, and government policies and other social forces further sapped family strength. These trends proceed apace today, aided by the widespread failure even to recognize the pressures on the black family as central to other problems and by the failure to devise both preventive and healing strategies."

NOTES

1. A version of this chapter will be incorporated in the National Academy of Science's report on the status of black Americans.

REFERENCES

FRANKLIN, J. H. (1987) From Slavery to Freedom, The History of Negro Americans. New York: Knopf.
GUTMAN, H. (1976) The Black Family in Slavery and Freedom, 1750-1925. New York: Pantheon.
A Policy Framework for Racial Justice (1983) Washington, DC: Joint Center for Political Studies.

2

INTERPRETING THE AFRICAN HERITAGE IN AFRO-AMERICAN FAMILY ORGANIZATION

NIARA SUDARKASA

Many of the debates concerning explanations of Black family organization are waged around false dichotomies. The experience of slavery in America is juxtaposed to the heritage of Africa as *the* explanation of certain aspects of Black family structure. "Class" versus "culture" becomes the framework for discussing determinants of household structure and role relationships. Black families are characterized either as "alternative institutions" or as groups whose structures reflect their "adaptive strategies," as if the two viewpoints were mutually exclusive.

Just as surely as Black American family patterns are in part an outgrowth of the descent into slavery (Frazier, 1939 [1966]), so too are they partly a reflection of the archetypical African institutions and values that informed and influenced the behavior of those Africans who were enslaved in America (Herskovits, 1941 [1958]). With respect to "class" and "culture," it is indeed the case that the variations in historical and contemporary Black family organization cannot be explained without reference to the socioeconomic contexts in which they developed (Allen, 1979). But neither can they be explained without

AUTHOR'S NOTE: I wish to thank Tao-Lin Hwang for his assistance with the research for this chapter, and Bamidele Agbasegbe Demerson for his helpful comments.

reference to the cultural contexts from which they derived (Nobles, 1974a, 1974b, 1978). Whereas Black families can be analyzed as groups with strategies for coping with wider societal forces (Stack, 1974), they must also be understood as institutions with historical traditions that set them apart as "alternative" formations that are not identical to (or pathological variants of) family structures found among other groups in America (Aschenbrenner, 1978).

After more than a decade of rethinking Black family structure (see, for example, Billingsley, 1968; Staples, 1971, 1978; Aschenbrenner, 1973; English,1974; Sudarkasa, 1975a; Allen, 1978; Shimkin et al., 1978), it is still the case that a holistic theory of past and present Black family organization remains to be developed. Such a theory or explanation must rest on the premise that political-economic variables are *always* part of any explanation of family formation and functioning, but that the cultural historical derivation of the formations in question helps to explain the nature of their adaptation to particular political-economic contexts.

Obviously, it is beyond the scope of this chapter to try to set forth such a holistic explanation of Black family organization. Its more modest aim is to take a step in this direction by laying to rest one of the false dichotomies that stand in the way of such an explanation. This review seeks to show how an understanding of African family structure sheds light on the form and functioning of Black American family structure as it developed in *the context of slavery* and later periods. It seeks to elucidate African institutional arrangements and values that were manifest in the family organization of Blacks enslaved in America, and suggests that some of these values and institutional arrangements continue to be recognizable in contemporary formations.

The relationships of causality, correlation, and constraint that exist between the political-economic sphere and that of the family cannot be dealt with here. What the chapter seeks to clarify is why Black familial institutions embrace certain alternatives of behavior and not others. It suggests a cultural historical basis for the fact that Black family organization differs from that of other groups even when political and economic factors are held relatively constant.

Thus, it is suggested that it cannot suffice to look to political and economic factors to explain, for example, the difference between lower-class Anglo- or Italian-American families and lower-class Afro-American families. One has to come to grips with the divergent culture histories of the groups concerned. In other words, one is led back to the institutional heritage stemming from Western Europe on the one hand and from West Africa on the other. Knowledge of the structure and functioning of kinship and the family in these areas helps to explain the structure and functioning of families formed among their descendants in America.

It might appear that this is too obvious a point to be belabored. However, when it comes to the study of Black American families, the scholarly community has historically taken a different view. Whereas it is generally agreed that the history of the family in Europe is pertinent to an understanding of European-derived family organization in America (and throughout the world), many—if not most—scholars working on Black American families have argued or assumed that the African family heritage was all but obliterated by the institution of slavery. This view has retained credence, despite the accumulation of evidence to the contrary, in large measure because E. Franklin Frazier (1939), the most prestigious and prolific student of the Black American family, all but discounted the relevance of Africa in his analyses.

This chapter takes its departure from W.E.B. DuBois (1908[1969]), Carter G. Woodson (1936), and M. J. Herskovits (1958), all of whom looked to Africa as well as to the legacy of slavery for explanations of Afro-American social institutions. Herskovits is the best-known advocate of the concept of African survivals in Afro-American family life, but DuBois was the first scholar to stress the need to study the Black American family against the background of its African origins. In his 1908 study of the Black family, DuBois prefaced his discussions of marriage, household structure, and economic organization with observations concerning the African antecedents of the patterns developed in America.

> In each case an attempt has been made to connect present conditions with the African past. This is not because Negro-Americans are Africans, or can trace an unbroken social history from Africa, but because there is a distinct nexus between Africa and America which, though broken and perverted, is nevertheless not to be neglected by the careful student [DuBois, 1969: 9].

Having documented the persistence of African family patterns in the Caribbean, and of African derived wedding ceremonies in Alabama, DuBois noted:

> Careful research would doubtless reveal many other traces of the African family in America. They would, however, be traces only, for the effectiveness of the slave system meant the practically complete crushing out of the African clan and family life [p. 21].

With the evidence that has accumulated since DuBois wrote, it is possible to argue that even though the constraints of slavery did prohibit the replication of African lineage ("clan") and family life in America, the principles on which these kin groups were based, and the values underlying them, led to the emergence of variants of African family life in the form of the extended families which developed among the enslaved Blacks in America. Evidence of the Africanity to which DuBois alluded is to be found not only in the relatively few "traces" of direct *institutional transfer* from Africa to America, but also in the numerous examples of *institutional transformation* from Africa to America.

No discussion of the relevance of Africa for understanding Afro-American family organization can proceed without confronting the issue of the "diversity" of the backgrounds of "African slaves" (read "enslaved Africans") brought to America. Obviously for certain purposes, each African community or each ethnic group can be described in terms of the linguistic, cultural, and/or social structural features which distinguish it from others. At the same time, however, these communities or ethnic groups can be analyzed from the point of view of their similarity to other groups.

It has long been established that the Africans enslaved in the United States and the rest of the Americas came from the Western part of the continent where there had been a long history of culture contact and widespread similarities in certain institutions (Herskovits, 1958: chs. 2 and 3). For example, some features of kinship organization were almost universal. Lineages, large co-resident domestic groups, and polygynous marriages are among the recurrent features found in groups speaking different languages, organized into states as well as "segmentary" societies, and living along the coast as well as in the interior (Radcliffe-Brown, 1950; Fortes, 1953; Onwuejeogwu, 1975).

When the concept of "African family structure" is used here, it refers to those organizational principles and patterns which are common to the different ethnic groups whose members were enslaved in America. These features of family organization are known to have existed for centuries on the African continent and are, therefore, legitimately termed a part of the African heritage.

AFRICAN FAMILY STRUCTURE: UNDERSTANDING THE DYNAMICS OF CONSANGUINITY AND CONJUGALITY

African families, like those in other parts of the world, embody two contrasting bases for membership: *consanguinity,* which refers to kinship that is commonly assumed or presumed to be biologically based and rooted in "blood ties," and *affinity,* which refers to kinship created by law and rooted "in-law." *Conjugality* refers specifically to the affinal kinship created between spouses (Marshall, 1968). Generally, all kinship entails a dynamic tension between the operation of the contrasting principles of consanguinity and affinity. The comparative study of family organization led Ralph Linton (1936: 159-163) to observe that in different societies families tend to be built either around a conjugal core or around a consanguineal core. In either case, the other principle is subordinate.

According to current historical research on the family in Europe, the principle of conjugality appears to have dominated family organization in the Western part of that continent (including Britain) at least since the Middle Ages, when a number of economic and political factors led to the predominance of nuclear and/or stem families built around married couples. Certainly for the past three or four hundred years, the conjugally based family has been the ideal and the norm in Western Europe (Shorter, 1975; Stone, 1975; Tilly and Scott, 1978). Whether or not the European conjugal family was a structural isolate is not the issue here. The point is that European families, whether nuclear or extended (as in the case of stem families), tended to emphasize the conjugal relationship in matters of household formation, decision making, property transmission, and socialization of the young (Goody, 1976).

African families, on the other hand, have traditionally been organized around consanguineal cores formed by adult siblings of the same sex or by larger same-sex segments of patri- or matrilineages. The groups which formed around these consanguineally related core members included their spouses and children, and perhaps some of their divorced siblings of the opposite sex. This co-resident *extended family* occupied a group of adjoining or contiguous dwellings known as a compound. Upon marriage, Africans did not normally form new isolated households, but joined a compound in which the extended family of the groom, or that of the bride, was already domiciled (Sudarkasa, 1980: 38-49).

African extended families could be subdivided in two ways. From one perspective, there was the division between the nucleus formed by the consanguineal core group and their children and the "outer group" formed by the in-marrying spouses. In many African languages, in-marrying spouses are collectively referred to as "wives" or "husbands" by both females and males of the core group. Thus, for example, in any compound in a patrilineal society, the in-marrying women may be known as the "wives of the house." They are, of course, also the mothers of the children of the compound. Their collective designation as "wives of the house" stresses the fact that their membership in the compound is rooted in law and can be terminated by law, whereas that of the core group is rooted in descent and is presumed to exist in perpetuity.

African extended families may also be divided into their constituent conjugally based family units comprised of parents and children. In the traditional African family, these conjugal units did not have the characteristics of the typical "nuclear family" of the West. In the first place, African conjugal families normally involved polygynous marriages at some stage in their developmental cycle. A number of Western scholars have chosen to characterize the polygynous conjugal family as several distinct nuclear families with one husband/father in common (Rivers, 1924: 12; Murdock, 1949: 2; Colson, 1962). In the African conception, however, whether a man had one wife and children or many wives and children, his was *one* family. In the case of polygynous families, both the husband and the senior co-wife played important roles in integrating the entire group (Fortes, 1949: chs. III and IV; Sudarkasa, 1973: ch. V; Ware, 1979). The very existence of the extended family as an "umbrella" group for the conjugal family meant that the latter group differed from the

Western nuclear family. Since, for many purposes and on many occasions, *all* the children of the same generation within the compound regarded themselves as brothers and sisters (rather than dividing into siblings versus "cousins"), and since the adults assumed certain responsibilities toward their "nephews" and "nieces" (whom they term sons and daughters) as well as toward their own offspring, African conjugal families did not have the rigid boundaries characteristic of nuclear families of the West.

The most far-reaching difference between African and European families stems from their differential emphasis on consanguinity and conjugality. This difference becomes clear when one considers extended family organization in the two contexts. The most common type of European extended family consisted of two or more nuclear families joined through the parent-child or sibling tie. It was this model of the stem family and the joint family that was put forth by George P. Murdock (1949: 23, 33, 39-40) as the generic form of the extended family. However, the African data show that on that continent, extended families were built around consanguineal cores and the conjugal components of these larger families differed significantly from the nuclear families of the West.

In Africa, unlike Europe, in many critical areas of family life the consanguineal core group rather than the conjugal pair was paramount. With respect to household formation, I have already indicated that married couples joined existing compounds. It was the lineage core that owned (or had the right of usufruct over) the land and the compound where families lived, farmed, and/or practiced their crafts. The most important properties in African societies—land, titles, and entitlements—were transmitted through the lineages, and spouses did not inherit from each other (Goody, 1976).

Within the extended family residing in a single compound, decision making centered in the consanguineal core group. The oldest male in the compound was usually its head, and all the men in his generation constituted the elders of the group. Together they were ultimately responsible for settling internal disputes, including those that could not be settled within the separate conjugal families or, in some cases, by the female elders among the wives (Sudarkasa, 1973, 1976). They also made decisions, such as those involving the allocation of land and other resources, which affected the functioning of the constituent conjugal families.

Given the presence of multiple spouses within the *conjugal* families, it is not surprising that decision making within them also differed from the model associated with nuclear family organization. Separate rather than joint decision making was common. In fact, husbands and wives normally had distinct purviews and responsibilities within the conjugal family (Sudarkasa, 1973; Oppong, 1974). Excepting those areas where Islamic traditions overshadowed indigenous African traditions, women had a good deal of control over the fruits of their own labor. Even though husbands typically had ultimate authority over wives, this authority did not extend to control over their wives' properties (Oppong, 1974; Robertson, 1976; Sudarkasa, 1976). Moreover, even though women were subordinate in their roles as wives, as mothers and sisters they wielded considerable authority, power, and influence. This distinction in the power attached to women's roles is symbolized by the fact that in the same society where wives knelt before their husbands, sons prostrated before their mothers and seniority as determined by age, rather than gender, governed relationships among siblings (Sudarkasa, 1973, 1976).

Socialization of the young involved the entire extended family, not just the separate conjugal families, even though each conjugal family had special responsibility for the children (theirs or their relatives') living with them. It is important to note that the concept of "living with" a conjugal family took on a different meaning in the context of the African compound. In the first place, husbands, wives, and children did not live in a bounded space, apart from other such units. Wives had their own rooms or small dwellings, and husbands had theirs. These were not necessarily adjacent to one another. (In some matrilineal societies, husbands and wives resided in separate compounds). Children ordinarily slept in their mothers' rooms until they were of a certain age, after which they customarily slept in communal rooms allocated to boys or girls. Children usually ate their meals with their mothers but they might also eat some of these meals with their fathers' co-wives (assuming that no hostility existed between the women concerned) or with their grandmothers. Children of the same compound played together and shared many learning experiences. They were socialized by all the adults to identify themselves collectively as sons and daughters of a particular lineage and compound, which entailed a kinship, based on descent, with all the lineage ancestors and with generations unborn (Radcliffe-Brown and Forde, 1950; Uchendu, 1965; Sudarkasa, 1980).

The stability of the African extended family did not depend on the stability of the marriage(s) of the individual core group members. Although traditional African marriages (particularly those in patrilineal societies) were more stable than those of most contemporary societies, marital dissolution did not have the ramifications it has in nuclear family systems. When divorces did occur, they were usually followed by remarriage. Normally, all adults other than those who held certain ceremonial offices or who were severely mentally or physically handicapped lived in a marital union (though not necessarily the same one) throughout their lives (for example, Lloyd, 1968). The children of a divorced couple were usually brought up in their natal compound (or by members of their lineage residing elsewhere), even though the in-marrying parent had left that compound.

Several scholars have remarked on the relative ease of divorce in some traditional African societies, particularly those in which matrilineal descent was the rule (for example, Fortes, 1950: 283). Jack Goody (1976: 64) has even suggested that the rate of divorce in precolonial Africa was higher than in parts of Europe and Asia in comparable periods as a corollary of contrasting patterns of property transmission, contrasting attitudes toward the remarriage of women (especially widows), and contrasting implications of polygyny and monogamy. If indeed there was a higher incidence of divorce in precolonial Africa, this would not be inconsistent with the wide-ranging emphasis on consanguinity in Africa as opposed to conjugality in Europe.

Marriage in Africa was a contractual union which often involved long-lasting companionate relationships, but it was not expected to be the all-encompassing, exclusive relationship of the Euro-American ideal type. Both men and women relied on their extended families and friends, as well as on their spouses, for emotionally gratifying relationships. Often, too, in the context of polygyny women as well as men had sexual liaisons with more than one partner. A woman's clandestine affairs did not necessarily lead to divorce because, in the absence of publicized information to the contrary, her husband was considered the father of all her children (Radcliffe-Brown, 1950). And in the context of the lineage (especially the patrilineage), all men aspired to have as many children as possible.

Interpersonal relationships within African families were governed by principles and values which I have elsewhere summarized under the concepts of respect, restraint, responsibility, and reciprocity. Common to all these principles was a notion of commitment to the collectivity. The family offered a network of security, but it also imposed a burden of obligations (Sudarkasa, 1980: 49-50). From the foregoing discussion, it should be understandable that, in their material form, these obligations extended first and foremost to consanguineal kin. Excepting the gifts that were exchanged at the time of marriage, the material obligations entailed in the conjugal relationship and the wider affinal relationships created by marriage were of a lesser magnitude than those associated with "blood" ties.

AFRO-AMERICAN FAMILY STRUCTURE:
INTERPRETING THE AFRICAN CONNECTION

Rather than start with the question of what was *African* about the families established by those Africans who were enslaved in America, it would be more appropriate to ask what was *not* African about them. Most of the Africans who were captured and brought to America arrived without any members of their families, but they brought with them the societal codes they had learned regarding family life. To argue that the trans-Atlantic voyage and the trauma of enslavement made them forget, or rendered useless their memories of how they had been brought up or how they had lived before their capture, is to argue from premises laden with myths about the Black experience (Elkins, 1963: 101-102; see also Frazier, 1966: ch. 1).

Given the African tradition of multilingualism and the widespread use of lingua francas (Maquet, 1972: 18-25)—which in West Africa would include Hausa, Yoruba, Djoula, and Twi—it is probable that many more of the enslaved Africans could communicate among themselves than is implied by those who remark on the multiplicity of "tribes" represented among the slaves. As Landman (1978: 80) has pointed out:

> In many areas of the world, individuals are expected to learn only one language in the ordinary course of their lives. But many Africans have been enculturated in social systems where multiple language or dialect acquisition have been regarded as normal.

The fact that Africans typically spoke three to five languages also makes it understandable why they quickly adopted "pidginized" forms of European languages as lingua francas for communicating among themselves and with their captors.

The relationships which the Blacks in America established among themselves would have reflected their own backgrounds *and* the conditions in which they found themselves. It is as erroneous to try to attribute what developed among them solely to slavery as it is to attribute it solely to the African background. Writers such as Herbert Gutman (1976), who emphasize the "adaptive" nature of "slave culture" must ask what it was that was being adapted as well as in what context this adaptation took place. Moreover, they must realize that adaptation does not necessarily imply extensive modification of an institution, especially when its structure is already suited (or "preadapted") to survival in the new context. Such an institution was the African extended family, which had served on that continent, in various environments and different political contexts, as a unit of production and distribution; of socialization, education, and social control; and of emotional and material support for the aged and the infirm as well as the hale and hearty (Kerri, 1979; Okediji, 1975; Shimkin and Uchendu, 1978; Sudarkasa, 1975b).

The extended family networks that were formed during slavery by Africans *and their descendants* were based on the institutional heritage which the Africans had brought with them to this continent, and the specific forms they took reflected the influence of European-derived institutions as well as the political and economic circumstances in which the enslaved population found itself.

The picture of Black families during slavery has become clearer over the past decade, particularly as a result of the wealth of data in Gutman's justly heralded study. Individual households were normally comprised of a conjugal pair, their children, and sometimes their grandchildren, other relatives, or nonkin. Marriage was usually monogamous, but polygynous unions where the wives lived in separate households have also been reported (Gutman, 1976: 59, 158; Blassingame, 1979: 171; Perdue et al., 1980: 209).

Probably only in a few localities did female-headed households constitute as much as one-quarter of all households (Gutman, 1976: esp. chs. 1-3). The rarity of this household type was in keeping with the African tradition whereby women normally bore children within the context of marriage and lived in monogamous or polygynous conjugal families that were part of larger extended families. I have tried to show elsewhere why it is inappropriate to apply the term "nuclear family" to the mother-child dyads within African polygynous families (Sudarkasa, 1980: 43-46). In some African societies—especially in matrilineal ones—a small percentage of previously married women, or married women living apart from their husbands, might head households that were usually attached to larger compounds. However, in my view, on the question of the origin of female-headed households among Blacks in America, Herskovits was wrong, and Frazier was right in attributing this development to conditions that arose during slavery and in the context of urbanization in later periods (Frazier, 1966; Herskovits, 1958; Furstenberg et al., 1975).

Gutman's data suggest that enslaved women who had their first children out of wedlock did not normally set up independent households, but rather continued to live with their parents. Most of them subsequently married and set up neolocal residence with their husbands. The data also suggest that female-headed households developed mainly in two situations: (1) A woman whose husband died or was sold off the plantation might head a household comprised of her children and perhaps her grandchildren born to an unmarried daughter; (2) a woman who did not marry after having one or two children out of wedlock but continued to have children (no doubt often for the "master") might have her own cabin built for her (Gutman, 1976: chs. 1-3).

It is very important to distinguish these two types of female-headed households, the first being only a phase in the developmental cycle of a conjugally headed household, and the second being a case of neolocal residence by an unmarried female. The pattern of households headed by widows was definitely not typical of family structure in Africa, where normally a widow married another member of her deceased husband's lineage. The pattern of neolocal residence by an unmarried woman with children would have been virtually unheard of in Africa. Indeed, it was also relatively rare among enslaved Blacks and in Black communities in later periods. Before the twentieth-century policy of public assistance for unwed mothers, virtually all young unmarried mothers in Black communities continued to live in households headed by other adults. If in later years they did establish their own households, these tended to be tied into transresidential family networks.

The existence during slavery of long-lasting conjugal unions among Blacks was not a departure from African family tradition. Even with the relative ease of divorce in matrilineal societies, most Africans lived in marital unions that ended only with the death of one of the spouses. In the patrilineal societies from which most American Blacks were taken, a number of factors, including the custom of returning bridewealth payments upon the dissolution of marriage, served to encourage marital stability (Radcliffe-Brown, 1950: 43-54). Given that the conditions of slavery did not permit the *replication* of African families, it might be expected that the husband and wife as elders in the household would assume even greater importance than they had in Africa, where the elders within the consanguineal core of the extended family and those among the wives would have had major leadership roles within the compound.

When the distinction is made between family and household—and, following Bender (1967), between the composition of the co-resident group and the domestic functions associated with both households and families—it becomes apparent that the question of who lived with whom during slavery (or later) must be subordinate to the questions of who was doing what for whom and what kin relationships were maintained over space and time. In any case, decisions concerning residence per se were not always in the hands of the enslaved Blacks themselves, and space alone served as a constraint on the size, and consequently to some extent on the composition, of the "slave" cabins.

That each conjugally based household formed a primary unit for food consumption and production among the enslaved Blacks is consistent with domestic organization within the African compound. However, Gutman's data, and those reported by enslaved Blacks themselves, on the strong bonds of obligation among kinsmen suggest that even within the constraints imposed by the slave regime, transresidential cooperation—including that between households in different localities—was the rule rather than the exception (Gutman, 1976: esp. 131-138; Perdue et al., 1980: esp. 26, 256, 323). One might hypothesize that on the larger plantations with a number of Black families related through consanguineal and affinal ties, the households of these families might have formed groupings similar to African compounds. Certainly we know that in later times such groupings were found in the South Carolina Sea Islands and other parts of the South (Agbasegbe, 1976, 1981; Gutman, 1976; Johnson, 1934: ch. 2; Powdermaker, 1939: ch. 8).

By focusing on extended families (rather than simply on households) among the enslaved Blacks, it becomes apparent that these kin networks had many of the features of continental African extended families. These Afro-American groupings were built around consanguineal kin whose spouses were related to or incorporated into the networks in different degrees. The significance of the consanguineal principle in these networks is indicated by Gutman's statement that "the pull between ties to an immediate family and to an enlarged kin network sometimes strained husbands and wives" (1976: 202; see also Frazier, 1966: pt. 2).

The literature on Black families during slavery provides a wealth of data on the way in which consanguineal kin assisted each other with child rearing, in life crisis events such as birth and death, in work groups, in efforts to obtain freedom, and so on. They maintained their networks against formidable odds and, after slavery, sought out those parents, siblings, aunts, and uncles from whom they had been torn (Blassingame, 1979; Genovese, 1974; Gutman, 1976; Owens, 1976). Relationships within these groups were governed by principles and values stemming from the African background. Respect for elders and reciprocity among kinsmen are noted in all discussions of Black families during slavery. The willingness to assume responsibility for relatives beyond the conjugal family and selflessness (a form of restraint) in the face of these responsibilities are also characteristics attributed to the enslaved population.

As would be expected, early Afro-American extended families differed from their African prototypes in ways that reflected the influence of slavery and of Euro-American values, especially their proscriptions and prescriptions regarding mating, marriage, and the family. No doubt, too, the Euro-American emphasis on the primacy of marriage within the family reinforced conjugality among the Afro-Americans even though the "legal" marriage of enslaved Blacks was prohibited. As DuBois noted at the turn of the century, African corporate lineages could not survive intact during slavery. Hence, the consanguineal core groups of Afro-American extended families differed in some ways from those of their African antecedents. It appears that in some of these Afro-American families membership in the core group was traced bilaterally, whereas in others there was a unilineal emphasis without full-fledged lineages.

Interestingly, after slavery, some of the corporate functions of African lineages reemerged in some extended families which became property-owning collectivities. I have suggested elsewhere that "the disappearance of the lineage principle or its absorption into the concept of extended family" is one of the aspects of the transformation of African family organization in America that requires research (Sudarkasa, 1980: 57). Among the various other issues that remain to be studied concerning these extended families are these: (1) Did members belong by virtue of bilateral or unilineal descent from a common ancestor or because of shared kinship with a living person? (2) How were group boundaries established and maintained? (3) What was the nature and extent of the authority of the elder(s)? (4) How long did the group last and what factors determined its span in time and space?

CONCLUSION

At the outset of this chapter it was suggested that a holistic explanation of Black family organization requires discarding or recasting some of the debates which have framed discussions in the past. I have tried to show why it is time to move beyond the debate over whether it was slavery *or* the African heritage which "determined" Black family organization to a synthesis which looks at institutional transformation as well as institutional transfer for the interplay between Africa and America in shaping the family structures of Afro-Americans.

Obviously, Black families have changed over time, and today one would expect that the evidence for African "retentions" (Herskovits, 1958: xxii-xxiii) in them would be more controvertible than in the past. Nevertheless, the persistence of some features of African family organization among contemporary Black American families has been documented for both rural and urban areas. Although this study cannot attempt a full-scale analysis of these features and the changes they have undergone, it is important to make reference to one of them, precisely because it impacts upon so many other aspects of Black family organization, and because its connection to Africa has not been acknowledged by most contemporary scholars. I refer to the emphasis on consanguinity noted especially among lower-income Black families and those in the rural South. Some writers, including Shimkin and Uchendu (1978), Agbasegbe (1976; 1981), Aschenbrenner (1973; 1975; 1978; Aschenbrenner and Carr, 1980) and the present author (1975a, 1980, 1981) have dealt explicitly with this concept in their discussions of Black family organization. However, without labelling it as such, many other scholars have described some aspects of the operation of consanguinity within the Black family in their discussions of "matrifocality" and "female-headed households." Too often, the origin of this consanguineal emphasis in Black families, which can be manifest even in households with both husband and wife present, is left unexplained or is "explained" by labelling it an "adaptive" characteristic.

In my view, historical realities require that the derivation of this aspect of Black family organization be traced to its African antecedents. Such a view does not deny the adaptive significance of consanguineal networks. In fact, it helps to clarify why these networks had the flexibility they had and why they, rather than conjugal relationships, came to be the stabilizing factor in Black families. The significance of this principle of organization is indicated by the list of Black family characteristics derived from it. Scrutiny of the list of Black family characteristics given by Aschenbrenner (1978) shows that 12 of the 18 "separate" features she lists are manifestations of the overall strength and entailments of consanguineal relationships.

Some writers have viewed the consanguineally based extended family as a factor of *instability* in the Black family because it sometimes undermines the conjugal relationships in which its members are involved. I would suggest that historically among Black Americans the concept of "family" meant first and foremost relationships created by "blood" rather than by marriage. (R. T. Smith

[1973] has made substantially the same point with respect to West Indian family organization.) Children were socialized to think in terms of obligations to parents (especially mothers), siblings, and others defined as "close kin." Obligations to "outsiders," who would include prospective spouses and in-laws, were definitely less compelling. Once a marriage took place, if the demands of the conjugal relationship came into irreconcilable conflict with consanguineal commitments, the former would often be sacrificed. Instead of interpreting instances of *marital* instability as prima facie evidence of family instability, it should be realized that the fragility of the conjugal relationship could be a consequence or corollary of the *stability* of the consanguineal family network. Historically, such groups survived by nurturing a strong sense of responsibility among members and by fostering a code of reciprocity which could strain relations with persons not bound by it.

Not all Black families exhibit the same emphasis on consanguineal relationships. Various factors, including education, occupational demands, aspirations toward upward mobility, and acceptance of American ideals concerning marriage and the family, have moved some (mainly middle- and upper-class) Black families toward conjugally focused households and conjugally centered extended family groupings. Even when such households include relatives other than the nuclear family, those relatives tend to be subordinated to the conjugal pair who form the core of the group. This contrasts with some older type Black families where a senior relative (especially the wife's or the husband's mother) could have a position of authority in the household equal to or greater than that of one or both of the spouses. Children in many contemporary Black homes are not socialized to think in terms of the parent-sibling group as the primary kin group, but rather in terms of their future spouses and families of procreation as the main source of their future emotional and material satisfaction and support. Among these Blacks, the nuclear household tends to be more isolated in terms of instrumental functions, and such extended family networks as exist tend to be clusters of nuclear families conforming to the model put forth by Murdock (1949: chs. 1 and 2).

For scholars interested in the heritage of Europe as well as the heritage of Africa in Afro-American family organization, a study of the operation of the principles of conjugality and consanguinity in these families would provide considerable insight into the ways in which these two institutional traditions have been interwoven. By looking at the differential impact of these principles in matters of household formation, delegation of authority, maintenance of solidarity and support, acquisition and transmission of property, financial management, and so on (Sudarkasa, 1981), and by examining the political and economic variables which favor the predominance of one or the other principle, we will emerge with questions and formulations that can move us beyond debates over "pathology" and "normalcy" in Black family life.

REFERENCES

AGBASEGBE, B. (1976) "The role of wife in the Black extended family: perspectives from a rural community in Southern United States," pp. 124-138 in D. McGuigan (ed.) New Research on Women and Sex Roles. Ann Arbor: Center for Continuing Education of Women, University of Michigan.

_____ (1981) "Some aspects of contemporary rural Afroamerican family life in the Sea Islands of Southeastern United States." Presented at the Annual Meeting of the Association of Social and Behavioral Scientists, Atlanta, Georgia, March 1981.

ALLEN, W. R. (1978) "The search for applicable theories of Black family life." Journal of Marraige and the Family 40 (February): 117-129.

_____ (1979) "Class, culture, and family organization: the effects of class and race on family structure in urban America." Journal of Comparative Family Studies 10 (Autumn): 301-313.

ASCHENBRENNER, J. (1973) "Extended families among Black Americans." Journal of Comparative Family Studies 4: 257-268.

_____ (1975) Lifelines: Black Families in Chicago. New York: Holt, Rinehart & Winston.

_____ (1978) "Continuities and variations in Black family structure," pp. 181-200 in D. B. Shimkin, E. M. Shimkin, and D. A. Frate (eds.) The Extended Family in Black Societies. The Hague: Mouton.

_____ and C. H. CARR (1980) "Conjugal relationships in the context of the Black extended family." Alternative Lifestyles 3 (November): 463-484.

BENDER, D. R. (1967) "A refinement of the concept of household: families, co-residence, and domestic functions." American Anthropologist 69 (October): 493-504.

BILLINGSLEY, A. (1968) Black Families in White America. Englewood Cliffs, NJ: Prentice-Hall.

BLASSINGAME, J. W. (1979) The Slave Community. New York: Oxford University Press.

COLSON, E. (1962) "Family change in contemporary Africa." Annals of the New York Academy of Sciences 96 (January): 641-652.

DuBOIS, W. E. B. (1969) The Negro American Family. New York: New American Library. (Originally published, 1908).

ELKINS, S. (1963) Slavery: A Problem in American Intellectual Life. New York: Grosset and Dunlap. (Originally published, 1959).

ENGLISH, R. (1974) "Beyond pathology: research and theoretical perspectives on Black families," pp. 39-52 in L. E. Gary (ed.) Social Research and the Black Community: Selected Issues and Priorities. Washington, DC: Institute for Urban Affairs and Research, Howard University.

FORTES, M. (1949) The Web of Kinship among the Tallensi. London: Oxford University Press.

_____ (1950) "Kinship and marriage among the Ashanti," pp. 252-284 in A. R. Radcliffe-Brown and D. Forde (eds.) African Systems of Kinship and Marriage. London: Oxford University Press.

_____ (1953) "The structure of unilineal descent groups." American Anthropologist 55 (January-March): 17-41.

FRAZIER, E. (1966) The Negro Family in the United States. Chicago: University of Chicago Press. (Originally published, 1939).

FURSTENBERG, F. , T. HERSHBERT, and J. MODELL (1975) "The origins of the female-headed Black family: the impact of the urban experience." Journal of Interdisciplinary History 6 (Autumn): 211-233.

GENOVESE, E. D. (1974) Roll Jordan Roll: The World the Slaves Made. New York: Random House.

GOODY, J. (1976) Production and Reproduction: A Comparative Study of the Domestic Domain. Cambridge: Cambridge University Press.

GUTMAN, H. (1976) The Black Family in Slavery and Freedom: 1750-1925. New York: Random House.

HERSKOVITS, M. J. (1958) The Myth of the Negro Past. Boston: Beacon. (Originally published, 1941).

JOHNSON, C. S. (1934) Shadow of the Plantation. Chicago: University of Chicago Press.

KERRI, J. N. (1979) "Understanding the African family: persistence, continuity, and change." Western Journal of Black Studies 3 (Spring): 14-17.

LANDMAN, R. H. (1978) "Language policies and their implications for ethnic relations in the newly sovereign states of Sub-Saharan Africa," pp. 69-90 in B. M. duToit (ed.) Ethnicity in Modern Africa. Boulder, CO: Westview Press.

LINTON, R. (1936) The Study of Man. New York: Appleton-Century-Crofts.

LLOYD, P. C. (1968) "Divorce among the Yoruba." American Anthropologist 70 (February): 67-81.

MAQUET, J. (1972) Civilizations of Black Africa. London: Oxford University Press.

MARSHALL, G. A. [Niara Sudarkasa] (1968) "Marriage: comparative analysis," in International Encyclopedia of the Social Sciences, Vol. 10. New York: Macmillan/Free Press.

MURDOCK, G. P. (1949) Social Structure. New York: Macmillan.

NOBLES, W. (1974a) "African root and American fruit: the Black family." Journal of Social and Behavioral Sciences 20: 52-64.

———— (1974b) "Africanity: its role in Black families." The Black Scholar 9 (June): 10-17.

———— (1978) "Toward an empirical and theoretical framework for defining Black families." Journal of Marriage and the Family 40 (November): 679-688.

OKEDIJI, P. A. (1975) "A psychosocial analysis of the extended family: the African case." African Urban Notes, Series B, 1(3): 93-99. (African Studies Center, Michigan State University)

ONWUEJEOGWU, M. A. (1975) The Social Anthropology of Africa: An Introduction. London: Heinemann.

OPPONG, C. (1974) Marriage among a Matrilineal Elite: A Family Study of Ghanaian Senior Civil Servants. Cambridge: Cambridge University Press.

OWENS, L. H. (1976) This Species of Property: Slave Life and Culture in the Old South. New York: Oxford University Press.

PERDUE, C. L., Jr., T. E. BARDEN, and R. K. PHILLIPS [eds.] (1980) Weevils in the Wheat: Interviews with Virginia Ex-Slaves. Bloomington: Indiana University Press.

POWDERMAKER, H. (1939) After Freedom: A Cultural Study in the Deep South. New York: Viking.

RADCLIFFE-BROWN, A. R. (1950) "Introduction," pp. 1-85 in A. R. Radcliffe-Brown and D. Forde (eds.) African Systems of Kinship and Marriage. London: Oxford University Press.

———— and D. FORDE [eds.] (1950) African Systems of Kinship and Marriage. London: Oxford University Press.

RIVERS, W. H. R. (1924) Social Organization. New York: Alfred Knopf.

ROBERTSON, C. (1976) "Ga women and socioeconomic change in Accra, Ghana," pp. 111-133 in N. J. Hafkin and E. G. Bay (eds.) Women in Africa: Studies in Social and Economic Change. Stanford: Stanford University Press.

SHIMKIN, D. and V. UCHENDU (1978) "Persistence, borrowing, and adaptive changes in Black kinship systems: some issues and their significance," pp. 391-406 in D. Shimkin, E. M. Shimkin, and D. A. Frate (eds.) The Extended Family in Black Societies. The Hague: Mouton.

SHIMKIN, D., E. M. SHIMKIN, and D. A. FRATE [eds.] (1978) The Extended Family in Black Societies. The Hague: Mouton.

SHORTER, E. (1975) The Making of the Modern Family. New York: Basic Books.

SMITH, R. T. (1973) "The matrifocal family," pp. 121-144 in J. Goody (ed.) The Character of Kinship. Cambridge: Cambridge University Press.

STACK, C. (1974) All Our Kin. New York: Harper & Row.

STAPLES, R. (1971) "Toward a sociology of the Black family: a decade of theory and research." Journal of Marriage and the Family 33 (February): 19-38.

———— [ed.] (1978) The Black Family: Essays and Studies. Belmont, CA: Wadsworth.

STONE, L. (1975) "The rise of the nuclear family in early modern England: the patriarchal stage," pp. 13-57 in C. E. Rosenberg (ed.) The Family in History. Philadelphia: University of Pennsylvania Press.

SUDARKASA, N. (1973) Where Women Work: A Study of Yoruba Women in the Marketplace and in the Home. Anthropological Papers No. 53. Ann Arbor: Museum of Anthropology, University of Michigan.

———— (1975a) "An exposition on the value premises underlying Black family studies." Journal of the National Medical Association 19 (May): 235-239.

———— (1975b) "National development planning for the promotion and protection of the family." Proceedings of the Conference on Social Research and National Development, E. Akeredolu-Ale, ed. The Nigerian Institute of Social and Economic Research, Ibadan, Nigeria.

———— (1976) "Female employment and family organization in West Africa," pp. 48-63 in D. G. McGuigan (ed.) New Research on Women and Sex Roles. Ann Arbor: Center for Continuing Education of Women, University of Michigan.

———— (1980) "African and Afro-American family structure: a comparison." The Black Scholar 11 (November-December): 37-60.

———— (1981) "Understanding the dynamics of consanguinity and conjugality in contemporary Black family organization." Presented at the Seventh Annual Third World Conference, Chicago, March 1981.

TILLY, L. A. and J. W. SCOTT (1978) Women, Work, and Family. New York: Holt, Rinehart & Winston.

UCHENDU, V. (1965) The Igbo of South-Eastern Nigeria. New York: Holt, Rinehart & Winston.

WARE, H. (1979) "Polygyny: women's views in a transitional society, Nigeria 1975." Journal of Marriage and the Family 41 (February): 185-195.

WOODSON, C. G. (1936) The African Background Outlined. Washington, DC: Association for the Study of Negro Life and History.

3

AFRICAN-AMERICAN FAMILY LIFE
An Instrument of Culture

WADE W. NOBLES

Given the critical importance of child-rearing practices and orientation in shaping the personalities, behaviors, and values of future citizens in any society, the parent-child relationship should be viewed as one of the major points at which the family's obligation to the state and the state's obligation to the family is crystallized. Unfortunately, a clear understanding of African-American parent-child relationships and their subsequent importance in our understanding of the African-American family's obligation to the state and the state's obligation to the African-American family has been clouded by racism.

A proper understanding of the strengths of African-American families, the difficulties they face, and the ways in which they are affected by public policy is confused and clouded by several co-mingling issues, among which the most prominent is racism. The issue of racism totally masks the understanding of African-American culture itself, to say nothing of the family as an instrument of culture.

It has been racism, primarily, that has allowed the guiding assumption of the "innate" inferiority of African people to go almost completely unchallenged in over 200 years of research and scientific investigation. It has been primarily the research guided by this assumption that has resulted in the examiners of African-American family life consistently offering evidence, information, theory, and analyses that focused solely on the so-called problems inherent in African-American family systems. Blinded by this racist assumption, these researchers have created what is the overwhelming historical character of the field: that the African-American family system was (is) an organization inherently laden with problems and inadequacies. Similarly, though far more subtle and sophisticated, the new thrust toward highlighting and examining only the African-American middle-class, well-to-do family creates the false image that the socioeconomic gap between African-Americans and white Americans has closed, that African-Americans are no longer victims of poverty and racism, and that all African-American people have benefited from the civil rights struggle. The basis of this false image is just as racist as the false image that all African-American families were on welfare. In a very sophisticated way, by overprojecting the image that there is nothing "wrong" with the African-American family, contemporary scientific researchers have participated in a scheme to simultaneously take away the gains of the 1960s and/or misdirect the blame for the concrete condition of African-American family life. The actuality is that generally there has been a perpetual state of disadvantage for most African-American families, yet the literature or data defines the condition of the African-American family as progressively more advantaged.

One need simply to recognize that our country is still a racist country (ergo: the continued popularity of KKK and Nazi parties) and that to be African-American in a white racist society is problematic by definition. Consequently, the family life of African-American people would be and is characterized by real and definite problems and conditions associated with racism and oppression.

Although a great deal of research has been done, the gap in useful, usable knowledge remains just as wide. In fact, the legacy of white-dominated research and racist scientific investigations has totally prevented us from understanding the nature of African-American family life; and, consequently, as a result of racist research, the understanding of African-American family life has been, in a very real way, held hostage by the intellectual instruments of the socioeconomic, political establishment.

DISCRIMINATION OR SCIENTIFIC COLONIALISM

AFRICAN-AMERICAN FAMILY LIFE HELD HOSTAGE BY WHITE-DOMINATED THINKING

There are two concepts that must be recognized if one is to see the pervasive and insidious nature of the phenomena that negatively affect African-American families. First, one must recognize that discrimination is an act designed to separate individuals or people for the purpose of allowing one group to receive preferential treatment and/or advantage; and second, that in a system characterized by racism and oppression, almost every element or process managed by the racist system is designed primarily to continue and secure the status of the "advantaged" by guaranteeing in all arenas their preferential treatment.

It is not difficult to equate the racist system with the act of holding a thing or a person hostage. The latter is an act designed to keep under one's control the person or thing held in order that the "hostage" can be used to bargain with or in exchange for one's own safety, benefit, or freedom. Combined, the almost total misrepresentation of African-American family life and the almost absolute control of the scientific understanding of African-American family life by non-African thinkers suggests that the African-American family has been and is being held hostage by white-dominated research and scientific studies. Some would argue that African-American families are not being held hostage physically; and, if anything, it is the understanding of African-American family life which is being held hostage. Given the concrete condition of African-American family life, this distinction is debatable.

Given that the first Africans came to these shores as enslaved captives in the mid-1700s, we could legitimately say that African-American families have been held hostage for over 87,000 days. From this historical perspective, one is able to see that the exploitation, domination, and control of African people in this country has been its most constant feature. Hence, it is fair to say that the state of African-American family life has been held hostage while other segments benefited from the disadvantage experienced by African people.

If, for example, one simply notes that white researchers from the early 1700s have consistently argued for and supported (without proof) the notion of African-American family inferiority (see Von Linnaes, 1735; Burmeister, 1835; Galton, 1969; Spencer, 1884; Hall, 1904; Thorndike, 1940; and Terman, 1916), then one is compelled to ask why. Given the prevalence of institutionalized racism in all areas of American life—politics, job opportunities, and education are three of the most noted areas—such a concerted effort suggests that science also was (is) being used as a tool of oppression and control and that indeed the creation of these findings were (are) beneficial, if no more than psychologically, to non-African people in this country. Of course, such information placed African-American people at a decided disadvantage. The African-American family as an area of investigation, for instance, has been examined from almost every conceivable orientation, and in almost every case it has been found to be less than viable (see Frazier, 1932; Bernard, 1966; Jeffers, 1967; Chilman, 1966; Willie, 1970; and Scanzoni, 1971). One cannot, in this regard, dismiss the relationship between the "results" of this line of research and the treatment of African-American families in the society at large.

It is in fact the case that, guided by the assumption that blackness is intrinsically inferior, racist models, theories, and/or orientations coupled with unsophisticated scientific treatments and analyses of African-American family life have not only led to mass confusion and an unusable body of knowledge, they have also translated to the direct maltreatment of African-American families (for example, forced sterilization).

Unfortunately, as long as this country remains racist, the need to hold African-American families hostage will exist and, with it, the continued uncritical adoption of non-African interpretations and/or analytical frameworks which will invariably result in both misdirected analyses of African-American life and blind acceptance of erroneous assumptions and "meanings" that "define" the reality of African-American family life.

This, in effect, is the legacy which we bring to the analyses of African-American life; and this is the legacy from which we must free ourselves as we go forward with the study and understanding of African-American family life.

PARENT-CHILD RELATIONSHIPS HELD HOSTAGE

THE 87,965TH DAY

The analogy of African-American families being held hostage is, of course, designed to refocus our attention on the real condition of African-American life in America and to the fact that, like those who were earnestly concerned about the Americans being held hostage in Iran, we know very little about what happened to them. The knowledge gap we face is extremely wide, even though a huge amount of data has accumulated over the years. The major gap is in studies that honestly reflect the condition of African-American family life and are not guided by various racist assumptions of African inferiority and negativity. The lack of a substantial body of studies (of all types) which from conceptualization to methods, from procedures to analyses, and from conclusions to interpretations, respect and reflect the cultural integrity of African-American family dynamics is the major gap in the field.

Despite this dilemma, there exist several classical contributions (Billingsley, 1968; Staples, 1976; Hill, 1971) which have addressed the mandate to find "What are the strengths?" Though none focused on the more narrow issue of parent-child relationships exclusively, the important works of Robert Hill, Andrew Billingsley, and Robert Staples have served as the cornerstones for the understanding of African-American family strengths. However, one must keep in mind, as did these authors, that to talk only about the strength of the African-American family without simultaneously recognizing that, without this dogged strength and resilience, African-American families would have been shattered and torn apart long ago is tantamount to closing one's eyes to the full complexity of the problem at hand. Given the continued and historical concrete conditions of racism and oppression, it is, in fact, a testimony to our humanity and a miracle of the human spirit that we even have an African-American family left to talk about.

Strengths and Interpersonal Relationships. The benchmark work on African-American family strength is Hill's classic documentation, *The Strength of African-American Families*. The focus of this discussion is interpersonal relationships, particularly parent-child, and the associated family strength found in that arena.

Traditionally, the analyses of parent-child relationships centered on understanding how parents instill in their children particular behavior repertoires, attitudes, and beliefs in their childhood training, child-rearing practices, and socialization strategies. Seldom did the attention turn to an examination of strengths implicit in the parent-child relationship. Though some researchers examined the psychological dispositions and/or behavioral or personality styles that emerged from the parent-child interaction, seldom did they turn their attention to an examination of the strengths and support implicit in the interpersonal relationships (parent-child and others) found in the family.

In his study of the African-American family system, Shimkin et al. (1974) isolated five critical elements of African-American family life that distinguish it from the family structure of other ethnic/racial groups. They noted that the traditional African-American family is a unique cultural form enjoying its own inherent resources. It is comprised of several individual households, with the channels of authority reaching beyond the household units that compose it. In periods of crises and at times of ceremony, the extended family is most visible and provides needed emotional support for its members. The family may (and often does) perform many ritual, social (and psychological) functions, including the education of its young and the adjudication of the family's internal conflicts. Even though some features of the African-American family can be explained "situationally" (that is, are adaptive responses to certain pressures of the moment), or through "borrowing," the underlying structure of the African-American extended family is ultimately traceable to Africa.

Almost ten years prior to Shimkin's work, Billingsley (1968) pointed out that the African-American family unit is itself an element embedded in a larger network of mutually interdependent relationships with the African-American community and the wider (white) society. Billingsley went on to point out that, even though the African-American family system is one institution in a complex of various American institutions, the African-American family cannot be totally understood or interpreted from a general (white) analytical framework. The limits of using a general analytical framework can be seen through an earlier study (Nobles et al., 1976) in which we found that a critical aspect of the parent-child relationship was that parents prepared their children to deal with racism. In fact, the unique child-rearing techniques found in African-American families seem to be geared to prepare the child for a *particular* kind of existence in a hostile racist environment. Children were in effect prepared to take on the appropriate sex and age roles as well as the racial role.

Consistent with Billingsley's conception of interlocking systems, Staples's (1976) work offers a valuable insight into the relation between African-American families and the wider society. Staples suggests that the African-American family has been a sanctuary that protected individuals from the pervasiveness of white racism and provided needed support systems that were unavailable in other majority group institutions. Consequently, the processes in the African-American family promoted and maintained the emotional well-being of its individual members in spite of the wider society.

In *A Formulative and Empirical Study of Black Families* (Nobles et al., 1976), we found that African-American parent-child interactions were characterized by an "atmosphere" or attitude that emphasized strong family ties or orientations, unconditional love, respect for self and others, and the assumed natural goodness of the child. Child-rearing techniques associated with the parent-child bond centered on the unconditional expression of love. That is, parents seldom made their love for their children a reinforcement contingency. The interpersonal relationship between parent and child could, therefore, be characterized by parent anger, punishment, and disappointment as well as the child's mistakes, failure, and misbehavior without canceling out the love associated with the parental-child bond.

A family strength, like the support network or system in which it operates, is any process or network of interactions that aid or help individuals in anticipating, addressing, interpreting, managing, and otherwise successfully responding to their concrete condition or situation. Within this definition, the kinds of elements or features mentioned previously are African-American families' strengths.

Upon further analyses of the interpersonal dynamics of African-American family styles and mental health support systems (see Nobles et al., 1979), five additional strengths were identified, classified, and defined.

Legitimation of Beingness. Through the parent-child (sibling and other familial relationships), the family provides its members with a source of connection, attachment, validation, worth, recognition, respect, and legitimacy. If one is secure in one's own personal meaning, then one is more capable of addressing and responding to complex, vague, and unfamiliar experiences confronted outside the home.

Provision of a Family Code. By providing its members with a "family code" (guidelines for behaving in novel and/or confusing situations), the family, via interpersonal relations, aids its members in interpreting, managing, and responding to both known and undefined situations.

Elasticity of Boundaries. Legitimation of Beingness and the provision of a family code produces an elasticity in African-American family interpersonal relationships. The unbreakable bond and associated rules of conduct give African-American family members the latitude and opportunity to stretch out and develop their own sense of "specialness" without fear of violating the familyhood. In a sense, the phrase or label, "the elasticity of boundaries," is indeed a literal interpretation of this phenomenon, in that family boundaries stretch to accommodate the various expressions of individual styles, personalities, and/or conditions. The sense of almost unconditional permanence or undeniable belonging strengthens family members' ability to respond to their unique concrete condition in ways that satisfy or are peculiar to their individual and personal needs.

The Provisions of Information/Knowledge. This feature gives members the benefit of shared insights and experiences and by so doing strengthens their ability to interpret and understand the events and happenings that affect their lives. The transgenerational mutual sharing of knowledge and experience heightens the individual member's (young and old) ability to address, manage, and respond to the rapidly changing as well as constant conditions in their reality.

Mediation of Concrete Conditions. The family kinships' ability to mediate the conflicts and other concrete conditions affecting its members provides a strength or support so obvious that it barely warrants explication. Clearly, the family's ability to provide its members with concrete aid and pragmatic help and to engage in interpersonal relations around problem solving and decision making (in response to both external and internal issues) while constantly buffering and repairing the damage resulting from racism and oppression directed at its members is a critical strength.

AFRICAN-AMERICAN FAMILY PARENT-CHILD RELATIONSHIP AND OUR OBLIGATION TO THE STATE

Given that African-American children must become adults during a period in which racism, discrimination, and oppression will change disguises and will not simply go away, the family parent-child relationship will have to center on the creation and maintenance of three senses: the sense of history, the sense of family, and the sense of the ultimate supreme power (God).

The sense of history will tell African-American children that they are first and foremost Africans and that we are Africans because of our common cultural orientation which gives us the same sense of the natural universe and human condition that characterizes all African peoples, and we have a common history of racial oppression which resulted in shared victimization. The sense of history will help African-American children to recognize that as Africans they must and will continue to struggle for the liberation of the human condition from oppression and racism. The sense of history will help them understand that the natural human condition is one of freedom and growth, and that any person, people, or invention which denies their freedom and potential to grow should be opposed and fought against. History will tell them that to resist and struggle against such a force is the only natural human response. To do otherwise is to conspire in the creation of their own dehumanization. The sense of history will also tell them that "the struggle" is by definition a human struggle and not an individual, personalized battle. Finally, the sense of history will tell African-American children that the enemies of human growth and freedom, wherever they are found in the world, are easily recognized by their behavior and attitude. History will show them that the historical enemy of our people is still our enemy today and that until that enemy changes its basic response to other human beings, it will always remain our enemy.

The sense of family is really the specific application of the sense of history previously defined. The sense of family will explicitly give African-American children the understanding that their identity and being is in the family—that, unlike the families of other groups, our family is a source of strength. It is not a burden to individual aspirations. In fact, in understanding the sense of family, African-American children will also understand that they will expand in personal strength as the family expands in size. The sense of family will give them the security of knowing that no matter what happens, the family love and protection will be unconditional and ever-present. The sense of family will help them realize that in their people (and not necessarily things) they will find a common meaning (definition) and a common ground.

The final sense that should emerge from the parent-child interaction is a sense of supreme being (God). The importance of formalized religion is in its ritual, which helps to replenish the necessity and the belief in the supreme force. It is important that African-American children engage in the religious ritual. It is even more important that African-American children understand, respect, and obey the supreme spirit which makes them human. The sense of the supreme being will help African-American children realize that there is a power and a will that is greater than all else. The sense of the force will tell them that the power is in us all and that its natural laws must be obeyed. Knowing that the force is in them will help them realize that in being the manifestation of the supreme force, they have no limitation—as long as they obey the natural (God's) laws of the universe. The sense of the supreme being will help them realize that just as the natural path of living plants is to grow toward the sun, our natural path is to grow (in understanding) toward the supreme force.

THE AFRICAN-AMERICAN FAMILY'S
OBLIGATION TO THE STATE

Ultimately, the African-American family parent-child relationship must become the focal point to which the African-American family's obligation to the state and the state's obligation to the African-American family is crystalized. For human beings, and especially those who are being oppressed and discriminated against, the parent-child relationship should make clear that the state's obligation to every family within its domain and jurisdiction is to guarantee each and every family a level of existence or a quality of life which ensures and guarantees the family's ability to advance and affirm the life and well-being of its members. In turn, and in tandem with the state's obligation, the human family's obligation to the state is to support the state in its correctness (in deed and action) and to never allow the state as the agent and instrument of the people to infringe upon or allow to continue in any form the dehumanization and degradation of its citizenry or in any way diminish, discriminate, or disallow the growth of the human potential.

REFERENCES

BERNARD, J. (1966) Marriage and Family Amongst Negroes. Englewood Cliffs, NJ: Prentice-Hall.

BILLINGSLEY, A. (1968) Black Families in White America. Englewood Cliffs, NJ: Prentice-Hall.

BURMEISTER, H. (1853) The Black Man: The Comparative Anatomy and Psychology of the African Negro. New York: W. C. Bryant.

CHILMAN, N. C. (1966) Growing Up Poor. Washington, DC: U.S. Department of Health, Education and Welfare.

FRAZIER, B. F. (1932) The Negro in Chicago. Chicago: University of Chicago Press.

GALTON, F. (1969) Hereditary Genius. London: Macmillan.

HALL, G. S. (1904) Adolescence. New York: Appleton-Century-Crofts.

HILL, R. (1971) The Strength of Black Families. New York: Emerson Hall.

JEFFERS, C. (1967) Living Poor. Ann Arbor, MI: Ann Arbor Publishers.

NOBLES, W. W. et al. (1976) A Formulative and Empirical Study of Black Families. Washington, DC: U.S. Department of Health, Education and Welfare.

————— (1979) Mental Health Support Systems in Black Families. Washington, DC: U.S. Department of Health, Education and Welfare.

SCANZONI, J. (1971) The Black Family in Modern Society. Boston: Allyn & Bacon.

SHIMKIN, D. et al. (1974) The Black Extended Family: A Basic Rural Institution and a Mechanism of Urban Adaptation. Cited in Ebony, March 1974.

SPENCER, H. (1884) The Man Versus the State. Baltimore: Penguin.

STAPLES, R. (1976) Introduction to Black Sociology. New York: McGraw-Hill.

TERMAN, L. M. (1916) The Measurement of Intelligence: An Explanation of and a Complete Guide for the Use of the Stanford Revision and Extension of the Binet-Simon Intelligence Scale. Boston: Houghton Mifflin.

THORNDIKE, E. L. (1940) Human Nature and the Social Order. New York: Macmillan.

VON LINNAES, C. (1735) Systema Natural. Luyduni: Butavurum.

WILLIE, C. (1970) The Family Life of Black People. Columbus, OH: Charles E. Merrill.

4

OLD-TIME RELIGION
Benches Can't Say "Amen"

WILLIAM HARRISON PIPES

Preaching and churches have traditionally been a mainstay of Black families. Among Blacks in the United States today, old-time preaching (the uneducated Black man's emotional type of preaching that came from slavery) is still a vital element. The fundamental reason why the Black man clings to the old-time religion is that he has been without a means of normal outward expression, due to his domination by powers beyond his control—in Africa, under colonial control; in America before the Civil War, the institution of slavery; in America today (especially in the "Black Belt" and to a lesser degree in other parts of the United States), the plantation system and/or "divine white right." In Africa and in America many Blacks have made their adjustment to an "impossible world" by means of an emotional escape—the frenzy and shouting of old-time religion.

To explain the preaching of this old-time religion, the author (1) investigated the African and slavery time characteristics of this type of preaching, and (2) compared and contrasted these findings with the characteristics of the preaching that was recorded in Macon County, Georgia.

Besides the religious motive, the chief purpose of old-time Black preaching appears to be to "stir up," to excite the emotions of the audience and the minister

AUTHOR'S NOTE: This chapter is condensed and adapted from the author's book, *Say Amen, Brother!* (New York: William-Frederick Press, 1951). Copyright by William Harrison Pipes.

as a means for their escape from an "impossible world." The old-time purpose of persuading people to come to Jesus is still present in varying degrees, but the emphasis here seems to be a secondary one.

EARLY AMERICAN AND AFRICAN HERITAGES

It cannot be overstressed that the "real" old-time Black preaching—undiluted by education and freedom—existed in America only during the days of slavery. Preaching in Macon County is merely its most immediate descendant. The rhythmical preaching of some sermons is illustrative. Indeed, it should be, for the preacher is a living example of the sudden crossing of two religious cultures.

This section seeks to show that the mixing of American and African backgrounds of religious practices produced old-time Black preaching. This was done by (1) considering the very earliest American background and the coming of enslaved Africans; (2) considering the African religious background of the slaves; (3) showing the actual mixing of the cultures; and (4) observing actual preaching of the Black church.

THE AMERICAN HERITAGE

It appears that there was Christian civilization in America, on the Island of Greenland, as early as the twelfth century (O'Gorman, 1895). But America had little pulpit eloquence until the sixteenth century, although it is said that Columbus's first act, in 1492, of kneeling to thank God for a safe journey might be considered preaching of a sort. It is known that, on returning to America in 1494, Columbus brought with him twelve priests. In the sixteenth century, Spanish Catholic priests wrote America's first real chapter in preaching, a chapter of humble missionary teaching.

It was the seventeenth century that marked the significant period in the development of the American heritage of preaching, especially as it was to influence Black preaching. Africans were first brought to America in large numbers in 1619 (Bacon, 1898). In this century there were two centers of preaching in America: Virginia and New England. Preaching activities in Jamestown, Virginia (settled in 1607) are very important, because this state fell within the "Black Belt" section, where there were many newly arrived enslaved Africans. "'About the last of August (1619),' says John Rolfe in John Smith's *Generall Historie,* 'came in a Dutch man of warre, that sold us twenty Negars.' These Blacks were sold into servitude, and Virginia . . . ; and thus slavery gained a firm place in the oldest of the colonies" (Brawley, 1921).

The Black slave faced a severe type of colonial religion in the beginning. But he had his own African religious heritage. The author is not unaware of Frazier's (1939) insistence that "African traditions and practices did not take root and survive in the United States" (pp. 7-8). Frazier attempted to destroy the contentions that Black religious practices in the United States may be attributed to African sources, but his attempts are feeble. For example, he stated:

> Of the same nature is the claim of Herskovits (1935, pp. 256-57) that the practice of baptism among Negroes is related to the great importance of the river-cults in West Africa, particularly in view of the fact that, as has been observed, river-cult priests were sold into slavery in great numbers. It needs simply to be stated that about a third of the rural Negroes in the United States are Methodists and only in exceptional cases practice baptism.

Frazier's refutation is fallacious for two reasons. First, he simply made a statement about the proportion of Blacks: who are Methodists without proof or documentation. The author knew from experience that some Methodists do baptise; but even if one accepted his unsupported implication that a third of the Blacks in the rural South do not practice baptism, Herskovits's contention that the American Black man's practice of baptism is related to the river-cults in West Africa may still stand. Over a period of 320 years, without contact with African religious practices, the American Blacks naturally have lost much of the African traditions and heritage. It is possible that they could have lost entirely the practice of baptism, but it is also possible that the continuity still remains. Frazier ignored these lines of reasoning, and labelled as "uncritical" and "absurd" the assertions of Herskovits, Woodson (1936), and others. Even if Africans were not allowed to bring actual religious practices to America, they certainly did bring with them their religious memories and their temperaments. As Park (1919) concluded, the tradition may have been American, but the temperament was African.

Contrary to John Hope Franklin (1947), Turner (1949), in an examination of the extent of Africanisms in the Gullah dialect, uncovered the use of 4000 African words, names, and numbers used by Blacks in the United States today. Good (1926) spoke even more specifically:

> Negroes have not lived in this country long enough to destroy the customs of the race developed in Africa. They hand down from generation to generation many of the customs and superstitions of the race, though most of them are greatly modified by life in the United States.

DuBois (1903) pointed out very definitely that the American Black's religion was influenced by African practices:

> It [the Negro church] was not at first by any means a Christian Church, but a mere adaptation of those heathen rites which we roughly designate by the term Obe Worship, or "Voodooism." Association and missionary effort soon gave these rites a veneer of Christianity, and gradually, after two centuries, the Church became Christian . . . , but with many of the old customs still clinging to the services. It is this historic fact that the Negro Church of today bases itself upon the sole surviving social institution of the African fatherland, that accounts for its extraordinary growth and vitality.

It is significant that Herskovits (1930) said that the African influence in America was strongest in the South and especially in Georgia.

It does seem reasonable that these Africans who were brought to America retained something of their African background. It cannot be denied that time and American influences modified and even eliminated some of this background. But it is inconceivable that a people could suddenly lose all of their religious practices. As Park (1919) said, "It is in connection with his [the Black man's] religion that we may expect to find, if anywhere, the indications of a distinctive Afro-American culture."

A STUDY OF BLACK PREACHING

This study was concerned with the preaching of the Black church, furthermore, because this phase of the creations of the American Black has not been studied extensively. As James Weldon Johnson (1932) pointed out, "A good deal has been written on the folk creations of the American Negro: his music, sacred and secular; his plantation tales, and his dances; but that there are folk sermons, as well, is a fact that has passed unnoticed." Since Johnson made this statement, some interest has been shown in old-fashioned preaching. The moving picture industry, newspapers, and radio have given attention to the subject. However, in almost every instance, the Black man's religion is used for entertainment; it is not considered seriously.

The fact that Black preaching has not been studied thoroughly in this field might not justify this investigation if it were not also true that for Black families within the Black man's most important institution (the church), the preacher (and his preaching, of course) is most important. "The Negro ministry is still the largest factor in the life of this [the Black] race" (Woodson, 1921). W. E. B. DuBois (1903), the eminent sociologist, evaluated the Black minister in these terms:

> The preacher is the most unique personality developed by the Negro on American soil. A leader, a politician, an orator, a "boss," an intriguer, an idealist—all these he is, and ever, too, the center of a group of men, now twenty, now a thousand in number.

It should be stressed here that the old-fashioned (old-time) Black is the unique personality referred to, for the more educated, unemotional Black ministers preach much the same as ministers of other races. But the

old-time Black preacher has not yet been given the niche in which he properly belongs. He has been portrayed only as a semi-comic figure. He had, it is true, his comic aspects, but on the whole he was an important figure, and at bottom a vital factor. . . . It was also he who instilled into the Negro the narcotic doctrine epitomized in the Spiritual, 'You May Have All Dis World, But Give Me Jesus.' This power of the old-time preacher, somewhat lessened and changed in his successors, is still a vital force; in fact, *it is still the greatest single influence among the colored people of the United States*. The Negro today is, perhaps, the most priest-governed group in the country [Johnson, 1932].

STUDY APPROACH

The purpose of this work was to make an interpretive study of old-time Black preaching as it was reflected during the late 1930s and early '40s in Macon County, Georgia, using the recordings of seven sermons.

Old-time Black preaching is important without a doubt, but James Weldon Johnson declared, "the old-time Negro preacher is rapidly passing." And this fact leads to the distinctive nature of this project: the recording of the sermons. Although the type of preaching under consideration is passing out of existence, students of American homiletics, of Black dialect, of public speaking, social sciences, and the general public may use the recordings made for this study as a basis for further study and understanding.

Without taking cognizance of the recording machine, Johnson (1932) declared of Black sermons: "There is, of course, no way of recreating the atmosphere—the fervor of the congregation, the amens and hallelujahs, the undertone of singing which was often a soft accompaniment to parts of the sermon." The recordings, even though they are unable to capture all of these aspects, go a long way toward a true presentation of these characteristics.

CHOICE OF MACON COUNTY

Throughout, the study had been confined to Macon County because conclusive proof had been given by Arthur Raper, an able sociologist, that among Blacks the closest parallel to pre-Civil War days (during which time old-fashioned Black preaching flourished on the big slave plantations) was to be found in the "Black Belt." The "Black Belt" is the name given to some 200 counties which stretch, crescent-like, from Virginia to Texas. The name has no reference to the color of the many Blacks who live in this section of the country, but to the rich, black soil of these counties. During slavery days, the large slave plantations, on which were found most of the Blacks in the United States, were to be found in the Black Belt (Raper, 1936).

It became a formidable task to record representative Black sermons which are delivered in almost every part of the country. Because the vast majority of Blacks live in the South, the problem became one of finding a typical Southern locality.

Since Reconstruction, and up to the present time, the Black Christian has become more and more like the white man; the former belief in the sinfulness of dancing and card-playing, for example, is being discarded. The author knew this to be true from actual experience as a member of a Black family in the Black Belt. In the course of this work, he often drew upon this experience but only when there was no better source of information available. His grandfather, Harrison Shaffer, a former slave, furnished much information concerning the days of slavery in the Black Belt.

Only in the Black Belt do we still have situations that are very close to the Black man's slavery days: the slave plantations with master and slaves become plantations with landlord and croppers; here alone have the Black man's earliest (old-time) religious practices been kept almost intact (Powdermaker, 1939). Macon County is typical of that part of the Black Belt which has clung most to the conditions of the old days. Macon County was acceptable as the "Middletown" of Black society.

These churches usually "hold services" (with preaching) on one regular Sunday in each month—every first Sunday, for example. This situation exists because one church alone is unable to pay a preacher a full salary. Consequently, a minister usually pastors four churches and preaches one Sunday a month at each church.

METHODOLOGY

The initial survey uncovered much interesting information on the Black man and many allusions to Black preaching; but, more significant to the investigator, it revealed that no detailed study with recordings had been made of genuine old-fashioned preaching among Blacks. From the beginning, it was felt that only by means of the recording machine could these sermons be put down accurately. Shorthand could not be depended upon. Yet, the sermons had to be taken down as delivered because this type of minister does not (often cannot) write his sermon. It was agreed, then, that the recording machine had to be used.

The following plan was followed:

(1) Study literature pertaining to the folkways, religion, beliefs, etc. of the audiences in the Black churches in Macon County.

(2) Attend church services to
   (a) record a representative number of sermons;
   (b) observe the practices of each preacher as to gestures, etc.
(3) Confer with each preacher and some of his members to learn the minister's training, preparation for a particular sermon, etc.
(4) Make the interpretation of Black preaching on the basis of accumulated data.

The original plan of procedure was followed closely, despite many difficulties. The Fort Valley State College purchased a Victor recording machine, and the college president kindly made the equipment available for recording Negro sermons over a period of three months.

Fortunately, Macon County is only a few miles from Fort Valley State College, where the author, during the summer of the recordings, was teaching a class in the Summer School's English Workshop. The students in this group were teachers from the high schools and grade schools of Georgia, and many of them came from Macon County. They knew where the churches were located, whether or not the churches had electricity, when preaching was "held," the denominations of the various churches, the ministers' names, and other information. This was very important, but even more important was the fact that these summer school teachers were known in the various communities in Macon County. Having them as members of the visiting party made it less likely to destroy the normalcy of the preaching situation. Rural teachers in Georgia often attend church services regularly; therefore, these teachers from Macon County were a part of the church audiences and were not considered strangers or outsiders.

Caution along this line was most important. An outsider has a difficult time learning anything about the inner thoughts and beliefs of Blacks in the Black Belt. They smile and act "nice" and the outsider thinks he has the facts. But the truth is often concealed. There are numerous sociological "investigations" which are supposed to reveal facts about the Black man; many of them only confuse the facts. As a Black who was born on a cotton plantation in the heart of the Black Belt and who grew up picking cotton and plowing as a typical "Black Belt" Black before leaving for Tuskegee Institute, the author knew this to be true from experience. It would be all but impossible for a white man to record sermons in Macon County without destroying the normalcy of the situation. (To make a successful study of the county, Raper, a white man, had to live in the county for the greater part of a year.) It was fortunate for this study that the author was able to joke with the people before church, talk their language in church and Sunday School, sing and pray and, in general become one of them.

The English Workshop Group and the author's wife, Anna Howard Russell Pipes, became the planning board for the recordings; Black preaching in Macon County became their project. First, it was agreed that, since of the 130 or more Black churches in Macon County, 78 were Missionary Baptist, 20 were Primitive Baptist, and 15 or 20 were Methodist, the six sermons to be recorded might be: 3, Missionary Baptist; 2, Primitive Baptist and 1, Methodist. We became known as the "Preaching Group."

The group left Fort Valley early on Sunday mornings and journeyed to the chosen church in time for Sunday School. Usually the investigator had to teach Sunday School (not a new experience for him) and the other members of the "Preaching Group" mixed with the church people and made friends. After these preliminaries, it was generally an easy matter to obtain permission to make the recording. Then the apparatus was set up outdoors and out of sight; only the microphone was visible to the audience during the recording. When there was a minister's study near the pulpit, it was used to house the apparatus; when it rained, the apparatus was set up inside the group automobile, which was parked close to the rear of the church.

The greatest difficulty in carrying out the recording project was due to the war and was beyond the power of this board: (1) recording discs (because of their rubber base) became almost unobtainable; the regular price doubled and tripled and then were not obtainable at any price; (2) gasoline rationing had come to Georgia. The four gallons per week would hardly take the group to some places in Macon County and back to Fort Valley. One student in the group was a minister himself and had an "X" card; thus he saved the project.

After the sermon was recorded, invariably the recorder was asked to play back the services and the sermon. The minister and the audience (now no longer religiously emotional) laughed and enjoyed hearing themselves. Frequently someone remarked, "Dat's jest whut he sed!" Others considered it "wonderful" that a member of their race could make records.

It is not likely that the recording tended to destroy the normalcy of the preaching situation to any great degree. Once or twice there was some artificiality at first, but the ministers and the audiences always accepted us or forgot about our presence when the "spirit" touched them. The recordings caught the spontaneity of the preaching and the reaction of the audience.

SERMONS[1]

SERMON III: "JOHN THE BAPTIST—A VOICE CRYING IN THE WILDERNESS"

It's very pleasant to be present here with you all today. Short service if possible. Got me kinda run-up; Communion at Smith Chapel, to preach Anniversary Sermon. Not feeling good. Ben on road, two weeks of service. Journeyed all night to git home. Don't feel good; got headache. You all peach-struck[2]; you all tired; been "gwine to it." Since you been "gwine to it" and am tired and I been "gwine to it" and am tired, don't 'spect too much. Omitted

Sunday School. Kinda late; hafta bear with you 'cause I know you ti'ed. *(Reads from the Bible in such a manner that one hardly can understand a word.)*

"In those days came John Baptist, preaching in the wilderness—*(of Judea).*[3] And saying, Repent ye: for the kingdom of heaven is at hand. For this is he that was spoken of by the prophet Esaias, saying, *The voice of one crying in the wilderness, Prepare* ye the way of the Lord, make his paths straight . . . (Matthew 3:1-17.)

"Then was Jesus led up of the spirit into the wilderness to be tempted of the devil. And when he had fasted forty days and forty nights, he was afterward an hungered. And when the tempter came to him, he said, If thou be the Son of God, command that these stones be made bread. But he answered and said, It is written, Man shall not live by bread alone, but by every word that proceedeth out of the mouth of God."[4] (Matthew 4:1-4.)

John was a preacher, baptizing folks. John the Baptist *(Loud cry of a baby in the audience.)*—and he was preaching to folks telling them about repentance of sin. Men don't lack you to tell them that.

Revival meeting about here. Been helping a man who gwine to help us. Gave me swell time down there. Only one thing: didn't have the spirit you got. *(Amens.)* I knocked 'round there. He will help us. We don't want to treat him no way but royal. If you want to be helped, have to help somebody. We wont to put him on a good revival. He got a home right there at home next to mine. If he don't treat me right, he's right there where I can hear what he say. *(Chuckles.)* We start now to make our aim. Five dollars or eight dollars ain't gwine to speak to no good preacher. Ten dollars ain't gwine to speak to no preacher. He gwine to preach! Every time I bring a man here, he better preacher'n me. *("No, he ain't," from the audience.)*

John was a preacher; preach 'pentance of sins. I *(have taken in a)* number of devils since I been here. Whether they converted or not, I don't know. I like that they sit down. But you'll do. Talk to me now. *(Asking for audience response.)* Them little black places dere ain't no good if you can just sit down. *(Humor; refers to the black faces of the audience.)* Consecrate myself now. *(Get serious.)* Get fair with you. I ain't got no need to come here; no one's a Christian here. Benches can't say, "Amen." You all can hear, can't yer? But John was a preacher and he went down there by himself. Wasn't no crowd down dere when he got dere.

Jesus said, "Lift Me up from the earth and I draw all men unto Me. And I draw all men unto Me." In the life you live—some us lives mighty—lift Him up. We live it while we at the church, in the church, in your songs, your moans, and your groans. Lift Him up. Let's see—er—John went down there and lift Him up. Jesus came to him and talked to him and when the Tempter came to Him, "If Thou the Son of Man, turn these rocks to bread."

He answered, "Man shall not live by bread alone." Testing Jesus, showing Him all the good things, calling Him in question. Ef he done got hungery, "Then make bread outta them stones lying around the mountain, jest like yer see 'em. Look at 'em!"

Then He got hungry, and they say to Him, "If Thou be the Son of God, command that these stones be made bread." Ain't that what he say? Preach it out there with me. I know what I'm talkin' 'bout; you too!

They thought that a fast change Him and carry Him their way. Some folks, if dey carry you their way, it's all right; ain't got nothin' to do for you if dey can't. After done been to wilderness, fast and pray. "Fast" mean don't eat, don't drink. After that, at a certain time, He got hungry. He thought *(The Tempter did.)* dat a fine time, fine time, fine chance to change Him—change His idea, change His mind—and he didn't stay 'way! You know, some folks belong to the church; long's dey can't carry you dey way, dey have nothin' for you to do. Ain't dat right? Now dat's de Lawd's turf! But as long as dey git you to do what dey want, dey wid you.

After he'd taken Him on the pinacke of dat temple, then He got hungry. He got—let me tell you, He don't eat, don't drink—after that, at a certain time, He got hungry, see? He got hungry. Then he[5] say that "this is my time." We're on our way. "Hungry; got nothin' to eat, but He says He's the Son of God." He said, "If you Christ, you outta prove it! You talk and don't prove it. Doing! He said that He God's Son; He always been with His Father; He hungry; got nothin' to eat and got no money and, quite natural, He'll yield to it." (You know, sometimes a fellow take things off people he wouldn't do it, but it's conditions.) Conditions make you do things that you wouldn't do. If conditions didn't have us so 'tight', have us going, don't you know you wouldn't work all day and all night Saturday? *(Amens.)*[6] Our conditions! Conditions! You look right at yer God sometime folks. God! Jesus look right at that rock. Rocks! Rock's something hard; something you can't bite; danger to swallow (Conditions make you do things that you wouldn't do, don't you know.) Rock's hard; bust fellow's brains out. "Turn to bread; make bread out of these" . . . .

John, forerunner of Jesus Christ, born of Elisha, come before Jesus Christ advertising Jesus Christ. One hundred years before His coming, Ezekiel—David say likewise. Daniel says he saw Him as a stone tore out of a mountain. "I'll give him all power." Ezekiel saw Him as a wheel; Ezekiel saw Him as a wheel comin' from—teeming. One Ezekiel saw Him; kept spying things—spectacle of force. Wheel in a wheel, little in big, Matthew—Luke—John—He's coming. John then grew up; maturity come up.

Don't know how much done in a run of a day. Lotta cussin' done in a run of a day; lotta disaster done in a run of a day; so much disaster done in a run of a day; no end to lying in the run of a day. Here's a day; another day. Grow—one day—days seem—. John Baptist preached in wilderness; say he go there by himself, holding up Jesus. Preached only one text. I'm got to git 'nother text every time I come here. Give up world; give 'self to God. Then you see Him, shall find the kingdom of Heaven at hand. He talk about Jesus; he talk about Jesus.

I know what I's telling you 'bout. "The Rose of Sharon, Knight of the Mornin' Star, come down to be ruler of the day. Kingdom of Heaven is at hand; Jesus not far off; always there to come to your need." That was spoke about by the prophet, the one crying in the wilderness: "Prepare ye the way of the Lord; make His paths straight; prepare the way for Him." Oh, brother, we ought to walk in such a life that somebody else ought to be prepare' through you for the Kingdom of God, the Kingdom of Heaven.

Heaven! I feel like it's a very splendid place. Heaven! I feel like it's the best place ever I have known. Wherever you at—in your state, in your field—when dat spirit of God hit you, you feel like you in Heaven right dare. You—ain't you never got happy? By yourself? You just done forgot everything and—and God knows you just feel like you in Heaven right then and there. *(Amens.)* Heaven is a spiritual place, spirit place. And Heaven make His paths straight—er—first why—.

Some folks say, "I'm a straight man myself; I'm a straight woman." Oh-oh-oh-oh, just follow on down the line; you just go her way; you'll find out whether she's straight or no. You'll find out whether she's straight or no, brother. You just deal with a man; you'll find out; you'll find out he's crooked as can be. Don't make 'em no crookeder'n him. He—. A straight man or woman don't care what time, when or where they are, they want to do right, want to walk out-right, plain before the world. Not ashamed of their lives; "I'm living straight." I ain't talking about walking straight and calmly, but your life! Straight! Straight! I ain't talkin. . . .

Forty days, forty nights—I told yo' what fasting mean. They got hungry. Bible said they tempted them. They—call Son of God, commanded stone be made bread. Testing—Jesus said, "Man, man shall not live by bread alone." Ain't dat true, man? *(The audience chants: "Man shall not live by bread alone.")* Man, God's word good. Hungry soul, hear somebody sing and pray. Certain, man can't get filled till he harken.

Uncle Sam calling for me; mighty war on calling for me. Dis last remark to you. Sit on a high hill, sit on a high hill—East and West—Lilly of the Valley—. Things of the world, things of the world, things of the world. This world—. Yes—oh, Jesus! Oh, Jesus! Sundown—. Pinackle of temple—. Lily of the Valley—. Beautiful things. "All this is mine, all this is mine. It is mine, it is mine, it is mine." Oh, Lord! "I tell you what you do now, if you just fall down and worship me."

"Get behind!" My Lord! God got His eyes on you. See all you do. Midnight! Save Jesus,[7] Save Jesus. Died on Calvary Hill. Save Jesus, save Jesus, save Jesus. Hint to the wise. Save Jesus. Get free. Save Jesus. Leper—save Jesus—take up your bed and go home. Save Jesus. Writing on the ground. Save Jesus, Man to depend on when trouble come. Put truth to him *(Devil)* and he go away. Truth breaks down things; truth washes down things. Last day—disciples—this Friday—took Him this night, took Him this night—all night long—now before Pilate. Judas, as he betrayed—little money—Judas as he betrayed, told 'em with a kiss. (Kiss ain't so good.) Judas, as he betrayed Jesus, betrayed with a kiss. Mighty man.

Hold it *(the spirit,)* hold it! Sometimes makes you cry, sometimes makes you cry, sometimes makes you pray, sometimes makes you moan, sometimes makes you right-living. If it makes you cry, I'll be with you, will not forsake you. Mother cry. Father fine. Everybody thinks you git it. Hold it. *(Moaning.)* Go with you to graveyard. He makes you your dying bed. Mercy! Hold it. *(Sings.)* I been had hold Him a long time; He ain't never let me down.

'Tis on cross, Friday evening. Lord! Right there Sunday morning soon, Sunday morning soon *(Christ)* rose out of the grave. Soon, soon, *(Sings it.)* soon *(Shouting in the audience—climax begins)*; watches 'round grave; felt like dead man on to himself. Oh—oh, knocked off dying smile; put back in one corner of grave. Angel sitting on Heavenly grave holding God's hand. Sat right there; nobody in the grave; saw it standing gaping open. He not there; somebody done stole Him away. I see Him go back. John go down to grave, go down to grave, go down to grave, go down to grave. Look-a-yonder, look-a-yonder; who do you see? Who you see? Jesus! Jesus! "I looked for Jesus, but shook and tremble." Jesus! Rocks began to roar. Jesus! "Got to tell my brother." Jesus! "I'm going before day."

Ahhhhhhh! Ahhhhhhh! *(Climax! General confusion.)*

Got my *(Pause.)* . . . in your soul. Got to cry sometime. Know I been born again. Git off by 'self and cry. My soul, *(Audience moans, "My soul.")* My soul have Savior. Have trouble and tribulation; sometimes afflicted; have to crawl into your home. Farewell; Farewell! *(Uniformed ushers come to administer to the shouting ladies.)* For motherless child, nowhere to go, nobody to go to. Fatherless child . . . *(Leaves pulpit and comes down to the audience.)* My! My! Don't you feel lonely sometime in world by yourself? Give me your hand. *(Picks up a tune on "Give me your hand." Audience joins in singing.)* Lord, give me your hand. Won't He lead you? *(Talking now.)* Won't He take care of you, chillun? Be consolation for you? My, my Lord! I done tried! I know He *do* care of you, preserve your soul, and den what I like about You, carry you home. Here rain wouldn't fall on you. Beautiful land. Gwine to sing and open de doors of the church.

OLD-TIME PREACHING

People listen attentively to a speaker if they feel that his message vitally concerns them. Are the speaker's ideas worthy of their sincere considerations? If they are, the speaker may be assured of their interest and goodwill. The emotions and the basic beliefs—friendship, duty, honor, fear, shame, emulation, patriotism, compassion—are the stuff of which emotional or pathetic appeal is made. These are the elements of emotional proof. Stripped of the unparalleled emphasis upon this appeal, old-time Black preaching is not unique. But, as James Weldon Johnson (1932) declared, the old-time Black preacher "had the power to sweep his hearers before him; and so himself was often swept away." This was the original old-time Black preacher. Do the original elements of pathetic proof appear in Macon County sermons? What is the nature of the new influence?

This question suggests the role of pathetic (emotional) appeal with the old-time Black audience. Blacks keep this emotional light burning within themselves constantly—in their moans, in their spirituals, and in their prayers; as they work the fields or walk the roads; as they shy down the streets of the country town or bow into some country store (always fearful of the Lords of the South and of Judge Lynch). They come to church with this emotional spark already within them; they only want the minister to fan it into a flame—to encourage them to let this light set them on fire with shouts and groans. This is their emotional escape from an impossible world; this action of shouting and moaning and laughing and crying relieves them. Therefore, a consideration of pathetic appeal with such people resolves itself into a determination of the methods the Black minister employs to fan these emotional sparks into flames. The audience's knowledge of the Bible (the chief source of information) equalled that of the speaker; the congregation and the minister share the same religious ideas. Therefore, this is not an intellectual occasion; this is not a time for thinking. The problem becomes one of arousing the emotions, of helping the tired, subdued Black man to associate his trials, sorrows, and joys with those of the Biblical characters.

The genuine old-time preacher knows that his mission in part is to fan emotions into flames. He accomplishes this by leading the audience to concentrate upon "getting happy" by suggestion (directly or indirectly)—through action, by the audience and by the minister (delivery). This initial action suggests the climactic emotional state which the audience and the minister seek.

The old-time Black preacher, although a master hypnotist, follows in the footsteps of great orators when he appeals to his audience's basic beliefs—Biblical ideas which have been adjusted to fit the descendants of Africans and of American slaves. The conception of God is at the center of these beliefs; to the

Black man, God is mysterious and all-powerful. The Black man's attitude toward God makes the congregation susceptible to certain emotional appeals. This preacher appeals to his audience's great *admiration* and *joy over* the power of God. Revealing how vital to them was his subject, ministers dwell on the audience's *love* for God and their *hope* for a new life to come.

The *fear* of God is another emotion to which the old-time Black preacher appeals:

> "My Lord! God got His eyes on you! See all you do."
> "Have mercy now; oh, Jesus, have mercy now."

Fear has consistently dogged the footsteps of the Black man—as an African, as an American slave, and now as a second-class citizen. Observe how a minister produces shouting by appealing to the *fear* of God:

> "Yonder He come. . . . God Almighty. . . . Thunder, your conscience; lightning in Your hand. . . . Everybody is gwine ter pray now!" *(Audience shouts wildly.)*

There is suggestion too in the last statement:

> "You may be too proud *(Suggests the preacher.)* to pray now; too proud to shout now, but you *will* shout and pray when God comes, so why not now?"

The people agree, and they do shout and pray. The audience's *fear* of God often approaches *awe* under the spell of the preacher's description of God's work.

But unadulterated *fear of death* is the emotion to which a minister appeals. The minister, even when not striking directly at fear-producing descriptions of death, likes to talk about things with which *death* has some connection. Any mention of the grave or of death serves the purpose—to produce shouting. Jesus' triumph over the great mystery, *death,* is most effective. The Biblical story of the strange death of Almighty God's Son is used frequently:

> Christ "kept on dying *(on the cross)*. He never stopped dying."

The preacher often stimulated the emotions of his audience by telling of his "call" to preach. In all instances, when the members of the audience are excited and open to the mildest suggestion, they are thinking of their own trials, joys, and sorrows, and their emotional condition is heightened by the rhythmical delivery and their own actions. For example, when the minister, after telling the Biblical story of Joseph the Dreamer, says:

> "I seed Him . . ., a shield over here one Sunday mornin'. He was takin' on board. . . . And I *dream, chillun,*" *(Sings the last two words; the audience joins in. Shouting.)*

he unlocks the door of his audience's world with the words *"dream, chillun,"* as did Martin Luther King in his "I Had a Dream" sermon. They too had trials and problems (like Joseph); they too were *dreaming* and hoping for a better day to come. When the preacher says "dream, chillun," he stimulates thoughts and emotions within the audience which lie too deep for words. The people understand; they shout. "How long" is the unlocking key to the door of frustration when a minister moans:

"*How long?* How long must I work in the vineyard?"

The words "how long" suggest to the Black his apparently endless chain of trials. How often he has wondered *how long* the Lord would permit his chosen servant to be mistreated in this world below. *"How long."* Pent up emotions overflow. Shouting.

WHEN IT COMES OUR TIME TO DIE[8]

The Black man's old-time religious prayer is not confined to the church. Outside the church, it keeps the emotional flame alive. It replaces the sermon at home, at the sick-bed, and at "wakes." Blacks in the Black Belt still observe the old custom of sitting up all night with the dead. Friends and relatives visit the house of the deceased on the night of the "wake"; the body is in plain view, and the night is spent in talking of death, of the dead person (especially, how the "end"—death—came), and in drinking coffee or something stronger.

This prayer given at a wake in the Black Belt is not unusual—and demonstrates too the new influences, which fight against the prayer's old-time emotional appeal:

"Oh, Gawd, we come this evenin' beared down wid the sorrows of this worl.' We come as paupers to Thy th'one o' grace. We been down in the valley o' the shadder, an' our hearts is heavy this evenin,' Lord. Thou's done thundered fo'th Thy will. Thou's done took from out our mist one o' Yo' lambs. Thou's done took a good brother who's done lived his 'lotted time an' died, Gawd, like we all mus' die. Ummmmmmmmmmmm. Thou's done come into this house o' sons an' wid Yo' own han', Yo' own grat han', Gawd—Ummmmmmmmmmmmm—Thou's done dashed down the vessel outa what Yo' po'ed life into them. Thou's done took a father an' a gran'-father. Thou's done beared down hearts. Thou's done put burdens on 'em. Thou's done whupped 'em wid stripes. 'Member dese hearts, great Lawd. Relieve 'em. You know when t' suns's been a-shinin' too long an' the earth's all parched an' barren, You sen's Yo' rain, Lord. You relieve the earth. When wars rage, like the one ragin' now, an' mens dies an' makes widders an' orfins, den, in Yo' own good time, Gawd—Yo' precious time Ummmmmmm— You sen's peace. You takes the burden off'n the hearts o' nations. An' You promise', Father, by the sweetflowin' blood o' Jesus, to rescue the perishin', suckle the needy, give health to the ailin' . . ."

(He did not pause at a piercing scream from Jamie. *She is shouting.* His extended fingers worked spasmodically, as if each had a life, independent of him.)

"An' sen' balm to the hearts o' sufferin'. Sen' it now, Lord. Let it flow like the healin' waters o' Gilead, an' ease the burden o' dese hearts broken by the fulfillin' o' Yo' almighty will. Amen."

(The preacher opened his eyes and looked around as he lowered his arms, shooting his cuffs as he did so. The three brothers stared at spots about six inches beyond their toes. One corner of his thick mouth drawn in a hard snarl, Paul lifted the pitcher *(of whiskey)* from the table and drank. In the other room there was a general snuffling and loosening of throats. Walter was the first to recover.)

"That was a fine prayer, Rev'ren'," he said. "Mighty fine."

"Thank you, brother."

. . . "That's fine. That's jus' fine,' the preacher said pompously. "Uncle Henry's *(Refers to the dead man.)* goin, a smile up there wid Gawd tomorrer. I'm aimin' to do him proud."

With that, he went back into the other room. Neely closed the door.

"He can lay a pow'ful prayer." [Redding, 1942].

The prayer, like the sermon, appeals to the emotions of gratitude to God, compassion, fear of death, fear of God, sorrow, shame; it, too, employs suggestion.

Like the prayer, the singing is important in stimulating the emotions. The hymn (like the spiritual) is really a blending of emotions. The words themselves are unintelligible unless they are "lined." That is, someone states a line or two before the audience sings them; the audience sings and pauses while additional lines are stated; the singing continues in this manner until the end; the audience is seated part of the time and stands part of the time. Even after the song is "lined," the words are so run together in the long-meter fashion that they are not distinguishable. Such singing is an emotional experience, like an instrumental rendition. Spirituals carry the same emotional charge. The singing is so important in setting the stage emotionally that the sermon is almost inconceivable without it.

DuBois (1903) said that "three things characterize the religion" of the Black man: the preacher, the music, and the frenzy. "The music is that plaintive rhythmic melody, which is touching in minor cadences, which, despite caricature and defilement, still remains the most original and beautiful expression of human life and longing yet born on American soil. Sprung from the African forests, where its counterpart can still be heard, it was adapted, changed, and intensified by the tragic soul-life of the slave, until, under the stress of law and whip, it became the one true expression of a people's sorrow, despair, and hope."

The old-time Black man is indeed a master of this art of emotional appeal. Even the order of services builds toward the desired emotional climax of shouting. Observe the order of services for the sermon, "Thou Shalt Love the Lord Thy God:"

1. *Song:* "My Faith Looks Up to Thee."
2. *Prayer:* A deacon thanks the Lord for having permitted *death* to leave them in the world "a little longer." *(The minister did not ordain the use of these exact words, but he knows the content of the average Negro old-time prayer.)*
3. *Song:* "I Love Jesus." *(A perfect selection.)*
4. *Song:* "Come, Thou Fount of Every Blessing."
5. *Hymn:* "Father, I Stretch My Hands to Thee."
6. *Responsive Reading from the Bible.*
7. *Song:* More of "Father, I Stretch My Hands to Thee."
8. *Prayer:* A preacher thanks the Lord for sparing them. The goodness of God is stressed.   •
9. *Song:* "Where He Leads Me I Will Follow."
10. *Scripture Reading:* "Thou Shalt Love the Lord Thy God."

In the order of services a prominent place is given to the prayer. Much can be said of the importance of prayer in emotional appeal. The prayer (or prayers) precedes the sermon and, using many of the same appeals to the emotions that are to be found in the sermons, serves to prepare the way, to set the mood, for the ultimate emotional frenzy caused by the sermon. The following prayer reveals the importance of the prayer for pathetic appeal:

> *(The congregation, bowed, hums the last verse of "My Faith Looks Up to Thee" as the deacon moves searchingly and rhythmically into his prayer.)* "Dear Lawd, we come befo' Thee and ask Thee ter stand by us. Thank Thee for ev'ry thing Thou's did for us. Christ, essemble between these four walls; git in the hearts uv men and women, boys and girls, Thou art God an' God alone.
>
> "Since the last time we's bowed, we's done things that we ought not uv done, an' we's left things undone what we ought uv done. Rule over Heav'n and earth; rule over these people down here, the sick an' afflicted and weary. And bind us one to another.
>
> "Now, Lawd, when it come our time to *die,* pray You receive us into Thy kingdom an' give us souls a resting place. Amen."

This prayer, given by another minister from the pulpit, revealed the effectiveness of prayer in emotional appeal: They "warm up" the emotions of the audience for the sermon.

THE PREACHER: MAN OF GOD

Some Blacks declared that the magnetism and power of the preacher solely are responsible for a "good meetin'," that the minister's ability to affect the emotions of the audience accounted for the shouting and the frenzy. Few observers accepted logical argument as an important element in old-time Black preaching.

The audience's conception of the Black minister as a "Man of God" is obviously a persuasive element. Even before the preacher speaks, his listeners are in a receptive mood, for the old-time Black preacher does not "just go to school" and then begin preaching; he is "called of God to preach." But what forces and influences develop this "man of God?" What is the nature of being "called?" What character qualities of the preacher make him persuasive? How does the "Man of God" differ from other Christians?

The preparation of the "man of God" often begins before birth, with the dedication of the child to God by a pregnant mother. Others are called after living a life of sin. There are "good" Negroes and "bad" Negroes who become ministers. The background of the "bad" Negro gives him ethical appeal because of the contrast between his new life and his old, "sinful" life. The people reason, "As bad as old Henry was, he surely must have been 'called' or he never would have become a preacher." Both types of preachers are "called" and both have appeal because of what they are.

Booker T. Washington (1924) implied that the Negro preacher is not always sincere in his claim that he has been called to preach. He tells the story of the Negro who, working along in the cotton field one day, suddenly stopped and cried in a pulpit voice:

> De sun am so hot and dis Nigger am so tired, bless my soul, I believe I done been called to preach! Glory!!

A common joke among Blacks is that such-and-such a preacher thought God said, "Go *preach*," when what He really said was, "Go *plow!*"

The character of Black preachers persuades their audiences—despite the moral weakness of some of them. The old-time Black preacher is "a good man." Blacks stress this point: the preacher must not dance, play cards, or drink. Yet some preachers are "the biggest devils" in the church. Members of the church can name the "sweethearts" of such pastors. Occasionally, a "sister's" husband or lover takes a knife or a razor and "cuts up" the minister. Almost every Black knows "dirty jokes" about the minister's lack of morals; it is a common saying that preachers love three things: money, women, and chicken. Yet the old-time Black preacher is respected and honored. (The author knows there are many upright and moral Black ministers. His intention here is not to disparage such ministers or their profession.) His being a "Man of God" is not the full answer. Other elements of his character are important to the understanding of this paradoxical situation.

Perhaps, above all, the old-time Black preacher was superior to his people in intelligence. As James Weldon Johnson (1932) said:

> The old-time preacher was generally a man far above the average in intelligence; he was, not infrequently, a man of positive genius. The earliest of these preachers

must have virtually committed many parts of the Bible to memory through
hearing the scripture read or preached from . . .

Native intelligence gives him leadership, for the old-time preacher lacked
education to give him prestige.

The Black preacher's small income meant that well-educated men did not
pastor these churches. This introduced other characteristics of these ministers.
"Pastoring" three churches, the typical minister received an average $546.60 a
year. He spent about one-sixth for traveling expenses. Even this small amount
was not paid as salary. It was charity. The minister had to "take up collection."
This explained two other characteristics of the preacher: first, why he was
extremely money-conscious and, second, why he must please the audience.
Only a burning desire to be a leader could compensate for this situation.

This *desire to lead* is an important element in the preacher's character; it
often accompanied natural leadership. Perhaps "leadership" is not the proper
word, but certainly these old-time preachers tackled any problem. James W.
Johnson tells of an old Black minister who opened his Bible one Sunday and
read from a rather cryptic passage. He did not understand a word of it, but
(always the leader) he removed his eyeglasses, slammed the Bible shut, stared
down at his respectful and expectant congregation, and said: "Brothers and
sisters, this morning—I intend to explain the unexplainable—find out the
undefinable—ponder over the impossible—and unscrew the inscrutable." Intelligence, leadership ability, and the "man of God" conception serve the Macon County preacher well.

SUMMARY

The methods of persuasion of the Macon County preaching demonstrate that
emotional appeal remains dominant; appeal through the character of the
preacher (the "Man of God") runs a close second. Logical argument is not
entirely absent. Especially in the sermons of the more highly educated ministers, there appear evidences of both inductive and deductive reasoning (at the
less emotional points of the sermon.) The method of instructing the audience
unemotionally is being ushered in by the more highly educated Black ministers.
Another modern influence seems to be the underlying purpose of soliciting
money.

The style of Macon County preaching is basically simple: short words which
are familiar to the audience (with a long word thrown in occasionally for
effect). Sentences are often elliptical (without complete subject and predicate).
Such sentences, however, are joined by conjunctions, to help maintain the
speaker's rhythmical flow of words. Slang and Black dialect (the language of
the audience) form the level of expression. But the style is figurative, with the

use of metaphor, based on the experiences of the audience or drawn from the Bible, taking the lead. The style is narrative—for the listener rather than for the reader. The amount of poetic, Biblical prose is decreasing, perhaps because education (newspapers, magazines, radio) is bringing in new expressions—a condition which is unlike the original complete dependency upon the Bible.

The delivery of the Macon County sermon is most characteristic of earlier old-time Black preaching. Entirely impromptu, it is rhythmical—which helps to heighten the emotions of the minister and the audience. It gains effect by the change from conversational to rhythmical speaking. The delivery is also made more effective by the preacher's appearance, his sincerity, his bombastic gestures, and his many movements in the pulpit. Possibly most important, the preacher's delivery is aided by his masterful modulation and control of his excellent voice. The recorded Macon County sermons indicate that old-time Black preaching today is still a vital part of the Black man's existence. Preaching is still the soul of a frustrated people.

The background of this study of American Blacks, A People in Bondage (from Africa, to American slavery, and to present-day second-class citizenship), explains old-time Black preaching partly as an escape mechanism for a frustrated people. This study also points up two conclusions: (1) the Black race in the United States has made unparalleled progress in normal adjustment (against odds), but the Black man should not expect to exercise first-class American citizenship immediately—unless America herself decides (probably beginning with a Supreme Court decision) to practice true democracy *for all people:* to remove from the American scene the half-century-old concept (based on a ruling of the United States Supreme Court) of "separate-but-equal"; (2) the crying need of the Black race in the United States is for improved leadership, regardless of the time-table of democracy: first-class citizenship for the Black man *now* as his American right.

First-Class Citizenship for the Black Man Now. If the masses of U.S. Blacks are to have their frustration-producing condition eliminated permanently in the near future, America must somehow come to realize the menace to the nation of racial prejudice in a nuclear age; she must realize in deed as well as in word that it is the American creed and law that no man deserves second-class citizenship because of race, color, or previous condition of servitude; she must realize that the best *preparation* for the Black man's wise use of first-class citizenship is to be found in the Black man's *practice* of first-class citizenship.

Long-range first-class citizenship will come to the Black man mainly through the unity of effort on the part of the Blacks themselves; this unity of effort must be used to prepare the race to exercise wisely his rights as a citizen and to prepare the minds of Southern white people to permit such democracy. If the Black man is frustrated because of persecution, the mind of the white man is warped because of the un-American practices of enslaving and degrading the

Black man; Booker T. Washington stated it in this manner: "You cannot hold a man down in a ditch without remaining there yourself."

Freedom for the Black man through unity of effort on the part of Blacks themselves? Is this not the blind leading the blind? Certainly, united action on the part of the Black Belt Blacks is in the distant future, for the Black man (due to his background of bondage) is far from belonging to a race that has solidarity. Old-time Black ministers often declare, "Negroes just won't stick together." As Gunnar Myrdal (1944) shows, however, the masses of a people *must* have education and some degree of economic security before they can unite to improve themselves permanently in a social, economic, and political way. The Black man as a group is still a semi-illiterate proletariate and, hence, cannot be expected to unite to improve the masses of his people until a sizable group of Blacks are both more highly educated and more economically secure. The Black man himself cannot make this a fact within the near future, nor is the white man likely to clear his mind of prejudice voluntarily within the near future. American democracy never had a greater command—for when the Black man is denied first-class citizenship, American democracy as a whole is debased.

Undoubtedly, the old-time Black preacher is *the* Black leader today; it is to him that the great majority of Blacks in this country look for guidance. The degreed and trained Black educators, ministers, writers, et al., should not delude themselves into thinking that they are the true Black leaders. The masses of Blacks seldom get to know these "leaders" and even when the opportunity does bring the highly trained leader into contact with the average Black the latter either does not understand the "highbrow" leader or distrusts his motives—and not always unjustly. But the old-time preacher is "one of the flock." He is trusted, listened to, and understood. Therefore, the crying need in improving the Black masses (whether first-class citizenship comes immediately or in the distant future) is for improved Black leadership.

As Richardson (1947) pointed out in his study, improvement of the Black ministry can do much to improve the condition of the Black masses, but the author is dubious of the leadership of any Black who is economically dependent on the goodwill of the prejudiced white persons (which eliminates many college presidents and teachers) or who is economically dependent upon the masses of Blacks (which seems to minimize the effectiveness of the leadership of the average Black minister, who is dependent upon Blacks for his income).

Without a feeling of despair or pessimism (but trying to read the timetable correctly, which is essential for the Black race in making the journey himself to first-class citizenship), the author does not conceive of Blacks possessing within the immediate future the educational and economical improvement necessary to wrest first-class citizenship from a reluctant country—and the country will be reluctant for some time to come. Will the greatest democracy on earth meet the challenge? Will the "Land of the Free" return to *her* old-time religion, *freedom for all people:* "All men are created equal and from that equal creation they derive rights inherent and unalienable, among which are the preservation of life and liberty and the pursuit of happiness?"

If America really wants to return to *her old-time* religion of freedom for all people, then let her say in deed—"Amen, Brother!" ("Benches can't say 'Amen.' You all can hear, can't yer?")

NOTES

1. Complete transcriptions of each of the sermons may be found in Say Amen, Brother! (Pipes, 1951).

2. It was peach-packing season in Georgia and most of the audience had worked until very late Saturday night, really until Sunday morning.

3. These words, like many others in this passage, he omitted. He often mumbled. It was discovered later that he could not read very well.

4. It appeared that the minister read on and on until he struck something in the Bible that appealed to him, something that would serve as his subject; entirely extemporaneous.

5. The Tempter.

6. He means the sermon, the emotional part, is getting underway.

7. Observe how "Save Jesus" becomes a refrain.

8. The minister, closing Sermon IV: "May the Lord bless us, may He help us, and may He save us when it comes our time to die. Amen."

9. Sermon III.

REFERENCES

BACON, L. W. (1898) A History of American Christianity. New York: Scribner.

BRAWLEY, B. (1921) A Short History of the American Negro. New York: Macmillan.

DUBOIS, W. E. B. (1903) Souls of Black Folk. Chicago: McClurg.

FRANKLIN, J. H. (1947) From Slavery to Freedom. New York: Alfred Knopf.

FRAZIER, E. F. (1939) The Negro Family in the United States. Chicago: University of Chicago Press.

GOOD, A. (1926) Sociology and Education. New York: Harper.

HERSKOVITS, M. (1930) "The Negro in the new world." American Anthropologist 32 (November).

JOHNSON, J. W. (1932) God's Trombone, Seven Negro Sermons in Verse. New York: Viking.

MYRDAL, G. (1944) An American Dilemma. New York: Harper.

O'GORMAN, T. (1895) A History of the Roman Catholic Church in the United States. New York: Christian Literature.

PARK, R. (1919) "The conflict and fusion of cultures with special reference to the Negro." Journal of Negro History 4, 2 (April).

PIPES, W. H. (1951) Say Amen, Brother! New York: William-Frederick Press.

POWDERMAKER, H. (1939) After Freedom. New York: Viking.

RAPER, A. A. (1936) Preface to Peasantry: A Tale of Two Black Belt Counties. Chapel Hill: University of North Carolina Press.

REDDING, J. S. (1942) No Day of Triumph. New York: Harper.

RICHARDSON, H. (1947) Dark Glory. New York: Friendship Press.

TURNER, L. D. (1949) Africanisms in the Gullah Dialect. Chicago: University of Chicago Press.

WASHINGTON, B. T. (1924) Up from Slavery. New York: Doubleday.

WOODSON, C. (1921) The History of the Negro Church. Washington, DC: Associated Publishers.

_____ (1925) Negro Orators and Their Orations. Washington, DC: Associated Publishers.

_____ (1936) The African Background Outlined. Washington, DC: Associated Publishers.

5

CONCEPTUALIZATIONS OF BLACK FAMILIES

JUALYNNE DODSON

CONTRASTING APPROACHES TO
THE STUDY OF BLACK FAMILIES

The pathological and dysfunctional view of black families has been primarily related to the cultural ethnocentric approach and associated with the work of E. Franklin Frazier (1939) and Daniel P. Moynihan (1965). The works of these scholars have culminated in the adaptation of social policies predicated on the assumption that the black family is unstable, disorganized, and unable to provide its members with the social and psychological support and development needed to assimilate fully into American society.

The cultural relativity school, on the other hand, begins with the assumption that black American culture and family patterns possess a degree of cultural integrity that is neither related to nor modeled on white American norms. Most members of this school trace the origins of these cultural differences back to black American's African cultural heritage, and all tend to focus on the "strengths" of black families rather than their weaknesses.

The cultural relativistic view, developed primarily as a reaction to the deficit view, maintains that the black family is a functional entity. This conceptualization is designed to challenge the theories and social policies emanating from the ethnocentric approach.

Underlying the theoretical and empirical arguments of the two schools is the common assumption that black families and white families are qualitatively different culturally. The schools diverge from each other, however, in their interpretation and explanation of the causes of these differences. The cultural ethnocentric school, operating on the assumption that America is culturally homogeneous and that there are universal norms for American cultural behavior to which all groups must conform, points to certain presumed inadequacies in black people to account for the differences. Similarly, it places a negative value judgment on the fact that black families deviate from the American norm. The cultural relativity school, on the other hand, assumes that America is a multicultural society and concludes that differences are largely accounted for by the variation in the cultural backgrounds and experiences of black and white Americans.

The assumption that black and white families are qualitatively different culturally is not shared by all students of black family life, however. A third set of studies that can be said to fall outside the two schools noted above emphasize the role of social class in determining family patterns and characteristics. The scholars of this perspective maintain that when you control for social class, no appreciable differences exist between black and white families. In-depth discussions of each of the two contrasting major approaches to the study of black family life follow. I will then consider some of the limitations of using social class as a variable in analyzing black family structure and functioning.

THE CULTURAL ETHNOCENTRIC SCHOOL

E. Franklin Frazier (1894-1962) was the leading twentieth-century exponent of the cultural ethnocentric school. He and W. E. B. DuBois pioneered in the study of the black family as a social phenomenon, but, unlike DuBois, one of Frazier's major concerns was understanding the process through which the black family became culturally assimilated into American life. It is important to note that Frazier's works, according to Lyman (1972), were influenced by his determination to (a) refute the argument advanced by Melville Herskovits (and DuBois) that much of black life is a continuation of African cultural forms and (b) empirically demonstrate Robert E. Park's race relations cycle. Frazier believed that black American marriage and family patterns, customs, and structures were the consequence of slavery and American culture, not African cultural transfers. He did not accept Herskovits's conclusion that black family structure, marital customs, and sexual practices were derived from African cultures. Rather, for example, Frazier (1939) interpreted "indiscriminate" and extramarital sexual behavior among blacks as being a product of slavery and unrelated to customs and practices in traditional polygamous African cultures.

Researchers attempting to discover possible African cultural transferences to the New World focused on the slavery period. At the time Frazier began his work, leading authorities on the history of American Negro slavery shared

Frazier's rather than Herskovits's position. Frazier's assertion that as "a result of the manner in which the Negro was enslaved, the Negro's African cultural heritage has had practically no effect on the evolution of his family in the United States" (1939: 66) reflected the views of both U. B. Phillips (1929), and, subsequently, Stanley Elkins (1959). Both concluded that while significant African cultural traits, such as names and folklore, did survive initially, they were eventually lost or distorted. Accordingly, Uncle Remus stories were altered to reflect the new animals and surroundings of the storytellers (Phillips, 1929: 195). If the culture of the African slaves was destroyed, then it is hopeless to expect that the evolution of the black family was influenced by that culture. So begins the logic of the cultural ethnocentric school.

The stability of the black family during slavery was controlled, they maintain, by the plantation owners. If a family arrangement failed to produce offspring, some slaveowners matched the couple, usually the woman, with other mates. Additionally, slave families were frequently broken up, its members sold individually. In spite of the slaves' unstable formal or legal marital and familial life, these authorities believed that blacks accepted and attempted to conform to the social norms of the majority society.

Frazier viewed blacks as an assimilation-oriented minority following the race-relations cycle as predicted and outlined by Ezra Parks (1926-1950). Indeed, Frazier saw the black family's assimilation toward the dominant American norms as part of the process by which it evolved from slavery and servitude toward freedom. In his study of blacks living in Chicago, Frazier found that as they moved outward from the inner city, black families appeared more culturally and physically assimilated, based on the proportion of interracial marriages (1939). It was his faithfulness to Park's race relations cycle which seemingly motivated Frazier to interpret black masses as assimilative and to ignore evidence to the contrary.[1] Although the race relations cycle has yet to be empirically validated, Frazier earnestly attempted to do so. It is, in a sense, a tragic conclusion to his intellectual career that he was forced to observe on the last page of one of his last books, *Black Bourgeoisie: The Rise of a New Middle Class in the United States,* that when blacks achieve "middle-class status their lives generally lose both content and significance" (1957: 238).

The line of research as pursued by Frazier was followed by a number of investigators and culminated in proposals for social policy. In 1965, the Office of Policy Planning and Research of the United States Department of Labor issued a 78-page document prepared by the assistant secretary, Daniel P. Moynihan, under the title, *The Negro Family–The Case for National Action.* This report repeatedly cited Frazier as support for its conclusions that the black community was characterized by broken families, illegitimacy, matriarchy, economic dependency, failure to pass armed forces entrance tests, delinquency, and crime. Moynihan placed the cause of these problems on a supposedly broken and unstable black family. Following his trend-making step, other investigators began to concentrate on the pathologies of black families.

In 1966, Elliot Liebow conducted a participant-observation study of 24 streetcorner black men. He concluded that the men had internalized the American norms for family roles, but that the oppressive conditions of their societal environment prevented their fulfilling these expectations. Lee Rainwater (1968), examining the matrifocal character of black American and Caribbean families, concluded that matriarchal families were pathological and detrimental to the personality development of black children. He also suggested that such families interfered with the ability of black males to develop normal heterosexual roles.

Jessie Bernard (1966) traced the evolution of the black family's stability from 1880 to 1963 and reported that the decrease in the proportion of black infants born out of wedlock was related to two distinct lifestyles independent of social class. One lifestyle was oriented toward the pursuit of pleasure and material consumption, while the other adhered to a firm belief in and acceptance of the Protestant ethic. This hedonistic orientation accounts for the decline in legitimate births among blacks. Having failed to internalize the marital norms of the American society, it is suggested that this subgroup ignores their responsibility when adherence becomes too difficult. The matrifocal family is seen as an outgrowth of the failure of black men to fulfill their paternal roles.

Parker and Kleiner (1966) contrasted the adjustment and attitudes of mothers in broken and intact families and examined the possible impact of these characteristics of their children. They found that mothers in broken family situations had poorer psychological adjustment and were less concerned about goals for their children. It was suggested that children raised in female-headed households would not have the psychological support of their mothers. Such research advances the argument that matriarchy and female-headed households are pathological and undermine any male-female relationship in the family (Blood and Wolfe, 1969; Duncan and Duncan, 1969; Bracey et al., 1971; Parker and Kleiner, 1966).

Other investigators have reported that the data supporting Moynihan's matriarchal concept are conclusive (Hyman and Reed, 1969). Investigators who focused on the validity of the female role in the black family have generally concluded that matrifocal families are not produced by values of the black community but by structural factors in the society which necessitate that males frequently abandon their roles (Yancy, 1972; Staples, 1974). Tenhouten (1970) was unable to substantiate the dominant role attributed to black mothers as implied in the Moynihan Report. Further, King (1967, 1969) found that black fathers were not perceived by their children as passive in decision making, and black mothers were perceived as less dominant than as reported in earlier studies. Delores Mack (1971) examined social class and racial differences in the distribution of power attributable to race. And Heiss (1972) found that instability in the black family does not necessarily lead to instability in future generations.

Studies which concentrated on the dysfunctional and disorganized aspects of black family life have deduced that the typical black family is fatherless, on welfare, thriftless, and overpopulated with illegitimate children. Inevitably, they have recommended economic reforms for "saving" black families from their own pathology (see, for example, Moynihan, 1965; Rainwater, 1965; Rodman, 1968). However, Andrew Billingsley (1968) challenged these stereotypes, pointing out that two-thirds of black families living in metropolitan areas are headed by husbands with their wives: Half have managed to pull themselves into the middle-class and nine-tenths are self-supporting.

There remains, then, considerable controversy among researchers concerning the ability of nonwhite Americans to establish and maintain viable marital and familial relations. Particularly, there are a large number of studies that underscore the dysfunctionality of black families. Implicit in the dichotomous conceptualization of functional versus dysfunctional capacities of black families is an assumption regarding normative model families. The belief that a statistical model of the American family can be identified and used to ascertain the character of the families of all American cultural groups is mythical at best. Further, such an assumption contradicts the ideals of a democratic society and the realities of a culturally plural one.

THE CULTURAL RELATIVITY SCHOOL

The cultural relativity view, primarily in reaction to the cultural ethnocentric view, advocates that the black family is a functional entity. This conceptualization is largely advanced and supported by Andrew Billingsley (1968), Virginia Young (1970), Robert Hill (1972), Wade Nobles (1974), and others. The perspective has been buttressed with old and new investigations which see black Americans' culture as different from that of whites (Valentine, 1968; Young, 1974) and possibly related to their African heritage (Herskovits, 1941; Nobles, 1974; Dodson, 1975, 1977). Although not all proponents of the cultural relativistic school agree on the degree to which African culture influenced the culture of black Americans, they do concur that black Americans' cultural orientation encourages family patterns that are instrumental in combating the oppressive racial conditions of American society.

American studies of the black family, and of blacks in general, have long ignored the works of Melville Herskovits (1885-1963), one of the first scholars to recognize similarities in African cultural patterns and those of African descendants living in the United States, the West Indies, and Brazil. Herskovits (1966) found what he considered to be authentic African cultural patterns reflected in language, music, art, house structure, dance, traditional religion, and healing practices. To many students of the black family, Herskovits's research raises the possibility that other aspects of "Africana" could have influenced the nature of the black family in the United States. Herskovits's works deal only limitedly with such possible relations. However, one of his major contributions was a truer conceptualization of family life in traditional African societies, which are characterized by unity, stability, and security (Herskovits, 1938).

Other writers have since reexamined the unity and stability of African families to refute any assertion that chaos and problems of African families paralleled the problems of contemporary black American families. From such studies, Billingsley concluded:

> Thus the men and women who were taken as slaves to the New World came from societies every bit as civilized and "respectable" as those of the Old World settlers who mastered them. But the two were very different types of society [sic] for the African family was much more closely integrated with the wider levels of kinship and society [1968: 48].

In examining the American black family, proponents of cultural relativism in North America point out that slavery did not totally destroy the traditional African base of black family functioning (Blassingame, 1972; Nobles, 1974; Turnbull, 1976). To these scholars, the black family represents a continuing fountain of strength and endurance built on, and issuing from, its African cultural heritage.

The field research of Young reflects that blacks are not merely versions of white Americans impoverished by lack of access to many of the rewards of American culture. She found that southern rural black families were culturally distinct from white families and demonstrated retention of African forms. This closely paralleled Herskovits's (1941) contentions. Her findings were especially supportive in the areas of interpersonal behavior and deep-level communication.

Similar to Charles Johnson (1934) and Hortense Powdermaker (1939), but contrary to Frazier (1939) and Moynihan (1965), Young did not find black families disorganized or dysfunctional. Young (1970) observed patterns of high illegitimacy rates and frequent marital dissolutions, which are usually associated with disorganization; however, she interpreted these patterns as natural to the emotional underpinnings of the family system and, thus, functional.

Nobles (1974, 1975) has indicated that the black community is oriented primarily toward extended families, in that most black family structures involve a system of kinship ties. This idea has been supported by Hayes and Mendel (1973), Billingsley (1968), Hill (1972), Stack (1974), and others. The extended family system is assumed to provide support for family members, either as assistance for protection or for mobility. It is argued that the extended family in the black community consists not only of conjugal and blood relatives, but of nonrelatives as well. Additionally, the prevalence of extended families, as compared with nuclear families, is held as another cultural pattern which distinguishes whites and blacks. However, the extent to which such families are characteristic of the black community has not been adequately substantiated.

Hayes and Mendel (1973) demonstrated that the extended family is a more prominent structure for black families and that blacks differ from whites in intensity and extent of family interaction. Their study of midwestern urban families, however, included a sample of only 25 complete and incomplete black and white families. The findings show that, with the exception of parents, blacks interact with more of their kin than do whites. Black families also receive more help from kin and have a greater number and more diversified types of relatives living with them than do white families. It is suggested by Hayes and Mendel that minority status in a hostile society strengthens kinship ties.

In a related study, Dubey (1971) examined the relationship between self-alienation and extended family using black, white, and Puerto Rican subjects. His data supported the hypothesis that subjects with a high degree of powerlessness were significantly more oriented toward the extended family. Dubey's study raises the question of whether the extended family is used as a buffer between oppression of the dominant society and the unmet needs of the family. Stack (1974) proposed that the extended family is, in part, a strategy for meeting physical, emotional, and economic needs of black families, and involves a reciprocal network of sharing to counter the lack of economic resources. McAdoo (1978) found that the reciprocal extended family-help patterns transcended economic groups and continued to be practiced even when families had moved from poverty to the middle-income level.

Nobles (1974) believes that the black kinship pattern was derived from African cultures not destroyed in the "Middle Passage" or in slavery; this suggests that perhaps the survival of "Africana" among black American families is not as remote as Elkins (1959) and Frazier (1939) have argued. Blassingame (1972) stated that not only did African cultural patterns survive American slavery, but new cultural patterns unique to black Americans were created. Even Frazier (1963) has noted indisputable non-Western religious practices in the black church. A more recent advocate of this view, Colin Turnbull, sums it succinctly: "(T)he slaves who were exported to the Americas were Africans before they were slaves and Africans afterwards, and *their descendants are still Africans today*" (1976: 242; emphasis added).

According to Turnbull, it is interesting to note that in some cases African cultural patterns were developed and preserved in the western hemisphere while they were lost in Africa. A case in point is Surinam (South America), where slaves escaped and recovered their independence. Although some of the ethnic cultures resemble original African cultures, Turnbull cautions that the Surinam cultures (comprising six "tribal" groups) could not have remained totally in isolation. With the exception of clearly identifiable African cultural patterns in islands along the Georgia coast, Turnbull stated that the splintering of ethnic clans during slavery, along with enforced acceptance of language and Western values, did much to repress African cultures in the United States.

A model that may prove useful for a further understanding of the New World "Africana" culture and black American families has been developed by Smith (1962). Equally important to the clarification of these issues is Nobles's work currently being conducted on African orientations in American families. However, we must await further research findings from the cultural relativistic perspective before determining the cultural origin of black family life.

AN ISSUE FROM BOTH SCHOOLS: SOCIAL CLASS

Research on racial differences in black family structure and function has been contaminated by methodological problems that make it difficult to conceptualize clear differences within and between groups. Social class has been widely employed as a variable in social science research. It is primarily used for classifying individuals into categories above or below one another on some scale of inferiority and superiority. The scale is intended to denote one's position in terms of social and economic prestige and/or power.

The most popular measure of social class in the United States is an occupation-scaled measure that is commonly used to reflect prestige. Other types of class measurement consist of single variables, such as education, income, and possessions. A number of multiple indices also exist. It has been questioned whether such measures can be applied equitable to all groups in an oppressive, pluralistic, and fluid society such as the United States. This is especially critical, since most measures of social class were developed by and for whites, and there is little convincing evidence that they accurately measure social class for black Americans.

A number of investigators, among them Drake (1965) and Jencks (1972), have demonstrated that education and income are less related for blacks compared to whites than may be expected. It has been shown that blacks are more frequently underemployed, in that they often have more education, training, or skills than their jobs require. Consequently, they receive salaries and wages disproportionate to their preparation. Since an underemployed black person has a lower income than a white with equivalent years of education, the former cannot afford the same standard of living as the latter. This lower standard of living requires the black person to adopt a different lifestyle than his or her status, as measured by education, would indicate.

Neither does occupation tend to indicate the same social classification for blacks as for whites. The owner of a small business in a black shopping area, for example, might not have nearly the same income as the owner of a similar business located in a white shopping area. However, according to the occupation categories of the Hollingshead-Redlich scale (1968), both persons would be designated in a middle-income social classification. Another problem with occupational ranking is that disparities exist within occupations as well as between them.

Jencks (1972) contends that one limitation to the definition of occupation as the indicator of social class is that it refers only to occupations, not to specific jobs within them. Accordingly, some jobs are more attractive and rewarding than others, even though they are classified together as a single occupation.

Billingsley's assertion that current indicators of social class are relatively more reliable when used for white ethnic groups than when used unmodified with black groups has never been adequately refuted. He believes that such indicators have resulted in an overestimation of the number of lower-class blacks and that this obscures rather than clarifies the variety of social class and behavior among black Americans (1968: 123). Although Billingsley accepts the utility of social class, he claims that current measures are mostly indicators of economic and social positions in the wider white community, not accurate descriptions of which blacks associate with whom and why.

It should be pointed out that social classification depends primarily on the degree to which an individual or individuals are held in esteem by their fellow group members. Social class, therefore, depends on the cultural values of the group. Deference is awarded according to what the group cherishes as being noble or worthy. Hence, social class could be based on such characteristics as age, wisdom, heredity, or economic power, and it could vary from one cultural group to another. Since the cultural distinctiveness of black Americans still warrants investigation, measures of social class also await clearer determination. The extent to which blacks possess different values regarding what is worthy in an individual determines their different orientation to family, to their community, and to the wider white community.

Cultural relativity becomes an important, yet complicated, factor when attempting to make social class comparisons of heterogenous groups within a single society. It appears logical to assume that different ethnic groups within the same society can be compared using the same social class criterion. However, this is not the empirical reality for the United States. The logical but incorrect assumption that because both peoples live within the same societal geography (nation), social class is perceived the same way in white and black communities is misleading.

I concur with Billingsley that the importance of social class is that the higher the social class of an individual, the greater will be his or her ability to survive with integrity in a hostile society. For a historically subjugated group such as black America, survival and dignity may be invaluable social qualities. Furthermore, given the nature of the historical and material experiences of, and relationship between, blacks and whites in North America, the extent to which they can be compared using similar social indicators is dubious. To ignore these fundamentally different realities and classify them into common social classes is to commit serious historical, methodological, and theoretical errors.

TOWARD REFLECTIVE ANALYSIS

This examination of major schools of thought in studies of the black family in the United States has been done to help direct thinking regarding prerequisite components of a "reflective analysis." Admittedly, this has been a limited review. For example, individual roles of family members have not been addressed. These are seen primarily as intertwined with the sociocultural patterns of marriage and family in contemporary black communities. For those who desire a more thorough and complete review of literature on black American families, there are at least three substantive sources: Allen (1976), Staples (1974, 1978), and Peters (1978). The particular approach I have taken has emphasized the ideological assumptions undergirding researchers' definitions of and approaches to research of black family life. This perspective was used because it is assumed that the ideological debate has indeed created the current impasse in black family research. Given the review of the debate, Walter Allen's conclusions about the status of studies on black family life is accurate:

> The literature on black families is characterized by inconsistent findings, poor problem conceptualization, overly simplistic research designs, questionable inferences from data and general disagreement over the relative appropriateness of competing perspectives of black family life. The question to be addressed now is: How might researchers go about the business of reconciling some of these problems and in the process strengthening the literature? To begin, theory construction/codification activities should be intensified. . . .

> The area of black family studies would also benefit from a change in focus of empirical research.

Any attempt to bring theoretical clarity to human phenomena must be informed by an understanding of the sociocultural, economic, and political contexts in which the phenomena occur. This axiom applies especially when exploring questions related to contemporary black family life in the United States.

In recommending the following components for a "reflective analysis" of black family life, my conceptualizations have been developed in concert with Ruth Dennis, Harriette McAdoo, Art Mathis, and Howard Dodson. This group of black scholars and researchers met and worked together from 1974 through 1977 to develop "Toward a Reflective Analysis" of black family life.

Drawing from the strengths and weaknesses of previous studies, a "reflective analysis" would minimally include the following:

(a) focus on socialization of black families as the process which brings together individual, cultural group(s), and society in a dynamic interactive process;

(b) account for the impact—positive and/or negative—of the relative unavailability of maximum social, economic, and political societal resources to black families and;

(c) account for the environmental reality that black families are forced to use relatively minimal resources to effect a socialization process and product which allows individuals to function in two social realities of the United States—a nonblack world of consistent, sufficient social support and a black world of fluctuating scarcity of resources.

Using these minimal components as a guide, a schema for evaluating black family socialization can be suggested. Positive evaluations can be placed on socialized behavior which allows the individual to interact with any segment of the society and maintain a sense of self-worth. However, because the realities of black family life are often contradictory, socialized behavior that may be evaluated as positive within one level of social functioning may be evaluated as negative within another. Black families must be able to socialize individuals who are able to participate in and yet protect self from the negative social attitudes and actions impinging on self-esteem, feelings of self-worth, and human evolutionary development.

NOTE

1. For example, the widespread support among black Americans for Marcus Garvey's Universal Negro Improvement Association (Cronon, 1964).

REFERENCES

ALLEN, W. R. (1976) Private correspondence in response to "Reflective Analysis" manuscript. Atlanta, Georgia.

———— (1978) "Search for applicable theories of Black family life." Journal of Marriage and the Family 40: 117-129.

AUSUBEL, D. P. and P. AUSUBEL (1963) "Ego development among segregated Negro children," in A. H. Passow (ed.) Education in Depressed Areas. New York: Bureau of Publications, Teachers College, Columbia University.

BERNARD, J. (1966) Marriage and Family Among Negroes. Englewood Cliffs, NJ: Prentice-Hall.

BETTELHEIM, B. (1964) Review of B. S. Bloom's Stability and Change in Human Characteristics. New York Review of Books 3: 1-4.

BILLINGSLEY, A. (1968) Black Families in White America. Englewood Cliffs, NJ: Prentice-Hall.

BLASSINGAME, J. W. (1972) The Slave Community: Plantation Life in Antebellum South. New York: Oxford.

BLAUNER, R. (1970) "Internal colonialism and ghetto revolt," in M. Westheimer (ed.) Confrontation. Glenview, IL: Scott, Foresman.

———— (1972) Racial Oppression in America. New York: Harper & Row.

BLOOD, R. and D. WOLFE (1969) "Negro-white differences in blue collar marriages in a northern metropolis." Social Forces 48: 59-63.

BRACEY, J. H., A. MEIER and E. RUDWICK [eds.] (1971) Black Matriarchy: Myth or Reality. Belmont, CA: Wadsworth.

BRONFENBRENNER, U. (1967) Paper read at Conference on Poverty, University of Wisconsin, Madison.

CLOWARD, R. A. and J. A. JONES (1962) "Social class: Education attitudes and participation," in A. H. Passows (ed.) Education in Depressed Areas. New York: Bureau of Publications, Teachers College, Columbia University.

CRONON, E. D. (1955) Black Moses: The Story of Marcus Garvey. Madison: University of Wisconsin Press.

DAVIS, A. and J. DOLLARD (1940) Children of Bondage. New York: Harper & Row.

DAVIS, A. and R. J. HAVIGHURST (1946) "Social class and color differences in childrearing." American Sociological Review 11: 698-710.

DODSON, J. (1975) Black Stylization and Implications for Child Welfare. Final Report (OCD-CB-422-C2). Washington, DC: Office of Child Development.

———— (1977) Afro American Culture: Expressive Behaviors. Atlanta: Atlanta University.

DRAKE, S. C. (1965) "The social and economic status of the Negro in the United States," in T. Parsons and K. B. Clark (eds.) The Negro American. Boston: Beacon.

DUBEY, S. N. (1971) "Powerlessness and orientation toward family and children: a study in deviance." Indian Journal of Social Work 32: 35-43.

DUNCAN, B., and O. D. DUNCAN (1969) "Family stability and occupational success." Social Problems 16: 273-285.

ELKINS, S. W. (1959) Slavery. Chicago: University of Chicago Press.

FOGEL, R. W. and S. L. ENGERMAN (1975) Time on the Cross, Volumes I and II. Boston: Little, Brown.

FRAZIER, E. F. (1932) The Negro Family in Chicago. Chicago: University of Chicago Press.

———— (1939) The Negro Family in the United States. Chicago: University of Chicago Press.

———— (1949a) "The Negro family in America," in R. W. Anshen (ed.) The Family: Its Function and Destiny. New York: Harper & Row.

———— (1949b) The Negro in the United States. New York: Macmillan.

———— (1957) Black Bourgeoisie: The Rise of a New Middle Class in the United States. New York: Free Press.

———— (1963) The Negro Church in America. New York: Schocken.

HAYES, W. and MENDEL, C. H. (1973) "Extended kinship in black and white families." Journal of Marriage and the Family 35: 51-57.

HEISS, J. (1972) "On the transmission of marital instability in black families." American Sociological Review 37: 82-92.

HERSKOVITS, M. J. (1938) Dahomey: An Ancient African Kingdom. New York: J. J. Augustin.

———— (1941) The Myth of the Negro Past. New York: Harper & Row.

HILL, R. (1972) The Strengths of Black Families. New York: Emerson-Hall.

HOLLINGSHEAD, A. B. and F. C. REDLICH (1968) Social Class and Mental Illness. New York: John Wiley.

HYMAN, H. H. and J. S. REED (1969) "Black matriarchy reconsidered: evidence from secondary analysis of sample survey." Public Opinion Quarterly 33: 346-354.

INKLES, A. (1966) "A note on social structure and the socialization of competence." Harvard Educational Review 36: 265-283.

JENCKS, C. (1972) Inequality. New York: Basic Books.

JOHNSON, C. S. (1934) Shadow of the Plantation. Chicago: University of Chicago Press.

KARDINER, A. and L. OVESEY (1951) The Mark of Oppression. New York: World.

KATZ, I. (1969) "A critique of personality approaches to Negro performance, with research suggestions." Journal of Social Issues 25: 12-27.

KING, K. (1967) "A comparison of the Negro and white family power structure in low-income families" Child and Family 6: 65-74.

———— (1969) "Adolescent perception of power structure in the Negro family." Journal of Marriage and the Family 31: 751-755.

LIEBOW, E. (1967) Tally's Corner: A Study of Negro Streetcorner Men. Boston: Little, Brown.

LYMAN, S. M. (1972) The Black American in Sociological Thought. New York: Capricorn Books.

MACK, D. E. (1971) "Where the black-matriarchy theorists went wrong." Psychology Today 4: 24, 86-87.

McADOO, H. P. (1974) The Socialization of Black Children: Priorities for Research in Social Research and the Black Community: Selected Issues and Priorities.

———— (1978) "Factors related to stability in upward mobile black families." Journal of Marriage and the Family 40: 761-766.

McCLELLAND, D. C. (1961) The Achieving Society. New York: Van Nostrand.

MOYNIHAN, D. P. (1965) The Negro Family—The Case for National Action. Washington, DC: Office of Policy Planning and Research, U.S. Department of Labor.

NOBLES, W. W. (1974) "Africanity: its role in black families." The Black Scholar 5: 10-17.

———— (1975) A Formulative and Empirical Study of Black Families. Publication No. OCD-90-C-255. San Francisco: Westside Community Mental Health Center.

PARK, R. E. (1939) "The nature of race relations," in E. T. Thompson (ed.) Race Relations and the Race Problem. Durham, NC: Duke University Press.

PARKER, S. and KLEINER, R. (1966) "Characteristics of Negro mothers in single-headed households." Journal of Marriage and the Family 28: 507-513.

PETERS, M. F. [ed.] (1978) Special issue of Journal of Marriage and the Family, Vol. 40, No. 4, November.

PETTIGREW, T. F. (1964) A Profile of the Negro American. Princeton, NJ: D. Van Nostrand.

PHILLIPS, U. B. (1929) Life and Labor in the Old South. Boston: Little, Brown.

POWDERMAKER, H. (1939) After Freedom: The Portrait of a Negro Community in the Deep South. New York: Viking.

RAINWATER, L. (1965) Family Design. Chicago: AVC.

———— (1968) "Crucible of identity: the Negro lower-class family." Daedalus 95: 258-264.

RIESSMAN, F. (1962) The Culturally Deprived Child. New York: Harper & Row.

RODMAN, H. (1968) "Family and social pathology in the ghetto." Science 161: 756-762.

SMITH, M. G. (1962) West Indian Family Structure. Seattle: University of Washington Press.

STACK, C. B. (1974) All Our Kin. New York: Harper & Row.

STAPLES, R. E. (1974) "The black family revisited: a review and a preview." Journal of Social and Behavior Sciences Spring: 65-77.

———— (1978) The Black Family: Essays and Studies. Belmont, CA: Wadsworth.

TENHOUTEN, W. (1970) "The black family: myth and reality." Psychiatry 33: 145-173.

TURNBULL, C. M. (1976) Man in Africa. Garden City, NY: Doubleday.

VALENTINE, C. A. (1968) Culture and Poverty. Chicago: University of Chicago Press.

WARNER, W. L., M. MEEKER, and K. EELLS (1949) Social Class in America. Chicago: Science Research Associates.

WILLIE, C. V. [ed.] (1970) The Family Life of Black People. Columbus, OH: Charles E. Merrill.

YANCEY, W. (1972) "Going down home: family structure and the urban trap." Social Science Quarterly 52: 893-906.

YOUNG, V. H. (1970) "Family and childhood in a southern Negro community." American Anthropologist 72: 269-288.

YOUNG, V. H. (1974) "A black American socialization pattern." in American Ethnologist 1: 405-413.

6

PERSPECTIVES ON BLACK FAMILY
EMPIRICAL RESEARCH: 1965-1978

LEANOR BOULIN JOHNSON

Guided by different perspectives while using the same data, Black and White social scientists often differ on the nature of Black family life and the direction social policies should take. The works of Moynihan (1965) and Hill (1972) demonstrate the critical link between data and interpretive frameworks (see Johnson, 1978). Although both analyzed the same U. S. Census data, they employed different theoretical perspectives and arrived at divergent conclusions. Moynihan reported a deteriorating Black family and recommended social policies that would encourage changes in the Black family's structure and values. Hill observed the resilience of Black families and recommended social policies that could build on the strengths of Black family values and structure. Without arguing the validity of either conclusion, the importance of studying perspectives governing Black family research should be evident. Yet, too often when trying to create a fit between scientific data and social needs, researchers argue over apparent discrepancies in the data or debate the merit of various statistical methods while ignoring another possible culprit—the subjective frame of reference (Gouldner, 1970; Van den Berghe, 1967; Mills, 1959; Mannheim, 1936; Adams, 1985).

AUTHOR'S NOTE: The author is indebted to Tony Haynes of Florida State University, whose original conceptualization contributed greatly to this chapter.

Recognizing both the limitations of scientific objectivity, particularly when racial groups are the target of analysis, and the tendency for policymakers to use social science research to guide policies on Black families, Staples (1974), Allen (1978), and Allen and Stokes (1981) identified major theoretical and value frameworks that either impede or facilitate a fuller understanding of Black families and the social policies that govern their lives. Notwithstanding these researchers' valuable contributions, they failed to document empirically the frequency of these frameworks and their occurrence over time. Further, their methodology prevents a systematic identification of changing perspectives in empirical Black family research. Thus, this chapter proposes to extend Staples's and Allen's studies by identifying journals that fostered empirical Black family studies: determining the frequency of their frameworks over time and identifying topics studied within each framework.

THEORETICAL PERSPECTIVES

The more than 500 Black family articles that appeared in the 1960s and 1970s represent five times more such literature than was produced during the preceding century (Staples and Mirande, 1980). With the exception of Allen (1978) and Staples (1974), social scientists have not categorized the various frameworks represented in this growing body of literature. Allen identifies three theoretical perspectives or value orientations: "Cultural Deviant" (CD), "Cultural Equivalent" (CE), and "Cultural Variant" (CV). The first framework views Black families as pathological; the second depicts Black families as legitimate when they adapt the lifestyle and norms of middle-class White families; and the third views Black families as different but functional family forms. Using a time typology, Staples identifies four eras through which Black family research has progressed: "Poverty/Acculturation," "Patholo-gists," "Reactive," and "Black Nationalist Family Studies." According to Staples, studies focusing on the pathological nature of Black families appeared during the thirties, forties, and sixties (that is, during the poverty/acculturation and pathologists eras). During the poverty/acculturation period—the thirties and forties—DuBois, Frazier, and others believed that the solution to Black family disorganization and poverty was conformity to White family norms. The pathologists differed from the poverty/acculturation approach in that pathologists' views emerged in the sixties and had significant impact on public policy; most scholars taking this view were White; and pathologists blamed Black families for Blacks' inferior social position. Studies reacting to this negative image of Black families emerged during the reactive era (approximately 1966-1977). Most recently, Black Nationalist Family Studies have depicted Black families as unique and functional.

TABLE 6.1   Theoretical Frameworks Used in Studying Black Families:
             Related Typologies

Staples	*Allen*
Poverty-Acculturated (e.g., Frazier, 1932, 1939; DuBois, 1909)	Cultural Deviant (e.g., Frazier, 1939; Moynihan, 1965)
Pathologist (e.g., Moynihan, 1965; Aldous, 1969)	Cultural Deviant (e.g., Frazier, 1939; Moynihan, 1965)
Reactive (e.g., Liebow, 1966; Billingsley, 1968)	Cultural Equivalent (e.g., Frazier, 1939; Scanzoni, 1971)
Black Nationalist (e.g., Cade, 1970; Hill, 1972)	Cultural Variant (e.g., Rodman, 1971; Ladner, 1971)

Common to both Allen's and Staples's categorization are basic value orientations (see Table 6.1). The cultural deviant perspective recognizes qualities that differentiate Black and White families and gives negative meaning, that is, pathological or dysfunctional attributes—to Black family traits. Both the poverty/acculturation and the pathologists eras manifest orientations similar to the cultural deviant perspective. During the poverty/acculturation era (early 1900s) the massive Black migration from the agrarian setting to the city uprooted a significant group in the Black community. DuBois (1908) and Frazier (1932, 1939) focused on the rate of illegitimacy and the number of female-headed households among this unstable Black group; both concluded that conformity to White middle-class family norms would eliminate family disorganization. Approximately 60 years later, the pathologists extended DuBois's and Frazier's thesis by blaming Black families for the deterioration of the Black community. The 1965 Moynihan report characterized this period.

The reactive era extended from approximately 1966 to 1971. During this period White and Black behavioral scientists reacted to Moynihan's "blame the victim" conclusions. By arguing that economic and racial discrimination victimized Blacks, they concluded that, given the same economic conditions, Black and White families are equivalent. Thus, the perspective of this era parallels Allen's cultural equivalent perspective. However, in addition to including authors of the late sixties and early seventies (such as Scanzoni, 1971; Bernard, 1966), Allen includes Frazier's writings of the thirties (those reports which describe Black families as "Black Puritans" when they adopt White morals). It must be remembered that while the Black Family was not being blamed for the problems it faced, little or no positive value was attributed to the unique traits of Black family structure.

The cultural variant perspective acknowledges certain family functions as universal, but recognizes that various constraints may produce culturally distinct structures and dynamics. Thus, the importance of cultural relativity is stressed. Although differences between Black and White families are noted, unique aspects of Black family life are not necessarily taken as reflections of pathologies (Allen, 1978). Consistent with this approach is the perspective used during the era of Black Nationalists research. In fact, it was the Black Nationalists who first began to delineate the strengths of Black families. Thus according to Staples (1974), they distinguished themselves from the reactive researchers, who also challenged the pathologists' position, but failed to attach positive value to the unique aspects of Black family life. Black Nationalists contend that if social scientists desire to report on the behavior of a culture other than their own, they must not use their own cultural framework and definitions to explain that behavior. Consequently, Black values cannot be used to explain White cultural patterns, nor can White values be used to explain Black cultural patterns (Johnson, 1978).

METHODOLOGY

In analyzing the treatment of Black families in the research literature of the 1965-1978 period, we first employ Allen's trichotomized typology which is free from a time sequence idea, yet captures the orientations underlying the stages presented by Staples. However, when focus is given to trends, Staples's stages will be the referent.

In some cases there appeared to be more than one perspective represented. An effort was made to label according to the most dominant theme. Since a clear distinction was not always possible, the reader may disagree with a particular interpretation. For the reader's benefit we have labeled each article by perspective (see Bibliography notes).

Articles were classified according to three criteria. Reports are labeled:

- *Cultural Deviant* (CD) if emphasis is given to White middle-class norms as the referent to which Black families are compared; and if deviation from these norms by Black families is explicitly or implicitly interpreted as pathological (Aldous, 1969);
- *Cultural Equivalent* (CE) if emphasis is given to White middle-class family norms as the referent to which Black families are compared; and if similarities between the two groups are explicitly or implicitly interpreted as support for shared cultural values (for example, Scanzoni, 1971); and

- *Cultural Variant* (CV) if White middle-class norms are not the primary referent and Black cultural patterns are primarily explained by use of Black values and experiences (Jackson, 1971).

The reliability of this content analysis was maintained by consistently applying these classification criteria (see Lantz, 1968).

We carefully scanned the table of contents in each periodical for titles and abstracts which involved aspects of Black family life (the unit of analysis). If, after reading the first few and the last paragraphs, the article appeared relevant, we examined the entire article and made the appropriate classifications. In order to minimize the sampling error, our list of articles was randomly checked against articles cited in the *International Bibliography of Research in Marriage and the Family, Vol. II.*

Journals from two fields were selected: sociology, because of its focus on social institutions and relationships, and social work, for its traditional concern with the welfare of families. From sociology we selected five journals; two specialized in family research and three were among the most widely circulated. From social work we selected the five most widely circulated journals.[1] The following list of ten journals was examined, and lengthy journal titles are abbreviated in the text.

Sociology: *Journal of Marriage and the Family (JMF)*
             Journal of Comparative Family Studies (JCFS)
             American Journal of Sociology (AJS)
             American Sociological Review (ASR)
             Social Forces

Social Work: *Child Welfare*
             Social Casework
             Social Service Review
             Public Welfare
             Social Work

In order to include representation from "established" Black periodicals, that is, journals in circulation for at least ten years—three additional journals were included: *Black Scholar, Journal of Social and Behavioral Sciences* (JSBS), and *Phylon*. We selected only those empirical articles which explicitly discussed some aspect of Black families.

FINDINGS

Although Moynihan's 1965 attack on Black families stimulated a plethora of articles on Black families, our selected journals reflect few empirical articles.

Of the 7017 articles published during the 13-year period, 3547 (51 percent) were empirical family studies. Empirical articles on Black families represented .01 percent (92) of all articles and .03 percent (107) of all empirical studies. The *JMF* special issue on Black families, edited by a Black scholar, and the Black journals accounted for 38 percent of all Black articles. Considering only the nonspecialized journals (that is, excluding *JMF* and *JCFS*) the Black journals contributed 57 percent of the empirical Black family studies. Although *JSBS* did not specialize in family articles, it devoted a slightly higher percentage of its articles to Black families than did *JMF* (6.0 percent versus 4.9 percent). Obviously, special issues and Black journals play an important role in publicizing the data from Black family research (see Table 6.2).

In the 1960s, 60 percent of the Black family studies were published by *JMF* and the remainder appeared in five other journals. In contrast, during the first five years of 1970, *JMF* published only 31 percent of the articles; the others were distributed among seven other journals, including two new journals— *Black Scholar* and *JCFS*. Even when we exclude the new journals, *JMF* published only 33 percent of the articles. Although *JMF*'s monopoly was weakened during this period, its 1978 special issue on Black families supplied 92 percent of the 12 articles published that year.

Given social work's traditional concern with family welfare, it is surprising that not only did *Social Casework* and *Social Work* each publish only one

TABLE 6.2　　Black Family Studies by Periodicals and Year

Periodical	Publication Year														Total
	65	66	67	68	69	70	71	72	73	74	75	76	77	78	
Journal of Marriage and the Family	1	3	2	3	6	2	0	5	2	2	4	2	3	11	46
*Journal of Social and Behavioral Sciences**	0	0	0	3	2	1	1	1	0	5	0	0	0	0	13
American Sociological Review	0	0	0	0	0	0	2	3	1	0	0	0	0	0	6
*Phylon**	1	0	0	0	0	0	0	1	0	0	0	1	5	1	9
American Journal of Sociology	0	0	0	0	1	0	1	0	2	2	0	0	0	0	6
Social Forces	1	0	0	0	1	1	0	0	0	1	0	0	0	0	4
Journal of Comparative Family Studies	**	**	**	**	**	0	1	0	0	0	2	1	0	0	4
*Black Scholar**	**	**	**	**	0	1	1	0	0	0	0	0	0	0	2
Social Casework	0	0	0	0	1	0	0	0	0	0	0	0	0	0	1
Social Work	0	0	0	0	0	0	0	0	0	0	0	1	0	0	1
Total	3	3	2	6	11	5	6	10	5	10	6	5	8	12	92

* Black journals
**Journal was not published in these years.

article in the 13-year survey period, but no empirical articles appeared in the other three selected social work journals. However, these latter journals did publish a few nonempirical Black family studies.

A greater percentage of articles was published between 1969 and 1972 (35 percent) than in the previous or following four years; 15 percent and 28 percent, respectively. Although these three years represented the zenith for empirical articles, the social work journals produced their articles prior to and after this period.

The frequency with which the theoretical perspectives appeared in the periodicals is shown in Table 6.3. Most journals contained studies that interpreted their data through a cultural equivalent framework. The cultural deviant perspective was absent from six of the ten journals. Although *JMF* gave preference to cultural equivalent, cultural deviant was represented in one-quarter of their articles. If we exclude *JMF*'s 1978 special issue on Black families, cultural deviant's representation in *JMF* increases to one-third and the cultural variant decreases from one-third to less than 12 percent. It should be noted that 69 percent of the cultural variant articles appeared in Black-edited journals. Black editors were generally more likely than non-Black editors to publish studies which used the cultural variant perspective; however, they were least likely to publish articles which used the cultural deviant perspective.

In tabulating Table 6.3 the three perspectives were evenly distributed among the six articles appearing in *ASR*, while all articles appearing in *Social Forces*, *JCFS*, and *Social Casework* used the cultural equivalent perspective.

Staples's unilinear evolutionary typology implies that each era will lead to and culminate in the next—poverty-acculturation to pathologists (both equiva-

TABLE 6.3   Black Family Studies by Periodical and Theoretical Perspectives, 1965-1978

Periodical	Total Reports	Theoretical Perspectives*		
		CD	CE	CV
Journal of Marriage and the Family	46	11	21	14
Journal of Social and Behavioral Sciences	13	1	8	4
American Sociological Review	6	2	2	2
Phylon	9	0	5	4
American Journal of Sociology	6	1	3	2
Social Forces	4	0	4	0
Journal of Comparative Family Studies	4	0	4	0
Black Scholar	2	0	0	2
Social Casework	1	0	1	0
Social Work	1	0	0	1
Total	92	15	48	29

*CD = cultural deviant; CE = cultural equivalent; CV = cultural variant.

lent to cultural deviant), to reactive (cultural equivalent) to Black Nationalist (cultural variant). Figure 6.1 gives moderate support to Staples's time typology. Although the cultural deviant perspective was present throughout the sixties and early seventies, it disappeared after 1974. Throughout the 13-year period, cultural equivalent tended to dominate the literature. No doubt this reflects America's long-standing commitment to the various forms of Anglo-conformity. The cultural variant perspective emerged in 1968, when Edwards, a Black researcher, published his *JMF* article, "Black Muslims and Negro Christian Relationships." Throughout the 1960s and continuing through 1976, this perspective maintained a low profile; its most recent two-year prominence resulted primarily from the *JMF* special issue.

Most writings of the sixties referenced Frazier's works, not Moynihan's. The first major response to Moynihan appeared in 1968, when Geismar and Gerhart published their *JMF* article, "Social Class, Ethnicity and Family Functioning: Exploring Some Issues Raised by the Moynihan Report." This article and Aldous's (1969) represent the most policy-oriented research of the sixties. Although both these articles appeared within the reactive era noted by Staples, the response to Moynihan appeared throughout the seventies (for example, Bould, 1977, Balkwell et al., 1978).

The conceptual framework of the areas studied is shown in Table 6.4. The cultural variant perspective was used in interpreting one-third of the family roles and structure articles, while approximately two-fifths and one-fifth were interpreted through the cultural equivalent and cultural deviant frameworks, respectively. Forty-four percent of the data on family roles, structure, and function were interpreted through the cultural equivalent perspective. In contrast, family roles, structure, and function represented 29 percent and 27 percent of the cultural deviant and cultural variant perspective, respectively. The cultural variant framework was absent in family function studies, and the cultural deviant perspective did not appear in studies on housing and mate selection and premarital sexual patterns.

Although a vast amount of literature on minority families and housing appears in economic journals, housing and its sociopsychological effects on minority families received insignificant attention in our selected journals. Only two studies (two percent of all reports) were published in the 13-year survey period.

One-half of the studies focused on family structure and roles—for example, role aspiration, attitude, and performance. Although not shown in Table 6.4, nearly two-fifths of these studies were published in the 1960s. More importantly, these two areas represented 75 percent of the studies published in that decade. During the next nine years the diversity of areas increased—the other five areas represented 55 percent during the 1970-1975 period; thereafter their representation increased an average of one percent each year. Focusing only on

Figure 6.1 Changes in Theoretical Perspective by Year, 1963-1978

99

TABLE 6.4   Area Studied, by Theoretical Perspectives

Area Studied	Total Reports	Theoretical Perspectives*		
		CD	CE	CV
Family roles	27	7	11	9
Family structure	18	3	8	7
Family functions	18	8	9	1
Mate selection and premarital sexual patterns	12	0	8	4
Fertility	8	1	4	3
Marital stability	7	1	5	1
Housing	2	0	1	1
Total	92	20	46	26

*CD = Cultural Deviant
 CE = Cultural Equivalent
 CV = Cultural Variant

the categories of "Marital Selection or Premarital Sexual Pattern" and "Fertility," we find that only one study in each category appeared during the sixties. By the end of 1978, an additional ten articles (five from a special issue) appeared in the former category and seven in the latter.

CONCLUSIONS

Empirical Black family studies represent less than one percent of all empirical family studies. Although a disproportionate number of these studies were published in Black-edited journals, *JMF* was the major source of Black articles, particularly during the sixties. Surprisingly, Black family articles were virtually absent from the social work journals.

Our analysis revealed variations in theoretical perspective by journals and across time. While most journals interpreted their data within the cultural equivalent perspective, the cultural deviant perspective was least likely and the cultural variant most likely to emerge in journals edited by Black scholars. For example, the cultural variant's rapid rise in 1979 resulted from a special *JMF* issue on Black families, which was edited by a Black scholar, Marie Peters. Generally, the cultural deviant and cultural variant perspectives followed Staples's typology. However, with the exception of 1978, the cultural equivalent framework was strong throughout the 13-year period, and reactions to the Moynihan Report continued throughout the seventies. The golden years for empirical studies were 1969 to 1972, during which virtually every journal published at least one article.

In reviewing the three perspectives, we note that Black-White comparisons have been an inherent bias of the cultural equivalent and deviant approaches. Thus, our understanding of the rich and complex variations among Black families has been limited. Perhaps this limitation will be overcome through the rise of the cultural variant frame of reference.

In contrast to the seventies, the sixties showed less variety in areas studied. Housing received the least attention (both publications appeared in the seventies). The emphasis given to roles and structure perhaps reflects the preoccupation with the stability of the Black family and its presumed inability to fulfill societal prerequisites—for example, the socialization of children. This concern, sparked by Frazier and revisited by Moynihan, has resulted in a narrow research agenda. While the Black matriarchy and its role in socializing children and marriage stability received enormous attention, no study focused on the interactions among cultural values, demographic factors (e.g., Black sex ratio), and family organization. Furthermore, given the tradition of multiearners within Black families, low family income, and the relatively high number of large families and Black youth, there exists a conspicuous absence of studies on dual-job/career families, sibling relationships, dating and courtship, and housing and social policies (particularly social security and tax laws). All these areas are of vital concern to Black families and represent tasks for future research.

Now that researchers appear to have abandoned the cultural deviant perspective and cultural variant is gaining prominence, many more culturally relevant empirical studies should emerge. It appears that Black researchers must take major responsibility for identifying the unique aspects of Black families.

NOTE

1. Based on Ulrich's International Periodical Directory, 1977-1978, these journals were among the most widely circulated:

Journal of Marriage and the Family	(Est. 1939/Cir. 11,000)
American Journal of Sociology	(Est. 1895/Cir. 10,892)
American Sociological Review	(Est. 1936/Cir. 15,000)
Social Forces	(Est. 1922/Cir. 5,000)
Child Welfare	(Est. 1922/Cir. 9,600)
Social Casework	(Est. 1920/Cir. 17,000)
Social Service Review	(Est. 1927/Cir. 6,736)
Public Welfare	(Est. 1943/Cir. 12,000)
Social Welfare	(Est. 1956/Cir. 85,000)

REFERENCES

ADAMS, B. N. (1985) "The family: problems and solutions." Journal of Marriage and the Family 47(3): 525-529.

ALLEN, W. (1978) "The search for applicable theories of Black family life." Journal of Marriage and the Family 40 (1): 111-129.

———— (1977) The Effects of Government Policies on Black Families. Division on Education and Research: Public Education, The Ford Foundation (October).

———— and S. STOKES (1981) "Black family life styles and mental health of Black Americans," in R. Endo and F. Munoz (eds.) Perspectives on Minority Group Mental Health. Chicago: Charter House.

DuBOIS, W. E. B. (1908) The Negro American family. Atlanta: Atlanta University Press.

FRAZIER, E. F. (1932) The Negro Family in Chicago. Chicago: University of Chicago Press.

———— (1939) The Negro Family in the United States. Chicago: University of Chicago Press.

GOULDNER, A. (1970) The Coming Crisis of Western Sociology. New York: Avon Books.

HILL, R. (1972) The Strength of Black Families. New York: Emerson Hall.

JOHNSON, L. (1978) "The search for values in Black family research," pp. 26-34 in R. Staples (ed.) The Black Family: Essays and Studies. Belmont, CA: Wadsworth.

JONES, M. (1976) "Scientific method, value judgments, and the Black predicament in the U.S." Review of Black Political Economy 7 (1): Fall.

LANTZ, H., R. SCHMITT, M. BRITTON, and E. SNYDER (1968) "Pre-industrial patterns in the colonial family in America: a content analysis of colonial magazines." American Sociological Review 33 (3): 413-426.

MANNHEIM, K. (1936) Ideology and Utopia. London: Routledge & Kegal Paul.

MILLS, C. W. (1959) The Sociological Imagination. New York: Grove Press.

MOYNIHAN, D. (1965) The Negro Family: The Case for National Action. Washington, DC: Office of Policy Planning and Research, U.S. Department of Labor.

NOBLES, Wade W. (1978) "Toward an empirical and theoretical framework for defining Black families." Journal of Marriage and the Family 40 (November): 679-688.

SCANZONI, J. (1971) The Black Family in Modern Society. Boston: Allyn & Bacon.

STAPLES, R. (1974) "The Black family revisited: a review and a preview." Journal of Social and Behavioral Sciences 20 (Spring): 65-78.

———— and A. MIRANDE (1980) "Racial and cultural variations among American families: a decennial review of the literature on minority families." Journal of Marriage and the Family 42 (4): 887-903.

Ulrich's International Periodical Directory (1978) New York: R. R. Bowker.

VAN DEN BERGHE, P. (1967) Race and Racism. New York: John Wiley.

BIBLIOGRAPHY

SELECTED RESEARCH REPORTS AND ASSIGNED CLASSIFICATIONS

(First parenthetical designation following the citation refers to area studied and the second to theoretical perspective: CD = Cultural Deviant; CE = Cultural Equivalent; CV = Cultural Variant.)

AMERICAN JOURNAL OF SOCIOLOGY

EPSTEIN, C. F. (1973) "Positive effects of the multiple negative explaining the success of Black professional women." 78 (4): 151-173. (Role: CV)

GOLDSCHIEDER, C. and P. R. UHLENBERG (1969) "Minority group status and fertility." 84 (4): 361-372. (Fertility: CE)

KANDEL, D. B. (1971) "Race, maternal authority, and adolescent aspiration." 76 (6): 999-1020. (Family functions: CE)

LOPATA, H. A. (1973) "Social relations of Black and White widowed women in a northern metropolis." 78 (4): 241-248. (Role: CE)

ROBERTS, R. E. and E. S. LEE (1974) "Minority group status and fertility revisited." 80 (2): 503-523. (Fertility: CD)

UDRY, J. R., K. E. BAUMAN, and C. CHASE (1971) "Skin color, status, and mate selection." 76 (4): 722-733. (Mate selection: CV)

AMERICAN SOCIOLOGICAL REVIEW

CENTERS, R., B. H. RAVEN, and A. RODRIGUES (1971) "Conjugal power structure: a re-examination." 36 (1): 1-17. (Role: CD)

HEISS, J. (1972) "On the transmission of marital instability in Black families." 37 (1): 82-92. (Marital stability: CV)

HERMES, G. (1972) "The process of entry into first marriage." 37 (2): 173-182. (Mate selection: CE).

REYNOLDS, F. and A. I. HERMALIN (1971) "Family stability: a comparison of trends between Blacks and Whites." 36 (1): 1-17. (Marital stability: CD)

ROLAND, J. and J. E. MARBLE (1972) "Family disruption and delinquent conduct: multiple measures and the effect of subclassification." 37 (1): 93-99. (Family functions: CE)

SAMPSON, W. A. and P. H. ROSSI (1975) "Race and family social standing." 40 (2): 201-214. (Role: CV)

BLACK SCHOLAR

JACKSON, J. (1971) "But where are the men?" 3 (4): 34-41. (Mate selection: CV)

REED, J. (1970) "Marriage and fertility in Black female teachers." 1 (3-4): 22-28. (Fertility: CV)

JOURNAL OF COMPARATIVE FAMILY STUDIES

MONAHAN, T. P. (1971) "Interracial marriage and divorce in Kansas and the question of instability of mixed marriages." 2 (1): 107-120. (Mate selection: CE)

_____ (1976) "The occupational class of couples entering into interracial marriages." 7 (2): 176-192. (Mate selection: CE)

JACKSON, R. N. (1975) "Some aspirations of lower class Black mothers." 6 (2): 171-181. (Family functioning: CE)

TOBIN, P. L., W. B. CLIFFORD, R. D. MUSTIAN, and S. C. DAVIS (1975) "Value of children and fertility behavior in a triracial rural county." 6 (1): 46-53. (Fertility: CE)

JOURNAL OF MARRIAGE AND THE FAMILY

AGRESTI, B. F. (1978) "The first decades of freedom: Black families in a southern county, 1870 and 1885." 40 (4): 697-706. (Family structure: CV)

ALDOUS, J. (1972) "Children's perception of adult role assignment: father absent, class, race, and sex influences." 34 (1): 55-65. (Role: CD)

_____ (1969) "Wives' employment status and lower-class men as husbands-fathers: support for the Moynihan thesis." 31 (3): 469-476. (Role: CD)

AXELSON, L. J. (1970) "The working wife: differences in perception among Negro and White males." 32 (3): 457-464. (Role: CE)

BALKWELL, C., J. BALEWICK, and J. W. BALKWELL (1978) "On Black and White family patterns in America: their impact on the expressive aspect of sex-role socialization." 40 (4): 743-747 (Role: CV).

BARTZ, K. W. and E. S. LEVINE (1978) "Childrearing by Black parents: a description and comparison to Anglo and Chicano parents." 40 (4): 709-719. (Family functions: CV)

BAUMAN, K. E. and J. R. UDRY (1972) "Powerlessness and regularity of contraception in an urban Negro male sample: a research note." 34 (1): 112-114. (Role: CE)

BERNARD, J. (1966) "Note on educational homogamy in Negro-White and White-Negro marriage, 1960." 28 (3): 274-276. (Mate selection: CE)

BOULD, S. (1977) "Female-headed families: personal fate control and the provider role." 39 (2): 339-349. (Family structure: CE).

BRODERICK, C. (1965) "Social heterosexual development among urban Negroes and Whites." 27 (2): 200-212. (Role: CE)

BROWN, P., L. PERRY, and E. HARBURG (1977) "Sex role attitudes and psychological outcomes for Black and White women experiencing marital dissolution." 39 (4): 549-561. (Role: CE)

CHRISTENSEN, H. T. and L. B. JOHNSON (1978) "Premarital coitus and the southern Black: a comparative view." 40 (4): 721-732. (Premarital sexual patterns: CV)

CROMWELL, V. L. and R. E. CROMWELL (1978) "Perceived dominance in decision making and conflict resolution among Anglo, Black, and Chicano couples." 40 (4): 749-759. (Family functions: CV).

DICKINSON, G. E. (1975) "Dating behavior of Black and White adolescents before and after desegregation." 37 (3): 602-608. (Mate selection CE)

DIETRICK, K. T. (1975) "A reexamination of the myth of Black matriarchy." 37 (2): 367-374. (Role: CE)

EDWARDS, H. (1968) "Black Muslim and Negro Christian relationships." 30 (4): 604-611. (Role: CV)

FISCHER, A., J. D. BEASLEY, and C. L. HARTER (1968) "The occurrence of the extended family at the origin of the family of procreation: a developmental approach to Negro family structure." 30 (2): 290-300. (Family structure: CD)

GEISMAR, L. L. and U. C. GERHART (1968) "Social class, ethnicity, and family functioning: exploring some issues raised by the Moynihan Report." 30 (3): 480-487. (Family functions: CE)

HANEY, C. A., R. MICHIELUTTE, C. M. COCHRANE, and C. E. VINCENT (1975) "Some consequences of illegitimacy in a sample of Black women." 37 (2): 359-366. (Role: CE)

HARRISON, A. O. and J. H. MINOR (1978) "Interrole conflict, coping strategies, and satisfaction among Black working wives." 40 (4): 799-805. (Role: CV)

HEER, D. M. (1966) "Negro-White marriage in the U.S." 28 (3): 262-273. (Mate selection: CE)
_____ (1974) "The prevalence of Black-White marriage in the U.S., 1960 and 1970." 36 (2): 246-258. (Mate selection: CE)

HOBBS, D. F. and J. M. WIMBISH (1977) "Transition to parenthood by Black couples." 39 (4): 677-689. (Family functions: CE)

KAMI, C. and N. L. RADIN (1967) "Class difference in the socialization practice of Negro mothers." 29 (2): 302-310. (Role: CD)

KING, C. A., T. J. ABERNATHY, and A. H. CHAPMAN (1976) "Black adolescents' views of maternal employment as a threat to the marital relationship: 1963-1973." 38 (4): 733-737. (Role: CE)

KING, K. (1969) "Adolescent perception of power structure in the Negro family." 31 (4): 751-755. (Role: CD)

KUVLESKY, W. and A. OBORDO (1972) "A racial comparison of teen-age girls' projections for marriage and procreation." 34 (1): 75-84. (Role: CD)

LAMMERMEIER, P. J. (1973) "Urban Black family of the nineteenth century: a study of Black family structure in the Ohio Valley, 1950-1980." 35 (3): 440-456. (Family structure: CE)

LANDRY, B. and M. P. JENDICK (1978) "Employment of wives in middle class Black families." 40 (4): 787-797. (Family functions: CV)

McADOO, H. P. (1978) "Factors related to stability in upwardly mobile Black families." 40 (4): 761-776. (Family functions: CV)

MELTON, W. and D. L. THOMAS (1976) "Instrumental and expressive values in mate selection of Black and White college students." 38 (3): 509-517. (Mate selection: CE)

MIAO, G. (1974) "Marital instability and unemployment among Whites and nonwhites, the Moynihan Report revisited—again." 36 (1): 77-86. (Marital stability: CE)

MERCER, C. V. (1967) "Interrelations among family stability, family composition, residence, and race." 29 (3): 456-460. (Family structure: CD)

NOLLE, D. (1972) "Changes in Black sons and daughters: a panel analysis of Black adolescents' orientations toward their parents." 34 (3): 443-447. (Family functions: CE)

PARKER, S. and R. KLEINER (1966) "Characteristics of Negro mothers in single-headed households." 28 (4): 507-513. (Family structure: CD)

PARKER, S. and R. J. KLIENER (1969) "Social and psychological dimensions of the family role performance of the Negro male." 31 (3): 500-511. (Role: CE)

POPE, H. (1969) "Negro-White differences in decisions regarding illegitimate children." 31 (4): 756-764. (Family structure: CV)

REED, F. W., J. R. UDRY, and M. RUPPERT (1975) "Relative incomes and fertility." 37 (4): 799-805. (Fertility: CE)

RODMAN, H., F. H. NICHOLS, and P. VOYDANOFF (1969) "Lower class attitudes toward 'deviant' family patterns: a cross-cultural study." 31 (2): 315-321. (Family structure: CV)

SAVAGE, J. E., A. V. ADAI, and P. FRIEDMAN (1978) "Community-social variables related to Black parent-absent families." 40 (4): 779-785. (Family structure: CV)

SCANZONI, J. (1975) "Sex roles, economic factors, and marital solidarity in Black and White marriages." 37 (1): 130-144. (Marital stability: CE)

STAPLES, R. (1978) "Race, liberalism, conservatism and premarital sexual permissiveness: a bi-racial comparison." 40 (4): 733-742 (Premarital sexual patterns: CV)

VINCENT, C. E., C. A. HANEY, and C. M. COCHRANE (1969) "Familial and generational patterns of illegitimacy." 30 (4): 659-667. (Family structure: CD)

WILLIAMS, J. A. and R. STOCKTON (1973) "Black family structure and functions: an empirical examination of some suggestions made by Billingsley." 35 (1): 39-49. (Family structure: CV)

WILLIE, C. V. and S. L. GREENBLAT (1978) "Four 'classic' studies of power relationships in Black families: a review and look to the future." 40 (4): 691-694. (Family functions: CE)

JOURNAL OF SOCIAL AND BEHAVIORAL SCIENCES

BILLINGSLEY, A. and M. G. GREENE (1974) "Family life among the free Black population in the 18th century." 20 (2): 1-18. (Family structure: CV)

EPPS, E. G. (1968) "Parent social status and personality characteristics of Negro high school students." 13 (2): 27-33. (Roles: CE)

HARRISON, A. E. (1974) "Dilemma of growing up Black and female." 20 (2): 28-40. (Role: CV)

JACKSON, J. J. (1974) "Ordinary Black husbands: the truly hidden man." 20 (2): 19-27. (Role: CE)

——— (1970) "Kinship relations among older Negro Americans." 16 (1-2): 5-17. (Family Structure: CE)

KENNEDY, E. J. (1968) "The relationship of maternal emotionality to obstetric complications and childbirth abnormalities." 13 (2): 3-8. (Family functions: CE)

KREPTAL, E. R. and E. G. EPPS (1968) "The 'father absence' effect aspirations: myth or reality." 13 (3): 9-17 (Family roles: CE)

KUTNER, N. G. (1974) "Differential adaptation among lower-class Black homemakers in a rural urban community." 20 (3): 55-65. (Role: CE)

LADNER, J. (1974) "Black women in poverty." 20 (2): 41-50. (Role: CV)

RHODES, E.C. (1969) "Family structure and the achievement syndrome among students at Tennessee A&I State University." 14 (1): 55-59. (Family functions: CD)

SHERMAN, E.G. (1969) "Urbanization and the Negro family: a case study in Florida." 14 (1): 36-41. (Family structure: CE)

SMITH, R. (1971) "Family life and environment in the Lincoln neighborhood community." 18 (1): 80-89. (Housing: CV)

STAPLES, R. (1972) "The influence of race on reactions to a hypothetical premarital pregnancy." 18 (3): 32-35. (Premarital sexual patterns: CE)

PHYLON

ANDERSON, J.E. (1977) "Planning of births: difference between Black and White in U.S." 38 (3): 323-296. (Family structure: CE)

BABCHUCK, N. and J.A. BALLWEG (1972) "Black family structure and primary relations." 33 (4): 334-347. (Family structure: CE)

CATES, W. (1977) "Legal abortion: are American women healthier because of it?" 38 (3): 267-281. (Fertility: CV)

HAWKINS, H.C. (1976) "Urban housing and the Black family." 37 (1): 73-84. (Housing: CE)

KOVAR, M.G. (1977) "Mortality of Black infants in the U.S." 38 (4): 378-397. (Fertility: CV)

LEE, A.S. (1977) "Maternal mortality in the United States." 38 (3): 259-266. (Fertility: CV)

SCHWARTZ, M. (1965) "The Northern U.S. Negro matriarchy: status vs. authority." 26 (1): 18-24. (Family structure: CE)

SIMON, R. (1978) "Black attitudes towards transracial adoption." 39 (2): 135-142. (Family functions: CV)

STOKES, C.S., K.W. CROKER, and J.C. SMITH (1977) "Race, education, and fertility: a comparison of Black-White reproductive behavior." 38 (2): 160-169. (Fertility: CE)

SWEET, J.A. and L.L. BUMPASS (1970) "Differentials in marital instability of the Black population: 1970." 34: 323-331. (Marital stability: CE)

SOCIAL CASEWORK

BILLINGSLEY, A. (1969) "Family functioning in the low-income Black community." 50 (1): 563-572. (Family structure: CE)

SOCIAL FORCES

BACON, L. (1974) "Early motherhood, accelerated transition, and social pathologies." 52 (3): 333-341. (Marital stability: CE)

BELL, R.R. (1965) "Lower class Negro mothers' aspirations for their children." 43 (4): 493-500. (Family functions: CE)

BLOOD, R.O. and D.M. WOLFE (1969) "Negro-White differences in blue-collar marriages in a northern metropolis." 38 (1): 59-64. (Role: CE)

MONAHAN, T.P. (1970) "Are interracial marriages really less stable?" 48 (4): 461-473. (Marital stability: CE)

SOCIAL WORK

BECKETT, J.O. (1976) "Working wives: a racial comparison." 21 (5): 463-471. (Role: CV)

PART II

DEMOGRAPHIC, ECONOMIC, MOBILITY, AND EDUCATIONAL PATTERNS

Poverty has been and continues to be the lot of most Blacks, as Glick indicated in his chapter on the demographic characteristics and as Hill, Moore, and Edelman pointed out in their chapters on social policy and advocacy. The goal of many Blacks has been to move from poverty to a more secure economic status. In spite of severe economic and occupational isolation and the lack of role models for many of the children, some Black families and individuals *have* managed to master the necessary skills, education, and jobs that allow them to move to a comparatively more secure situation. However, this situation is not secure—it is tenuous, and because there is so little inherited wealth among Black families, it tends to depend totally on wage earnings in service fields. This requires that each generation of a Black family must recreate the effort needed to climb the mobility ladders itself, unlike majority families where the status of the father can be transferred to that of the sons and future generations. The major contribution that Black families have traditionally been able to bestow on their children has been the drive to succeed and the motivation to achieve within the school setting. Ogbu pointed out the futility dreams sometimes meet: the child wants to succeed, but the society has decided that it is hopeless and transmits this to the child, who then turns away from the goal of academic excellence.

The goal of many Blacks has been to move from poverty to a more secure economic status. The authors in several chapters point this out strongly. Glick clearly indicates this in his chapter on the demographic characteristics of family life; Malveaux in the economic chapter; McAdoo in the chapter on mobility; and Edelman and Hill, in their chapters on social policy and advocacy.

The increases in upwardly mobile Blacks, while the lower group decreases, are discussed in light of the changes that are occurring within

107

the Black community. No longer are we able to talk about "the" Black family or even a "bifurcated" family. Recognition must be made that there are many mobility patterns that Blacks have taken over the years. As we cannot simplify the mobility patterns of whites or Chinese into one or two patterns, it becomes increasingly evident that there is a complexity to the economic and social life of Blacks. This complexity becomes even more evident when the social and economic connotations of skin color, hair type, and the absence or presence of Negroid facial features are discussed. Economic mobility and geographic mobility are also examined in light of the changes that have occurred.

Glick documents the changes that have occurred in Black family life in his updated chapter. He reemphasizes the reality that there is no such thing as "the Black family," for different forms exist at different classes and levels. Three areas are covered in detail in the chapter: family compositions, marriage and divorce, and employment and income. Within this chapter he points to the fact that Black families tend to have more younger children; that there is short joint survival of the unit after the children leave the home; that one-half of Black children now live only with their mothers; and that Black men tend to be less educated than their wives, although the level of education as a whole is increasing. Other trends highlighted are that the number of children in one-parent homes grew at a slower rate than in non-Black homes and that more adult children now remain in the family because of the inability to maintain separate households. The notorious imbalanced sex ratio is predicted to decline by the mid-1990s. Glick recognizes the centrality of children in Black families and predicts that there will be a decrease in the differences between Black and other families in the future, if there is less stratification by race.

Glick's chapter is packed with demographic background data that effectively pull together sources from multiple locations and will prove to be of great value to other writers in the field. This clear presentation is deceptive of the complexity of the mass of information covered. Glick presents the most current analyses and portrayal of the Black family one could possibly find.

Malveaux covers the philosophic background of the popular view of Black families. Yet she refutes the popular conception of the "typical" family. The diverse complexities of families and the public policy debates are presented. The income, family economics, the labor market are examined in detail. The labor market status of the Black male is related to the position of families and to the welfare availability. Black female versus white female income gaps and labor force participation are presented. The important concern with Black youth and their potential losses is related to the overall poverty of families. This important chapter clearly brings home the basic need for economic parity within our society.

The transgenerational mobility patterns of African families is presented by Harriette McAdoo in a theoretical discussion of the role the extended family has played in assisting Black family members to avoid the destructive cycle outlined by Ogbu. McAdoo found that the educational achievements were the result of personal perseverence, strong support, and often sacrifice by other family members. They did not have to cut themselves off from the reciprocal obligations of the kin support network in order to be mobile. This network was not felt to be only a coping strategy of poverty, but evolved into a cultural pattern that tended to transcend social class. The barriers to mobility were so great that it took more than one generation to move from abject poverty to middle-income status. One mobility pattern was found to have families who appear to be operating with a minimum amount of stress, with the highest educational, occupational, and economic rewards. These were families who had been upwardly mobile in three generations, from poverty status and into middle-income status. Family members were found to remain in the supportive network even after mobility, for cultural/family reasons. Those who had been middle class tended not to remain at that level but to gradually slip back down through the succeeding generations, falling victims to their own lowered academic attainments and discrimination within the labor market.

Ogbu also offers an explanation for why the educational level of young Blacks is low, an explanation that is counter to some well-accepted theories. His main thesis is that Black youth and their educators and parents are all locked into a caste-like status from which there is no exit. Ogbu's work has shown the futility of a nature-nurture argument on lower Black school achievement by clearly articulating the effect of being in a caste-like minority. Black youth, upon receipt of deliberate inferior education, correctly perceive the lack of comparable payoff of advanced education and are molded by both Black and white to enter and remain in their lower-status position.

Ogbu rejects the four major excuses that have been put forward for the lack of Black academic achievement: home environment, school environment, genetics, and different cultural values that reinforce different skills utilized in school. He finds all of the above faulty. They do not adequately compare data and they do not perceive the role that racial discrimination plays in the situation of Blacks. Most theories of poor achievement, and the policies that are implemented to overcome the differences, are color-blind and see that the life experiences of Blacks and non-Blacks are alike. This is a false assumption, for Blacks and other poor minorities are unable ever to escape their caste-like positions. The achievement of Blacks is compared to that of other "immigrant minorities" with an explanation of the differences that exist in their perceptions of job opportunities and thus are provided a different motivation to prepare themselves for these jobs.

Ogbu points to the collective historical experience of discrimination, the structural barriers that have a reciprocal influence on the employer and students' perceptions of their ability to get jobs. This circular interaction of perceptions and actual barriers results in a job ceiling that is obvious to youth, who then stop attempting to move out of their castes. Schools play their part in reinforcing children in the directions that would ensure that they remain in this status, making them the victims of the "double stratification of class and race caste."

Ogbu's analyses are refreshing and are free of the customary defenses or negative explanations that often appear in explanations of Black schooling. As a Nigerian, trained as an anthropologist, he may have the objectivity that many of us may lack, allowing him to clearly analyze the downward spiral within which Black youth find themselves caught.

7

DEMOGRAPHIC PICTURES OF BLACK FAMILIES

PAUL C. GLICK

Among the many well-recognized differences between Black families and families of other races in the United States, some have been converging, some diverging, and others simply persisting. These differences are important but can be overemphasized because all families tend to share in the periodic changes that occur in economic opportunities and in other aspects of the cultural environment, even though the sharing is not always equal. During periods of economic expansion, Black families have tended to improve their relative position, but during recessions they have tended to lose some of their gains. Also, in recent decades, Black families have been sharing in certain benefits, such as those resulting from the decreasing burden of large families and from an especially rapid increase in the educational level of their young adults, but they have had more than their share of the deprivation associated with the increase in the number of one-parent families.

This chapter will throw light on recent changes in the United States concerning the diversity of Black family patterns and those of all races combined. The presentation will confirm that "'the' Negro family is itself a fiction. Different family forms prevail at different class and income levels throughout our society" (Willie, 1970). The chapter is organized around three major demographic areas: family composition; marriage and divorce; and education, employment, and income. The concluding section will present a discussion of some implications of the outstanding features of Black family life.

FAMILY COMPOSITION

According to the traditional norm, families are formed through marriage, and couples who marry remain married until one spouse dies. The extent to which current marital behavior differs from the norm will be examined in this section, along with some of the implications for the living arrangements of children, for young adults leaving home and establishing new families, and for the composition of households as distinct from families.

VARIETY OF FAMILY TYPES

Most of the families in the United States are maintained (1) by a married couple or (2) by one parent and one or more of the parent's own young children. Fully 82 percent of Black families in 1985 were of one or the other of these types, and the corresponding proportion for all families without regard for race was 91 percent (Table 7.1). But at the same time, twice as large a proportion of Black families as of all families were *not* of either of these two types (18 percent versus 9 percent). Many of the families not of these two types consist of such groups of relatives as grandparents and their grandchildren, brothers and sisters, and other relatives, including neither a married couple nor a lone parent and young children.

A continuing feature of Black families is that they are more likely than other families to have young children among their members. By 1985, 57 percent of Black families as compared with 50 percent of families of all races included one or more sons or daughters under 18 years of age in the home. The larger proportion of Black families with children reflects, among other things, the higher birth rate of Black women and the shorter survival of Black marriages after their children leave home (Norton and Glick, 1986). There was a decline since 1980 in the proportion of Black married-couple families with young children present, but little change in the quite high proportion of lone parents with children present.

Among Black families in 1985 with young children in the home (57 percent of all Black families), actually about as many were one-parent families (30 percent) as were married-couple families (27 percent). This situation stands in stark contrast with that in families of all races, in which only 11 percent were one-parent families and 38 percent were married-couple families. As far back as 1950, twice as large a proportion of Black families as families of all races were of the one-parent type (9 percent versus 4 percent). Consequently, this is one feature of family life in which the gap between Black families and families of all races has been growing.

TABLE 7.1 Families by Type, Race, and Presence of Own Children Under 18 Years Old: United States, 1985, 1980, and 1970

Type of Family and Presence of Own Children under 18	All Races			Black			Percentage Black, 1985
	1985	1980	1970	1985	1980	1970	
All families (thousands)	62,706	58,426	51,586	6,778	6,042	4,887	11
Percentage	100	100	100	100	100	100	—
With own children	50	52	56	57	62	61	13
No own children	50	48	44	43	38	39	9
Married-couple families	80	83	87	51	55	68	7
With own children	38	42	50	27	31	41	8
No own children	42	41	37	24	24	27	6
Parent-child families	11	10	6	30	31	20	30
Mother and own children	10	9	5	28	29	18	32
Father and own children	1	1	1	2	2	2	14
Other families	9	7	7	18	14	12	23
Female householder	7	5	5	15	11	10	25
Male householder	2	2	2	3	3	2	16

SOURCE: U. S. Bureau of the Census, 1986a, 1981b, and 1971.

LIVING ARRANGEMENTS OF CHILDREN

Some of the sharpest differences between the family life of Black and other races can be found in the living arrangements of young children. For example, of all children under 18 in 1985, 15 percent were Black, but only 8 percent of those living with two parents were Black and 35 percent of those living with a lone mother were Black (Table 7.2). The most extreme contrast is found among children living with a mother who had never been married; two of every three (67 percent) of these children in 1985 had a Black mother. In fact, as many Black children were living with a never-married parent as with a divorced or separated parent (26 percent and 24 percent respectively). By comparison, less than one-half as many children of all races were living with a never-married parent as with a divorced or separated parent (6 percent versus 15 percent).

Nearly all of the racial differences that can be demonstrated from the data in Table 7.2 present a picture of much greater family disorganization in the living arrangements of Black children than of other young children. Even though there was about a one-third downturn between 1980 and 1985 in the proportion of Black children living with a separated or widowed mother, there was a doubling of the proportion with a never-married mother (from 13 percent up to 25 percent). There was also a doubling of the proportion of children of all races living with a never-married mother, but that was only from 3 percent to 6 percent—the latter being the same as the proportion for Black children 15 years earlier in 1970. A continuing small proportion of children live with a lone father (3 percent in 1985).

The rapid growth in the number of young children living with a never-married mother is closely related to the sharp upturn in the proportion of births occurring to unmarried mothers. Vital statistics reveal that the proportion of births to unmarried mothers rose from 35 percent in 1970 to 59 percent in 1984 for Black births, and from "only" 6 percent to 21 percent for all races. Although the rate of increase for Black births to unmarried mothers was not as great as that for other races, the level is still close to three times as high as that for all races (59 percent versus 21 percent).

As recently as 1960, there were more young children living with a widowed parent as with a divorced parent, but now four times as many live with a divorced parent as with a widowed parent. This shift resulted from both a declining mortality rate for young mothers and a vast increase in the divorce rate.

A continuing larger proportion of Black than other children under 18 live apart from either parent. According to the 1980 census, these children represented 4.5 percent of the children of all races and 11 percent of Black

TABLE 7.2 Living Arrangements of Noninstitutional Children Under 18 Years Old by Race: United States, 1985, 1980, and 1970

Living Arrangements	All Races			Black			Percentage Black, 1985
	1985	1980	1970	1985	1980	1970	
All children under 18 (thousands)	62,475	61,744	69,162	9,479	9,290	9,406	15
Percentage	100	100	100	100	100	100	—
Living with:							
Two parents	74	76	85	39	42	58	8
One parent	23	20	12	54	46	33	35
Mother only	21	18	11	51	44	30	37
Divorced	8	7	3	11	11	5	20
Married	5	6	5	12	16	15	35
Separated	5	5	3	11	15	13	36
Widowed	2	2	2	2	4	4	25
Never married	6	3	1	25	13	6	67
Father only	3	2	1	3	2	3	18
Divorced	1	1	*	1	1	*	12
Married	1	1	1	1	1	2	16
Separated	1	*	*	1	1	1	18
Widowed	1	*	*	*	*	1	15
Never married	*	*	*	1	*	*	19
Other relatives only	3	3	2	6	11	7	41
Nonrelatives only	1	1	1	1	1	2	22

SOURCE: U.S. Bureau of the Census, 1986b, 1981a, and 1973.
*Base less than 75,000.

115

children. About two-thirds of the children living apart from parents were residing with relatives, and the rest were living with foster parents or in institutions. Again, about two-thirds of those living with relatives apart from parents were living with their grandparents. In these circumstances, many of the mothers must have left their children in the care of older relatives, then the mothers—being younger, better educated, and more employable—must have gone elsewhere to increase their opportunities to earn a living.

As a noteworthy sidelight, census data show that young boys are more likely than young girls to be living in a home where a father is present. In 1985, there were 105 boys for every 100 girls under 18 years of age in Black families maintained by a father and mother; the corresponding ratio for families with a lone mother was only 98, whereas that for lone fathers was 179. In families of divorced mothers there were only 92 boys to 100 girls. (Corresponding results for families of divorced fathers is not shown because of the small numbers involved.) The results are similar for children in families of all races combined. Evidently, marriages are more likely to remain intact if boys are present, and divorced mothers are more likely to be willing to remarry (or are more likely to be asked to remarry) if they have custody of sons rather than daughters. Studies show that boys tend to be harder than girls to rear, and at least for that reason, divorced mothers of young sons usually have a special need to remarry, just as married mothers of young sons have a need to remain married.

A rapidly increasing but still small proportion of Black children live in the suburbs of metropolitan cities. During the 1970s the number of suburbanites increased three times as fast for the Black population as for persons of all races (45 percent versus 14 percent). In 1980, however, only 21 percent of the Black population, as compared with 40 percent of the entire population of the United States, lived in metropolitan suburbs.

The median age of Black children under 18 increased by about two years between 1970 and 1985, mainly because of the declining birth rate. This change must have made it easier for divorced parents to maintain a home without a spouse, to the extent that fewer custodial parents had very young children who required close supervision.

YOUNG ADULTS LEAVING HOME

The departure of young adults from their parental home generally occurs during their late teens or their twenties and is a critical period for all concerned. In 1940, near the end of the Depression, 32 percent of the Black population 18 to 29 years old were still living in their parental homes or had returned to live there. In 1960, near the end of the baby boom, there were still 31 percent of these Black youths living with their parents. But by 1970, the trend had turned upward and has continued to rise. In that year, the figure had gone up to 40 percent, and by 1984 it stood at 46 percent, well above the 36 percent for those of all races in 1984. This recent upward movement of late departure (or return to) the parental home has also been characteristic of young adults of all races. It has been attributed, among other things, to relatively high rates of unemployment, divorce, and unmarried parenthood, as well as to more young adults delaying marriage while they attend the rapidly growing number of community colleges near their parents' homes (Glick and Lin, 1986).

CHILDBEARING AND CHILDLESSNESS

After young adults leave their parental homes, most of them eventually marry, establish separate homes, and begin childbearing. Historically, Black families have had more children than other families, but there are signs that the average number of children born to mothers in the two racial groups may be in a current phase of convergence. This assertion is based in part on answers received by the Census Bureau from women about how many children they had already borne and how many more they expected to have. In 1983, among women 18 to 34 years of age, regardless of marital status, Black women had so far had an average of 1.5 children, or 36 percent above the 1.1 children for women of all races combined. However, the average number of "lifetime births expected" by Black women was 2.2 children, or only 5 percent higher than the 2.1 for all women. Incidentally, an average of 2.1 children per woman will reproduce the population from one generation to the next, aside from any net immigration.

Other evidence of a somewhat larger decline in the fertility of Black women than other women is found in the results for women with nearly completed childbearing. Thus, during the 15 years between 1969 and 1984, the average number of children ever born to Black women 35 to 44 years old declined by 0.9 of a child, from 3.8 to 2.9 children, while the corresponding average for women of all races declined by 0.7 of a child, from 3.1 to 2.4 children. These findings indicate that the rate of childbearing for those nearing the end of childbearing in 1984 was more than enough to replace the population, regardless of race.

Poorly educated Black women tend to have more children than their counterparts of other races, but highly educated Black women have about as few children as those of other races. For example, 1982 data for Black women 35 to 44 years old with less than a full high school education had borne 3.8 children, on the average, as compared with 3.1 children for comparable women of all races. But the same type of rate for college graduates was 1.8 children for Black women and also for all women. Thus, at the higher educational level, the average sizes of family for the two racial groups have completely converged.

Childlessness is another measure of fertility, which generally varies conversely with the birth rate, and which has declined sharply during the last quarter of a century. Among women 35 to 44 years old in 1960, who had borne most of their children before the baby boom, fully 22 percent of the Black women had given birth to no children; for women of all races the figure was 13 percent. By 1984, the childlessness rate for those 35 to 44 had declined dramatically to only 8 percent for Black women, even lower than the 10 percent for women of all races. These women had been at the crest of their childbearing during the transition from the baby boom to the baby bust. From another angle, women 18 to 34 years of age in 1982 were asked by the Census Bureau how many children they had borne and how many more they expected to have. Overall, 10 percent of the Black women reported that they expected to have no more, again a level slightly lower than the 12 percent for women of all races. Therefore, in respect to childlessness to date and expected future childlessness, the trends for the two racial groups have not only converged but appear to be crossing over.

FAMILY HOUSEHOLDS AND OTHER HOUSEHOLDS

Family households are households maintained by householders who share their living quarters with one or more relatives. Nonfamily households are maintained by householders with no relatives in their home. The latter type of household has been growing much more rapidly than the former type because of such factors as delayed marriages, which postpone the establishment of married-couple households; more women outliving their husbands and being able to enjoy the privacy (or being required to endure the loneliness) of living alone; more formerly married couples becoming divorced and creating a one-parent family and a one-person household; and many more nonfamily households consisting of unmarried couples cohabiting outside marriage (Glick and Spanier, 1980; Glick, 1984).

About 3 of every 10 households in 1985, regardless of race, were nonfamily households. The vast majority of these households consisted of persons living alone and were divided about evenly among never married, separated or divorced, and widowed persons. Nearly all the rest are informally cohabiting couples.

Unmarried couples of all races quadrupled in number from 0.5 million in 1970 to 2.0 million in 1985, but this includes little change after 1983.

Incidentally, these unmarried couples have been referred to as POSSLQs, that is, partners of opposite sex sharing living quarters. Information on the total number of Black unmarried couples was obtained from the 1980 census (U.S. Bureau of the Census, 1985). At that time there were 1.8 million cohabiting couples, of whom 0.6 million were in households maintained by Black adults. Among all couples (married and unmarried combined), 7.7 percent of the Black couples, as compared with 3.4 percent of couples of all races, were unmarried. Another way of showing the relatively heavy concentration of unmarried couples in the Black population is to point out that 16.5 percent of all *unmarried* couples in 1980 were maintained by Black adults, far higher than the figure of 6.8 percent of all *married* couples being maintained by Black adults.

The proportion of couples in 1980 that were cohabiting was especially large among couples in interracial unions. Thus fully 27 percent of Black husband/White wife couples were not married to each other; for White husband/Black wife couples the corresponding figure was also quite high, 21 percent.

Despite the sharp increases during recent decades in one-parent households, one-person households, and unmarried-couple households, the fact remains that about one-half of the Black people in the United States live in households that are maintained by a married couple. Yet the corresponding figure for persons of all races is significantly higher, about three-fourths. Within this context, the most common living arrangement of the population is a household containing a married couple and one or more children under 18 years of age; one of every three Black persons, as compared with one of every two persons of all races, was living in this type of a home in 1985.

MARRIAGE AND DIVORCE

Changes in marriage and divorce are reflected in marital status trends, and each marital status category depends strongly on a given range of ages. Consequently, the following treatment of the subject focuses on the most relevant age range for a given marital status.

DELAY OF MARRIAGE

Young adult Black persons have a consistent pattern of postponing marriage longer than persons of other races. A sharply increasing delay of marriage between 1970 and 1985 is shown in Table 7.3 in the form of a rising percentage of persons in their twenties who had never married. The median age at first marriage for both men and women occurs during this period of life. During the 15 years since 1970, the level of the percentage of those who had never married was more than one-half for young men and nearly doubled for young women, regardless of race. By 1985, 72 percent of the Black men in their twenties, and 64 percent of the Black women in the same age group had never married. Corresponding figures for young adults of all races were distinctly lower, 57 percent and 42 percent, respectively. Among the factors contributing to the increasing delay of marriage have been continued high unemployment rates, especially among Black persons seeking their first permanent job, more time devoted to advancing their education, more persons opting for cohabitation before marriage, and the effects of a phenomenon called a "marriage squeeze" (Glick and Norton, 1979).

The recent marriage squeeze resulted from the upturn in births during the late 1940s and 1950s, and the tendency for young men to be two or three years older than the women they marry. Thus a woman born in 1947, when the birth rate had risen, was likely to expect to marry a man born in 1944 or 1945, when the birth rate was still low. Accordingly, about 20 or 25 years later, there was an excess of women of marriageable age, and this situation has persisted for those born throughout the baby boom. Here, the most marriageable ages for men is taken to be 18 to 27 years, and for women 16 to 25 years. In 1970, there was only 74 percent as many Black men as Black women in these ages. By 1980, the ratio had risen to 80 and by 1985 to 99. Looking ahead, those born during the baby bust will experience a reversal of the marriage squeeze, when there will be a shortage of young men of marriageable age. Thus by 1995 there are expected to be 102 Black men for every 100 Black women in this age range. The earlier marriage squeeze made it difficult for women to marry, but the future marriage squeeze will make it harder for men to marry. The ratios for young adults of all races are considerably higher because a smaller percentage of Black births are boys and because there is a larger undercount of young Black men than of other men in censuses and surveys.

SEPARATION AND DIVORCE

Since 1970 there has been not only a delay of marriage but also an acceleration in the extent of marital disruption, defined as separation or divorce. As seen in Table 7.3, the level of disrupted marriages is much higher for Black women than for Black men. In fact, more women than men of all races combined are reported as separated, whereas the numbers should be the same. One likely reason is that more women with a premarital

TABLE 7.3 Marital Status of the Noninstitutional Population in Selected Age
Groups by Race and Sex: United States, 1985, 1980, and 1970

Marital Status, Age, and Race	Men			Women		
	1985	1980	1970	1985	1980	1970
Percentage never married, 20 to 29 years old						
All races	57	51	39	42	37	25
Black	72	62	44	64	53	34
Percentage separated or divorced, 25 to 34 years old						
All races	12	9	5	17	14	8
Black	19	13	9	29	28	20
Percentage in intact marriage, 35 to 44 years old						
All races	76	81	84	72	84	79
Black	57	61	69	46	49	58
Percentage widowed, 55 years old and over						
All races	9	9	11	36	37	38
Black	16	14	16	46	45	44

SOURCE: U.S. Bureau of the Census, 1986b, 1981a, and 1972.

birth who have never married incorrectly report themselves as separated. However, separation has been increasing less rapidly than divorce, apparently implying that more separated persons have been dissolving their marriages by divorce so that they can remarry or at least "make a clean break" from their marriages.

The "divorce ratio" shows how many divorced persons there are for every 100 in intact marriages. In 1985, there were 25 percent as many Black divorced persons as Black married persons—18 percent for men and 33 percent for women. These ratios are extremely high, far above those for their counterparts of all races—10 percent for men and 15 percent for women.

The likelihood of divorce is negatively correlated with income for men and positively correlated for women, regardless of race. Evidently, relatively affluent men are not only less likely to become divorced, but if they do, they are more likely to remarry rather quickly. On the other hand, relatively affluent divorced women tend to be more deliberate about remarrying, and then if they want to remarry they are likely to find that most of the desirable unmarried men have already become married or remarried.

Black women with an incomplete college education, as well as other such women, are more likely than those in any other education group to be divorced before they reach middle age. Many of these women started toward the goal of achieving a full college education, but because of adverse circumstances did not achieve it. Those with graduate school training also have rather high divorce probabilities. Women with advanced college degrees are most often absorbed in career interests that compete with the desire to maintain a permanent marriage.

INTACT MARRIAGES

As marital disruption has become more frequent, the proportion of persons who are in intact marriages at mid-life has been on the decline. Both this trend and racial differentials accelerated during the 1980s as is evident from the data for persons 35 to 44 years old in Table 7.3. Regardless of the trend, men with a high income level are more likely to be continuing an intact first marriage. This situation suggests that men who are financially successful in their line of work tend to have a continuing experience in an intact marriage, but this relationship is strongest at the lower end of the income distribution, apparently implying that marital permanence for men depends less on their being well-to-do than it does on their not being poor. Among men in 1980 who were simultaneously in the highest educational level and the highest income level, there was no significant racial difference with respect to the proportion still in their first marriages at the age of 45 to 54 years.

The pattern for women is different. Those with high earnings are generally less likely, regardless of race, to be in intact first marriages by middle age. Married women with high incomes may find that the demands of their work interfere with their marital adjustment, and such a situation may be the worst for that one-sixth of wives who earn more than their husbands, even though there is evidence that men are becoming increasingly tolerant of their wives having the higher income.

The extent to which marital stability has been affected by changes in the proportion widowed above the mid-fifties is very slight (Table 7.3). At that period of life, widowhood continues to be much more prevalent among women than men, largely because of lower death rates for women and higher remarriage rates for men, regardless of race.

REMARRIAGE

Black persons who remarry after divorce are less likely than persons of other races to do so at the usual ages, that is, when they are 25 to 44 years of age. However, according to the 1980 census, Black persons who were the most likely to remarry were those with a partial high school education. Specifically, among Black ever-married high school dropouts 25 to 44 years old, only 14 percent of the men and women had remarried. For ever-married persons of all races, 21 percent of the men and 25 percent of the women had remarried. These findings are consistent with those of Eckhardt et al. (1980) to the effect that the proportion of divorced persons who remarry is lower among Blacks than Whites at each interval since divorce.

Teenage marriage, regardless of race, is much more likely than marriage at more mature ages to be associated with divorce followed by remarriage within 5 to 10 years after first marriage. In fact, the likelihood is twice as great. Here, more mature ages refers to 20 to 24 years for women and 25 to 29 for men. These ages include the period when college graduates are most likely to marry.

A study by Glick (1980) demonstrated that remarriage is more likely to be followed by redivorce among Black women 35 to 44 years old than among women of other races of the same age. It also showed that Black women 35 to 44 with no young children were more likely to become redivorced than were those with children, especially those with preschool-age children. This result may reflect the greater ease of childless women than mothers to be self-sustaining.

INTERRACIAL MARRIAGE

At the time of the 1980 census of the United States, there were 1,012,000 interracial couples reported in which both the husband and the wife were in their first marriage. This was three times as many as the 330,000 reported in 1970 and six times as many as in 1960. Some of this phenomenal increase may have resulted from more willingness to report accurately, but it could have reflected a growing acceptance by young adults of interracial marriage as a tolerable life-style, especially among better educated persons. The 121,000 Black/White couples in 1980 (both married once) were close to twice the 65,000 in 1970. Three-fourths (78 percent) of these couples in 1980 involved a Black husband and a White wife, as compared with two-thirds (63 percent) in 1970. Although the Black/White married couples in 1980 represented 3.4 percent of all Black couples, they represented only 0.3 percent of all White couples. Incidentally, one-half of Native American first marriages among couples in 1980 were mixed; for Japanese (wives) it was 40 percent, for Chinese it was 10 percent, and for Filipinos 23 percent—all much higher than Black intermarriage.

Interracial married couples have a greater probability of having a short marriage than married couples with the husband and wife of the same race, whether Black or White. Heer (1974) analyzed 1970 census data for first marriages contracted in the 1950s that were still intact in 1970. The results showed that 90 percent of the White/White couples were still living together and that 78 percent of the Black/Black couples were also still together. However, much smaller proportions of the mixed racial couples had a continuing marriage: 63 percent of the couples with a Black husband and a White wife (Black/White); and only 47 percent of the couples with a White husband and a Black wife (White/Black). Comparable figures from the 1980 census on first marriages during the 1960s that were still intact in 1980 have the same pattern, but the proportions are smaller: 79 percent, 68 percent, 58 percent, and 44 percent, respectively. Evidently Black/White couples are not only more numerous at marriage, but they also tend to have longer marriages than White/Black couples.

EDUCATION, EMPLOYMENT, AND INCOME

In this final major section, the units in the treatment of education will be children, and will feature the extent of their parents' schooling, whereas the units to be featured in the presentation about employment will be wives and mothers, and the units in regard to income will be primarily families by type.

EDUCATION OF PARENTS

The great majority of young children live with parents who are under 45 years old. Moreover, nine-tenths of Black families maintained by adults of this age have children under 18 years of age in their homes. As for the education of Black children's parents, it may come as a surprise that in 1985, a total of 27 percent had a parent with at least one year of college training (Table 7.4). This figure is far higher than in 1970 and one-third higher than it was only five years earlier in 1980.

Turning to Black children under 18 in one-parent families, it is significant that the proportion of their parents who had not completed a full high school education *declined* by about one-eighth during the short span of five years between 1980 and 1985. Meanwhile, the proportion of Black children under 18 whose parents had finished at least some college education *increased* at a much higher rate, by about one-third.

Therefore, it is correct to infer that Black children currently live in the homes of much better educated parents now than just a few years ago. Also,

TABLE 7.4 Years of School Completed by Parents Under 45 Years Old of
           Noninstitutional Children Under 18 Years Old by Type of Family
           and Race: United States, 1985 and 1980

Family Type and Parent's Education[a]	All Races			Black		
	1985	1980	Percentage Change	1985	1980	Percentage Change
All Children in Families						
Total under 18 (thousands)	48,797	46,102	—	6,719	6,369	—
Percentage	100	100	6	100	100	5
Parent's education						
0-8 years	7	9	−16	7	11	−27
9-11 years	13	15	−7	24	28	−13
12 years	40	40	6	42	41	8
13-15 years	19	17	15	18	15	33
16 or more	21	19	17	9	5	73
Children in Families of Lone Mothers						
Total under 18 (thousands)	9,747	8,624	—	3,563	3,344	—
Percentage	100	100	13	100	100	7
Mother's education						
0-8 years	11	12	3	9	12	−17
9-11 years	23	26	−1	28	33	−10
12 years	42	41	15	44	39	18
13-15 years	17	15	29	15	13	28
16 or more	7	6	41	4	3	51

SOURCE: U. S. Bureau of the Census, 1986a and 1981b.
a. Years of school completed by fathers under 45 years of age in families with a male householder and by mothers under 45 years old in families with a female householder.

the rate of improvement in the education of Black parents has been much higher than that of other parents. The fact remains, however, that the average educational level of Black parents is still substantially lower than that of parents of all races combined. Thus the gap between the educational levels of Black and other parents has been narrowing, but differences still persist.

Another kind of racial difference is found in the gap between the educational attainments of husbands and their wives. Specifically, Black women are more likely than other women to be married to men with less education than they have. This situation is exaggerated among women in their second and subsequent marriages (Spanier and Glick, 1980) and is related to the much smaller proportion of Black husbands than other husbands who are college educated. Again, this differential has been decreasing.

WORKING WIVES AND MOTHERS

Most of the Black husbands as well as husbands of other races are in the labor force, but an increasing proportion of men have been retiring at an earlier age. Thus 84 percent of the Black husbands were in the labor force in 1970, but the corresponding figure in 1984 was 78 percent (U.S. Bureau of the Census, 1973a; U.S. Bureau of Labor Statistics, 1984). For husbands of all races the rate went down from 86 percent in 1980 to 79 percent in 1984.

By contrast, the labor force participation rate for wives, regardless of race, has been increasing, with the rate for Black wives continuing to be especially high. To illustrate, 51 percent of Black wives in 1969 and 63 percent in 1984 were in the labor force, as compared with 40 percent and 53 percent, respectively, for wives of all races. The worker rate for divorced women was still higher than that for married women, but here the rate of 70 percent for Black women was not quite as high as the 74 percent for women of all races. The growth in the proportion of women in the labor market reflects many other social and economic changes, including the decline in the birth rate, an upgrading of the educational level—and therefore the employability of women, and the expansion of employment opportunities for clerical and professional employees.

Wives with no children under 18 years of age have continued to include a high and increasing proportion in the labor force. In 1984, Black childless wives had a worker rate of 54 percent, a few points above the 47 percent for childless women of all races. Likewise, Black married mothers had a higher worker rate than all married mothers, 70 percent versus 59 percent. However, childless divorced women had the highest rates of all, 80 percent for Black divorcees and 85 percent for divorcees of all races. Meanwhile, Black fathers in 1984 had a much higher unemployment rate than that for fathers of all races, 13 percent as compared with 9 percent. The especially high unemployment rate and a relatively low average educational level of Black fathers no doubt discourages many of them from even looking for work.

FAMILY INCOME

Changes in family income by race during recent years have been profoundly affected by the changing mix of families by type as well as by the changing proportion of wives in the labor force. This generalization can be verified by studying the rows of figures at the bottom of Table 7.5. As can be seen, the median income of Black families in 1984 was 58 percent as large as that for families of all races. Although this percentage is quite low, it is at least somewhat higher than the 54 percent in 1979 and 53 percent in

TABLE 7.5 Type of Family in 1985, 1980, and 1970 and Median Family Income in 1984, 1979, and 1969 by Race: United States

Year and Race	All Families	Married-Couple Families		Male Householder, No Wife Present	Female Householder, No Husband Present
		Wife in Paid Labor Force	Wife Not in Paid Labor Force		
All races (percentages)					
1985	100	43	37	4	16
1980	100	40	42	3	15
1970	100	34	53	2	11
Black (percentages)					
1985	100	33	18	5	44
1980	100	33	23	4	40
1970	100	36	32	4	28
Median Family Income					
All races					
1984	$26,433	$34,668	$23,582	$23,325	$12,803
1979[a]	$29,050	$33,709	$24,014	$22,795	$13,408
1969[a]	$25,211	$31,079	$23,729	$22,289	$12,887
Black					
1984	$15,432	$28,775	$14,502	$15,724	$ 8,648
1979[a]	$15,723	$27,946	$15,679	$16,868	$ 9,323
1969[a]	$13,385	$20,381	$12,522	$13,888	$ 7,455
Black as percentage of all races					
1984	58	83	61	67	68
1979	54	83	65	74	70
1969	53	66	53	62	58

SOURCE: U. S. Bureau of the Census, 1986 c, 1980, and 1970.

a. In 1984 dollars.

1969. Moreover, for each type of family, shown in the box heading of the table, there was an appreciable improvement between 1969 and 1984 in the family income of Blacks as compared with that for all families, even though there was a decline for several types between 1979 and 1984. The greatest improvement since 1969 was that for Black families with the wife in the paid labor force; by 1979 and also 1984, the median income of these families was 83 percent as large as that for families of all races, whereas it had been only 66 percent as large in 1969.

An important reason for the relative position of Black families with the wife in the paid labor force is the much larger proportion of Black wives than wives of all races who work year round full time (48 percent versus 32 percent in 1984). Moreover, the median income of Black wives who worked year-round full time in 1984 ($14,700) was almost as high as that for all wives ($15,100). And perhaps surprisingly, the median income of *all* Black wives in 1984 was actually 14 percent higher than that of *all* wives regardless of race ($8,500 as compared to $6,600). Meanwhile, Black men were less likely to work full time and had lower average wages than other men. These are among the reasons why the median income of families with the wife in the paid labor force was "only" 83 percent as high for Black families as for families of all races. Incidentally, Black wives had the same or more income than their husbands in 25 percent of the families as compared with 15 percent for wives of all races, according to a study made with census data in 1978. By 1984, the corresponding figure for wives of all races was 18 percent.

For this complex set of reasons, the net effect has been a substantial increase in the relative income position of Black families of each type since 1969, as well as a moderate increase in the position of Black families as a whole. Nonetheless, the income level for Black families remains comparatively low for each family type. A much fuller exposition of this situation is presented in Chapter 9 of *Social Indicators III* (U.S. Bureau of the Census, 1980b).

The poverty rate for Black families in 1983 was 32 percent, somewhat above the 28 percent in 1973. During the same period, the poverty rate for all families increased from 9 percent to 12 percent (U.S. Bureau of the Census, 1984). Accordingly, the poverty rate has continued to be about three times as high for Black families as for all families. Again, a prime reason is the higher poverty rate for the increasing proportion of Black families maintained by a woman with no husband in the home.

Even though the poverty rate for Black families was quite high during the last 15 years, it was still much higher back in 1959, when it was 48 percent for Black families of all types combined, and even higher, 65 percent, for families maintained by Black women. Comparable rates for families of all races were much lower, 19 percent and 43 percent, respectively.

Per capita income is a measure that assesses the relative income standing of different population groups at least partially independent of the type of family structure. Information for 1984 shows that the average income per Black person in the noninstitutional population was $6,070, whereas that for persons of all races was $10,200, making per capita income for the Black population 60 percent of that for persons of all races. In 1970, the corresponding figure was also 60 percent, implying no change in the gap by race for this measure.

Child support and alimony are also important aspects of family income in this era of large proportions of women who are divorced, three of every eight of whom have children under 18 in their homes. According to a special study in 1983 conducted by the U.S. Bureau of the Census (1986d), only 34 percent of the Black women who had sole custody, as compared with 58 percent for similar women of all races, were awarded child support payments. Moreover, a smaller proportion of Black women than women of all races who were supposed to receive child support payments actually received them (two-thirds as compared with nearly three-fourths). And for custodial mothers regardless of race, the amount of child support received constituted only about one-fourth of their total income. Those who received child support payments had larger total incomes, on the average, than those who received none. This fact is no doubt related to the husbands' income level and the effectiveness of mothers at obtaining the payments that had been awarded to them.

Only about 6 percent of Black women in 1984 were awarded alimony at the time of divorce, and about four-tenths of those who were supposed to receive alimony actually did receive it.

DISCUSSION

This chapter represents the author's attempt to add to the growing number of "works on Black families that tend to view them from a positive rather than a negative perspective" (Wilkinson, 1978). From a balanced viewpoint, Black families are regarded as "an important subculture of American society, different in many ways from White families, but possessing a value system, patterns of behavior, and institutions which can be described, understood, and appreciated for their own strengths and characteristics" (Peters, 1978).

A strength, as well as a liability, that is prominent among Black families is "the centrality of children," to borrow an apt expression from Cazenave

(1980). As Table 7.1 has demonstrated, a larger proportion of Black families than families of other races include young children among their members. Another distinguishing feature of Black families has been the large and continually growing proportion that are maintained by women. These prevailing Black family life-styles have been interpreted, in part, as adaptations to the special circumstances in which many Black persons find themselves and, in part, as preferences for certain values that often differ from those of members of other races. Yet Black families vary widely in the personal and social characteristics of their members; moreover, Black family members tend to be concentrated somewhat more in selected parts of the range of these characteristics than family members of other races because of differing circumstances or matters of choice.

Some of the apparent differences between Black and other families are probably the result of unequal amounts of misreporting in censuses and surveys on such subjects as the absence of the husband from the household. Most likely many poor couples, regardless of race, yield to the temptation to report that the husband is absent if they believe that doing so will improve their chances of receiving welfare benefits; if such reporting is more likely to occur among Black families, it could be at least in part because a larger proportion of Black families than other families are poor. Also, Black husbands are more likely than other husbands to live apart from their wives because larger proportions of them are serving in the Armed Forces or are residing in an institution.

Some of the signs of diminishing differences between Black and other families also deserve to be mentioned. For example, even though a larger proportion of Black children live in one-parent families, the rate of increase in this proportion has been less rapid since 1970 among Black children than children of other races. Therefore, this gap has been narrowing. Other demonstrations of converging tendencies since 1970 include the more rapid increase in the (generally lower) average educational level of Black women as compared with other women who maintain homes; the less rapid increase in the (generally higher) proportion of households maintained by unmarried Blacks than is the case with other couples; and the more rapid increase in the (generally lower) median incomes of Black families compared with other families of each type. In some respects these developments are evidence that "Black families have managed to sustain their families under pressures that are now being shared by a growing number of non-Black families" (McAdoo, 1978).

Many of the racial differences in family characteristics persist but are demonstrably smaller within socioeconomic levels than they are for all levels combined. If racial differences in socioeconomic stratification should diminish during coming years, one might reasonably expect that more of the residual differences in family characteristics will become matters of choice to fulfill aspirations rather necessary to cope with their unique problems of adjustment.

REFERENCES

CAZENAVE, N. A. (1980) "Alternate intimacy, marriage, and family lifestyles among low-income Black Americans." Alternative Lifestyles 3 (November): 425-444.

ECKHARDT, K. W., W. R. GRADY, and G. E. HENDERSHOT (1980) "Expectations and probabilities of remarriage: Findings from the National Survey of Family Growth, Cycle II." (unpublished)

GLICK, P. C. (1980) "Remarriage: some recent changes and variations." Journal of Family Issues (December): 455-478.

_____ (1984) "American household structure in transition." Family Planning Perspectives (September/October): 205-211.

GLICK, P. C. and S. L. LIN (1986) "More young adults are living with their parents: who are they?" Journal of Marriage and the Family (February): 107-112.

GLICK, P. C. and A. J. NORTON (1979) "Marrying, divorcing, and living together in the U.S. today." Population Bulletin (February): 1-41.

GLICK, P. C. and G. B. SPANIER (1980) "Married and unmarried cohabitation in the United States." Journal of Marriage and the Family (February):19-30.

HEER, D. M. (1974) "The prevalence of Black-White marriage in the United States, 1960 and 1970." Journal of Marriage and the Family (May): 246-258.

McADOO, H. P. (1978) "Factors related to stability in upwardly mobile Black families." Journal of Marriage and the Family (November): 761-776.

NORTON, A. J. and P. C. GLICK (1986) "One parent families: a social and economic profile." Family Relations (January): 9-17.

PETERS, M. F. (1978) "Black families: notes from the guest editor." Journal of Marriage and the Family (November): 655-658.

SPANIER, G. B. and P. C. GLICK (1980) "Paths to remarriage." Journal of Divorce (Spring): 283-298.

U.S. Bureau of the Census (1970) Income in 1969 of Families and Persons in the United States. Current Population Reports, Series P-60, No. 75. Washington, DC: Government Printing Office.

_____ (1971) Household and family characteristics: 1970. Current Population Reports, Series P-20, No. 218. Washington, DC: Government Printing Office.

_____ (1972) Marital Status. 1970 Census, II: 4C. Washington, DC: Government Printing Office.

_____ (1973a) Employment and Work Experience. 1970 Census, II: 6A. Washington, DC: Government Printing Office.

_____ (1973b) Persons by Family Characteristics. 1970 Census, II: 4B. Washington, DC: Government Printing Office.

_____ (1980a) Money income and poverty status of families and persons in the United States: 1979. Current Population Reports, Series P-60, No. 125. Washington, DC: Government Printing Office.

_____ (1980b) Social Indicators III. Washington, DC: Government Printing Office.

_____ (1981a) Marital Status and Living Arrangements: March 1980. Current Population Reports, Series P-20, No. 365. Washington, DC: Government Printing Office.

_____ (1981b) Household and Family Characteristics: March 1980. Current Population Reports, Series P-20, No. 366. Washington, DC: Government Printing Office.

_____ (1984) Statistical Abstract of the United States: 1985: Washington, DC: Government Printing Office.

_____ (1985) Living Arrangements of Children and Adults. 1980 Census, II: 4B. Washington, DC: Government Printing Office.

_____ (1986a) Household and family characteristics: March 1985. Series P-20, No. 411 Washington, DC: Government Printing Office.

_____ (1986b) Marital Status and Living Arrangements: March 1985. Series P-20, No. 410 Washington, DC: Government Printing Office.

_____ (1986c) Money Income of Households, Families, and Persons in the United States: 1984. Series P-60, No. 151. Washington, DC: Government Printing Office.

_____ (1986d) Child Support and Alimony: 1983. Current Population Reports, Series P-23, No. 148. Washington, DC: Government Printing Office.

U. S. Bureau of Labor Statistics (1984) "Working mothers reach record number in 1984." Monthly Labor Review, December 1984.

WILKINSON, D. Y. (1978) "Toward a positive frame of reference for analysis of Black families: a selected bibliography." Journal of Marriage and the Family (November): 707-708.

WILLIE, C. V. (1970) The Family Life of Black People. Columbus, Ohio: Charles E. Merrill.

8

THE ECONOMIC STATUSES OF BLACK FAMILIES

JULIANNE MALVEAUX

The status of the Black family, especially in the 1980s, has been examined and analyzed by a number of researchers. Many, reviewing frequently touted statistics on the number of Black female-headed households, rates of Black teen pregnancy, and high rates of Black male unemployment, have returned to the controversial findings of Daniel Patrick Moynihan's 1965 report, noting that "Moynihan was right." Others have reviewed strengths of the Black family and relied on discussions of Black extended families to paint a more optimistic picture of Black households. For many researchers, some discussion of the appropriate framework from which to analyze Black families becomes tantamount. Johnson (1981), for example, writes that the literature on the Black family may fall into one of three frameworks: culturally equivalent, culturally deviant, or culturally variant.

Although the academic literature that describes and discusses the Black family may not have changed since Johnson's article (nearly half of the theoretical articles about the Black family approached the issue from the culturally equivalent point of view, "popular wisdom" of the 1980s has described the Black family as culturally deviant. Economist Glenn Loury, for example, has written not of economic variations between Blacks and whites, but of variations in "family values" and "moral values," as if these factors alone cause income and economic differences between Blacks and whites. Similarly, an effect of the federal budgets that cut social programs in every year since FY 1981 has been to attack the survival of Black families. "Popular wisdom" maintains that these families might survive economically if they were only able to work harder. In perhaps the most disturbing manipulation of public perceptions about the Black family, CBS news correspondent Bill Moyers (1986) produced a CBS Special Report, *The Vanishing Black Family: Crisis in the Black Community*, which portrayed not the Black *family*, but Black youth from Newark, New Jersey. The lurid documentary dealt not with vanishing families (the majority of all Black families are husband-wife families), but with the "popular" crisis of teen parenting and pregnancy. Slightly less alarmist, but equally disturbing, was the manner in which *Washington Post* columnist Leon Dash (1986) inserted himself into the life of Black teens in Southeast Washington, D.C., and wrote about their family formation.

Although no discussion of the status of the Black family is completely irrelevant, Dash and Moyers and many others have a tendency to describe a certain type of Black family as "typical." Such a family, according to popular wisdom, is headed by a single woman likely to have borne her children in her teens. Her daughters, too, are likely to follow a similar pattern. Popular wisdom would describe this family as impoverished, perhaps dependent on public assistance.

Such a family is not a "typical" Black family. Although 42 percent of all Black families were female-headed in 1984, 51 percent were married couple families. Although nearly a third (30.9 percent) of all Black families lived in poverty in 1984, nearly the same number (29.4 percent) of Black families had earnings above $25,000 (white median family income was $27,000 that year). Whether Black families experience poverty, receive public assistance, or maintain relatively high earnings, disparities between Black and white families at every income level are important. (U.S. Department of Commerce, 1985.)

It is important to emphasize the diverse complexion of Black families. They range from single mothers who receive public assistance and raise their children against all odds. Black families also include upwardly mobile, two-earner families with incomes above $50,000 per year. Although a profile of Black families would reveal enormous diversity, Black families share the common experience of institutional racism.

A set of external and internal forces determines the status of Black families. Externally, the macroeconomy determines the economic condition of Black families. As America recovers from repeated recessions, so does the Black community, though in trickled-down and diluted form. Because Blacks are not evenly distributed among industries, industrial policy questions are also important to the economic status of Black families.

The employment outlook for Black workers is of major significance to Black families. Black workers experience unemployment at more than twice the rate of white workers. Black male workers participate in lower levels of the labor force than do white male workers. In addition, Black male workers maintain more lower-status, poorer-paying jobs than white male workers. Similarly, though Black women mirror white women in their concentration in "typically female" jobs, Black women earn less than do their white counterparts, and work in lower-status, female-dominated jobs.

A broad range of sociological and demographic factors also affect the status of Black families. Black families are not immune to the higher divorce rates, higher rates of female-headed households, deferred marriages, and the social changes that have affected all of society. These factors contribute to a decline in the number of Black married couple families in the same sense that they have contributed to the decline in the number of white married couple families. These same factors indirectly affect the economic status of Black families.

The multiple factors that influence the economic status of Black families include those factors that affect the employment status of both Black men and women, especially the shifting structure of the economy, the decline in manufacturing jobs, and the accompanying decline in the participation of Black men in the labor market. Other factors include those policies that encourage (or discourage) the availability of child care, those macro-economic policies that affect overall well-being (and that of Black families in particular). The federal budget strategies that have favored high defense spending (as opposed to social programs that emphasize job training and income maintenance) may also contribute to the economic status of the Black family.

The economic status of Black families has become a recent focus of public policy. Researchers have attempted to minimize the effects of race, stating that if Black families started families at a later age, had fewer children, worked in more remunerative occupations, or had families with two wage earners, then the economic status of Black families would be improved. Such arguments fail to account for the impact of institutional racism on Black workers, on the children of these workers, and ultimately on the future of Black communities. These arguments also tend to focus on pathologies instead of strategies for strengthening Black families. In poverty and on public assistance, or with progress and relatively well-salaried, Black families share the yoke of institutional racism. The economic status of Black families reflects this shared heritage.

THE DEMOGRAPHICS OF BLACK FAMILY INCOME

There were 6.8 million Black families in the United States in 1984, 3.5 million of which were married couple families. The majority (64 percent) of

TABLE 8.1 Family Status by Race, 1984

	Number of Black Families (thousands) 6,778	Median Income $15,432	Number of White Families (thousands) 54,400	Median Income $27,686	Ratio B/W Income 55.7
Married couple families	3,469	23,418	45,643	30,058	77.9
Percentage of total families that are married couple families	51.2		83.9		
Excess of married couple income over total income (percentage)		51.7		8.6	
Number of families with wives in the labor force	2,221	28,775	23,979	35,176	81.8
Percentage of married couple families with wives in the labor force	64.0		52.5		
Excess of two LF family incomes over married couple income (percentage)		22.9		17.0	
Two LF families as a percentage of total families	32.7		44.1		
Excess of two LF family income over total family income (percentage)		86.5		27.1	
Female headed families	2,964	8,648	6,941	15,134	57.1
Percentage of total families that are female-headed	43.7		12.8		
Female-headed family incomes and a percentage of total incomes		56.0		54.7	

SOURCE: U.S. Bureau of the Census, Current Population Reports, Series P-60, No. 149, *Money, Income and Poverty Status of Families and Persons in the United States: 1984*. Washington, DC: Government Printing Office, 1985.

married couple families had working wives. A significant number of Black families (nearly 3 million, or 44 percent) were female-headed. Table 8.1 details the status of both Black and white families.

Income varies widely among Black families by family composition. While median income for all Black families totaled $15,432 in 1984, it totaled $28,775 in married couple families with the wife in the labor force, but just $8,648 for female-headed households.

An income gap exists between Black and white families regardless of family composition, but the gap is most narrow for married couple families with working wives, in which Black families earn almost 82 percent of what white families earn. Black married couple families are more likely than white married couple families to have wives in the labor force; furthermore, Black married couple families with working wives have median incomes that are nearly double (186 percent) median incomes of all Black families. In contrast, white married couple families with working wives have median incomes just 27 percent higher than median incomes of all white families. Thus, the work effort of Black women contributes more toward maintaining the income level of Black families than that of white women. Although a more detailed examination of the data will provide a fuller explanation of this phenomenon, the fact that white men earn significantly more than Black men partly explains this.

Tables 8.2 and 8.3 show Black and white family income for selected years in constant (1984) dollars (the use of constant dollars controls for the effects of inflation). Although these tables do not provide information about family composition, they do show more detail on the income distribution of families. Both tables demonstrate the effects of economic cycles on family income in addition to the economic vulnerability of Black families to recession.

For example, the proportion of Black families with incomes over $25,000 (in constant dollars) was higher in 1970 than it was in 1984. Though the proportion of families with such income levels has fluctuated, the decline in the number of families with earnings between $25,000 and $34,000 indicates the fact that some Black families have slipped back into poverty. In contrast, the number of Black families with incomes above $35,000 has increased, suggesting progress for an upper tier of Black families. Much of this progress represents a recapturing of old gains—15.8 percent of Black families had incomes above $35,000 in 1980; this proportion dropped in 1982, but rose by 1984.

In contrast, the proportion of white families with incomes in excess of $35,000 declined somewhat in 1982, but exceeded its 1980 level by 1984. Black families experienced both absolute and relative reductions in

TABLE 8.2   Black Family Income for Selected Years
              in (constant) 1984 Dollars

	1984	1982	1980	1976	1974	1970
Families (in thousands)	6,778	6,530	6,317	5,804	5,491	4,928
Percentage	100.0	100.0	100.0	100.0	100.0	100.0
Under $10,000	34.0	35.6	32.1	29.4	28.9	28.4
$10,000-$14,999	14.9	15.4	15.4	16.2	16.0	16.2
$15,000-$19,999	12.3	11.0	12.2	11.7	13.2	16.5
$20,000-$24,999	9.4	10.2	9.8	10.4	10.5	9.3
$25,000-$34,999	13.1	14.5	14.7	19.9	20.0	19.0
$35,000-$49,999	10.5	9.5	10.9	7.9	7.5	7.0
$50,000 plus	5.3	3.6	4.9	4.5	3.9	3.6
Median income	$15,432	$14,633	$15,976	$16,863	$16,863	$16,796
Ratio B/W income	55.7	55.2	57.9	59.5	59.7	61.3

SOURCE: U.S. Bureau of the Census, Current Population Reports, Series P-60, No. 149, *Money, Income and Poverty Status of Families and Persons in the United States: 1984.* Washington, DC: Government Printing Office, 1985.

TABLE 8.3   White Family Income for Selected Years
              in (constant) 1984 Dollars

	1984	1982	1980	1976	1974	1970
Families (in thousands)	54,400	53,407	52,710	50,083	49,440	46,535
Percentage	100.0	100.0	100.0	100.0	100.0	100.0
Under $10,000	11.9	12.8	11.4	10.3	9.9	11.1
$10,000-$14,999	10.3	11.0	10.3	10.1	9.7	9.5
$15,000-$19,999	10.7	11.4	11.1	10.2	10.7	14.3
$20,000-$24,999	11.0	11.8	11.0	11.0	12.0	9.3
$25,000-$34,999	19.8	20.3	21.8	28.3	28.0	29.3
$35,000-$49,999	19.4	18.2	19.5	15.2	15.0	14.5
$50,000 plus	16.9	14.6	14.8	14.9	14.8	12.1
Median income	$27,686	$26,475	$27,611	$28,349	$28,241	$27,381

SOURCE: U.S. Bureau of the Census, Current Population Reports, Series P-60, No. 149, *Money, Income and Poverty Status of Families and Persons in the United States: 1984.* Washington, DC: Government Printing Office, 1985.

income. The absolute percentage point decline between 1980 and 1982 was 1.5 percent for white families and 2.7 percent for Black families. In relative terms, the proportion of Black families with incomes in excess of $35,000 dropped by 17 percent, while the proportion of white families dropped by 4 percent.

Although erosion in the incomes of both Black and white families between 1980 and 1982 comes as no surprise, especially given recession and high unemployment rates, the fact that middle-income Blacks bore a heavier burden of this status than whites has roots in the "last hired, first fired" concept that makes Blacks more vulnerable during periods of economic fluctuation. Furthermore, Black professionals had a higher concentration in public sector employment during a period when both the federal and state governments reduced employment levels.

A corollary to the decrease in the proportion of Black families with incomes of more than $25,000 is the increase in the number of families with low incomes. The proportion of Black families with incomes under $10,000 rose from 1970 to 1984, with a major increase taking place between 1980 and 1982. Though the proportion of Black families with incomes under $10,000 declined between 1982 and 1984, more than one third of all Black families earned less than $10,000 during that year.

While the proportion of Black families with incomes under $10,000 increased between 1970 and 1984, the proportion of families with incomes between $10,000 and $14,999 declined slightly. The proportion of Black families with incomes under $15,000 went from 44.6 percent in 1970 to more than 50 percent in 1982, falling to 48.9 percent in 1984. In contrast, 22 percent of white families had incomes of under $15,000, with nearly 12 percent having incomes under $10,000 in 1984. Though the number of families with incomes under $15,000 rose slightly (from 20.6 percent to 22.2 percent) between 1970 and 1984, this increase is both absolutely and relatively smaller than the increase in the proportion of Black families with incomes at that level.

The income distribution of Black families, then, has changed in these ways since 1970: (1) the proportion of Blacks in poverty has increased; (2) the proportion of Blacks at the highest income levels (over $35,000) has risen by almost a third since 1970; (3) the proportion of Blacks with "middle incomes" (broadly defined as incomes between $15,000 and $34,999) declined between 1970 and 1984. These changes are similar to changes in the income distribution of white families, among whom proportions of those in poverty and at the top income levels rose. Differences are summarized in Table 8.4. There was about a 10 percent decline in the proportion of both Black and white families with "middle" incomes (between $15,000 and $34,999) between 1970 and 1984. Among whites, most of the decline in middle income families results in an increase in the proportion of higher income families. On the other hand, for Black families, nearly half of the decline in the proportion of middle income families resulted in an increase in the proportion of lower income families. This discussion of the demographics of Black income status began with some analysis of the income gap between Black and white families. Tables 8.2 through 8.4 reinforce this point clearly. What is especially notable

TABLE 8.4   Black and White Income 1970 and 1984
             in (constant) 1984 Dollars

		Black (percentage)	White (percentage)
1984			
Low income	(less than $15,000)	48.9	22.2
Middle income	($15,000-$34,999)	34.8	41.5
Upper income	($35,000-$50,000)	15.8	36.3
1970			
Low income	(less than $15,000)	44.6	20.6
Middle income	($15,000-$34,999)	44.8	52.9
Upper income	($35,000-$50,000)	10.6	26.6

SOURCE: U.S. Bureau of the Census, Current Population Reports, Series P-60, No. 149, *Money, Income and Poverty Status of Families and Persons in the United States: 1984.* Washington, DC: Government Printing Office, 1985.

about the income gap is the fact that it has widened, not narrowed, since 1970. Despite the fact that the proportion of Black families with high incomes grew faster than the proportion of white families with high incomes (the proportion of Black families with incomes over $50,000 grew by 47 percent between 1970 and 1984, while the proportion of such white families grew by 40 percent), the base of Black families with such incomes was so small at the outset that even with greater growth, the proportion of white families with high incomes was almost three times the proportion of similar Black families in 1984.

Some social scientists have argued that affirmative action is no longer an effective remedy to combat discrimination and to improve the economic status of Black families (Murray, 1984). The slightly accelerated pace of Black income gains over white gains suggests that affirmative action has been effective in increasing the proportion of Black families at high income levels. The income gap persists, though, because affirmative action can do little to combat the structural shifts in the economy (as well as those monetary and fiscal policies) that leave a third of Black families poor.

BLACK FAMILY ECONOMICS AND THE LABOR MARKET

Because labor market earnings represent a major portion of Black families' incomes, it is important to examine the status of Blacks in the labor market in the context of Black family economics. The basic data mirror the income gap: Blacks have higher unemployment rates, lower labor force participation rates (in general, though Black women have higher participation rates than white women), a higher incidence of part-time employment, and lower earnings than whites, even in the same occupations.

In September 1985, for example, adult (20 years old or more) Black men experienced unemployment rates of 13.4 percent. Black men had labor force participation rates of 64.7 percent, about 12 percentage points lower than white male participation rates. Wilson (1985) reports that while the economic status of employed Black men has improved, the proportion of employed Black men has dropped from 80 percent in 1930 to 56 percent in 1983.

How does the labor market status of Black men relate to the status of Black families? Wilson suggests that Black male joblessness, morality, and incarceration rates restrict the ability of Black men to support their families. From a policy standpoint, this suggestion is important. If an interest exists in strengthening the economic status of Black families, efforts might be targeted on creating jobs for Black men, not on restricting welfare availability to Black women.

In addition to joblessness, the occupational status of Black men is important. While the number of Black men employed in managerial and professional jobs has increased, the majority of men remain employed in blue-collar and service jobs. The occupational status of Black men differs significantly from that of white men. For example, the largest concentration of Black men in the labor market (36 percent) work as operatives, laborers, and assemblers. These Black men had median earnings of $287 per week in 1984 (compared to $304 median earnings for all Black men). In contrast, a small number of white men (22 percent) worked in these jobs for higher median earnings of $324 per week (compared to $403 per week median earnings for all white men).

Two kinds of wage gaps reveal themselves in this discussion: (1) Black male operatives, laborers, and assemblers earned 89 percent of what their white male counterparts earned; and (2) full-time, full-year employed Black men earned 75 percent of what their white male counterparts earned. Employed Black men experience other wage gaps and occupational differences that contribute to wage gaps. For example, 22.6 percent of all white males worked in crafts jobs, with median earnings of $402 per week. Fewer Black men (16 percent) worked in similar jobs. Their earnings were also lower—$348 per week.

Although the Black men who worked full-time, full-year experienced wages that ranged from 58 percent of white male wages to wage parity with white men, comparing full-time, full-year men ignores differences in unemployment and in labor force participation. The combination of occupational concentrations and unemployment make Black men particularly vulnerable to cyclical shifts in the labor market. And, though the Wilson argument is not conclusive, it suggests that the joblessness that accompanies these cyclical shifts also contributes to the economic status of Black families.

Black women in the labor market, too, experience differences in status that have implications for the status of their families. The very high number of Black female-headed families has been the target of much policy concern. But Table 8.1 suggests that female headship alone does not imply poverty. The average white female-headed family had median income of $15,384 in 1984, an income only slightly lower than the median for *all* Black families. Because Black female headship is so highly correlated with poverty (51.7 percent of Black female-headed households have poverty status), it is appropriate to examine the role employment plays in determining the economic status of Black families.

Wage gaps between full-time employed Black and white women are narrower than those between Black and white men. In 1984, the median wage per week was $264 for full-time white women and $242 for full-time Black women. Full-time Black women's earnings were 92 percent of full-time white women's earnings. At the same time significant differences arose between the status of Black and white women (Malveaux, 1985a). Black women have consistently experienced higher unemployment rates than have white or Hispanic women, with Black women's unemployment levels tending to be twice those of white women. In December 1985, for example, the unemployment rate for adult white women was 5.4 percent, while the unemployment rate for adult Black women was 12.6 percent.

Black women lose their jobs more quickly than do white women during recession. They also find jobs more slowly than Black men, white men, and white women in periods of economic recovery. Black women's unemployment rates showed less cyclical sensitivity than did the rates of Black and white men, and unemployment rate improvement during recovery correlates more highly with the length of recovery than does unemployment rate improvement for other race-sex groups (Malveaux, 1985b).

Labor force participation rates, a measure of labor supply, are measured as that proportion of the population either working or looking for work. Black women have always had high labor force participation rates, but the gap between Black and white women's labor force participation has narrowed considerably in the past 15 years. In 1960, for example, a 12-point gap developed in the labor force participation rates of Black and white women. By December 1985, Black female labor force participation was 59.2 percent, compared to white female labor force participation of 54.4 percent.

The labor force participation of young Black women has been dropping for some time, with participation for those 16-24 below 30 percent in 1984. Barbara Jones (1985) cites the declining employment opportunities and increased competition for unskilled jobs as part of the reason labor force participation rates for young women remain so low. The paucity of affordable child care and job training programs, especially given high rates of teen pregnancy, may also be factors in the declining participation of young women.

Perhaps the greatest difference in the status of Black and white women lies in the difference in occupational status. At first glance, Black and white women seem to be distributed similarly in occupations. A third of all white women are clerical workers, as are 30 percent of all Black women workers. A total of 23 percent of all Black women work in service jobs, as do 16 percent of white women. In all, 15 percent of Black women workers and 17 percent of white women workers work in professional jobs.

Beneath surface similarities lie key differences. Black women tend to be employed in lower-paying, lower-level, pink- and blue-collar occupations, such as manufacturing, service, and private household work (44 percent of Black women). Black women also experience an occupational segregation distinct from the occupational segregation white women experience. In addition to being employed in jobs that are "typically female," Black women are also employed in jobs that are "typically," or disproportionately, Black female. If Black women are either deliberately or traditionally "crowded" into a few low-paying jobs, they lower wages in those jobs in which they cluster, and reduce competition (or increase wages) in the jobs from which they are excluded. This concept of Black women's crowding explains, in part, why Black women receive lower pay than white women in similar occupations.

"Typically Black female" occupations are those in which Black women's representation is more than twice their representation in the labor force. In service jobs, for example, Black women are overrepresented by a factor of 3 or 4 (or, at 3 or 4 times their representation in the labor force) as chambermaids, welfare service aides, cleaners, and nurse's aides. Some 41 percent of the Black women who work in service occupations are employed in these four jobs (Malveaux, 1985a).

Similarly, nearly a quarter of all Black women are concentrated in just six of 48 clerical occupations. They are overrepresented by a factor of four as file clerks, typists, teacher aides, keypunch operators, calculating machine operators, and social welfare clerical assistants.

Part-time work is common in those occupations in which Black women are concentrated. Many women work part-time for "economic reasons," officially defined as accepting part-time work when full-time work is unavailable. For example, more than a third of all service workers work part-time. Some 16 percent work part-time for economic reasons. The part-time characteristics of jobs Black women tend toward hold disadvantages for them in the labor market. The official definition of "economic reasons" excludes other reasons that are also "economic": the paucity of child care, the unavailability of flexible schedules, and so on.

Another aspect of the occupational status of Black women rests with the disproportionate number of Black women concentrated in government employment. While 16 percent of all workers were employed by the government in 1981, 26 percent of Black women workers were so employed. Nearly a third of the Black women employed in clerical jobs worked for the government. While the high level of government employment means that many Black women are covered by collective bargaining agreements in public employee unions, the fiscal uncertainties that the government faces make it likely that many of these Black women find their employment in jeopardy.

The result in differences, whether differences exist in Black male or Black female status in the labor market, is that more Black families have low earnings than white families. In fact, while most Black people in poverty did not work (66 percent), one in six did not work because they could not find work. Nearly half reported that they "keep house" and so could not work, but one might argue that the availability of child care might attract more of these women into the labor market. Most importantly, though, a third of those Blacks in poverty worked. Their poverty status is a function of occupational segregation and joblessness (70 percent of those Black workers in poverty worked fewer than 50 weeks per year).

FAMILY FORMATION AND BLACK YOUTH: POTENTIAL LOSSES IN TWO GENERATIONS

Much of the alarm about the status of Black families focuses on issues of Black teen pregnancy and Black male unemployment, underemployment, and criminal activity. The alarm has been translated into so many well-publicized "special reports" and "investigations" that it would appear that Black teen families compose the bulk of all Black families. Nothing could be further from the truth—Black families headed by 15- to 25-year old women represent 16 percent of all Black female-headed families in poverty, and 10.3 percent of all Black female-headed families. Poverty is disproportionate among families headed by young Blacks, but young Blacks by no means represent the majority of Black families (U.S. Department of Commerce, 1985).

Instead, although some aspects of youth's lives explain the incidence of poverty among young Black families (such as educational attainment, number of children, and work experience), the incidence of poverty among adult female-headed families is equally alarming. Nearly a third (31.8 percent) of the Black families headed by Black women who have attended college are families with incomes below the poverty line. So too, a third of the Black female-headed families in which women worked. Although rates of poverty are lower when families are not female-headed, there is a significant poverty incidence in married-couple families in which the householder has attended college, in those in which the householder has worked full-time, and even in those in which there are two workers in the household.

This data on poverty status does not mean to detract from the problems of families headed by young Blacks, but merely to put these families in perspective. Some young Blacks will leave poverty as they age; others, based on data about the current Black population, may remain in poverty even after they reach adulthood.

Although the dimensions of the teen pregnancy problem have been overstated, the concern about Black teen parenting and pregnancy is important. But it is notable that Black teen birthrates are falling, while white teen birthrates are rising. The popular media would portray teen pregnancy as a uniquely "Black" problem, but issues of teen sexuality, parenting, and pregnancy are issues that confront the entire population.

Black teen parenting is important because Black teens are less likely than others to marry, and thus will be dependent on their parents, or on one income (which is likely to be consumed by child care costs), or on public assistance for survival. Even when young Black men attempt to meet their responsibilities as parents by sharing child care costs, their attempts may be frustrated by the bleak labor market prospects they face.

It is clear, as well, that labor market prospects for Black teens are bleak. Black teen (16-19) labor force participation rates were 39.6 percent in September 1985, and averaged less than 40 percent for that entire year. Unemployment rates were 38.3 percent, higher for men (at 41 percent) than for women (at 35 percent). The combination of low participation rates and high unemployment rates meant that just one in four Black teens held jobs in 1985 (U.S. Bureau of Labor Statistics, 1986).

The fact that so many Black children grow up in poverty is of as much concern as the levels of teen parenting and pregnancy. But all Black children in poverty are not the sons and daughters of teen parents. More than half of Black children under age 3 lived in poverty in 1984, as did just half of those between three and five. The older children were, the lower were their poverty rates, but the overall rate of Black child poverty was 33.8 percent in 1984 (compared to 11.5 percent for white children).

The Children's Defense Fund (CDF) has produced voluminous work on the status of children in poverty. Their work has followed patterns in federal budgets, demonstrating losses in levels of funding for education, mental health, welfare services, juvenile justice, and other programs. CDF's work on child poverty focuses both on the extent of child poverty and the extent to which government policy has exacerbated levels of child poverty (Children's Defense Fund, 1986).

CDF reports suggest in many ways that two generations fall at risk because of policies that exacerbate child poverty. When young girls have children, they are "least likely to receive early and continuous prenatal care." Their children have higher death rates and lower than average rates of growth. Teen mothers and fathers stay in jeopardy because social programs that support them have been eliminated. Their children, too, are at jeopardy, both because of a paucity of programs to support them and because their parents are placed at risk and unable to provide for them.

POLICIES TO STRENGTHEN THE ECONOMIC STATUS OF BLACK FAMILIES

This chapter portrays Black families under siege: Black families in poverty; Black families with near-poverty earnings; Black families with earners subject to high levels of unemployment rates; Black female-headed families with no access to child care; Black families headed by teens who may be locked out of both educational systems and social service networks.

Can policies be developed to strengthen the status of Black families? Clearly, policies that improve the labor market status of Black men and Black women will improve the status of Black families. These policies include affirmative action strategies and their subsets, such as comparable worth strategies (Malveaux, 1985a), as well as policies and programs that increase the availability of employment and training programs. Policies that provide increased educational access to Black students and workers relate to the set of labor market policies suggested. Additionally, policies that increase the availability of child care to working women will improve the status of Black female-headed families.

It is equally important to understand those circumstances under which targeted policies are more useful than macroeconomic policies. Black workers experience a disadvantaged status in the labor market and should, perhaps, experience a disproportionate advantage when policy is formulated. Otherwise, as mentioned earlier, even an accelerated pace of Black progress is insufficient for catch-up.

This chapter opened with the concept of shared legacies among Black families, despite class status. Discussion reinforces the fact that while there has been economic progress in the 1970-1984 period, there remain problems for Black families. When public policy is designed to strengthen the status of Black families, not highlight perceived pathologies, then Black child futures will be ensured. Without enlightened public policy, the economic status of Black families is both at jeopardy and under siege.

REFERENCES

Children's Defense Fund (1986) An Analysis of the FY 1987 Federal Budget and Children." Washington, DC: Author.

DASH, L. (1986) "At risk: chronicles of teenage pregnancy." The Washington Post.

JOHNSON, L. B. (1981) "Perspective on Black family empirical research: 1965-1978," in H. P. McAdoo (ed.) Black Families. Beverly Hills: Sage.

JONES, B. (1986) "Black women and labor force participation: an analysis of sluggish growth rates." Review of Black Political Economy (Winter).

MALVEAUX, J. (1985a) "Similarities and differences in the economic interests of Black and white women," Review of Black Political Economy (Summer).

_____ (1985b) "Black women's employment in recession and recovery." Presented at AEA meetings (December).

MOYERS, B. (1986) The Vanishing Black Family: Crisis in the Black Community." CBS Special Report.

MOYNIHAN, D. P. (1965) The Negro Family: The Case for National Action. U.S. Department of Labor. Washington, DC: Government Printing Office.

MURRAY, C. (1984) Losing Ground: American Social Policy 1950-1980. New York: Basic Books.

U.S. Bureau of Labor Statistics (1984a) The Employment Situation: September 1985. Washington, DC (USDL 85-416): Government Printing Office.

_____ (1984b) Data on occupation and income. (unpublished)

_____ (1986) Employment and Earnings. (January) Washington, DC: Government Printing Office.

U.S. Department of Commerce, Bureau of the Census (1985) Current Population Reports, Series P-60, No. 149, Money Income and Poverty Status of Families and Persons in the United States: 1984. Washington, DC: Government Printing Office.

WILSON, W. J. (1985) Congressional Black Caucus Newsletter. Washington, DC.

9

TRANSGENERATIONAL PATTERNS
OF UPWARD MOBILITY
IN AFRICAN-AMERICAN FAMILIES

HARRIETTE PIPES McADOO

The transgenerational mobility patterns of African-American families have ebbed and flowed along with the country's patterns of economic changes. Blacks as a group made important mobility changes from the point of arrival on the continent into this century. Significant improvements were made over the past decades of the 1940s through the 1970s. Many families were able to be upwardly mobile and to enable their children to have greater opportunities. The progress toward the American dream of improved circumstances peaked and then declined during the 1980s.

The overall impression presented in the public media is that a growing number of Black families have become middle class through the opportunities provided through higher education and affirmative action. Some now feel that affirmative programs are no longer needed and that Blacks may have gotten greater economic rewards than they deserve. In fact, the number of Black middle-class families has declined since the mid-1970s. A steady erosion has occurred in the proportion of Blacks preparing for and being employed by the traditional professions. The recessions of the mid-1970s dealt serious blows to the progress of the Black middle class, while intensifying the decline in all other groups. The economic decline continued through the 1980s. College attendance declined for Blacks, especially males. The increase in the need for technological skills, even in entry-level jobs, will make it more difficult for Black individuals and families to maintain themselves at levels of self-sufficiency and will preclude mobility into more secure status. Earning power per family unit has decreased for Black families in relation to all other families in the United States (Hill, 1981). More families are being forced to "double up" with other family members as a result of the high unemployment rate and growing inflation. The growing underclass entrapment of Blacks, including the working poor, prevents any consideration of upward mobility (Glasgow, 1980).

The increasing numbers of single mothers will have a definite impact on families' abilities to be upwardly mobile into or even to remain in the middle class. The earnings of two adults who are sharing parenting and financial support are needed for families to maintain their economic levels and to garner the resources to move into higher statuses. Black families have historically been more vulnerable to external economic and policy environments and have been affected earlier than have other groups.

Even when middle-class status is obtained, the changes in governmental policies, technological advances, and the restrictions caused by the growing national deficits will contribute to the decline of families who are able to be upwardly mobile. The supportive help provided by the wider extended families and other networks of support is expected to be even more important in the near future than it has been in the past.

One Black subgroup has reached economic parity with non-Blacks of the same age group—the "golden cohort" of young male and female professionals, aged 25-35, who delayed childbearing and are concentrating their energies on their careers (Malveaux, 1981). They are college graduates who are now employed at a salary level equal to that of whites. This new element has led some writers to believe that race is no longer an important element in employment for these select people who have obtained advanced education (Wilson, 1978). Though racial differences are minimal now in this younger professional group, no data have yet emerged on the differential changes that may occur as the two racial groups mature and attempt to climb the occupational ladder. Initial employment and increases may be on a par while employees are in their early professional and occupational careers. However, with time, solidarity and racial preferential patterns are expected to become more evident as promotions, salary increases, and transfers into managerial positions are unequally distributed and continue to reinforce the older patterns built on racial group membership.

One contributing factor that has been proposed as another barrier to mobility of the very poor families is the bifurcation of Black families into diverse economic groups and the movement of the more affluent families into white urban and suburban communities (Wilson, 1987). The rigidly segregated communities of the pre-1960s were restrictive to those who had the resources to move into more affluent neighborhoods, and poor and wealthy Blacks lived in the same neighborhoods. They lived in the same areas, attended the same schools and churches, and participated in the parallel Black institutions. However, their social lives were as strictly segregated along economic lines as along racial lines. The professional Blacks provided resident role models for the poorer individuals. The concentration of poor Blacks within urban centers, the intensification of the impoverishment of single mothers, and the isolation from exposure to persons who are attempting to be upwardly mobile, will probably contribute to the greater decline in middle-class families. However, one must be careful to avoid blaming upwardly mobile Blacks for the conditions of the remaining poor. External pressures, discrimination, and changes in governmental policies are the forces that sap individual initiative of poor with mobility aspirations.

When looking at income mobility, factors other than simple ability are obviously at play. Blacks get a lower dollar return for their education in general and in proportion to the number of years spent in school (Schwartz and Williams, 1977). Regardless of test scores, similarity of background, or length of time spent in getting advanced education, the data clearly show that employers hire and promote on the basis of the race of the person, regardless of which factors are controlled in statistical calculations (Corcoran, 1977). They unfailingly become victims of the Black job ceiling (Ogbu, this volume).

To concentrate upon only those Blacks with higher levels of education and the enthusiasm of youth is misleading, for the vast majority of Blacks do not have those resources. The elimination of affirmative action programs will also truncate the career mobility of those who are fully qualified but lack the opportunity to realize their potential fully. Only time will tell.

BACKGROUND

Three theoretical considerations must be examined when focusing on mobility within Black families. The first relates to the disagreement within the field of Black family studies about the relative merits of the African-linked cultural patterns. Some writers feel that no such links exist and that any deviations from the mainstream are the result of class, race, and poverty (Heiss, 1975; Hill, 1981). Existing family forms are thus seen as an adaptation of individuals within a poverty status to the mainstream family structures and organization (Shimkin et al., 1978; Aschenbrenner, 1973). This view is also supported by the belief that nonpoor Black families are indistinguishable from nonpoor non-Black families (Heiss, 1975).

Some writers prefer to use ethnicity to focus on Black families, combining class level and castelike status (Scanzoni, 1971; Ogbu, 1974). Others have posited that to look at class only without some cultural framework is to view the families within a vacuum, even when extensive assimilation has occurred (Herskovits, 1941; Nobles, 1976; Sudarkasa, 1980) This last group emphasizes the cultural continuity of Black family patterns. The position adopted by writers is often a reflection of their academic disciplines; sociologists rely more on income and class data, and anthropologists, along with some psychologists, lean toward cultural data.

The second theoretical consideration is whether the kin-support networks help or hinder upward mobility. Some writers have stressed the draining aspect of this mutual aid because of the lack of support from community institutions (Pleck, 1979; McQueen, 1971). Most have indicated that this mutual aid was essential, in that it extended the economic reach of all the family members (Hill, 1971; Stack, 1975; McAdoo, 1978). The inherent reciprocity of the obligation requires family members to keep their resources fluid and open to the emergencies of those within the extended circle. Although this prevents individuals from focusing their resources only on the family of procreation, the assurance of available help is deemed to far outweigh the negative aspects of involvement within the kin insurance network.

The third theoretical consideration is that extended patterns are only an element of sheer poverty. The lack of resources for poor Blacks requires a continuation of kin-help patterns as a coping strategy. This point of view predicts that extended kin patterns no longer exist for families above the poverty level. This view states that there is no basis in fact for the belief that some continuity of present Afro-American families and distant African family patterns were lost during and after enslavement. All of these varying views are discussed in detail in other chapters.

Supports that were made available to some Black families during the period of enslavement and in the decades immediately afterwards resulted in certain families being given advantages or head starts over other families. Many of these same families have been able to consolidate their gains and achievements and have maintained these advantages to the present time. These were the families whose adults were able to receive or earn their freedom early, who were taught to read during enslavement (an illegal activity), who developed skills, or who acquired land or other valuable attributes that allowed them an advantage over the other families.

They often were able to obtain apprenticeships, normal school education, and advanced college and graduate degrees while the vast majority of freedmen were still in rural poverty. The children and grandchildren of many of these families went on to become the leading educators, religious and civil rights leaders, and medical and scientific front-runners of the twentieth century.

Many of these skills and acquisitions were the result of the efforts, special talents and intelligence, fortunate circumstances, and intense hard work of the individuals themselves. Some advancement came from the collective efforts of entire families, who "invested" in the most talented of their families' youth. These extended family efforts were often the important ingredient that allowed them to be upwardly mobile (McAdoo, 1978; Martin and Martin, 1978; Wilkinson, 1987).

Other early advancements were the result of assistance provided by non-Blacks. This help may have come from missionaries who went south to set up freedmen's schools or persons who provided college tuition for gifted students (Haley, 1976). In other instances, the help was provided by white relatives who openly funded the education of their offspring or who quietly facilitated the entrance of close relatives into historically Black colleges or northern white schools. This latter group was a remnant of the miscegenation that occurred during and after enslavement.

All these elements and sources of support provided "screens of opportunity" to some families that incurred advantages that persisted for generations (Billingsley, 1968; Horton and Horton, 1979; Pleck, 1979). Other families had greater obstacles to overcome. They often took more than one generation to move from poverty to solid working-class status, and finally, in the third or fourth generation, into comfortable middle-class status (McAdoo, 1978).

SOURCES OF STATUS WITHIN BLACK COMMUNITIES

Franklin E. Frazier (1939) made two divisions within the Black middle class. The first mobile group was composed of more established, well educated, puritanical, quiet persons who were closely tied to the Black community. The second wave, rich as the result of industrial growth or war economy, became the notorious "Black bourgeois" with conspicuous consumption and less emphasis on education. These two groups have blended in the present-day younger and middle-age groups, along with the newly mobile who fit neither earlier class. The two older groups, however, are clearly evident in the older society of most urban centers.

Several forms of status demarcation have existed within the Black community that includes the standard differentiation that comes with advanced economic, educational, and occupational status. In addition, high status is afforded those in the public entertainment and athletic fields who have recognition and finances, but not necessarily the education and security of other mobile groups. Status also comes from the political and community influences; of elected officials. Status is sometimes given to wealthy individuals who live at the outer limits of legal activities. There are those within the community who, independent of their jobs, wield tremendous influence through leadership in church or social organizations. The Black church has provided leadership roles and sources of status for generations.

A status differentiations unique to Blacks has been based upon skin color, hair types, and the absence or presence of Negroid or Caucasoid facial features. It is the direct result of the internalization of a preference for European characteristics to the denigration of African physical characteristics. This is remnant of the period of exploitative miscegenation during enslavement and reflects the sexual vulnerability of females of African descent within this century.

Earlier, one route of upward mobility within Black communities was to marry a person who was lighter in color, for skin color was often an attribute used to establish attractiveness. This element of mate selection was most obvious in the preferred choices of wives by Black males who had "moved up."

Skin color now is not as important a component of status. However, some light-skinned Blacks still feel superior and prefer to socialize with those of similar appearance, while others who are very dark continue to harbor feelings of group-imposed inferiority or insecurity. This can lead to certain levels of antagonism between light and dark-skinned Blacks. Though diminished in importance, skin color differentiation can still be a viable, though usually unspoken, criterion of status. Though not totally reflective of a "self-hatred" philosophy (McAdoo, 1977; Cross, 1987), color preferences represent a devaluation of the external representation of the castelike status of African-Americans within American society (Ogbu, 1986). It reflects the continuing preferences of the wider society for white over Black.

One of the major contributions of the Civil Rights and Black Consciousness movements were the attempts that were made to defuse the importance of physical appearance in the attribution of social status and upward mobility. For a period of time, a reaction formation occurred in some younger groups, in which dark skin rather than lighter skin was verbally preferred. Ideally, skin color should be irrelevant to status or mobility. Within recent generations, skin color advantages have lessened as Blacks, regardless of SES or skin color, have been able to obtain some of the benefits of higher education in a variety of settings and locations. Physical appearance is not as important a mobility criterion now as is individual achievement, other than to mark a person permanently within a racial caste in our society.

PATTERNS OF MOBILITY

EDUCATIONAL MOBILITY

Despite the thrust of discrimination and the pall of poverty that lies over so many Black families, some have managed to acquire the needed education, skills, and achievements to become economically secure. This security is tenuous and depends, for the most part, on the good health and employment of wage earners. Successful Blacks have had to overcome the adaptive reaction to the castelike status of Blacks that leads to the expectation and realization of lowered school achievement that inhibits mobility (Ogbu, 1974).

Few Black families have wealth they are able to pass on to the succeeding generation. Each generation of Blacks thus must recreate the mobility cycle and generate the effort necessary to succeed and move upward again. The greatest gift a Black family has been able to bestow upon its children has been the motivation and the skills necessary to succeed in school.

Only through their achievements, with the support of the wider community and extended family help, have individual Blacks been able to get the advanced education needed to move into higher status jobs and positions. Although proclaimed "self-made" persons may now be in high-income positions, a close examination usually reveals that these persons were the recipients of "screens of opportunities" (Billingsley, 1968)—special efforts of relatives, school teachers in segregated school systems, community groups—or were fortunately picked up and protected by mentors as they worked on their higher degrees or status (Franklin, 1979; Hill, 1971; Martin and Martin, 1978; McAdoo, 1978; Manns, this volume).

Although education for the next generation has been valued, it has often been difficult for the youth to obtain this education. The life circumstances, the educational programs that are available for their children, and the socialization practices within Black families often make educational achievement very difficult. The coping strategies that are protective within urban poor communities may be the very characteristics that interfere with their ability to take advantage of the opportunities within school systems (McAdoo, 1981). This dissonance is particularly salient for young Black males. These young men often are unable to make the proper "match" between their own characteristics and those attributes that are most successful in facilitating relationships with teachers and the educational systems. The subtle, and sometimes not so subtle, denigration of Black males tends to stifle their academic pursuits and channel them into sports (Rasberry, 1987). It therefore becomes more difficult for males to meet their own mobility goals. As a result, fewer males are now attending college than are females.

Enrollment in public school increased from 1970 to 1977, but has declined since then. The racial gap in school attendance rate was eliminated as a result of compulsory attendance laws. Educational attainment rates improved during this same time. The high school graduation rate increase for Blacks (from 53 percent to 79 percent in 1982) was twice that of whites, but Blacks still had a lower overall level.

The difficulty that many urban Black children have in school has also been attributed to the conscious and unconscious attempt that children make to maintain their identity and acceptance with their peers, who may not be oriented toward educational attainment. Fordham and Ogbu (1986) have clearly demonstrated that in order to be accepted, bright Black children often behave in ways that ensure that they are not perceived, by their peers or their teachers, as achievers. They tend to avoid concentrated efforts toward achievement in order to maintain their perceptions of what it is to be "Black," to avoid "acting white" or being seen as "brainiacs." Their experiences have been referred to as "cultural inversion," in which verbal support is given to academic achievement, but actual achievement behavior is avoided. These cultural frames of reference continue even when children are raised within middle-class Black homes. Improvements in educational and occupational opportunities are not taken advantage of because of the unconscious fear of a loss of cultural identity. Ogbu (1986) further explained the difficulties that Blacks have in being upwardly mobile by referring to the social context of subordination that is experienced by Blacks. The subordination limits access to the most valued and highly remunerative occupational positions and thus mobility is limited.

The cultural dimensions and the devaluation of the individual of color that exist in educational institutions contribute to the difficulties that Blacks encounter when they attempt academic mobility. But the greatest deterrent to college enrollment and completion, that overshadows all other factors, continues to be the socioeconomic situation of so many Black families. The continuing segregation and financial differentiation of the public schooling of Black children are only manifestations of the socio-economic pressures.

According to the Census data, more men are in college now than 10 years ago. During the early 1970s the tendency was for more men than women to be enrolled, and during the late 1980s more women tended to be enrolled. In 1987, the Black female college enrollment was higher than that of males. However, the gender gap is less important than the overall racial pattern. Both men and women are less likely to enroll in and complete college in the late 1980s than they were in the mid- to late-1970s. Black college enrollment increased from 7 percent of total college enrollment in 1970 to 11 percent in 1981. Most of this increase occurred in the early 1970s.

College enrollment does not give the total picture, for many Blacks are in junior colleges that do not provide the degrees and skills that allow them to be upwardly mobile. The shifts in financial aid for higher education, from grants to loans, make it more difficult for students to obtain advanced degrees. More Blacks are enrolled in white institutions, but more receive degrees in Black colleges. More go on to obtain professional degrees when the undergraduate degree was earned at a Black college.

ECONOMIC MOBILITY

Economic upward mobility of families has been reflected more in the attainment of family units in which two parents are present and are in the marketplace. Mobility is extremely difficult for family units that are composed only of women and children, regardless of race. Census data showed substantial improvements during the 1960s and early 1970s in the incomes, educational attainment, school enrollment, and home ownership of Black married couples (U.S. Department of Commerce, 1983). Between 1971 and 1981, the number of owner-occupied housing units increased 45 percent. This progress occurred while other groups (unmarried mothers, youth, elderly) were experiencing marked declines in these same areas.

In 1980, Blacks accounted for 10 percent of the civilian labor force and were underrepresented in managerial and professional occupations (6 percent) and technical and administrative (8 percent). More men were in these higher categories, with a male/female ratio of .71. Women in managerial or professional fields tended to remain in the traditional female jobs of teacher, social worker, or nurse. Blacks who held professional-level jobs represented 11 percent of total employed Black adults.

The special stresses of single mothers are again shown in the level of professional occupations, probably reflecting their difficulty in obtaining advanced education and training. In 1986, only 8 percent of female single parents were at the professional level, compared to 13 percent of males who were parenting alone and 14 percent of married couples (U.S. Department of Commerce, 1986). Only 7 percent of single mothers with minor children in the home were employed in professional positions.

TABLE 9.1   Types of Families, Median Incomes, and Income Ratios by Race
and Joint Educational Levels of Married Couples in 1985

Race	All Married Couples	Both High School	College Graduates		
			Husband Only	Wife Only	Both
Median Incomes					
Black	$23,418	$25,507	$36,681	$32,776	$46,483
Hispanic	22,599	26,275	34,171	34,010	46,957
White	30,058	29,041	42,222	37,620	48,017
Median Income Ratios					
Black/White	.78	.88	.87	.87	.97
Black/Hispanic	1.04	.97	1.07	.96	.99

SOURCE: U.S. Bureau of the Census (1986). Current Population Reports, Series P-20, No. 411, Household and Family Characteristics: March 1985. Washington, DC Government Printing Office, Table 18, p. 97.

Married couples had a 6.9 percent gain in real median income between 1970 and 1980. In 1985, 41 percent of married couples had median incomes of $25,000-$49,999, while 19 percent had a median income of $50,000 or more. However, as more single-parent families were created, married couples represented a smaller proportion of all Black families, moving from 64 percent in 1972, to 55 percent in 1981, to 51 percent in 1985 (U.S. Department of Commerce, 1986). The median income of Black single-parent women in 1984 was $8,648, or 57 percent of income for white single mothers (U.S. Department of Commerce, 1985).

Middle class Black parents who are able to obtain college degrees have median earnings almost on a par with non-Blacks. When both parents were college graduates in 1985, the median family income was $46,483, a ratio of .97 of white and .99 of Hispanic median incomes (see Table 9.1.) However, race differences have not been eliminated. For example, white couples composed of fathers with a college degree and mothers with no degree earned 90 percent of the median income of Black couples when both of them were college graduates. The median income of all Black married couples was $23,418, only 78 percent of white married couple median income.

GEOGRAPHIC MOBILITY

Blacks have traditionally sought better economic conditions by moving from the rural South to southern cities, from the South to the industrial

North, and from the mid-Atlantic and southern coastal regions to the New York and Boston areas. The present pattern appears to be the return of older workers to their native South in search of a slower pace, or the movement of young workers from depressed northern cities to the Sunbelt for immediate employment. Northern urban patterns have often consisted of an urban-to-inner-suburban-to-outer-suburban movement as families searched for the perceived better life and education for their children. Each wave of migrants hopes that a better economy will provide greater resources for the family members. Not all are successful, but enough have been able to improve their condition to fuel the continual search for a better place.

Mobility in order to take advantage of perceived increased opportunities has continued to the present generation (U.S. Department of Commerce, 1985). Movements to new areas have often been within the sponsorship of the broader extended family. These chain migrations of geographic mobility often operated when one person moved to the site and became established. This person, in turn, sponsored other relatives, friends, and church members as they relocated to the same area (Pleck, 1979; Horton and Horton, 1979). The support chains resulted in the relocation of practically entire youth cohorts of a community. They ensured that a person who moved to an area was not totally isolated, but was met with an existing supportive network that would give assistance until a niche was found.

AN EMPIRICAL EXAMINATION OF UPWARD MOBILITY AND EXTENDED-FAMILY INTERACTIONS IN BLACK FAMILIES

In our examination of mobility patterns in a representative sample of Black families, it was impossible to articulate support or rejection of the source of the cultural patterns that were predicted to exist. Rather, we looked at whether some of the traditional "strengths" of Black families actually do exist and can be empirically examined. This study was able to examine whether involvement within the extended-family support network was a help or a hindrance to upper mobility. Theories related to the value of support networks as a coping strategy of poverty and not of culture were directly addressed.

Literature reviews indicated an absence of good descriptive material on mobile Black families. Several questions on these families had simply not been answered. Therefore, the primary purpose of the study was to obtain good descriptive data on upwardly mobile Black families.

The secondary purpose of the present examination was to test the hypothesis that certain family cultural patterns are a viable element within Black family life and that these patterns remain as families move upward. One pattern that was selected was extended-family support networks, operationally defined as close and frequent interactions between kin and the frequent exchange of emotional support, goods, and services.

The second hypothesis was that active extended-family support patterns would be found in all mobility patterns and would be similar regardless of the length of time the family had been at this economic level, either newly mobile or middle class for two or more generations. It was assumed that the extended-family patterns were more than a coping mechanism of poverty, and that individuals would retain their cultural pattern of close involvement with kin and fictive kin when they were no longer poor.

In order to test these hypotheses and to examine some of the mobility patterns of Blacks, we selected a group of currently middle-class persons and traced with them the geographic, educational, and occupational mobility their families had followed over the past three generations. This study was designed to answer the following questions:

(1) What are the characteristics and mobility patterns of upwardly mobile Black families?

(2) Are currently middle-class Black families involved in extended-family support patterns?

(3) Are the family support patterns for those who were born poor different from those who were born middle class?

(4) Is the reciprocity inherent in support networks felt to be excessive?

(5) Are family characteristics different in the three mobility patterns?

METHODS

The data used to answer these questions were obtained from surveys of an urban and suburban sample of middle-income Black families with school-aged children and parents who had some college education and were above the age of 25. Suburban families were randomly selected, with replacement, from a list of all Blacks living in the town. Once they were interviewed, their educational and occupational levels were matched with a comparative sample from a nearby mid-Atlantic city.

Families were interviewed for about five hours each. Attempts were made to control as many external variables as possible. Each parent was interviewed by Black, college-educated adults, with the fathers interviewed by males and the mothers by females. The interviewing was done only after the questions had been field-tested twice and extensively modified to be sensitive to the race-related and personal topics that were covered.

Because of the rigid segregation of Black communities in the past and because of the duality of Black existence, some criteria of socioeconomic status apply that are identical to that of the majority society; but unique criteria are also applied within the Black community to differentiate between high- and low-rank status. The view that Blacks have only one status, low, only leads to the stereotypical view of Blacks and does not recognize the diversity within and between Blacks.

To avoid the difficulties of applying standardized SES scales to Blacks, five different procedures were used: the modified scoring of the Hollingshead-Redlich scale, self-ratings of social class status, educational rankings, occupational rankings, and the standard Hollingshead-Redlich scale. For this report, only the modified SES, in which education is given a higher factor loading than occupation, is used. Income was obtained but not used in SES classifications because of the lower incomes of Blacks in spite of their occupations.

RESULTS

FAMILY DESCRIPTIONS

Data were obtained from 178 domestic units including 305 parents—131 fathers and 174 mothers. Although no control was made for family type (one-/two-parent families), 28 percent were one-parent homes, a close approximation of the proportion of single-parent homes in current census reports. A total of 93 percent of the families were nuclear in structure, comprising either one or two parents. Only 6 percent were extended in structure, while 2 percent were augmented in form, with nonrelatives living in the home. They had an average of 2.37 children each, consistent with the low number of children traditionally born to middle-income families. The average income was $20,000 for fathers and $11,000 for the 85 percent of the mothers who worked. The mean ages were 41 years for the fathers and 37 years for the mothers.

These parents had not moved a great deal during their lives; 85 percent had never moved or had moved only once. Almost half had been born in the mid-Atlantic area, and one-fourth were born in the South and had moved North. They were the children of migrants from the South who had moved to this area and had remained geographically close to their kin.

Religion continued to play an important role in the lives of only half of the parents, a direct contrast to the important role of the church in their parents' and grandparents' lives. One-fourth indicated that religion had no role in their lives. There was a definite move across the three generations from the fundamental denominations as income increased. For example, the Baptists were the largest group in all three generations, but membership declined from over 60 percent in the grandparents' generation to 32 percent in the subjects' generation. Meanwhile, Catholic membership doubled (7 to 15 percent) and Episcopal membership tripled (3 to 9 percent).

Fathers' occupational status was high, but still was not commensurate with their very high educational achievement, as shown by the SES differences when the two status codings were made. The occupations of the employed mothers had much lower status than would be expected based on their education. The mobility or financial stability of these families was clearly tied to the occupation and income of the father. The maternal occupation dominance stereotype was not supported for these families. Although these mothers had jobs of generally lower status than the fathers, in earlier generations the mothers' families had higher status for both male and female. The males' fathers were skilled workers and the females' fathers held higher clerical positions.

The stereotype of the woman being better educated did not hold in the present generation. In two-parent homes, the fathers were significantly better educated than the mothers (χ^2 (12) = 29.90, p < .003). When their education was compared by their status at birth, no educational difference was found between the fathers who were born middle class and those who were born working class. However, mothers who were born working class had significantly higher educations than those born into middle-class families (χ^2 (4) = 15.69, p < .001). In earlier generations, the mother tended to be better educated than the male. It appears that education peaked at the point of mobility. It was maintained in the second generation and began to decline in the third generation of middle-class status.

SUPPORT NETWORK INVOLVEMENT

The hypothesis that families would be involved in the kin-help exchange network, even after obtaining middle-class status, was supported. Parents indicated an extensive and intensive involvement with the network. The majority tended to live within 30 miles of their family members, which facilitated interaction. They felt that it was relatively easy for them to stay in contact with their kin.

Family members were seen as the most important source of outside help. Overall, 80 percent of the families had a reciprocal involvement with their kin. They gave and received help with child care, financial aid, and

TABLE 9.2   Four Cross-Generational Mobility Patterns

Patterns	Grandparents	Parents	Subjects	Percentage
I	working	working	middle*	62
II	lower*	working*	middle*	23
III	working	middle*	middle	6 } 15
IV	middle	middle	middle	9 }
Total				100

*Point of upward mobility.

emotional support. The reciprocal obligations that involved the support network were not felt to be excessive and were part of everyday life. The pressure on the newly mobile to help kin who were less fortunate was significantly stronger than for those who were born middle class. This was not perceived as a burden, but simply the way that things are done in the family. Many mentioned that their advanced education was possible only because of family help.

When the three mobility patterns were combined into those who were born working class versus those born middle class, no significant differences appeared between the two social classes of origin in the amount or kind of help given to or received from family members, nor in the attitudes about the reciprocity. The hypothesis that extended-family involvement would extend beyond the point of mobility was supported.

CROSS-GENERATIONAL MOBILITY PATTERNS

Four generations of SED status were computed for 128 of the families, going from the children of the subjects (all born middle class) back to the subjects' grandparents. The patterns had three possible points of mobility. The mobility patterns revealed, surprisingly, that no one was able to move from abject poverty into middle-income status in just one generation. Several subjects said that they went from being poor to where they are now, but a closer examination of the data indicated that although their parents had low incomes, they had higher educations than expected. They would not be considered as part of the permanent underclass, but rather as solid working class but poor individuals.

The original nine mobility patterns were condensed into four, shown in Table 9.2.

Pattern I: Born working class, newly mobile. Families in the largest group represented the typical Black who is now of middle-class status. The parents were born into solid working-class families—poor, but self-supporting and independent of government support. They were able to achieve this status through the acquisition of professional degrees that allowed them to move into higher status jobs. Some 79 percent had college or professional training. As the first generation to move up, they had relatives who were much poorer but with whom they kept in frequent contact.

Their parents usually had grade school or less than high school educations. Their mothers tended to be better educated than their fathers. Their grandparents had grade school educations, although 17 percent of them did attend some college. As a group, the grandparents and the parents had just a little more education than the average Black, and they were able to get solid, respectable working-class jobs within the community.

Pattern II: Upwardly mobile in each generation. Over three generations these families had been in three different levels. Their grandparents had been reared in lower-class poverty families, the parents had moved to working class, and the subjects were mobile in the middle class. Subjects in this group had the highest academic training—almost all had college or advanced degrees. Their fathers had high school and their grandparents had junior high or grade school educations. Again, their mothers were better educated: 14 percent had college degrees and 24 percent had some college training. The mobility in the second generation may have been helped a great deal by the education of the mother. Of all four patterns, this one had the highest educational, occupational, and income levels and the lowest level of stress.

Pattern III: Upwardly mobile in parents' generation. These subjects had all been born into middle-class status, whereas their grandparents had been born into working-class families. The mobility occurred in their parents' generation. Educational achievement had decreased in the present generation: only 29 percent had graduate or professional training, compared to 63 percent of their fathers and 50 percent of their mothers. The group's second generation was better educated than any of the other four patterns. In the paternal grandparents' generation, one-third of each sex had high school training. In the maternal line, the males had completed grade school and the females had finished high school, and 14 percent of the maternal grandmothers had graduated from college. Education clearly was a goal within these families. The small cell size for which we have three generations of information, however, limits the implications that can be drawn from this group.

Pattern IV: Middle class over three generations. For these families, the subjects' grandparents had been middle class, and this had been maintained into the subjects' generation. In all, 9 percent of the families were in this group. A subset of this pattern, 3 percent of all families, had parents and grandparents who were at a higher level than they had reached. This was usually because the subjects had received less education and were earning a much lower salary than had the past two generations. Because these subjects were clearly still middle class, they are included in the fourth group.

An interesting finding for this three-generation middle-class group was that they had the lowest level of education—33 percent had college and only 9 percent had advanced professional degrees. The parent generation had the same level of achievement as the subjects (father, 42 percent; mother, 25 percent). They had maintained their accomplishments but had not moved beyond their parents. However, grandfathers (born in the late 1800s) on both sides were very well educated, even by today's standards. In all, 60 percent of the paternal grandfathers and 20 percent of the maternal grandfathers had college and advanced degrees.

MATERNAL ROLE IN MOBILITY

The overall mobility was dependent on the education and income of the father. However, because of the inequity of pay, the cross-generation data indicate that the point of mobility for the family coincided with employment outside the home of both mother and father. Mobility would not have been possible without the dual income and could not be maintained without the continued employment of both parents.

While the level of maternal employment was high in all patterns, there were some indications that the present level of maternal employment was related to the father's ability to maintain the middle-income life-style on one income. More mothers worked when income tended to be low, and fewer worked when the father's income, education, and occupational status were high. When a choice was feasible, more tended not to work and to concentrate on the home and the family.

The role model provided by an employed grandmother was not a factor, for only 30 percent of the grandmothers worked in all of the patterns. However, the role model of a working mother may be a salient point for the fathers. For the mobility pattern in which almost all of the mothers now work, the male subjects' mothers worked outside of the home.

Sons who were born to families in which the mothers had higher-level occupations than the fathers are currently the highest achievers. Their motivation may be attributed, in part, to the drive of the employed mother with limited education who was able to move to a responsible position that was higher than the subject's father's.

The most important factor for the mother in deciding to work was economic necessity and the precariousness of Black middle-class families who are, because of the dearth of inherited wealth and unearned income, only one paycheck from poverty. Despite their high educational level, Blacks' lower payoff has meant that they have little surplus income to invest and use to augment their wage earnings. Families are where they are because of their own efforts and not because the financial benefits of earlier generations have been passed on, as is frequently done in non-Black populations.

SOURCES OF STATUS

Because differential skin color and hair type were the traditional status criteria for many Blacks, the parents were asked how important these were in Black life. Physical characteristics that are race-related still appear to be an important element for these adults. One-half felt that higher status was afforded to non-Black characteristics, and one-third felt that it was of less importance now but of serious concern in the past. This becomes operational in mate selection and in job promotions. Parents appeared to assume that everyone had internalized a status preference for the characteristics of the majority group but that attitudes were not as important as in the good 1930s. Other than skin color, status was assigned to families within the community in a manner indistinguishable from other groups.

DISCUSSION

MIDDLE-CLASS DECLINE

When the educational levels of each pattern were reviewed over the generations, it was obvious that the level of education peaked at the point of mobility. The level was maintained in the second and definitely declined in the third generation of middle-class status. These families seemed unable to pass on the major benefits from one generation to the next, except when they are upwardly mobile. Once mobility occurred, it was difficult to maintain this higher status. The highest levels of education, occupational status, and income were found in the pattern that had been upwardly mobile for each of the three generations.

There are many explanations for this decline. It could be a function of a regression toward the mean in education and achievement. Or it could be that the comparative security these families experienced as the children were growing up tended to sap the achievement of youth. Another alternative may be that since they did not feel the need to select a job for basic survival, they were allowed to select occupations on the basis of interest rather than financial security. Another explanation could be that the parents were both deeply involved in their jobs and may not have given the children the guidance and structure they needed in order to match successfully the academic excellence of their parents. An indulgent life-style may be the middle-class "dream" for which they worked so hard to give to their children, but this may be the same type of environment that would not reinforce the drive toward achievement. Society was not supportive of the maintenance of Black upward mobility. Therefore, unless the drive to achieve remained active and sacrifices were made, the status declined.

FAMILIAL SOCIAL SUPPORT AND MOBILITY

This examination of upwardly mobile patterns in Black families has indicated that the education and achievement of the individuals were often impossible without the support of extended family. Mobility, the result of the acquisition of professional training that leads to high-paying jobs, appears to require intensive effort by family members, and without perseverance there is a tendency to experience a decline in status. The employment of both parents is required for initiation and maintenance of mobility, but maternal employment appears to lessen if the husband is able to support the family adequately on his salary. Families with only one parent are at a distinct disadvantage and find it difficult to maintain their hard-earned status. The positions many of the parents held were not as high as would be expected, but the racial "job ceiling" effect became evident even within the professions and with people who had special talents.

The continuation of the extended-family support system reflects continued cultural patterns and is a factor in countering the vulnerability of the Black middle class. Both factors are operational within all of the mobility patterns. The kin support network is as essential now as it was in earlier generations, for it involves cultural patterns created and retained from earlier times that are still functional and supportive of Black family life.

REFERENCES

ASCHENBRENNER, J. (1973) "Extended families among Black Americans." Journal of Comparative Family Studies 4.

BILLINGSLEY, A. (1968) Black Families in White America. Englewood Cliffs, NJ: Prentice-Hall.

CORCORAN, M. (1977) "Who gets ahead: a summary," in C. Jencks (ed.) Who Gets Ahead? The Determinants of Economic Success in America. New York: Basic Books.

CROSS, W. (1987) A two-factor theory of Black identity: implications for the study of identity development in minority children, in J. Phinney and M. J. Rotherman (eds.) Children's Ethnic Socialization, Pluralism, and Development. Newbury Park: Sage.

FORDHAM, S. and J. OGBU (1986) Black students' school success: coping with the burden of acting "white." The Urban Review 36(3).

FRANKLIN, V. (1979) The Education of Black Philadelphia, The Social and Educational History of a Minority Community, 1900-1950. Philadelphia: University of Pennsylvania Press.

FRAZIER, E. (1939) The Negro Family in the United States. Chicago: University of Chicago Press.

GLASGOW, D. (1980) The Black Underclass, Poverty, Unemployment and Entrapment of Ghetto Youth. San Francisco: Jossey-Bass.

HALEY, A. (1976) Roots. New York: Doubleday.

HEISS, J. (1975) The Case of the Black Family, A Sociological Inquiry. New York: Columbia University Press.

HERSKOVITS, M. (1941) The Myth of the Negro Past. New York: Harper & Row.

HILL, R. (1971) Strengths of Black Families. New York: Emerson-Hall.

——— (1981) "The Black family and national policy." Presented at the University of Wisconsin Black History Week.

HORTON, J. and L. HORTON (1979) Black Bostonians, Family Life and Community Struggle in the Antebellum North. New York: Holmes and Meier.

McADOO, H. (1977) "The development of self-concept and race attitudes of young Black children over time," pp. 46-82 in W. Cross (ed.) Empirical Research in Black Psychology III. Washington, DC: National Institute of Education, HEW.

——— (1978) "Factors related to stability in upwardly mobile Black families." Journal of Marriage and the Family 40(4): 761-778.

——— (1981) "Youth, school, and the family in transition." Urban Education 16(3): 261-277.

McQUEEN, A. (1971) "Incipient social mobility among poor Black urban families." Presented at Howard University Research Seminar, Spring.

MALVEAUX, J. (1981) "Shifts in the occupational and employment status of Black women: current trends and future implications." Presented at the Conference on Black Working Women, University of California, Berkeley, May 21.

MARTIN, E. and J. MARTIN (1978) The Black Extended Family. Chicago: University of Chicago Press.

NOBLES, W. (1976) "A formulative and empirical study of Black families." Washington, DC: Department of Health, Education and Welfare.

NOBLES, W. and L. GODDARD (1977) "Consciousness, adaptability and coping strategies: socioeconomic characteristics and ecological issues in Black families." Western Journal of Black Studies 1(2): 105-113.

OGBU, J. (1974) The Next Generation, An Ethnography of Education in an Urban Neighborhood. New York: Academic Press.

——— (1986) The Consequences of the American Caste System (pp. 19-56) in U. Neisser (ed.) The School Achievement of Minority Children: New Perspectives. Hillsdale, NJ: Lawrence Erlbaum.

PLECK, E. (1979) Black Migration and Poverty, Boston 1865-1900. New York: Academic Press.

RASBERRY, W. (1987) "Missing: Black men on campus." Washington Post (July 21): A15.

SCANZONI, J. (1971) The Black Family in Modern Society, Chicago: University of Chicago Press.

SCHWARTZ, J. and J. WILLIAMS (1977) "The effects of race on earnings" in C. Jencks (ed.) Who Gets Ahead? The Determinants of Economic Success in America. New York: Basic Books.

SHIMKIN, D. B., E. M. SHIMKIN and D. A. FRATE [eds.] (1978) The Extended Family in Black Societies. The Hague: Mouton.

STACK, C. (1975) All Our Kin: Strategies for Survival in a Black Community. New York: Harper & Row.

SUDARKASA, N. (1980) "African and Afro-American family structure." The Black Scholar, Journal of Black Studies and Research 2(8).

U.S. Department of Commerce, Bureau of the Census (1983) America's Black Population: 1970 to 1982, A Statistical View. Special Publication P10/POP-83-1, July. Washington, DC: Government Printing Office.

_____ (1985) Current Population Reports, Series P-60, No. 149, Money, Income and Poverty Status of Families and Persons in the United States: 1984. Washington, DC: Government Printing Office.

_____ (1986) Current Population Reports, Series P-20, No. 411, Household and Family Characteristics: March 1985. Washington, DC: U. S. Government Printing Office.

WILKINSON, D. (1987) "Ethnicity" (pp. 182-210) in M. Sussman and S. Steinmetz (eds.) Handbook of Marriage and the Family. New York: Plenum.

WILSON, J. (1978) The Declining Significance of Race: Blacks and the Changing American Institutions. Chicago: University of Chicago Press.

WILSON, J. W. (1987) The Truly Disadvantaged: The Inner City, the Underclass, and Public Policy. Chicago: University of Chicago Press.

10

BLACK EDUCATION
A Cultural-Ecological
Perspective

JOHN U. OGBU

In this chapter I will attempt to explain why black children do less well in school than other children. The chapter will also discuss the effects of these perceptions and academic efforts on black upward mobility. I want to explore how black school performance is related to black perceptions of social and occupational opportunity structure as well as educational opportunity structure.

The chapter is divided into four parts. The first outlines the problem and some of its current explanations; the second examines the structural context of the problem; the third describes the cultural-ecological framework and the mechanisms of maintaining the disproportionately high rate of school failure; the concluding part of the chapter considers some of the policy implications of the cultural-ecological perspective.

THE PROBLEM AND
SOME CURRENT EXPLANATIONS

One baffling educational problem in the United States is the persistence of low academic performance among Black Americans and other caste-like minorities with similar features—Chicanos, Indians, Native Hawaiians, and Puerto Ricans. These minorities not only do less well in school than white Americans, they also do less well than other minorities, including Chinese Americans and Japanese Americans. It is true that children from poor families of all groups do less well in school than children from affluent families; it is also true that a disproportionate number of black children come from poor families. However, differences between blacks and whites in academic achievement remain when children from similar socioeconomic backgrounds are compared (Jensen, 1969: 81-82; Baughman, 1971: 5-8; Jencks, 1972: 154; Mayeske et al., 1973; CEMREL, 1978; Haskins, 1980).

Since the sixties special efforts have been initiated to help "disadvantaged" black and other children improve their school performance. These efforts have had some positive results; but they have not significantly changed the relative academic position of black children, especially those of the inner city (CEMREL, 1978; Ogbu, 1978).

The failure of these efforts lies, in part, in the theories undergirding the rationale with which they are approached. Social scientists assumed in the sixties that school performance depends on three factors: home environment, school environment and genetic endowment (Bloom et al., 1965; Coleman, 1966; Jensen, 1969; Guthrie et al., 1971). Given these assumptions, it follows that blacks are relatively unsuccessful in school because they come from homes or attend schools or have genetic endowment less conducive to school success. Social scientists continue to argue about the relative weight of each of these three factors in influencing school performance. Policymakers have generally been more sympathetic to theories emphasizing the deficiencies of the home or school. Consequently they have based their programs for change on such theories.

In more recent years a cultural difference or cultural discontinuity perspective has emerged to explain the disproportionately high rate of school failure among blacks and other caste-like minorities. This perspective argues that blacks have their own culture with its own child-rearing practices through which distinctively black instrumental competencies are inculcated; and that black children probably fail in school because schools do not recognize and utilize black children's competencies for teaching, learning, and testing (Wright, 1970; Gibson, 1976; Boykin, 1980).

Elsewhere I have analyzed the strengths and weaknesses of these explanations (Ogbu, 1978, 1980a, 1980b, 1981a). Here I will briefly summarize three issues most relevant to the present chapter. First, these explanations are not based on adequate comparative data. They are based on data from one type of minority group, *caste-like minorities*, and fail to explain why other types of minorities with similar features of poverty and cultural differences succeed in the same schools. Second, although proponents of these views want to assist black children to improve their school performance in order to better their chances of obtaining good jobs with good wages after graduation, they do not usually consider the possible effects of job discrimination against black parents on their children's education. They do not, for example, ask how black perceptions of job discrimination influence their perceptions of and responses to schooling. On the whole, current explanations generally neglect the reciprocal influence of employment opportunities and schooling. Third, some of the explanations erroneously assume that the educational and economic problems of Black Americans are the same as those of lower-class whites. In reality this is a false assumption, because blacks occupy more or less a caste-like position in a racial stratification system. Other weaknesses of these explanations will become apparent when we consider the structural position of Black Americans as the context for understanding their lag in school performance. Traditional educational research has considered neither the collective historical experience of blacks nor the structural barriers of the wider society.

The term "caste-like" minorities is used for two reasons. It contrasts this type of minority with "immigrant minorities" in terms of both structural and school experiences. Many wonder why some minorities do well in school and others do not. The term is also used in reference to some minority groups which are not racially different from the dominant group and yet are doing poorly in school. Chicanos, for instance, cannot as a group be racially defined as different from whites; many of them call themselves "white" and are officially defined as "white" or "Caucasian." However, in my analysis in terms of structural barriers and school experiences, they qualify as a "caste-like" minority group.

RACIAL STRATIFICATION AS A STRUCTURAL CONTEXT OF SCHOOL FAILURE

Social scientists concerned with the problem of lower school performance among blacks have long recognized "race" as a variable but not "racial stratification." If they consider American society stratified at all, their preferred model is class stratification (Coleman, 1966; Jensen, 1969; Jencks, 1972; Mosteller and Moynihan, 1972; Ogbu, 1977, 1981b). They have ample data on parental education, occupation, and income to show that a disproportionate number of black children come from "lower-class" backgrounds. From this classification they argue that school performance among blacks is class-related. But this class model is only one of several that can be constructed for American society, and it is probably not the one that most accurately reflects the position of blacks, who are a racial caste. However, I am using the concept of caste or caste-like advisedly, as a methodological tool to emphasize the structural legacy of black subordination. I am not suggesting that Black Americans are a caste in the classical Hindu sense. One of the questions, then, is: How does the stratification of racial castes differ from class stratification?

CLASS VERSUS RACIAL CASTE STRATIFICATION

In general, stratification of racial castes differs from class stratification with regard to closure, affiliation, status summation, social mobility, and cognitive orientation.

Closure and Affiliation. Class stratification is based on economic relations, an acquired characteristic, whereas racial stratification is based on "status honor," regarded as an inborn quality (Berreman, 1977). Social classes are more or less permanent entities but have no clear boundaries; nor is their membership necessarily permanent, because people are continually moving in and out of them. Furthermore, children of interclass marriage can affiliate with the class of either parent. Racial castes, on the other hand, are permanently hierarchically organized into more or less endogamous groups, clearly bounded, publicly recognized and named. Interracial/caste marriage is often prohibited, but where it is allowed there is usually a formal or informal rule as to which parent's group the children must affiliate (Berreman, 1967: 279-280). For example, before their emancipation in 1871, the Japanese Buraku outcastes were legally forbidden to intermarry with the dominant Ippan group (Mitchell, 1967); in contemporary South Africa, intermarriage between blacks and whites is legally forbidden (van den Berghe, 1967); and in the United States, "it was not until 1967 that the United States Supreme Court finally declared unconstitutional those statutes (in 16 states at that time) prohibiting interracial marriage" (Higginbotham, 1978: 41; see also Franklin, 1971). In the United States the rule of affiliation has always been that any children of known black-white mating must affiliate with the black. In very rare cases do some "blacks" covertly become "whites" through the painful and noninstitutionalized process of "passing" (Warner et al., 1941; Burma, 1946; Eckard, 1946).

Status Summation. In a class stratification, such as exists among American whites, occupational and other status positions are based on training (for example, on formal education) and ability. This is much less true for racial minorities because of a *job ceiling* and other barriers. A job ceiling is composed of the highly consistent pressures and obstacles that selectively assign minorities (and women) to jobs at the low level of status, power, dignity, and income, while allowing white males to compete more easily and freely for the more desirable jobs above that ceiling on the basis of individual training and ability. The job ceiling and other barriers have been the object of racial minorities' struggle for equal social, economic, and political opportunities (Drake and Clayton, 1970; Newman et al., 1976; Ogbu, 1978).

Social Mobility. Vertical social mobility is built into class stratification and the means of achieving it are usually prescribed. Mobility from one racial stratum to the next is proscribed.

Cognitive Orientation. Class and racial castes differ also in cognitive orientation (Berreman, 1977). For instance, blacks and other caste-like minorities do not accept their low social, political, and occupational status as legitimate outcomes of their individual failures and misfortunes, whereas lower-class whites often do (Sennett and Cobb, 1972). Blacks see racial barriers in employment and education as the primary causes of their low social status and poverty. Most Black Americans, regardless of their class positions, blame "the system" rather than themselves for their failure to get ahead as individuals and as a group, an orientation which underlies their collective struggle for equal employment and educational opportunity.

In contrast, there is neither a conscious feeling among white Americans of any given class "that they belong together in a corporate unity" nor a feeling that their common interests are different from those of other social classes (Myrdal, 1944). Not even the lower-class whites share a collective perception of their social and economic difficulties as stemming from "the system." *What distinguishes Black Americans and similar minorities from lower-class whites is not that their objective material conditions are different but that the way the minorities perceive and interpret their conditions is different.*

Blacks are, of course, internally stratified by social class, as whites are internally stratified. But the black classes and the white classes differ both in development and attributes. They are unequal in development because historically blacks have had less access to the number and types of jobs and training that facilitate class differentiation and mobility. Black social classes are also qualitatively different because the historical circumstances that created them and the structural forces that sustain them are different from those that created and sustain white social classes. For example, the narrow base of black class differentiation began during enslavement rather than, as among whites, with differences in education, ability, and family background. During enslavement most blacks had no access to schooling and were relegated to slave status, regardless of their individual abilities; among the few free blacks, most were confined to menial jobs and social position through legal and extralegal mechanisms. After enslavement, racial barriers in employment—*the job ceiling*—continued to limit their base of class differentiation and mobility. These collective experiences resulted in the shared perception of the lack of equal opportunity for blacks of any social class; that is, blacks came to believe that it is much more difficult for *any black* than for *any white* to achieve economic and social self-betterment in the mainstream economy *through free competition based on training and ability*. Another reason for the qualitative difference is the forced *ghettoization* of blacks. Until recent decades whites created and maintained clearly defined residential boundaries of the city to which they restricted the black population. Many relatively well-to-do blacks who preferred to live elsewhere were forced to share the ghetto with poorer blacks. This involuntary segregation of blacks further reinforced their shared sense of oppression.

In summary, then, the economic and educational problems of Black Americans, even poor blacks, are not merely those resulting from lower-class status. They are, instead, consequences of the *double stratification of class and racial caste*. As a result, lower-class blacks share certain attributes common to all lower-class people everywhere; but they also have distinctive attributes because they belong to a subordinate racial caste. This additional impact of double stratification is apparent in the black status mobility system described in the next section.

CASTE-LIKE MINORITIES VERSUS OTHER MINORITIES

Some minorities do relatively well in American schools, and it is important to distinguish them from those who do not. Generally, blacks fit into a category I call *caste-like minorities* (Ogbu, 1978). Such minorities are characterized by a greater lag in school performance. They are distinguished from other minorities by four factors. First, they have usually been incorporated into "their country" involuntarily and permanently. Blacks are a classic example, having been brought to America as slaves. As a result, they occupy a more or less permanent place in society from which they can escape only through "passing" or emigration—options not always open. Second, membership in a caste-like minority is acquired permanently at birth. Third, caste-like minorities have limited access to the social goods of society by virtue of their group membership rather than because they lack training and ability. More specifically, *they face a job ceiling*. Finally, having been incorporated into society involuntarily and then relegated to menial status, caste-like minorities tend to focus on their economic and social problems in terms of collective institutional discrimination, which they perceive as more than temporary.

These then, are the structural features that distinguish blacks from whites, poor blacks from lower-class whites, and blacks from such immigrant minorities as Chinese Americans and Japanese Americans, who came to America more or less voluntarily for social and economic self-betterment. The occupational and educational implications of this structural position of blacks are expressed through their unique status mobility system.

STATUS MOBILITY SYSTEM
AND SCHOOL PERFORMANCE

STATUS MOBILITY SYSTEM

A status mobility system is the way of getting ahead in a society or social group. Members of a society or social group usually share a theory about how their status mobility system works or how one gets ahead or "makes it," however "making it" is defined (LeVine, 1967). The theory or folk assumptions generally cover the range of available status positions (for example, types of jobs open to members), rules for eligibility to compete for the available positions, and how to qualify for successful competition. A status mobility system works insofar as the actual experiences of a large proportion of the population confirm the folk beliefs about it. And how the system works influences the values and practices of parents and others entrusted with the upbringing of children as well as how children themselves strive to be as they get older. People's theory of how their status mobility system works is the cognitive basis of their behaviors with regard to child rearing and schooling as well as strategies for subsistence and self-advancement (Ogbu, 1980a, 1980b, 1980c).

In a relatively open class system, such as exists among white Americans, differences in the status mobility systems of the different classes are minor. But for stratified racial castes, such as blacks and whites, the status mobility system of each stratum is unique in many respects. For example, the status mobility system of the subordinate racial caste is distinctive in two ways that have important implications for schooling. First, the minority status mobility system offers access to fewer social goods such as high-paying jobs than the status mobility system of the dominant group; and second, the minority status mobility system embodies two sets of rules of behavior for achievement: one imposed by the dominant group and the other evolved within the subordinate population. In the United States whites "impose" educational credentials on blacks; as a consequence, blacks have developed a number of alternative or "survival" strategies, including collective struggle, clientship, and hustling for making it. Black Americans employ these two sets of rules differentially according to their circumstance.

Caste-like minority schooling reflects these two features of their status mobility system for two reasons. On the one hand, the dominant group's perceptions of how the minorities get ahead or should get ahead influence how it defines and provides for the minorities' educational needs; on the other hand, how the minorities perceive their opportunity structure and the role of schooling within it influences their response to schooling. In this situation caste-like minority schooling generally functions to prepare children to participate as adults in the minority rather than the dominant group's status mobility system. From this point of departure, I would suggest that a clue to the differences in the education and school performance of whites and blacks lies in the nature of their status mobility systems. Specifically, the caste-bound black status mobility system traditionally offers fewer jobs requiring high-level schooling or credentials and also embodies two sets of rules of behavior for achievement. The black status mobility system makes both whites and blacks behave in a manner that promotes black school failure. Perceptions of dominant whites of how blacks ought to get ahead leads them to provide blacks with inferior education. For blacks, their own perceptions of the limited opportunities to get ahead in the conventional economy and their perceptions of inferior education generate attitudes and behaviors that are often not conducive to school success. Among the black responses to the job ceiling and to inferior education discussed below are disillusionment and lack of persevering academic efforts because of low educational payoffs. Other responses are alternative or survival strategies that may require skills and attitudes incongruent with attitudes and skills required for classroom teaching and learning; and hostility and lack of trust toward the public school. Let us briefly examine in more detail how white and black responses to black status mobility systems cause the disproportionately high school failure among blacks.

Inferior Education. Many public and private schools now profess to offer blacks some quality education provided whites and have even established special programs to enable black children to "succeed" like the whites. These are, however, recent developments which must not mask the fact that before the sixties there was no explicit or implicit goal to educate blacks and whites equally for adult occupational and social positions. Also, while it is true that lower-class white education has always been inferior to that of the white middle class (Warner et al., 1944; Hollingshead, 1949; Sexton, 1961), it is equally true that at every class level blacks have been provided still more inferior education. For example, as late as 1972 the money spent by the school district of Washington, D.C., for each child decreased as the proportion of black children in a given school increased (Hughes and Hughes, 1973), a situation also documented for Chicago and other cities (Sexton, 1968: 228).

In general, prior to Emancipation, blacks were systematically excluded by law from formal education. Thereafter they were given an inferior education in segregated schools. Segregation was legal nationwide, though it lasted longest in the South (Pierce, 1955: 35-36; Bond, 1966: 374-384; Bullock, 1970; Weinberg, 1977). In the separate schools the inferiority of black education was maintained through inadequate funding, facilities, and staffing; through a shorter school year and a curriculum which emphasized manual rather than academic training (Pierce, 1955: 234; Bond, 1966: 97-99, 1969: 132, 235-265; Thomas and Noblitt, 1978). Blacks who attended integrated schools received inferior education through more subtle mechanisms—negative teacher attitudes and low expectations (Knowles and Prewitt, 1969; U.S. Senate Select Committee, 1972; Hobbs, 1975); biased testing and classification (Mercer, 1973; Children's Defense Fund, 1974: 101-114; Illinois Advisory Commission on Civil Rights, 1974); tracking or ability grouping (Findley, 1973; Ogbu, 1974: 169); biased textbooks and inferior curriculum (Kane, 1970; U.S. Senate Select Committee, 1972). They also generally received academic and career guidance which reinforced their preparation for inferior positions in adult life (Ogbu, 1974a: 120, 1974: 193). Extracurricular activities were race-typed. These subtle devices were also present in segregated schools. Today, both gross and subtle mechanisms still exist in many schools, as evidenced by many lawsuits for school integration and from protests against testing, tracking, and related matters in many American cities (U.S. Commission on Civil Rights, 1967, 1977).

One subtle mechanism now receiving increasing attention is the disproportionate labeling of black children as having "learning handicaps" and channeling them into special education which prepares them for inferior occupations. In a recent court case brought by blacks against the San Francisco school district, for instance, evidence was presented showing that black children who made up only 31 percent of the school enrollment in the 1976-1977 school year constituted 53.8 percent of all children in the educable mentally retarded classes. In the same year, in 20 California school districts, which enrolled 80 percent of all black children in public schools in the state, blacks constituted 27.5 percent of the school population but 62 percent of the educable mentally retarded population. The judge in the case ruled against the San Francisco school district, noting that the disproportionate placement of blacks in the special education classes could not have occurred by chance (U.S. District Court for Northern California, 1979). The figures for San Francisco are similar to those for other large American cities, including Chicago and New York.

Some evidence suggests that in many instances blacks are provided inferior education deliberately. We find in the South purposive misappropriation of black school funds for white schools, legislation to legalize such misappropriation, and employment of less qualified teachers for black schools, less pay for the teachers, and a disproportionate workload (Pierce, 1955; Bond, 1966; Bullock, 1970).

Even northern philanthropists who helped make public school education more available to blacks and whites in the South endorsed an explicit policy to give whites superior academic education for superior jobs and other adult positions, and to give blacks an "industrial" or manual education. They did, however, make some provision for a few blacks to receive academic training to serve the black community as preachers, teachers, doctors, and lawyers (Harlan, 1968: 76-80; Bullock, 1970: 93-98). Interestingly enough, when industrial education became an asset to acquiring well-paying industrial jobs and attracted state and federal financial support, black participation was curtailed (Pierce, 1955). Myrdal (1944: 877) explains this policy reversal by saying that southern whites believed that blacks should receive an industrial education so long as it did not mean preparing them to compete more effectively with whites for skilled and economically rewarding jobs (see also Frazier, 1957: 439; Bond, 1966: 404).

In the North the policy of differential and inferior education has been more covert and, partly because records are not kept by race, less adequately documented. But it has existed as a deliberate policy in many instances. Evidence presented in various desegregation cases shows the prevalence of inferior education for blacks in the North (Sexton, 1968; U.S. Commission on Civil Rights, 1967, 1977). And many blacks educated in the North who discussed their experiences with me usually recounted how they and other blacks were channeled into "dead-end courses" in segregated and integrated schools.

The possibility of blacks receiving inferior education has also been reinforced by many school personnel sharing the general folk assumptions of whites that blacks are less "intelligent" than whites and therefore apparently not capable of mastering the type of education required for the more desirable jobs and social positions (Johnson, 1930: 224; Pierce, 1955: 20; Conant, 1961). These folk beliefs, which predate the invention of modern psychometric measures of "intelligence" (Bullock, 1970: 68), have had a considerable influence on the type of curriculum school personnel consider appropriate for black children and on perceptions of how black children should be treated. Another factor contributing to the inferior education is that well-meaning school personnel with an awareness of the limited chances of black school leavers obtaining good jobs tended to channel black pupils into those educational programs which prepared them mainly for traditional "Negro jobs."

Black Responses. It would appear from their long history of collective struggle for equal education that blacks see formal education as a means to improve their social and economic status. But their expectations have not been met, partly because their education has not been designed to do this. It appears that this dilemma has caused blacks to appear to respond to both the inferior education and to the job ceiling in some ways that actually promote school failure and preparation for marginal economic participation. These responses are considered next.

Disillusionment and Lack of Effort Optimism. Disillusionment is one of the responses blacks have made to the job ceiling with adverse effects on academic behavior. Blacks do not believe that American society is a land of equal opportunity; they often point out that racial discrimination has historically prevented them from obtaining desirable jobs, good wages, and promotions commensurate with their education and ability; discrimination has also prevented them from owning houses and living in better parts of the community.

One result of this perception of limited opportunity structure is disillusionment about the real value of schooling. Another is lack of perseverance in academic pursuits. The disillusionment is summed up in the maxim, "What's the use of trying?" From my own observations of black children in the classrooms and community of Stockton, California, I would conclude that the children do not take their schoolwork seriously and do not persevere at it, even though they acknowledge that a serious attitude toward school and perseverance or hard work are necessary for doing well in school. Furthermore, interviews with parents suggest that they, too, may be teaching their children ambivalent attitudes toward schooling. On the one hand, parents espouse the need to work hard in school and to get more education than they themselves did. On the other hand, the same parents teach their children verbally and through their own life experiences of unemployment, underemployment, and other discriminations, as well as through gossip about similar experiences among relatives, neighbors and friends—*through the actual texture of life in the home and community*—that even if the children succeed in school they may not make it as adults in the wider society. Eventually black children become disillusioned and "give up"; and they learn to blame "the system" for their school failure as their parents blame "the system" for their own failures.

The historical barriers confronting blacks have restricted educational payoffs. Blacks do not remain passive, but respond actively and creatively to these barriers. The important consideration is if the nature of these responses have facilitated or hindered the successful pursuit of formal education. My observations have been that some reactions have been incongruent with the maximization of school efforts. It is my theses that as structural barriers are removed and as blacks experience and perceive the barriers as eliminated, they will respond with perceptions and behaviors that facilitate a greater degree of school success.

SURVIVAL STRATEGIES AND INCONGRUENT ATTITUDES AND SKILLS

Another response to the job ceiling which has some adverse effects on black school performance is what blacks call "survival strategies." These fall into two categories. One consists of those strategies directed toward increasing conventional economic and social resources of the black community and obtaining conventional jobs and other social rewards. These strategies include *collective struggle* or civil rights activities (Scott, 1976; Newman et al., 1978) and *clientship* or "uncle tomming" (Myrdal, 1944; Dollard, 1957; Farmer, 1968; Powdermaker, 1968; Ogbu, 1981b). The other category includes *hustling* and related means—strategies directed toward exploiting nonconventional economic and social resources or "the street economy" (Heard, 1968; Milner, 1970; Wolfe, 1970; Bullock, 1970; Foster, 1974).

Within the black community success in obtaining conventional jobs and other social resources often requires collective struggle (at least to make them available) and/or clientship, *in addition to educational credentials*. There are also other survival strategies which provide alternative ways of making a living and achieving status to school credentials and conventional jobs. People who succeed in the conventional economy and status system, either through school credentials only, through a combination of school credentials and clientship or other form of survival strategy, or through hustling and related activities in the street economy—all are "legitimately successful" in the eyes of the community. Such people are admired, and they influence the ways others, including children, try to make it.

I suggest that the survival strategies may require knowledge, attitudes, and skills not wholly compatible with those required for white middle-class classroom and school behavior. I also suggest that children probably begin to learn the survival strategies from preschool years as part of their normal "enculturation." As a result, they may begin school with potential dispositions for academic and behavioral difficulties. But whether or not and to what extent they experience learning problems depends on their encounter with school personnel and other children.

CONFLICT AND DISTRUST

A third response to the job ceiling is hostility and distrust toward the public schools, which has grown out of a long history of unpleasant experiences with the schools and with white society in general. Throughout the history of public school education in America blacks have learned to perceive their frequent exclusion and discriminatory treatment as designed to prevent them from qualifying for the more desirable jobs open to whites. Consequently, a significant thrust of black collective struggle has been forcing whites and the schools to provide them with equal education.

Thus, initially we find blacks fighting against total exclusion from the public schools. For over one century they have fought against inferior education in segregated and integrated schools. Where blacks attend segregated schools, these schools are theoretically black schools, so that one might expect blacks to identify with and work with such schools. However, the identification and cooperation of blacks have often been undermined by simultaneous perceptions of segregated schools as inferior to white schools. This results in diverting attention and efforts toward integration and equalization of education. These events frequently generate a feeling that the public schools cannot be trusted to educate black children because of their gross and subtle mechanisms of discrimination. The conflicts also force the schools to treat blacks defensively, often resorting to various forms of control, paternalism, or contest. The schools' responses, too, divert their efforts from educating black children. On the basis of these observations, which can be documented in many American cities, I would suggest that black-school relationship, riddled with conflicts and suspicion, would make it difficult for blacks to accept and internalize the schools' goals, standards, and teaching and learning approaches, and that this situation would contribute to the school performance lag of black children.

POLICY IMPLICATIONS

Given this analysis of the sources of the lag in black school performance, there seem to be three prerequisites for eliminating the lag. These prerequisites are to recognize, first, that stratification of racial castes exists in America, second, that the disproportionately high rate of school failure is a kind of collective adaptation to the job ceiling and other features of the black status mobility system. The adaptation was historically engendered by policies and actions of whites and their institutions and has been maintained by the same; it has also been sustained by black responses to their situation. The third prerequisite for a change is to recognize that *real change* depends on opening up decent jobs and other opportunities to black youths and adults, not just on patching up individuals' supposed past or present "deficiencies." The solution requires both short-range and long-range policies and programs. Short-range remedies may include some current programs to assist the present generation of children experiencing difficulties in school. The long-range goal is, however, to develop policies and programs that will ensure that future generations of black children will not experience a disproportionately high rate of school failure and that the solution is the ultimate destruction of the caste system, particularly the element of the job ceiling.

REFERENCES

BAUGHMAN, E. (1971) Black Americans. New York: Academic Press.
BERREMAN, G. D. (1967) "Caste in cross-cultural perspective: organizational components," in G. DeVos and H. Wagatsuma (eds.) Japan's Invisible Race: Caste in Culture and Personality. Berkeley and Los Angeles: University of California Press.
———— (1977) "Social inequality: a cross-cultural paradigm." Unpublished manuscript, Department of Anthropology, University of California, Berkeley.
BLOOM, B. S., A. DAVIS, and R. D. HESS [eds.] (1965) Compensatory Education for Cultural Deprivation. New York: Holt, Rinehart & Winston.
BOND, H. M. (1966) The Education of the Negro in the Negro Education in American Social Order. New York: Octagon.
———— (1969) Negro Education in Alabama. New York: Atheneum.
BOYKIN, A. W. (1980) "Reading achievement and the social cultural frame of reference of Afro

American children." Presented at NIE Roundtable Discussion on Issues in Urban Reading, Washington, D.C.

BULLOCK, H.E. (1970) A History of Negro Education in the South: From 1619 to the Present. New York: Praeger.

BURMA, J.H. (1946) "The measurement of Negro passing." American Journal of Sociology 52: 18-22.

CEMREL, Inc. (1978) Minority Education 1960-78: Grounds, Gains, and Gaps, Vol. 1. Chicago: CEMREL, Inc.

Children's Defense Fund (1974) Children Out of School in America. Washington, DC: Washington Research Project, Inc.

COLEMAN, J.S. (1966) Equality of Educational Opportunity. Washington, DC: Government Printing Office.

COLLINS, T.W. and G.W. NOBLITT (1978) Stratification and Resegregation : The Case of Crossover High School, Memphis, Tennessee. Final Report, NIE Contract Grant 400-76-009. Washington, DC: National Institute of Education.

CONANT, J.B. (1961) Slums and Suburbs. New York: McGraw-Hill.

DOLLARD, J. (1957) Caste and Class in a Southern Town. Garden City, NY: Doubleday.

DRAKE, S.C. and H. CAYTON (1970) Black Metropolis: A Study of Negro Life in a Northern City, Vols. 1 and 2. New York: Harcourt Brace Jovanovich.

ECKARD, E.W. (1946) "How many Negroes pass?" American Journal of Sociology 52: 498-500.

FARMER, J. (1968) "Stereotypes of the Negro and their relationships to his self-image," in H.C. Rudman and R.L. Featherstone (eds.) Urban Schooling. New York: Harcourt Brace Jovanovich.

FINDLEY, W.G. (1973) "How ability grouping fails." Inequality in Education 14: 38-40.

FOSTER, H.L. (1974) Ribbin', Jivin', an Playin' the Dozens: The Unrecognized Dilemma of Inner-City Schools. Cambridge, MA: Ballinger.

FRANKLIN, J.H. (1971) The Free Negro in North Carolina, 1790-1860. New York: W.W. Norton.

FRAZIER, E.F. (1940) Negro Youth at the Crossways. Washington, DC: American Council on Education.

GIBSON, M.A. (1976) "Approaches to multicultural education in the United States." Anthropology and Education Quarterly 7: 7-18.

GUTHRIE, J.W., G.B. KLEINDORFER, H.M. LEVIN, and R.T. STOUT (1971) Schools and Inequality. Cambridge: MIT Press.

HARLAN, L.R. (1968) Separate and Unequal. New York: Atheneum.

HASKINS, R. (1980) "Race, family income and school achievement." Unpublished manuscript.

HEARD, N.C. (1968) Howard Street. New York: Dial Press.

HIGGINBOTHAM, A.L. (1978) In the Matter of Color: Race and the American Legal Process: The Colonial Period. New York: Oxford University Press.

HOBBS, N. (1975) The Future of Children. San Francisco: Jossey-Bass.

HOLLINGSHEAD, A. (1949) Elmtown's Youth. New York: John Wiley.

HUGHES, J.F. and A.O. HUGHES (1973) Equal Education: A New National Strategy. Bloomington: Indiana University Press.

Illinois Advisory Commission on Civil Rights (1974) Bilingual/Bicultural Education—A Privilege or a Right? Washington, DC: U.S. Government Printing Office.

JENCKS, C. (1972) Inequality. New York: Basic Books.

JENSEN, A.R. (1969) "How much can we boost IQ and scholastic achievement?" Harvard Educational Review 39: 1-123.

JOHNSON, C.S. (1930) The Negro in American Civilization. New York: Holt.

KNOWLES, L.L. and D. PREWITT (eds.) (1969) Institutional Racism in America. Englewood-Cliffs, N.J.: Prentice-Hall.

LEVINE, R. A. (1967) Dreams and Deeds. Chicago: University of Chicago Press.

MAYESKE, G. W., T. OKADA, A. E. COHEN, A. E. BEATON, and C. E. WISLER (1973) A Study of the Achievement of our Nation's Students. Washington, D.C.: U.S. Government Printing Office.

MERCER, J. R. (1973) Labeling the Mentally Retarded. Berkeley: University of California Press.

MILNER, C. A. (1970) "Black pimps and their prostitutes." Unpublished Ph.D. dissertation, Department of Anthropology, University of California, Berkeley.

MITCHELL, R. H. (1967) The Korean Minority in Japan. Berkeley: University of California Press.

MOSTELLER, F. and D. P. MOYNIHAN (eds.) (1972) On Equality of Educational Opportunity. New York: Random House.

MYRDAL, G. (1944) An American Dilemma. New York: Harper.

NEWMAN, D. K., B. K. AMIDEI, D. D. CARTER, W. J. KRUVANT, and J. S. RUSSELL (1978) Protest, Politics and Prosperity: Black Americans and White Institutions, 1940-1975. New York: Pantheon Books.

OGBU, J. U. (1974a) The Next Generation. New York: Academic Press.

—————— (1974b) "Learning in Burgherside," in G. M. Foster and R. V. Kemper (eds.) Anthropologists in the City. Boston: Little, Brown.

—————— (1977) "Racial stratification and education: The case of Stockton, California." IRCD Bulletin 12 (3): 1-26.

—————— (1978) Minority Education and Caste. New York: Academic Press.

—————— (1980a) "Caste and IQ in cross-cultural perspective," to appear in D. A. Wilkerson (ed.) Human Diversity and the Assessment of Intellectual Development.

—————— (1980b) "Equalization of educational opportunity and racial/ethnic inequality: A cross-cultural perspective," to appear in P. Altbach, R. Arnove, and G. Kelley (eds.) Comparative Education. New York: Macmillan.

—————— (1980c) "Societal forces as a context of ghetto children's school failure," to appear in L. Feagans and D. Darran (eds.) The Language of Children Reared in Poverty. New York: Academic Press.

—————— (1981a) "Minority schooling and transition to labor force." Paper presented for a seminar Youth Education and Employment: Policy Issues for the 1980s, Madison, Wisconsin.

—————— (1981b) "Schooling in the ghetto: A cultural-ecological perspective on community and home influences." Paper presented at the NIE Conference on Follow Through, Philadelphia, Pennsylvania.

POWDERMAKER, H. (1968) After Freedom. New York: Atheneum.

SCOTT, J. W. (1976) The Black Revolts. Cambridge: Schenkman.

SENNETT, R. and J. COBB (1972) The Hidden Injuries of Class. New York: Random House.

SEXTON, P. C. (1961) Education and Income. New York: Viking Press.

—————— (1967) Racial Isolation in the Public Schools: A Report, Vol. 1. Washington, D.C.: Government Printing Office.

—————— (1968) "Schools: Broken ladder to success," in L. A. Ferman (ed.) Negroes and Jobs. Ann Arbor: University of Michigan Press.

U.S. Commission on Civil Rights (1977) The Unfinished Business. U.S. Government Printing Office.

U.S. District Court for Northern California (1979) Opinion: Larry P. vs Riles. San Francisco, California Mimeo.

U.S. Senate Select Committee on Education (1972) Report: Toward Equal Educational Opportunity. Washington, D.C.: U.S. Government Printing Office.

VAN DEN BERGHE, P. (1967) Race and Racism: A Comparative Perspective. New York: Wiley.

WARNER, W. L., R. J. HAVIGHURST, and M. B. LOEB (1941) Color and Human Nature: Negro

Personality Development in a Northern City. Washington, D.C.: American Council on Education.

_____ (1944) Who Shall Be Educated? The Challenge of Equal Opportunity. New York: Harper.

WOLFE, T. (1970) Radical Chic and Mau-Mauing the Flack Catchers. New York: Strauss and Giroux.

WEINBERG, M. (1977) A Chance to Learn: A History of Race and Education in the United States. New York: Cambridge University Press.

WRIGHT, N. (ed.) (1970) What Black Educators are Saying. New York: Hawthorn Books.

PART III

MALE-FEMALE RELATIONSHIPS IN
AFRICAN-AMERICAN COMMUNITIES

The section of this book on male-female relationships gives an overview of the roles and the attitudes that Black males and Black females hold towards each other. This too has become an issue that has attracted much attention within the community. An overview of marital relations is followed by a discussion on male-female relations, then a discourse is presented on Black women's values regarding marriage, ending with their attitudes towards child-bearing.

Robert Staples gives an overview of race and marital status and their impact on Black families. He gives a historical basis to the present relationship between Black males and females and explains some of the unique patterns that are sometimes found. The equalitarian relations, the role overload of women, and the greater independence of women within the families are based on historical and financial reasons and may have implications for marriage relations. Regardless of these pressures, Blacks are heavily committed to marriage in former years, with a postponement occurring in the younger age groups, consistent with other families. The increasing level of singlehood is explained, as are the structural restraints that are faced at the lower- and middle-income levels. The complexity for the relations in the pair-bonding process are begun by Staples and detailed by Cazenave, Heiss, and Harrison.

Audrey Chapman explores the recent media attention that has been given to the situation of the relationship between Black males and females. This is an area of growing concern both inside and outside of marriage. Chapman takes us through history, showing how stereotypes have played havoc, how the pressures build, as both males and females seek to survive economically in a society that is growing toward more high technology. Educational changes have played a part, as well as employment conditions. But the crucial element of relationships is where it is all focused.

Jerold Heiss presents a clear articulation of the different points of view that have been presented in the literature in relation to the association of family values and race or SES. He uses a national probability sample to test Ladner's hypothesis that Black women reject society's expectation and create alternative family forms that result in different values. He tackled the difficult task of looking at family and marriage values from three points: Is race associated with values? If race does matter, then what is the impact of the differential SES? Which is greater? And if one controls all other variables, is race still important? He began with the premise that SES, not race or culture, was the key variable, and he found that the racial differences were minor, indicating a divergence projected by Glick of values and structure. The instrumental concerns were more salient for Black women in terms of marriage partners, and SES had less influence on Blacks than on whites. There were no race differences in attitudes toward divorce, and there was an increase in the acceptance by Blacks for out-of-wedlock parentage.

Algea Harrison, in an updated review of attitudes toward procreation, points to the importance of parental role expectations and how they have changed and how they affect the procreational attitudes of Black adults. While little was found about the male role in parenting and in procreation planning, there were many studies about the women. Black families were found to provide modeling that would lead the children toward androgynous roles. The importance of the active maternal roles, as noted also by Staples, and the centrality of children in the women's lives often lead to subsequent prioritization of the mother over the wife role. The decline of the fertility levels and the increase in the use of effective birth control, along with the delay in parenting of younger career-oriented women, will have an influence on the pair-bonding and on the attitudes toward procreation in the future.

11

AN OVERVIEW OF
RACE AND MARITAL STATUS

ROBERT STAPLES

Relationships between Black men and women have had a peculiar evolution. Unlike the white family, which was a patriarchy and sustained by the economic dependence of the female, the Black dyad has been characterized by more equalitarian roles and economic parity in North America. The system of slavery did not permit Black males to assume the superordinate role in the family constellation, since the female was not economically dependent on him. Hence, relationships between the sexes were ordered along sociopsychological factors rather than economic compulsion to marry and remain married. This fact, in part, explains the unique trajectory of Black male/female relationships.

In the past slavery era, the economic parity of Black men and women continued. Due to the meager wages of most Black males, women were forced to enter the labor market and contribute to the maintenance of the households. Such a strong economic role in the family had certain consequences for the marital relationship. The stability of the white, patriarchal family was based on the economic dependence of the female member, forcing her into the prescribed role of a passive, subordinate female. Because Black females were more economically independent, many developed attitudes of freedom and equality unknown to most women in the nineteenth century. While this trait may be currently perceived as a healthy predecessor to the modern women's liberation movement, it produced tensions in Black marriages that were less prevalent in white marriages. The independent woman, in the past, and present, is more likely to be party to a dissolved marriage than her more reliant and passive counterpart.

Economic factors, however, provide only the foundation for dyadic conflict, which is subject to the interplay of other psychosocial forces. Another cause of male/female conflict is the often ignored consequences of the dual role Black women play in the family: worker and mother. The heavy concentration of Black women in domestic service often meant that they held the unenviable position of caring for two households: their own and that of their employer. It has seldom been questioned that the negative effects of doing double duty in two households has created competition between obligations to the two households and could tear at the fabric of the Black woman's marital relationship. Certainly, it could lead to role overload that might compound the difficulties of prosaic marital interaction. It might be noted that this same role overload continues to be extant, albeit in a slightly different form. Many Black women remain burdened by the multiple roles they must play—worker, mother, and wife. Surely, it partly explains the resultant tension and high rate of marital dissolution among so many Black couples.

Despite the problematic aspects of marriage, Blacks continued to marry in record numbers. When one looks at the marital status of Black women over the age of 65, only 3.5 percent had never married in comparison to 6.5 percent of white women.[1] However, the younger group of Blacks appear to have abandoned marriage as a viable institution. At least, the figures which show only a minority of them married and living with a spouse indicates that to be the case. Upon closer inspection, it seems that the desire to marry and remain married has not diminished, only the conditions for doing so have altered.

One can best understand the high rate of singlehood among Blacks by examining it along class and gender lines. The basic causes are structural constraints and ideological preferences. Among lower-income Blacks, the structural constraints consist of the unavailability and undesirability of Black males in the eligible pool of potential mates. Due to the operational effects of institutional racism, large numbers of Black males are incarcerated, unemployed, narcotized, or fall prey to early death. There may actually be an excess of three million Black women without the opportunity to find an available or desirable mate. As a result, many Black women have children out of wedlock and raise them with the assistance of extended family members and the biological father.

Similar structural constraints are operative among the Black middle class. Assuming a desire for homogeneity in mate selection, it is not possible for every Black female college graduate to find a mate among her peers. In 1975, there were 68,000 more Black female college graduates than males. Overall, the ratio of single college-educated Black women to similar men is two to one. In certain categories the ratio is as low as 38 women to every male. This gap, while currently wide, will continue to widen, as there are 150,000 more Black women than men currently enrolled in college. A very different demographic picture exists among whites, where there are a million more white male college graduates than females. This difference can originally be attributed to the historical practice of Black families sending their daughters to college because the males had a wider variety of occupations open to them. The daughters either went to college and became schoolteachers or went into domestic service, an occupation fraught with risks for young Black women in the postbellum south.

However, it is among this middle-class group that ideological preference—that is, the desire not to marry—is more prevalent. Because the women in this group earn 90 percent of a similar male's income, they do not need to marry for economic support. It is more often the satisfaction of psychological needs that is the dominant reason for entering into marriage. Yet, the satisfaction of psychological needs is not the forte of American males. Moreover, the greater a woman's educational level and income, the less desirable she is to many Black males. While a male's success adds to his desirability as a mate, it detracts from a woman's. Hence, the women in this group are less likely to marry and remain married, if they do marry. It is a classical case of success in the labor market and failure in the marriage arena.

Relationships between Black men and women are probably more complex than spelled out in this brief overview. Certainly the dominant factors are contained in the interplay of institutional racism with individual traits. The problems of Black male/female conflict are ultimately a function of political and economic forces beyond their control. Even within the context of economic and racial oppression, many Black men and women share happy moments with each other. For many of them, the relationship lasts a lifetime. There are also those for whom the tension of living in a racist society filters into their most intimate relationships. Relationships between the sexes is, at best, fragile in a society undergoing such rapid social change as occurs in the United States. Rapid social change, no matter in what direction, can cause dislocation in individuals and institutions. The dyadic relationships of Blacks, America's most vulnerable group, to economic and political change, are most sensitive to those changes.

NOTE

1. All figures used are taken from Staples (1981).

REFERENCE

STAPLES, R. (1981) The World of Black Singles. Westport, CT: Greenwood Press.

12

MALE-FEMALE RELATIONS
How the Past Affects the Present

AUDREY B. CHAPMAN

With all the recent media attention to the plight of the Black family, it would be hard to ignore the fact that great problems still exist between Black men and women. However, it is a mistake to view these problems in a vacuum. Any objective observer can see that family relations have changed throughout American society as a whole, not just within the Black community. Yet it is probably true that economics compounds the problems in the Black community more so than in the white community.

A thorough discussion of the future for Black family structure calls for an examination of the historical chasm between Black men and women. Powerful controlling myths surround the relationship between Black men and women, and those myths still influence Black thinking and behavior. It is baffling to contemplate how some of the myths that took hold during slavery still cripple us today.

Rodgers-Rose indicated in the book, *The Black Woman* (1980), how devastating the stereotypes of the shiftless Black male and the hostile woman have been to Blacks. Blacks internalize these feelings and bring them into their relationships. Many women say that Black men can't be counted upon, because they have met a few who can't give Black women the support they need. Another persistent and damaging myth is that of a controlling Black woman.

These stereotypes serve as two examples of myths from the past that continue to plague relationships today. Ideas like these have been perpetuated by society, and Black males and females collude in them, consciously and subconsciously. Thus, they continue to struggle with each other, instead of uniting against the external forces that keep them in turmoil. Some Blacks remain bent on merely surviving, rather than devoting their energies toward controlling their lives.

Since the 1960s, Blacks have experienced many external negative pressures, at a time when many Blacks expected to be doing better. Social changes that occur in the larger society filter out and affect the Black community, as well. The sexual revolution, a climbing divorce rate, and a return to conservatism and subtle racism have brought new challenges for many Black families. Although many Black families surmounted these pressures, many others still anguish in the hopelessness of the situation. Obviously, these factors greatly affect relationships. As Black Americans, we witness the fallout today.

Some 59 percent of all Black families will be female-headed households by 1990. With these larger responsibilities, women are bound to feel some anxiety and hostility toward men. And men are feeling confused and less involved. The latest statistic from the Children's Foundation reported 13.8 million children lived in poverty in 1983, an increase of more than four million since 1973. The plight of Black children and their families has worsened dramatically compared with whites since 1980. Black children are three times as likely to live in poverty or in female-headed households. Many of these children are born to unwed teenage mothers.

Americans are aware of how the economy has always played a central role in causing hardships for men and women. This has caused the divorce rate to double among Black couples since 1980. These results challenge the future of Black relationships more than ever before.

For those who have never married, the social arena has changed so that many women face a future without the prospect of marriage partners. Some blame this dynamic on the male shortage. In 1980 there were just under 30 million unmarried women within the total population, compared to 21.5 million single men. What prevails today is a large number of middle-class single men and women who need security but fear commitment. This fear of commitment dominates relationships, dating back to several decades of changing sex roles.

There is yet another group that has been affected also by the social change of the last 15-20 years—married couples. They now face tension because of competing career and roles, problems of remarriages, and stepchildren. These couples must meet many needs and demands, while having little time and energy for themselves.

WHAT IT'S LIKE TODAY

Presently relationships seem influx. Since the women's movement and the sexual revolution, Blacks have taken on a "yo-yo" or approach-avoidance mentality, in which two people interact briefly (often only physically), only to reunite several weeks later or never again. If married, some focus less on intimacy and more on superficiality.

Alvin Toffler in *Future Shock* (1970) attempted to prepare Americans for what he referred to as the "SuperIndustrial Revolution." In his book he suggests that this phase would place more of an emphasis upon "freedom" instead of commitment. Whereas previous generations stayed in marriages because of societal expectations, today Americans witness a new attitude of "doing your own thing." The result has been an increase in the single population, serial monogamy with several marriages of short duration, and an increase in unwed mothers.

A recent *U.S. News and World Report* (February 1986) article indicated that among the baby boomers between ages 25 and 29, 39 percent of the men have delayed marriage, while 26 percent of the women remain single—substantial increases since 1970 for both sexes. More than 60 percent of those living alone are female. About half of this group earn middle-income salaries, while 44 percent earn under $10,000. It is estimated that there are 20.6 million single adults.

Economics has grave effects upon marital prospects for Blacks. There is an estimated excess of one million women in the Black population, resulting in a ratio of 90 males per 100 females. So there are many more Black females who are single, never married, or divorced than there are white counterparts. In 1985, there were 39.5 percent Black never-marrieds and 8.5 percent divorcees.

The shift from an industrial to high tech economy has pushed a great number of Black males into unemployment. Unemployment rates rose higher in 1982-83 for Black men than for women between 18 and 44 years of age. Job prospects have been decreasing for Black men in all age groups since 1955, while increasing for Black and white females. Black males between 35 and 44 years of age experienced a 14.2 percent rate of unemployment, compared to 10.1 percent for Black females during 1983 (U.S. Bureau of Labor Statistics, November 1983). This dismal fact leaves the Black women (with the exception of Black single mothers) miles ahead of Black men in the labor force, thus creating obvious social problems for both sexes.

The social rift between Black males and females begins at an early period of development. The same internal and external forces of family and society that encourage young Black females toward scholastic achievement discourage the young Black males from attaining this same goal. Society teaches Black males instead to prove their manhood through excelling in sports, music, and hustling. Therefore, some young Black men learn early in life how to gain status in a system hostile to them.

Black society loses its young men early in the educational system, which creates the imbalance in economic strata. The lack of competitive skills reduces access into the professional job market, where the real economic gains exist. In 1972, Blacks represented 12.7 percent of all 18-year-olds, 10.5 percent of all high school graduates, 8.7 percent of all college freshmen, and 6.5 percent of all graduates awarded bachelor's degrees. By 1979, Blacks represented only about 4 percent of all professional and doctoral degree recipients (Berryman, 1983).

Between 1976 and 1981, Black women increased their number of doctoral degrees by 29 percent and their number of first professional degrees by 71 percent over the six-year period. Doctoral degrees awarded to Black men decreased by 10 percent and first professional degrees by 12 percent during the same period of time, 1984.

An estimated 40 percent of the Black male population is functionally illiterate. Also, during adolescence, there is often an increase in homicide, suicide, incarceration, and substance abuse among Black men. The depressing news about these threatening statistics is that these circumstances leave a large number of Black women available in America without Black partners. What are the results? Black women focus more upon their education as a possible means of economic, social, and sexual independence, instead of their reliance upon a man. Black men, on the other hand, seem confused today about how to provide the needs for the "new Black woman" who seems so self-sufficient. Because the professional Black man is not available in large numbers, the ones who are risk rejection because they do not meet certain standards.

Some men who are desirable do not concern themselves with lacking partners and the other men avoid approaching women in order to avoid vulnerability.

Women then feel less powerful to assert themselves when they are in a relationship because the opportunity to find another one is not great.

Women feel more responsible for the outcome of relationships than do men. This applies equally to white women and Black women. They persevere in unsatisfying situations just to keep peace within the relationship, only to discover that behavior creates other dynamics—confusion. This reaction often creates rivalry, jealously, and competition among women, and hostility toward men.

Some men, on the other hand, approach stress in relationships with what may seem a cavalier attitude. Whereas many women tend to devote more attention toward maintaining relationships, men, who are in a more advantageous position, tend to end them more readily since they are, unlike women, always in demand.

But society seems to be in the throes of a period of a "throwaway" style of relating, with brief emotional ties. Women emerged from the women's movement feeling autonomous, with less need for permanent commitments. Sexual liaison sex became "in" and intimacy "out." This new way of relating left many feeling unfulfilled and lacking emotional connections. For Blacks not actively taking part in the movement, many took part by conveniently adopting various aspects of this new life-style. Many experts believe the imbalance between the sexes further aggravates this problem.

The status of relationships is of great importance today. Many people are concerned about the apparent chasm between men and women, and the resulting ill effects on the future of the family. The problem is that the society has been slow in adjusting to some very powerful social changes of the last few decades. The resulting confusion and tension for individuals and families is what Americans are witnessing today. Many men and women struggle without really understanding the underlying reasons for the new tensions between them. This lack of understanding makes change or improvement most difficult.

WHERE ARE BLACKS HEADING

Perhaps the best place to begin exploring where relationships stand is with the current structure of the Black family in America. The family is changing because of certain external issues, causing the natural balance in relationships to be in flux. Households headed by females increased from 28 percent to 41 percent between 1970 and 1982. This is partially a result of a rise in the divorce rate and an increase in the numbers of unwed mothers. By 1982, only 49 percent of Black children lived with one parent, and 8 percent lived with neither parent. William Julius Wilson, University of Chicago, predicts that by the end of the century, 70 percent of Black men will be unemployed.

The New York Times reported in 1982 that the divorce rate had doubled for Black women. There are 257 divorces to every 1,000 Black women, a ratio that rose 104 percent since 1970. For Black males, *The New York Times* reported that there were 151 divorced to every 1,000 who were married, up from 62 in 1972. The difference in the rates for Black men was the fact that they marry sooner and at higher rates than do divorced Black women. Remarried on the census statistics is counted as a marriage.

The divorce rate counts as the second largest category for singles in this country. The first is the never married persons, who these days are forestalling marriage over longer periods. The 1986 U.S. Census indicates that there are now 39.5 percent more Black singles who never married in this country, compared to 54.6 percent for their white counterparts. This leaves more Black women single (divorced, widowed, or never married) than men, creating a sex ratio imbalance of 76 Black males per 100 Black females nationally. There is an estimated excess of one million women in the Black population. The other condition that creates a greater imbalance is the selection process that middle-class women use in selecting a potential mate. Many men are considered "unacceptable," if they are not good looking, professional, with an income of at least $90,000, well-bred, with degrees, and so on.

During the research effort on the book *Mansharing: Dilemma or Choice* (1986), 2,000 women were interviewed nationally on why mate selection was difficult. Over 75 percent (1,580) of them reported having fewer problems meeting men than identifying someone who would fulfill many of their needs. Most of the women answered to the survey by indicating, "It's not who he is, but what the possibilities are for him to gain access to power." Because of unequal economic factors, more Black men do not fit into these categories.

Aside from the economic unsuitability of Black men, other factors contribute to the shortage of available Black men. There is also a high mortality rate among Black men; many are incarcerated, in mental hospitals, drug addicts, in the military (overseas), or simply not interested in Black women. Most recently, the rate of Black homosexuality appears to be more visible in the Black community. All of these factors reduce the eligibility pool of Black men, creating more women who desire partners at an age when fewer exist.

The imbalance promotes an interesting social structure for Black men— a situation sometimes referred to as mate sharing. Mate sharing occurs in a situation in which two or more women may share one man. They may be married or single, aware or unaware of the status.

In 1982 a workshop was offered on man sharing for Washington, D.C. women. At the first session, 120 women attended in order to understand more fully man sharing. Others, however, attended because they had chosen to share men. These women usually ranged between the ages of 35 and 45 and were divorced or widowed. They were in search of companion- ship, not marriage. More often, these women viewed sharing as a dilemma and were in conflict and depressed about the lack of an exclusive relationship.

The interesting reaction was the difference in some women who were opposed to sharing, but who had information that they had shared many times.

Harriette McAdoo conducted a research study on single parent mothers in Washington to determine how they felt about sharing men. The study found that while these women reported having difficulty with sharing, there was a discrepancy in their behavior. Although only a small number agreed to a shared arrangement, almost four times that number reported that they had participated nonetheless.

Documented in the book *Too Many Women* (1983), Secord found whenever there has been an excess of females in society, there was a devaluing of marriage and monogamy. In 1986 a sexual survey was conducted by *New Women Magazine,* in which 65 percent of the men admitted they had been unfaithful to a wife or lover and 34 percent of the women had suggested that they had also been unfaithful. Given the statistical ratio between Black men and women, it creates an atmosphere in which many women unknowingly share a partner.

Robert Staples, in *The World of Black Singles* (1981), noted that because of the surplus of Black women, it's a "buyer's market" in the marital arena for Black men.

It is clear that the numbers affect the problems of stability in relationships, but that is not the entire issue. The other factor is that Black men and women, as well as whites, embraced the changing gender role issues with much anxiety.

Christopher Lasch suggests in his book *The Culture of Narcissism* (1979) that American men and women have taken flight from "feelings" and have entered an era of sexual warfare. It seems that relations between the sexes have become characterized by a greater investment in sexual freedom, but with diminishing emotional returns. Americans are into a period of living for the moment.

The appearance that everything that happens between a man and woman is okay, and that everything includes anything has become a tempting illusion for many, resulting in an escalating tension between men and women. Much of this tension stems from the collapse of "chivalry ethics." Lasch describes the outcome when men and women pursue sex for sex itself—"the efficient contraceptive, legalized abortion, and a realistic and healthy acceptance of the body have weakened the links that once tied sex to love, marriage and procreation. Men and women now pursue sexual pleasure as an end in itself, unmediated even by the conventional trappings of romance."

So both sexes, in order to survive in an era of detached unions, must work hard to manipulate their emotions to protect themselves against pain and rejection. That is why relationships appear so shaky that they cannot accommodate mutual demands or expectations—not to mention commitment and monogamy. Both sexes invest in playing it safe.

Informal interviews in counseling practice indicate that men and women feel lonely, sad, and scared about the lack of stable relationships with the opposite sex. This awareness usually occurs for both after many years on the social circuit. These individuals often begin to realize that developing loving bonds need not be such a scary undertaking. With that they can learn that positive relationships are at the root of strong families for Black people.

Some Black couples have always managed to avoid the "1970s-1980s" trend of relating. A closer investigation of how these Black couples are faring is essential in the development of a model for those still seeking a new way to interact emotionally with the opposite sex.

THOSE WHO ARE MAKING IT WORK

Many today struggle with the question of how they can maintain "good" relationships. Some believe that the importance of friendship supersedes the importance of sexual union, social commitments, and other short-term affairs. Love is a natural and basic need; every living object needs it.

Because greater numbers of men and women discover the importance of spiritual bonding, many newly experience what love and friendship really are. Some are aware that what was abandoned in the 1970s needs to be recouped for survival in today's world. Many realize that a good friendship forms the basis of strong, durable relationships.

Many couples take their relationships so seriously that they structure time for communication, relaxation, and spiritual union. They work very hard on fairness within the union. Some even have weekly meetings to keep tensions from mounting in the household. These couples relate spiritually as friends long after the glow is gone. For example, one couple who both maintained high-powered jobs and travelled extensively, decided to hold weekly family meetings just to keep communications open and conflict at a minimum in their household.

For married couples in the past, friendship was the basis of their commitment to each other. They learned how to understand each other's needs, likes, and dislikes. They learned the process of give and take and the ability to be less selfish. There was an acceptance of the total person that allowed patience and endurance during trying times. Black men and women need to relearn some of the "old ways." Single persons need to gain closeness in similar ways.

Many single women form support groups to further unite around a common concern or need. This allows them to share and not compete with other women over personal relationships. It allows them to know they're not alone in their experiences. Civic organizations, sororities, singles' associations, church groups, also provide a base for meeting and developing friendships. Developing cross-sex friendships is another way of extending one's self. Friendships will provide important support networks when families are often far away.

Cross-sex friendships can be difficult for some to formulate, mainly because few role models for doing so exist. Time was that many patterns of cross-sex friendships existed. For example, if a man was working in another town, a friend of his might oversee his household needs while he was away. Examples in the Black community of this type occur today, but the community needs many more.

Black men have formed several groups around the country addressing the need to support single heads of household. Concerned Black Men and Adopt A Family are but a two organizations that address these needs in the community.

Another trend in relationships today for some Blacks is the new response to crossing the color line. According to the 1984 Census, of the total population of 46 million white males, 64,000 are married to Black women. And of the total population of 3.5 million Black couples, 100,000 Black men are married to white women.

In an informal interview with 350 Black single women, 205 stated that they had dated a white male and the others believed at some point that they would. When asked why they would consider this, they all said they "want more economic options and a chance at identifying a partner where (they believed) less hassles would exist."

Of Black men, according to Robert Staples's study, 85 percent had had at least one interracial experience. The report on the Educational Status of Black Americans, from the 1985 College Board Report, recorded even more interracial couples paired with white male/Black female. It is suspected that as more Black women attend higher education and move further up in status, they may move away from Black men. Thus the traditional Black family unit is at stake.

Blacks must be concerned about the educational and psychological status of Black men because of the implications for the survival of Black family life. If Black males continue to be an endangered species through social oppression while some Black females continue to succeed, there may be the potential for a tremendous gulf between the sexes. This wedge would affect Black people by creating a different life-style for future generations. It will promote other dynamics as well.

There will be unorthodox ways of relating—older women will be seeking younger men at greater rates; communal households of women and children (divorced and unwed) will join together for support; and the selection of mates from the cross-cultural pool of men will be more inviting.

Most fear provoking, though, is the possibility that the Black population may end up with the single, unwed women (adolescent or adult) as the only ones producing families, while the middle-class population postpones marriage as an alternative to careers or finding "Mr. or Ms. Right."

Blacks need to recognize that they still have choices. We need to challenge the awful myth that we cannot get along. The statistics don't have to be strong indicators of the future, unless Blacks allow them to be. Blacks must strive toward empowerment, making decisions that are based upon what's real in America, rather than what they would like to experience through false expectations from material gains. The middle class must reach back and invite those less fortunate to come along.

Blacks must become more comfortable with the fact that total dependence upon the system that oppresses the race will never set Blacks free. Blacks must also realize that they will survive more effectively if they have each other, regardless of the availability of men. Blacks must applaud those who are making professional strides, because they may have the clout to make the difference for the race as a whole. By this gain, everyone gains.

Black men and women must realize their joint responsibility for today's tensions in relationships and therefore strive to join together to create healthy connections. Values and ethics have been challenged in the past few years. Sexual health problems and the lack of closeness and intimacy cause many to reconsider the old style of relating. Even though these ways were not perfect, they did create relationships of substance. So if Blacks want successful relationships, they must be willing to take some risks. This may mean, even if the male shortage continues, that people will recommit themselves to mutually monogamous relationships. Conceptualizing relating on a more humanistic basis, friendship will become more vital as the basis for developing realistic love.

Love is the pulse of spirituality and bonding. No race of people has ever succeeded without it. Blacks have always gotten through difficult times through strong efforts of brotherhood and sisterhood.

Once Blacks accept total responsibility together, women can be relieved of bearing alone the social burdens and men can stop feeling undervalued and threatened. With this in mind, men and women must reexamine their own values and needs. Put simply, Black men and women must decide to structure their personal lives in more respectful and loving ways for the future of the race. The next generation's very existence depends upon this premise.

REFERENCES

BERRYMAN, S. (1983) Who Will Do Science? New York: Rockefeller Foundation.
CHAPMAN, B. A. (1986) Mansharing: Choice or Dilemma. New York: William Morrow.
LASCH, C. (1979) The Culture of Narcissism. New York: Warner Communications.
McADOO, H. (1983) Extended Family Support of Black Single Mothers. DHSS Research Report #5701 MH32159, March. Washington, DC: Government Printing Office.
RODGERS-ROSE, L. [ed.] (1980) The Black Woman. Beverly Hills, CA: Sage.
SECORD, P. (1983) Too Many Women. Beverly Hills, CA: Sage.
STAPLES, R. (1981) The World of Black Singles. Westport, CT: Greenwood.
TOFFLER, A. (1970) Future Shock. New York: Random House.
U.S. News & World Report (1986) "Among baby boomer memories." Horizon Section, 4.
WILLIAMS, J. D. [ed.] (1984) The State of Black America. New York: National Urban League.

13

WOMEN'S VALUES REGARDING MARRIAGE AND THE FAMILY

JEROLD HEISS

After a number of years of sociological investigation, it is now clear that the distributions of several family variables are different for blacks and whites. Black families, for example, tend to be somewhat larger, they are more likely to be female-headed, they are more likely to be extended in form, and so forth (Jackson, 1973; Baughman, 1971; Heiss, 1975). However, the reasons for this racial variation remain unclear. Some authors argue that there are important differences in family values, and they see the differences in family behavior as a reflection of these psychological differences. Others deny the existence of attitudinal differences. They contend, for example, that blacks and whites are equal in their acceptance of the values underlying what is often called the "mainstream family model"—a husband, a wife, their children, and no others; with the wife as a full-time homemaker and the husband the sole breadwinner.[1] These authors believe that variation by race occurs because the situations of blacks and whites differ in ways that produce differential access to the resources that are required if one is to live by that model.

Ladner (1972: 247) expresses the "attitude difference" view when she says that many of the girls in her study of the lower-class "reject larger societal expectations of them and *realistically* adapt to as well as create their own alternatives and norms." Peters and de Ford (1978: 193) express a similar sentiment when they list three family values that they say black families subscribe to, "unlike most families in the dominant culture." And, of course, the value difference view is held by those who place the sources of the contemporary black family in Africa and/or slavery (see, for example, Nobles, 1978; Herskovits, 1941).

Scanzoni (1971: 3), by denying attitudinal differences, is stating part of the "situational" view when he argues that "the *dominant* family form throughout western society at the level of values . . . is what the majority of adults (black and white) prefer." Along the same lines, Hannerz (1969: 71) suggests, in speaking of lower-class blacks, that "there is an idealization of the mainstream model of marriage. People get married and hope to make a go of it largely along its lines." And, similarly, "no ghetto-specific model for a male-female union has anything close to the normative validity which the mainstream model enjoys in the ghetto as well as outside it" (Hannerz, 1969: 102).

According to these authors, the differences in family form emerge from situational differences. Hannerz contends, for example, that conflict and disruption arise in lower-class black families because "the rights and duties prescribed in the mainstream model are applied to the situation so that facts of limited access to resources are transformed into ambiguities and deviations in the definition of the conjugal relationship. . . . In such cases the influence of the mainstream model prevents a stable settlement on the basis of ghetto-specific macrostructural conditions" (1969: 89; see also Rainwater, 1970; Schulz, 1969; Liebow, 1967; Staples, 1978; Ladner, 1972).

Cutting across the lines drawn by the two positions just described is a difference of opinion that relates to the contribution of socioeconomic status (SES) to the differences between the races. Some of those who posit the existence of attitudinal differences see them as a function of the differential distribution of SES. Their view is that SES is the major factor affecting these attitudes, and they believe that the racial difference is due to the fact that the races differ in SES. Others suggest that the racial differences would remain even if the races were equal on SES. They argue that the experiences that cause the supposed attitudinal differences are associated with racial status at all SES levels, though perhaps to different degrees. Similarly, those who focus on situational factors may claim that the situations of blacks tend to differ from those of whites regardless of social class, or they may posit that racial differences reflect social status differences between the races (see Udry, 1966; Billingsley, 1968; Frazier, 1939; Jackson, 1973).

The goal of this chapter is to cast some light on these matters by considering data drawn from a national sample of women. It will not be possible to settle the issue completely, but we will be able to test the "attitude-difference" theory by directly comparing the attitudes of women of the two races. Furthermore, when such differences are found, we will be able to estimate the degree to which they are a function of SES by comparing the attitudes of the racial groups with SES held constant.[2]

In addition, we will attempt to push the matter somewhat further by determining the independent effect of race, SES, and other variables[3] upon the variation in attitudes. By comparing the magnitude of these various effects we will be able to determine the relative significance of the racial effect. In sum, and more specifically, the research to be reported here is intended to provide answers to the following questions:

(1) Do black and white women differ in their attitudes regarding family-related issues?
(2) If there are differences on these issues, are they a result of differences in SES between the races?
(3) Are the SES or racial effects greater?
(4) If the racial groups showed the same distribution on SES, and other variables (age, religion, current marital status, number of children, and work status), would they differ in their responses?
(5) Are the racial differences that remain after the effects of other independent variables are ruled out greater or less than the SES differences that remain when the other independent variables are controlled?
(6) After race and SES have explained as much of the variance in responses as they can, how much more of the variation is explained by the other variables?

The answers to these questions will allow us to estimate the independent effects of racial status and will provide us with standards by which to judge the relative significance of these effects.

The data will also permit us to determine the relationship between SES and the dependent variables for each race separately. This will allow us to discover if the patterning of responses is the same in the two races; if variables which affect attitudes in one race have similar effects in the other. If this is the case, it would suggest that if the races become more similar in social status, they would probably become more similar in family attitudes. Also, since we have available surveys conducted in 1974 and 1979 which asked some of the same questions, it will be possible to determine whether the attitudes of the races are converging or diverging.

HYPOTHESES

Our basic hypothesis is that the attitude differences between the races are of minor significance. We expect that they will be rather small in absolute size, that they will be no larger than those associated with SES and the other demographic variables, and that they are at least partially a function of the differential distribution of SES and the other variables to be considered.

It is our belief that the family values held by an individual are a result of his or her particular socialization experiences, and that the relevant experiences are not strongly affected by race and the other demographic variables that are used in this study. This view is based, to begin with, on a rejection of the "Africanist" and "slavery" positions. Certainly, African ancestry and the experience of slavery represent two major differences between blacks and whites. We believe, however, that these differences have relatively little direct impact on the family attitudes that are taught contemporary blacks. Further, we assume, consistent with recent research (Gutman, 1976), that if there is any remaining effect of slavery, it does not push in the direction of a markedly distinctive family value set.

This is not to deny that there are relevant differences in the *recent* histories of blacks and whites. Racial status is a significant element in the lives of people in this society, and it is quite probable that race has an effect on the family attitudes that people encounter and on the choices they make among the attitudes presented to them. At the same time, however, we would note that both races are constantly exposed to the general American culture, and this would serve to reduce the difference between them.

It also seems likely that some of the differences in the experiences of blacks and whites are as much a function of differences in SES and other demographic variables as they are of racial status, per se. Thus we would expect that when SES and the other demographic variables are controlled, the differences between the races would be reduced. Given this, and the known relevance of some of the other variables—for example age and marital status—we would expect that the *independent* effect of racial status would prove to be no greater than the independent effects of the other factors.

We further assume that SES is related to family attitudes in a similar manner in both races. This hypothesis rests on the assumption that the situations of blacks and whites are sufficiently alike to ensure that the implications of possessing a particular trait are the same in both races—even if the magnitude of the effect is not the same in all cases. For example, regardless of race, people who are well educated are likely to have important socialization experiences that differ from those of the less well educated. The former are, for one thing, more likely to be economically secure. Such differences may very well be reflected in similar intraracial SES effects.

Finally, we expect to find that the races have come closer together on family attitudes over the last few years. This prediction is based on the assumption that recent societal events have brought many additional blacks into the mainstream of American life. This would have had the effect of further reducing the influence of the relevant parts of black culture, it would have increased blacks' exposure to the secondary agencies of socialization, and it would have reduced the differences between their life experiences and those of the typical white. All of these would lead to a convergence in attitudes over time.

METHODS

The data to be considered in this study were obtained from surveys of national samples conducted in 1974 and 1979 under the sponsorship of Virginia

Slims cigarettes. A multistage, stratified, probability design was used to choose sampling units to the level of blocks, and beyond this level there was a combination of random and quota methods. (The quotas were for sex, age level, and employment status.) The subjects of this study are the 2566 white women and the 318 black women of the 1974 survey and the 2607 white women and 296 black women questioned in 1979.

The SES scale is a factor-analytic score using respondents' education, family income, and a complex occupational prestige code. This code used the respondent's occupation if she was unmarried and employed, husband's occupation for married women not in the labor force, and a composite of husband's and respondent's occupation for married women who held outside employment. The factor analysis and scoring were done separately for the 1974 and 1979 samples so that changes in the distribution of socioeconomic characteristics in the society would not produce a higher set of scores for the 1979 respondents.

RESULTS

The first set of questions bears on motivations for marrying. The respondents' views were determined by giving them a list of ten possible reasons for marrying and asking them to choose the two or three they considered the most important. The responses were analyzed by means of factor analysis, and a clear expressive-instrumental factor emerged. Those who scored high on this factor tended to choose items which referred to instrumental concerns related to responsibilities, income, and the quality of life. On the other hand, high scorers were less likely than other respondents to choose the expressive reasons which related to being in love, liking and wanting to be with a particular person, having children, and so forth.

The respondents were also asked to rate 13 marital outcomes in terms of their importance "for a good marriage,"[4] and their responses provide us with an index of their motivations for marriage. When these responses were factor analyzed, two useful factors were found: an expressive factor, which had its major impact on the items that had to do with sexual relationships and the survival of love, and a companionship factor indexed by items dealing with understanding the spouse's life, sharing the humorous side of things, and the sharing of feelings. The analysis which follows utilizes these factors plus two items which did not weight heavily on either factor: the necessity of financial security and children for a good marriage.

The goal of this section is to test the general validity of Ladner's (1972) conclusion that the motivations that led the lower-class black women in her sample to marry differ from those of whites. She states that the former enter marriage after "a more realistic cold assessment of the chances of its succeeding. . . . Love, emotional security, etc. are actually 'luxury' reasons for getting

married. Thus, Black females . . . are using more sophisticated and rational
reasons for entering the marriage contract" (Ladner, 1972: 247).

Our data bearing on this issue are presented in Table 13.1. Since they are
complex and presented in a somewhat unusual format, I will begin with a
detailed reading of the data bearing on the first dependent variable to ensure that
the reader will be able to follow the argument in the later sections despite the use
of cursory references to the tables.

Section 1 of the table presents Pearson correlations between race, SES, and
the dependent variables. The figures in column A show that race and SES are
both weakly related to the number of instrumental reasons for marriage chosen
by the respondent. Blacks are more likely than whites to choose such reasons (r
= .18), and the higher the SES, the smaller the number of instrumental reasons
chosen (r = −.13).

The numbers in Section 2 are the standardized regression coefficients
(Betas) for race and the dependent variable controlling for SES, and for SES

TABLE 13.1   Analysis of Responses to Questions Bearing on Marital Motivations
and Goals

Statistic: Variable; Constants	Motives and Goals				
	(A) Instru-mental[1]	(B) Expres-sive[1]	(C) Companion-ship[1]	(D) Financial Security[2]	(E) Having a Child[2]
1. Correlation: race	.18	−.01	−.10	.12	.02
SES	−.13	−.01	.06	−.13	−.16
2. Beta: race; SES constant	.16	−.01	−.09	.10	−.02
SES; race constant	−.09	−.02	.04	−.11	−.16
3. Final Beta: race	.15	−.03	−.11	.10	.00
SES	−.07	−.03	.04	−.10	−.13
4. R: race + SES	.20	.02	.11	.17	.16
R added by 5 other variables	.04	.09	.04	.01	.12
5. b: SES, no variables constant					
Black	−.10	−.03	−.04	.01	−.09
White	−.09	−.01	.04	−.07	−.10
6. b: SES; 5 variables constant					
Black	−.04	−.06	−.06	.05	−.06
White	−.06	−.02	.04	−.06	−.08
7. Trend, 1974-1979[3]					
Black	−.14	−.11	−.11	+1.8%	−6.9%
White	−.03	−.06	−.08	+8.3%	−5.2%

[1] For numerical scores a positive sign indicates that blacks or higher-status persons tended to get the
higher scores.
[2] For nonnumerical variables a positive sign means that blacks or high-status respondents were more likely to
say the goal was important.
[3] A positive sign means that people in the 1979 study had higher scores or a greater likelihood of saying
the goal was important.

and the dependent variable controlling on race. In column A we see that when SES is controlled the association of race and instrumental score is about the same as it was when SES was not held constant, and the relationship for SES is reduced slightly when race is controlled (cf. Section 1 and Section 2). This means that race and SES are weakly related to the score independently of each other, and that a small part of the association between SES and instrumentality that was seen in Section 1 was owing to racial differences among the SES groups.

The figures in the third section are the Betas for race and SES when they and age, religion, marital status, number of children, and employment status are all in the equation. For instrumental score these Betas are approximately equal to the SES and race betas without the other variables held constant. This means that the "other" variables do not explain the effects of SES and race on the dependent variable.

The first row of Section 4 presents the multiple correlation of race and SES with the dependent variable. In the case of instrumental score, the multiple correlation is quite small. When taken together, race and SES explain only a small amount of the variation in instrumental scores.[5] The second row of Section 4 shows how much the other five variables add to the multiple correlation if they are put into the equation after race and SES have been entered. In this case, the addition of the other variables does not raise the multiple R very much. The other variables do not increase our ability to explain variations in instrumental score.

In summary, none of the variables is strongly related to variations in response to the measure of instrumental motivations, but race has a somewhat stronger effect than SES, and the other five variables do not increase the correlation by any significant amount.

Sections 5 and 6 present *unstandardized* regression coefficients (b's) for SES for each race separately, with and without the other variables held constant. These figures tell us how SES affects the dependent variables in each race, another way of judging the extent to which the races are similar or different.

The data in column A suggest that for instrumental scores the patterning by SES is similar in the two races. The coefficients for SES and instrumental score are in the same direction for whites and blacks, and they are about the same magnitude. Controlling the other variables reduces both coefficients, but the reduction is slightly greater for blacks. The general conclusion is that there are similar differences between SES groups in both races, that these SES differences are small, and that they are partially a result of the associations among SES, age, and so forth.

The trends from 1974 to 1979 are presented in Section 7. As is indicated by the negative signs, both races had lower instrumental scores in 1979 than they had in 1974. Importantly, however, the change is somewhat greater for blacks.

Since in the 1974 study the blacks had higher scores than the whites, this means that there has been a small convergence of the races between 1974 and 1979.

The items bearing on the criteria for a good marriage show a variety of patterns. Section 1 indicates that neither SES nor race is related to choosing expressive criteria (column B). In fact, none of the independent variables shows a substantial association with this dependent variable. As compared with whites, however, blacks do show a tendency to give less importance to companionships (column C), and they emphasize financial security more than whites (column D), even when other variables are held constant. The racial effect on the rating of companionship is stronger than the SES effect; for financial security it is the same strength. And the ratings on the importance of children for a good marriage (column 3) are related to SES but not to race.

This diversity makes it difficult to present a general conclusion, but it does seem that there are small racial differences on some marital goals and motivations. And, just as Ladner (1972) suggested, blacks tend to be more instrumental. The differences are small, to be sure, and they are not found on all variables, but they do seem to exist and, importantly, none of them is a reflection of racial differences in SES or the other variables being considered here.

In general, the social status patterns are about the same in the two races. For two of the variables, the signs of the b's are different, which implies that in one race high-SES people tend to have higher scores and in the other race lower-status people have the higher scores. But for both variables the effects are small.

The time trends are all in the same direction for the two races, and generally they do not differ much in magnitude. This suggests that there is neither convergence nor divergence. The financial security item is an exception, however. Both races rated this higher in 1979 than in 1974, but the increase was greater for whites. This caused the races to converge on this matter, since in 1974 the blacks were more likely to respond that financial security was important.

Turning now to other matters, we note that many authors have reported that the structural patterns prescribed by the mainstream model are followed less often by blacks than they are by whites.[6] For example, maternal employment outside the home is more common for blacks (Nye, 1974); the black rate for extramarital parenthood is higher (White, 1979); black families are more likely to be female-headed (Rodgers-Rose, 1980); and there is a greater likelihood that the household will contain people who are not members of the nuclear family (Hill and Shackleford, 1978). The purpose of this section is to determine if there are attitudinal differences behind such structural differences.

Column A of Table 13.2 analyzes the responses to an item which asked the respondents to choose among a variety of family forms. For our purposes the item was dichotomized into "mainstream" and "nonmainstream" categories. The former is comprised of those who chose the option of a nuclear family with a "traditional" division of labor. The second category was comprised primarily

Jerold Heiss

TABLE 13.2   Analysis of Responses to Questions Bearing on Acceptance of "Nonmainstream" Family Forms

Statistic: Variable; Constants	Family Forms Accepted			
	(A) Accepts Nontrad. Form[1]	(B) Respects House Husband[1]	(C) Kids w/o Marriage[2]	(D) Accepts Child Who Cohabits[1]
1. Correlation: race	.04	−.10	.07	−.04
SES	.15	.23	.11	−.14
2. Beta: race; SES constant	.08	−.05	.11	−.08
SES; race constant	.17	.22	.14	−.16
3. Final Beta: race	.06	−.05	.08	−.05
SES	.10	.21	.10	−.10
4. R: race + SES	.17	.24	.15	.16
R added by 5 other variables	.20	.02	.14	.16
5. b: SES, no variables constant				
Black	.12	.16	.13	−.06
White	.09	.12	.08	−.16
6. b: SES; 5 variables constant				
Black	.11	.18	.08	−.01
White	.05	.12	.06	−.11
7. Trend, 1974-1979[3]				
Black	+3.0%	—[4]	.16	+13.7%
White	+7.6%	—[4]	.04	+12.2%

[1] For nonnumerical variables a positive sign means that blacks or high-status respondents were more likely to say the form was acceptable.
[2] For numerical scores a positive sign indicates that blacks or higher-status persons tended to get the higher scores.
[3] A positive sign means that people in the 1979 study had higher scores or a greater likelihood of saying the form was acceptable.
[4] The question was not asked in 1974.

of people who preferred a nuclear family with an equal sharing of responsibilities for housework, children, and "breadwinning."[7] The item considered in Column B asks the respondents whether they would respect a man who stayed home and did the housework while his wife worked, more, less, or about the same as a man who was a wage earner. The remaining two variables also deal with variant family forms; cohabitation without marriage (for one's child), and parenthood without marriage.[8]

Despite the behavioral differences that exist, the races show very little difference on these attitude items. None of the racial correlations is above .10, which indicates that blacks are not *substantially* more accepting of these "nonmainstream" family forms.[9] It is also clear that this failure to find racial differences is not due to a lack of patterned variation. The SES differences are all .10 or above, even when other variables are held constant. In addition, the demographic factors, particularly age, add a reasonable amount to the multiple R's for three of the variables.

The patterns of response are generally the same for both races (Sections 5 and 6). The only notable difference is that SES has less of an independent effect on attitudes toward cohabitation for blacks than for whites. This notwithstanding, these data give further evidence of the similarity of the races.

The data for trends over time show that for two of the three items for which there are data, the movement is in the same direction at about the same speed. Blacks, however, increased their acceptance of parenthood without marriage to a greater degree than did whites. Since blacks were originally more accepting, this produces a small widening of the gap between the races.

With the exceptions noted, it may be concluded that the hypotheses of this study are generally supported by the data on acceptance of "nonmainstream" family forms.

Finally, we turn to the subject of divorce, a matter about which there has been considerable controversy. That blacks have higher divorce rates than whites is beyond dispute by now (see Ross and Sawhill, 1975; Heiss, 1975), but we still do not know if this is due to a greater acceptance of divorce by blacks or to situational factors which make it more difficult for blacks to achieve a stable marriage (Hannerz, 1969; Liebow, 1967; Heiss, 1975; Ross and Sawhill, 1975).

The first matter to be considered is responses to a general item that asked the respondents whether they would favor or oppose divorce as a solution to a marriage which was "not working out." The second variable is the number of reasons the respondent accepted as valid reasons for divorce. (The list given the respondents contained items that referred to such things as the loss of love, different ideas about how children should be raised, and a severe drinking problem.) Thus, we can determine whether the races differ in their general willingness to resort to divorce if a marriage is defined as bad, and we can also determine their reactions to particular kinds of problems. The final two variables are factor-analytic scores which group the reasons into an expressive group which included such reasons as feeling the romance has gone out of the marriage, and a conflict group which contained items dealing with matters such as conflict over how money should be spent.

Our discussion of Table 13.3, which contains the relevant data, is brief, for the races show no differences on any of the items. Thus, several of the other questions lose their relevance. We simply note that SES differences are also quite trivial, though they are generally larger than the race differences; that the races are quite similar in their patterning of responses; and that from 1974 to 1979 there is essentially no change in acceptance of divorce for whites or blacks.

TABLE 13.3 Analysis of Responses to Questions Bearing on Attitudes
Toward Divorce

Statistic: Variable; Constants	(A) Accepts Divorce[1]	(B) Number of Reasons Accepted[2]	(C) Expressive Reasons[2]	(D) Conflict Reasons[2]
		Divorce Attitudes		
1. Correlation: race	−.02	.01	.06	.01
SES	−.05	.09	.01	.13
2. Beta: race; SES constant	−.03	.03	.06	.05
SES; race constant	−.06	.10	.02	.14
3. Final Beta: race	−.01	.01	.05	.03
SES	−.05	.09	−.01	.14
4. R: race + SES	.06	.10	.06	.14
R added by 5 other variables	.10	.09	.10	.06
5. b: SES, no variables constant				
Black	−.02	.29	.01	.14
White	−.03	.29	.03	.13
6. b: SES; 5 variables constant				
Black	.01	.39	.03	.14
White	−.03	.25	−.01	.13
7. Trend, 1974-1979[3]				
Black	+3.0%	—[4]	—[4]	—[4]
White	−0.1%	—[4]	—[4]	—[4]

[1] For nonnumerical variables a positive sign means that blacks or high-status respondents were more likely to say the reason was acceptable.
[2] For numerical scores a positive sign indicates that blacks or higher-status persons tended to get the higher scores.
[3] A positive sign means that people in the 1979 study had higher scores or a greater likelihood of saying the reason was acceptable.
[4] The question was not asked in 1979.

SUMMARY AND CONCLUSION

The data suggest the following answers to the questions that were posed at the beginning.[10]

1. Though there are differences between the family attitudes of black and white women, the evidence of this study suggests that they are trivial in size, more often than not. The prime exception to this generalization seems to be that black women are more instrumental in their motivations for marriage and in their marital goals. Even here, however, the racial correlations are not large.

2. The differences that were found do *not* seem to be a reflection of SES differences. The control for SES does not typically reduce the race-attitude correlations, even though race and SES are correlated.[11]

3. There is not much difference in the magnitude of the race and SES differences; race is certainly not more important than SES. In fact, in most cases the SES betas are somewhat larger.

4. As noted before, the racial differences are quite small, but in almost no case are they made significantly smaller by controlling for the other variables considered in this study. The racial differences are not due to differences in these social characteristics.

5. When the other variables are controlled, SES still seems to have a somewhat greater independent effect than race.

6. In general, the other variables do not add much to the multiple correlations obtained by using only SES and race. Variations in the dependent variables are not strongly related to any of the independent variables for which there is information in these surveys.

In addition, we conclude that SES tends to show similar relations to the dependent variables in both races, and between 1974 and 1979 the races have not changed their relative positions very much. However, there is more evidence for convergence that there is for divergence.

The major general conclusion is that the differences in the history and present experiences of blacks and whites have not produced major differences in their attitudes toward the family matters considered here. Despite the differences in their situations there is a common core of experience, and that core seems to include exposure to the "mainstream model." It is clear that racial status does not hold the key to family attitudes. In some cases, for example, the SES differences within each race are considerably larger than the difference between the races. Undoubtedly, racial differences in family attitudes are neither as large nor as important as some have claimed.

Finally, it does not seem likely that attitudinal differences of the size we have found could account for the differences in family behavior that have been reported in other studies. It seems extremely likely that much of the racial variance in family behavior is a function of situational and resource differences rather than attitude differences.

NOTES

1. A more accurate term would perhaps be the "stereotypical model," for less than 15 percent of contemporary American homes are of this type. It should also be noted that as used here the term *mainstream model* is not intended to have any value connotations. There is no implication that American families should fit this model or that such families are necessarily preferable to other types. They are simply the type that, until recently at least, were considered to be the norm.

2. There is, of course, a basic problem involved in the attempt to control for SES when racial comparisons are being made, for people of different races who are equal on *objective* indicators of SES do not necessarily occupy comparable positions in the status hierarchy (see Dodson, this volume; Heiss, 1975; Jackson, 1973). There does not seem to be an adequate operational solution to this problem, though the use of a composite indicator such as is used here does reduce its magnitude. The reader should keep in mind that when we speak of comparisons with SES controlled, we are not in fact dealing with groups that are equal in social status, broadly conceived.

3. The "other" variables are age, religion, current marital status, number of children, and work status.

4. For these questions, the subjects were asked to rate the importance of each item. They were not asked to choose the few they considered most important, as in the previous set.

5. To make the figures in the table more comparable, R rather than R^2 is presented. The increase in variance explained is, of course, indicated by R^2.

6. No value judgment is implied by this statement. We do not believe that it is necessarily desirable for a group to live by the mainstream model (see Heiss, 1975).

7. This category also includes those who choose other forms such as the communal family. However, over 90 percent of the subjects chose one of the responses that involved a nuclear family unit.

8. The latter variable was a factor-analytic scale. Some of the items which loaded heavily on this factor referred to single people having children, and others asked about them raising children. A question that asked if a couple should marry for the sake of the child if the woman was pregnant did *not* load heavily on this factor.

9. The strongest correlation is found for the item that asks about respect for a man who keeps house. It is negative, which means that blacks are a little less favorable to this variant form.

10. It should be emphasized that these conclusions should not be generalized to aspects of family life not covered here. Even within the areas we have considered we have found that the findings are not totally consistent.

11. The reductions do not occur because in most cases when there is a correlation between race and attitude, the correlation of SES and the attitude is quite small.

REFERENCES

BAUGHMAN, E. E. (1971) Black Americans. New York: Academic Press.

BILLINGSLEY, A. (1968) Black Families in White America. Englewood Cliffs, NJ: Prentice-Hall.

FRAZIER, E. F. (1939) The Negro Family in the United States. Chicago: University of Chicago Press.

GUTMAN, H. G. (1976) The Black Family in Slavery and Freedom. New York: Pantheon.

HANNERZ, U. (1969) Soulside. New York: Columbia University Press.

HEISS, J. (1975) The Case of the Black Family. New York: Columbia University Press.

HERSKOVITS, M. J. (1941) The Myth of the Negro Past. New York: Harper & Row.

HILL, R. B. and L. SHACKLEFORD (1978) "The Black extended family revisited," pp. 201-206 in R. Staples (ed.) The Black Family: Essays and Studies. Belmont, CA: Wadsworth.

JACKSON, J. J. (1973) "Family organization and ideology," pp. 405-445 in K. S. Miller and R. M. Dreger (eds.) Comparative Studies of Blacks and Whites in the United States. New York: Seminar Press.

LADNER, J. A. (1972) Tomorrow's Tomorrow: The Black Woman. Garden City, NY: Anchor.

LIEBOW, E. (1967) Tally's Corner. Boston: Little, Brown.

NOBLES, W. (1978) "Africanity: its role in Black families," pp. 19-26 in R. Staples (ed.) The Black Family: Essays and Studies. Belmont, CA: Wadsworth.

NYE, F. I. (1974) "Sociocultural context," pp. 1-31 in L. W. Hoffman and F. I. Nye (eds.) Working Mothers. San Francisco: Jossey-Bass.

PETERS, M. and C. de FORD (1978) "The solo mother," pp. 192-200 in R. Staples (ed.) The Black Family: Essays and Studies. Belmont, CA: Wadsworth.

RAINWATER, L. (1970) Behind Ghetto Walls. Chicago: AVC.

RODGERS-ROSE, L. F. (1980) "Some demographic characteristics of the Black woman: 1940 to 1975," pp. 29-41 in L. F. Rodgers-Rose (ed.) The Black Woman. Beverly Hills, CA: Sage.

ROSS, H. L. and V. SAWHILL (1975) Time of Transition. Washington, DC: Urban Institute.

SCANZONI, J. H. (1971) The Black Family in Modern Society. Boston: Allyn & Bacon.

SCHULZ, D. (1969) Coming Up Black. Englewood Cliffs, NJ: Prentice-Hall.

STAPLES, R. (1978) "The Black family revisited," pp. 13-18 in R. Staples (ed.) The Black Family: Essays and Studies. Belmont, CA: Wadsworth.

UDRY, J. R. (1966) "Marital instability by race, sex, education and occupation using 1960 census data." American Journal of Sociology 72: 203-209.

WHITE, L. K. (1979) "The correlates of urban illegitimacy in the United States, 1960-1970." Journal of Marriage and the Family 41: 715-720.

14

ATTITUDES TOWARD PROCREATION
AMONG BLACK ADULTS

ALGEA O. HARRISON

The purpose of this discussion is to examine attitudes toward procreation among black adults. The attitudes were examined by reviewing the literature on family planning, specifically birth rates and birth control practices. It was assumed that an important indicator of attitudes toward procreation was birth rate figures and that planned family size reflected attitudes toward incorporating parenting into a life-style. In addition, behavior in parental roles was considered another indicator of one's attitude toward procreation. Hence, studies and investigations that examined paternal and maternal roles among black adults were reviewed. Importantly, the black community was not viewed as monolithic; instead, important demographic differences were delineated and noted. The discussion of these issues is pertinent since improvements in scientific technology and health care delivery systems have increased opportunities for blacks to consider the options of childlessness or limiting the number of offspring. One of the important issues regarding procreation is teenage pregnancy, however, the topic is discussed in detail in another chapter.

FAMILY PLANNING

BIRTH RATES

The birth rate for blacks has declined over the past two decades from 31.9 in 1960 to 20.9 in 1983 (U.S. National Center for Health Statistics,

1986). Between 1959 and 1967 there was a 30 percent decline in the general fertility rates for nonwhites (Farley, 1970). This decline in average number of births continued during the decade between 1967 to 1977 among black women who had expected to have fewer children. There was a decline in births from 3,191 in 1967 to 2,364 in 1977 among black wives in the 18-39 age range. (All figures are bases per 1,000 women.) At the same time, there was a decline in birth rates for women of all races in the 18-39 age category from 2,427 in 1967 to 1,860 in 1977 (U.S. Bureau of the Census, 1977). The birth rate leveled off for black women in 1978 with very little change through 1983. This general trend was apparent for nonblacks also.

Black women also have limited the size of their families drastically in the past two decades. In 1960, black women between the ages of 15-44 had their fifth child at the rate of 14.1, and by 1983, the rate had dropped to 2.8. The greatest change in number of children was between a family size of two or three. By 1983, the birth rate for the second child was 24.1 compared to 24.3 in 1960, however, it was 13.7 in 1983 for the third child as compared to 24.0 in 1960. Indeed these occurrences are consistent with the number of children black wives expected to have. In 1975, 50.4 percent of black women between the ages of 25-29 and 38.3 percent between 30-34 years expected two children in contrast to the 23.3 percent and 26.8 percent in the same age categories who expected three children. In 1983, 49.9 percent of black women in the younger age group expected two children as compared to 45.7 percent in the older group. On the other hand, 23.5 percent in the younger age group and 21.8 percent in the older age group expected three children. Black women at the prime childbearing years are successfully planning their families. Indeed in 1982, 80.1 percent of the children born to black women between the ages of 25-34 were wanted, as compared to 19.6 percent that were unwanted at conception. The percentages change to 84.3 wanted and 15.5 unwanted if the mother was married at the time of conception. One speculates that the major reason for the successful family planning by black adults is the availability of improved birth control techniques.

BIRTH CONTROL PRACTICES

The early studies of birth control use among blacks in the latter part of the nineteenth century are controversial (McFalls and Masnick, 1981). There was a sharp decline in the fertility rates among blacks from 1880 to 1940 and many demographers concluded that the decline was owing to health factors, particularly venereal disease. The willingness of social scientists to accept this health explanation prevented more thorough examination of the issue. Recent examination of the evidence has suggested that blacks did use birth control at a much higher rate than the demographers believed. Furthermore, contraception and induced abortion were practiced in tribal Africa and among slaves, so black women had some knowledge of techniques to control fertility. After World War II, increased health and medical services, urbanization, and improved general living conditions had an impact on birth control use among the black population (Farley, 1970). There were, however, demographic differences with more favorable attitudes reported by urban than rural females and more positive orientations the higher the educational levels (Furstenberg et al., 1969; Ladner, 1972; Valien and Fitzgerald, 1949). Nevertheless, urban black middle-class females preferred smaller families, used the most effective available birth control method—pills and IUD—and had lower fertility rates. In contrast, urban and rural poor females also preferred smaller families, yet were using less effective birth control methods—preparations available at drug stores and condoms—and as a result, had higher fertility rates than they desired (Furstenberg et al., 1969; Linn et al., 1978; Westoff, 1970).

Moreover, there was evidence that both partners wanted to use some type of contraceptive and felt the decision should not be the sole responsibility of either partner (Johnson and Samples, 1979; Vadies and Hale, 1977). Yet studies have indicated that some black women are poorly informed regarding the human reproductive system and lack accurate information regarding birth control. Johnson and Snow (1982) in their assessment of low-income, undereducated black clientele at a prenatal clinic regarding their knowledge of family planning found that majority of the women had had at least one unwanted pregnancy. Their lack of knowledge concerning reproduction and the appropriate use of birth control contributed to these unwanted pregnancies. Furthermore there were sex differences in motives to act to control family size patterns among blacks. Data indicated that feelings of powerlessness, value of children, and fear of racial genocide were important variables in explaining and predicting birth control use among black males (Bauman and Udry, 1972; Treadwell, 1972; Tobin et al., 1975). In contrast to black males, poor black females in 17 cities failed to support the idea that high feelings of powerlessness lead to selection of poor or no contraceptive methods (Morris and Sison, 1974). Furthermore, among black females, the most frequently cited reason for wanting to limit family size were economics and desire to control their lives (Cochrane et al., 1973; Gustavos and Mammen, 1973; Treadwell, 1972). The best predictors of birth control use among black females were information about contraceptives, past experiences of failure with birth control methods, and intention to act (Haney et al., 1974; Kothandapani, 1971; Linn et al., 1978). Hence there were sex differences among blacks in motivations to practice birth control. Nevertheless, although black adults wanted to control for the probability of pregnancy, the role of parent was considered a significant indicator of adulthood (Scott, 1976). Therefore, a review of literature on behavior of black adults in parental roles follows.

PARENTAL ROLE

PATERNAL ROLE

Historically, the role of black males as fathers has been controversial (Cross, 1978; Elkins, 1959; Frazier, 1939; Herskovits, 1958; Hill, 1971; Moynihan, 1965; Staples, 1971b; Wilkinson and Taylor, 1977). Moreover, it has been suggested that lover and sexual partner were the most salient interpersonal adult roles for black males, and paternity was viewed as a mark of masculinity and not an adult role to implement (Buckhout, 1971; Staples, 1978). This lack of understanding and knowledge about the contributions of fathers to the socialization process has been true also for white fathers (Lamb, 1976). In contrast to black fathers, however, it was assumed that white fathers functioned in their role, and the reason there was limited scientific evidence concerning their influence was the fault of social scientists, who frequently used mothers as subjects in investigating parental roles (Lamb, 1976).

Subsequently, in recent years there were attempts to fill this void in scientific knowledge concerning white fathers as a result of inquiries into the social affectional systems of infants and changes in the family structure in contemporary society (Lamb, 1976). In the same manner, there was an increase in investigations of the role of black fathers, but these studies were generated for different reasons. Research projects and articles were initially reactions to the reported matriarchal black family structure (Moynihan, 1965). Later explorations continued as a result of the shortcomings in the literature and limited knowledge regarding demographic differences among black fathers.

The major shortcomings in the body of scientific knowledge were that researchers (a) failed to recognize the existence of a black culture and the antecedent African experience and examine social roles in that context (Nobles, 1980; Peters, 1974); (b) neglected to interview black fathers and observe father-child interactions for demographic differences (J. McAdoo, 1979); (c) observed and investigated black family life using the very poorest families as subjects and generalized the findings to all black families (Billingsley, 1968); and (d) used theoretical models limited to Western cultural life-styles (Nobles, 1980).

Indeed, the devaluing of black fathers in data analysis and policies implemented by social agencies was not lost on black males. Studies revealed that they resented being treated as absent and ineffectual fathers and viewed themselves as salient figures in the lives of their children and active participants in the child rearing process (Cazenave, 1977; Coles, 1977; Hopkins, 1977; J. McAdoo, 1979). In addition, consistent with the customs of their culture, black males have assumed the paternal role in the status of boyfriend and as members of a kinship network system (Schultz, 1971; Stack, 1974). Importantly, because black males were thwarted in their role as economic provider—one aspect of the father role—did not preclude failure in all aspects of the father role.

In the socialization process, parents function as models, socializing agents, and figures for identification. Several reports of black family life indicated that black males fulfilled these psychological aspects of the father role (Aseltine, 1978; Billingsley, 1968; Blassingame, 1972; Gutman, 1976; Hill, 1971; H. McAdoo, 1978; J. McAdoo, 1979). Indeed, highly mobile, as compared to less mobile, black males reported strong attempts to identify with their fathers and pressure from their mothers to be like him (Moulton and Stewart, 1971). In contrast, there were reported findings of failures of black males in the father role (Frazier, 1939; Rainwater, 1970). It is difficult to ascertain, however, whether these and similar studies were reporting that black fathers had no impact or influence, or whether their reported values and behaviors were inconsistent with middle-class and Western theoretical models of parenting and thus were negative and ineffectual.

From the start, research investigations of parental roles among black men were more concerned with effects of father absence rather than presence. Psychoanalytic theoretical discussions suggested that the combination of absent fathers and mother-dominated household structures among black families would have a negative impact on socialization of black children (Thomas and Sillen, 1972). The subsequent studies of black family life were criticized for several reasons (Billingsley, 1971; Breyer and May, 1970; Gary, 1974; Scott, 1976). Notably, social scientists generally compared children from poor black families with multiple problems, one of which was father absence, to children from white middle-class families, with father present, on a number of child behavioral variables. The negative findings for black children were attributed directly to the effect of father absence or mother-dominated households, and there were no attempts to control for the effects of confounding of variables.

In the same manner, critics noted how investigations failed to acknowledge the impact of the wider black community, culture differences in role prescriptions, and importance of kinship systems, which were documented and postulated as important mediating variables (Barnes, 1980; H. McAdoo, 1978; Stack, 1974). Furthermore, the accumulated evidence on the impact of father absence reflected an inconsistency in findings (Badaines, 1976; D'Andrade, 1973; Earl and Lohmann, 1978; Keller and Murray, 1973; Longebaugh, 1973; Rubin, 1974). This inconsistency may be explained by the criticisms discussed previously. This position does not dismiss father absence as inconsequential; rather, it states what scientific data are needed for more definite statements of effects and how black culture and life-style might mitigate the impact of the socialization process. Besides, there was evidence that black mothers functioned in an instrumental and expressive manner (Beckett, 1976; Hannerz, 1977), and father absence was shown to alter the mother-child relationship (D'Andrade, 1973; Longebaugh, 1973). Hence, a discussion of the maternal role of black females follows.

MATERNAL ROLE

The contributions of black women in their role as mother in Africa and America were acknowledged and described (Billingsley, 1968; Blassingame, 1972; Herskovits, 1958; Gutman, 1976; Staples, 1971a, 1971b, 1973). Indeed the most prevalent image of black women in poetry by blacks is the image of mother (Rushing, 1978). Yet performance of black women in their role of mother has generated myths and stereotypes that have dominated the research literature on black families for the past decade. Data generated from numerous studies were most critical of the behavior of black mothers as reinforcing agents. Generally, mother-child interactions were viewed as detrimental to sex-role socializations, cognitive development, and a variety of personality traits in black children (D'Andrade, 1973; Lott and Lott, 1963; Thomas and Sillen, 1972). As noted previously, these studies of black family life were subsequently criticized. Consequently, research projects were designed and discussions initiated to note the limitations of previous studies and view the parenting style of black mothers from the perspective of their own culture (Banks et al., 1979; Boykin, 1979; Gary, 1974; Franklin, 1979; Willie, 1974). Data indicated and discussions suggested that black mothers were reinforcing behavior that facilitated the coping skills of black children in dealing with a dualism in their lives, being black in a racist society and acquiring the necessary skills to advance in the dominant culture.

Similarly, performance evaluations of black mothers as role models and figures of identification were inconsistent (Halpern, 1973; Peters, 1974; Scott, 1976). Interestingly, research investigations have found, when black and white children were compared, that blacks had less sexual dimorphism of expression of pleasure (Balkwell et al., 1978), more androgynous attitudes (Johnson, 1977; Kleinke and Nicholson, 1979), and a less stereotypic view of sex role (Gold and St. Ange, 1974). In short, data suggested that the feminine behavior model that black mothers presented shaped the sex-role perceptions of black children toward a more androgynous view. Still, more investigations are needed. Mothers were presenting behaviors of a more active involvement in their world that contributed to the androgynous attitudes that were being formulated by the children. Indeed, there is evidence on the implementation of the maternal role among black mothers for clarification and correction of criticism noted earlier.

Black women have consistently indicated that they value the role of mother and consider it an important aspect of their sex-role identity (Harrison, 1977). Indeed, there was evidence that black women sometimes gave the mother role priority over the wife and worker roles (Blood and Wolfe, 1971; Harrison and Minor, 1978). In other words, it is evident that conflict will arise between these social roles because of personal time and energy constraints. Whenever interrole conflicts emerge, some black women attempt to resolve the conflict by putting their children's needs before their husbands' or employers' demands. In families headed by women with no husband present, the woman has a heavy load from the demands of adult roles. Clearly these women can benefit from a more aggressive governmental policy that speaks to their problems (Simms, 1986).

In addition, black women generally have internalized the black community's perceptions of them as strong, independent, and resourceful persons (Ladner, 1972; Watson, 1974). Recently this image has been criticized as dehumanizing because it lacks consideration of human frailties and complexities (Walker, 1983). During the 1960s and 1970s, the image of the strong black woman was criticized and attacked as inappropriate and counterproductive to a healthy black community by black civil rights organizations that were extremely sexist (Giddings, 1984). As noted by Giddings, "Historically, racial necessity has made black women redefine the notion of womanhood to integrate the concepts of work, achievement, and independence into their role as women" (p. 356). Indeed it was within the domestic life style of slaves where egalitarianism between the sexes emerged. According to Davis (1983), "They transformed that negative equality which emanated from the equal oppression they suffered as slaves into a positive quality: the egalitarianism characterizing their social relations" (p. 18). Thus black mothers have placed a high value on their femininity as self-defined and their role as mothers.

SUMMARY

There has been a decline in birth rates among blacks for the past three decades and further decline is predicted for the future. Nevertheless, black adults have not concurrently devalued parental roles.

Implementations of the paternal role by black males were controversial in the research literature, and the need for further scientific investigations was discussed. Black fathers valued their role, yet few studies have revealed their perspective of role prescriptions. The reasons for this lack of knowledge can be attributed to several criticisms of studies of black family life.

In the past decade, studies of parental roles were dominated by investigations of the performance of black females in their role as mother. Theoretical postulations and data from several studies were critical of their performance as reinforcing agents, models, and figures of identification. The reactions to this negative portrayal have resulted in critical examinations of the body of scientific knowledge and creation of innovative and sensitive approaches to the study of black culture.

REFERENCES

ASELTINE, G. (1978) "Family socialization perceptions among black and white high school students." Journal of Negro Education 47 (Summer): 256-266.

BADAINES, J. (1976) "Identification, imitation, and sex-role preference in father-present and father-absent black and Chicano boys." Journal of Psychology 92 (January): 15-24.

BALKWELL, C., J. BALSWICK and J. BALKWELL (1978) "On black and white family patterns in America: their impact on the expressive aspect of sex-role socialization." Journal of Marriage and the Family 40(4): 743-747.

BANKS, W., C. McQUATER, and J. L. HUBBARD (1979) "Toward a reconceptualization of the social-cognitive bases of achievement orientations in blacks," pp. 294-311 in A. W. Boykins, A. J. Franklin, and J. F. Yates (eds.) Research Directions of Black Psychologists. New York: Russell Sage.

BARNES, E. (1980) "The black community as the source of positive self-concept for black children: a theoretical perspective," pp. 106-1130 in R. J. Jones (ed.) Black Psychology. New York: Harper and Row.

BAUMAN, K. and R. UDRY (1972) "Powerlessness and regularity of contraception in an urban Negro male sample: a research note." Journal of Marriage and the Family 34(1): 112-114.

BECKETT, J. O. (1976) "Working wives: a racial comparison." Social Work 21 (November): 463-471.

BILLINGSLEY, A. (1968) Black Families in White America. Englewood Cliffs, NJ: Prentice Hall.

———(1971) "The treatment of Negro families in American scholarship," in R. Staples (ed.) Black Families in America: Essays and Studies. Belmont, CA: Wadsworth.

BLASSINGAME, J. (1972) The Slave Community. New York: Oxford Press.

BLOOD, R. O. and D. M. WOLFE (1971) "Negro-White differences in blue-collar marriages in a northern metropolis," pp. 171-177 in R. Staples (ed.) The Black Family: Essays and Studies. Belmont, CA: Wadsworth.

BOYKIN, A. W. (1979) "Black psychology and the research process: keeping the baby but throwing out the bath water," pp. 85-103 in A. J. Boykin, A. J. Franklin, and J. F. Yates (eds.) Research Directions of Black Psychologists. New York: Russell Sage.

BREYER, N. L. and J. C. MAY (1970) "Effect of sex and race of the observer and model on imitative learning." Psychological Reports 27(2): 639-646.

BUCKHOUT, R. (1971) "The war on people: a scenario for population control." Environment and Behavior 3 (September): 322-344.

CAZENAVE, C., C. VINCENT, C. HANEY, and R. MICHIELUTTE (1973) "Motivational determinants of family planning clinic attendance." Journal of Psychology 84 (May): 33-43.

CAZENAVE, N. (1977) "Middle-income black fathers: an analysis of the prouder role." The Family Coordinator 28 (October): 583-593.

COCHRANE, C. C., V. C. HANEY, AND R. MICHIELATTE (1973) "Motivational determinatants of family planning clinic attendance." Journal of Psychology 84 (May): 33-43.

COLES, R. (1977) "Black fathers," pp. 85-101 in D. Wilkinson and R. Taylor (eds.) The Black Male in America. Chicago: Nelson-Hall.

CROSS, W. E. (1978) "Black family and black identity: a literature review." Western Journal of Black Studies 2 (Summer): 111-124.

D'ANDRADE, R. (1973) "Father absence, identification, and identity." Ethos 1 (Winter): 440-445.

DAVIS, A. Y. (1983) Women, Race and Class. New York: Random House.

EARL, L. and N. LOHMAN (1978) "Absent fathers and black male children." Social Work 23 (September): 413-415.

ELKINS, S. (1959) Slavery. Chicago: University of Chicago Press.

ENTWISTLE, D. and E. GREENBERGER (1972) "Adolescents' views of women's work roles." American Journal of Orthopsychiatry 42 (July): 648-656.

Family Coordinator (1979) "Men's Roles in the Family." Special issue, Vol. 28 (October).

FARLEY, R. (1970) Growth of the Black Population. Chicago: Markham.

FRANKLIN, A. J. (1979) "Recall and memory organization from variations in list content: a test of the culture-specific hypothesis," pp. 241-252 in A. W. Boykin, A. J. Franklin, and J. F. Yates (eds.) Research Directions of Black Psychologists. New York: Russell Sage.

FRAZIER, E. F. (1939) The Negro Family in the United States. Chicago: University of Chicago Press.

FURSTENBERG, F., L. GORDIS, and M. MARKOWITZ (1969) "Birth control knowledge and attitude among unmarried pregnant adolescents." Journal of Marriage and the Family 31(1): 34-42.

GARY, L. E. [ed.] (1974) Social Research in the Black Community. Washington, DC: Howard University Press.

GIDDINGS, P. (1984) When and Where I Enter: The Impact of Black Women on Race and Sex in America. New York: William Morrow.

GOLD, A. and C. St. ANGE (1974) "Development of sex-role stereotypes in black and white elementary school girls." Developmental Psychology 10(3): 461.

GUSTAVOS, S. and K. MAMMEN (1973) "Black-White differentials in the family size preferences among youth." Pacific Sociological Review 16: 107-119.

GUTMAN, H. (1976) The Black Family in Slavery and Freedom, 1750-1925. New York: Pantheon.

HALPERN, F. (1973) Survival: Black/White. New York: Pergamon.

HANEY, C., R. MICHIELUTTE, C. VINCENT, and C. COCHRANE (1974) "Factors associated with the poverty of black women." Sociology and Social Research 59(1): 40-49.

HANNERZ, V. (1977) "Growing up male," pp. 33-59 in D. Wilkinson and R. Taylor (eds.) The Black Male in America. Chicago: Nelson-Hall.

HARRISON, A. (1977) "Black Women," pp. 131-146 in V. O'Leary, Toward Understanding Women. Monterey, CA: Brooks/Cole.

HARRISON, A. and J. MINOR (1978) "Interrole conflict, coping strategies, and satisfaction among black working wives." Journal of Marriage and the Family 40 (November): 799-805.

HERSKOVITS, M. J. (1958) The Myth of the Negro Past. Boston: Beacon.

HILL, R. B. (1971) The Strength of Black Families. New York: Emerson Hall.

HOPKINS, T. (1977) "The role of community agencies as viewed by black fathers." American Journal of Orthopsychiatry 42 (April): 508-516.

JOHNSON, J. (1977) "Androgyny and the maternal principle." School Review 86(1): 50-69.

JOHNSON, L. and R. STAPLES (1979) "Family planning and the young minority male: a pilot project." The Family Coordinator 28 (October): 535-543.

JOHNSON, S. M. and L. F. SNOW (1982) "Assessment of reproductive knowledge in an inner-city clinic." Social Science Medicine 16(19): 1657-62.

KELLER, P. and E. MURRAY (1973) "Imitative aggression with adult male and female models in father absent and father present Negro boys." Journal of Genetic Psychology 122 (June): 217-221.

KLEINKE, C. L. and T. NICHOLSON (1979) "Black and white children's awareness of de facto race and sex difference." Developmental Psychology 15(2): 84-86.

KOTHANDAPANI, V. (1971) "Validation of feeling, belief, and intention to act as three components of attitude and their contribution to prediction of contraceptive behavior." Journal of Personality and Social Psychology 19 (September): 321-333.

LADNER, J. (1972) Tomorrow's Tomorrow. Garden City, NY: Doubleday.

LAMB, M. E. (1976) The Role of the Father in Child Development. New York: John Wiley.

LINN, M., J. CARMICHAEL, P. KLITENICK, and N. WEBB (1978) "Fertility related attitude of minority mothers with large and small families." Journal of Applied Social Psychology 8 (January-March): 1-14.

LONGEBAUGH, R. (1973) "Mother behavior as a variable moderating the effects of father absence." Ethos 1 (Winter): 456-465.

LOTT, A. and B. LOTT (1963) Negro and White Youth: A Psychological Study in a Border-State Community. New York: Holt, Rinehart and Winston.

McADOO, H. (1978) "Factors related to stability in upwardly mobile black families." Journal of Marriage and the Family 40 (November): 761-776.

McADOO, J. (1979) "Father-child interaction patterns and self-esteem in black preschool children." Young Children 34 (January): 46-53.

McFALLS, J. F. and G. S. MASNICK (1981) "Birth control and the fertility of the U.S. black population, 1880 to 1980." Journal of Family History 89 (Spring): 89-105.

MORRIS, N. and B. SISON (1974) "Correlates of female powerlessness: parity, methods of birth control pregnancy." Journal of Marriage and the Family 36(4): 708-713.

MOULTON, R. and L. STEWART (1971) "Parents as models for mobile and low-mobile black males." Vocational Guidance Quarterly 19 (June): 247-253.

MOYNIHAN, D. P. (1965) The Negro Family: The Case for National Action. U.S. Department of Labor. Washington, DC: Government Printing Office.

NOBLES, W. (1980) "African philosophy: foundations for black psychology," pp. 23-36 in R. L. Jones (ed.) Black Psychology. New York: Harper and Row.

PETERS, M. F. (1974) "The black family-perpetuating the myths: an analysis of family sociology textbook treatment of black families." The Family Coordinator 23 (October): 349-357.

RAINWATER, L. (1970) Behind Ghetto Walls. Chicago: AVC.

RUBIN, R. (1974) "Adult male absence and the self-attitudes of black children." Child Study Journal 4(1) 33-46.

RUSHING, A. B. (1978) "Images of black women in Afro-American poetry," pp. 74-84 in S. Harley and R. Terborg-Penn (eds.) The Afro-American Woman: Struggles and Images. Port Washington, NY: Kennikat.

SCHULTZ, D. (1971) "The role of the boyfriend," pp. 94-100 in R. Staples (ed.) The Black Family: Essays and Studies. Belmont, CA: Wadsworth.

SCOTT, P. B. (1976) "A critical overview of sex roles research on black families." Women Studies Abstracts: 1-13.

SIMMS, M. C. (1986) "Black women who head families: an economic struggle," pp. 141-151 in M. C. Simms and J. M. Malveaux (eds.) Slipping Through the Cracks: The Status of Black Women. New Brunswick, NJ: Transaction.

SLY, D. (1970) "Minority group status and fertility." American Journal of Sociology 76(3): 443-450.

STACK, C. B. (1973) The Black Woman in America. Chicago: Nelson-Hall.

⸺ (1974) All Our Kin: Strategies for Survival in a Black Community. New York: Harper and Row.

⸺ (1978) "Masculinity and race: the dual dilemma of black men." Journal of Social Issues 34 (Winter): 169-183.

STAPLES, R. (1971a) "The myth of the black matriarchy." The Black Scholar 2: 2-9.

⸺ (1971b) "Towards a sociology of the black family: A theoretical and methodological assessment." Journal of Marriage & the Family 33: 119-138.

⸺ (1973) The Black Woman in America: Sex, Marriage, and the Family. Chicago: Nelson Hall.

⸺ (1978) "Black family life and development," pp. 73-94 in L.E. Gary (ed.) Mental Health: A Challenge to the Black Community. Philadelphia: Dorrance.

THOMAS, A. and S. SILLEN (1972) Racism and Psychiatry. New York: Brunner/Mazel.

TOBIN, P. W., W. CLIFFORD, R. MUSTIAN, and A. DAVIS (1975) "Value of children and fertility behavior in a tri-racial, rural county." Journal of Comparative Family Studies 6 (Spring): 46-55.

TREADWELL, J. (1972) "Is abortion black genocide?" Family Planning Perspectives 4(1): 4-5.

U.S. Bureau of the Census (1977) Population Reports. Washington, DC: Government Printing Office.

U.S. National Center for Health Statistics (1986) Advance Data from Vital and Health Statistics. Washington, DC: Government Printing Office.

VADIES, E. and D. HALE (1977) "Attitudes of adolescent males towards abortion, contraception, and sexuality." Social Work in Health Care 3 (Winter): 169-174.

VALIEN, P. and A. FITZGERALD (1949) "Attitudes of the Negro mother toward birth control." American Journal of Sociology 55(3): 279-283.

WALKER, A. (1973) In Search of Our Mothers' Gardens. San Diego: Harcourt Brace Jovanovich.

WATSON, V. (1974) "Self-concept formation and the Afro-American woman." Journal of Afro-American Issues 2(3): 226-236.

WESTOFF, C. (1970) "Contraceptive practice among urban blacks in the United States, 1965." Milbank Memorial Fund Quarterly 48(2): 215-233.

WILKINSON, D. and R. TAYLOR [eds.] (1977) The Black Male in America. Chicago: Nelson-Hall.

WILLIE, C. (1974) A New Look at Black Families. Englewood Cliffs, NJ: Prentice-Hall.

PART IV

SOCIALIZATION WITHIN
AFRICAN-AMERICAN FAMILIES

Marie Peters begins this section with a historical overview of the Black family socialization literature. She shows how the early works were descriptive and used the comparative deficit-oriented approach, finally becoming more value free in the ecological approach. In her excellent review, she points out the major contributions made by the various studies and gives a critique of the weaknesses of several of the noted studies. For instance, many studies did not mention race; others focused only on the mother-child relationship and no other or used simplistic correlation and excluded possible influences of other factors. There are critiques also of the different intervention methods and of the questionable research methodology used in earlier studies. Peters traces the literature through the early stages on through the war on poverty to the present. Several key variables are then detailed: protectiveness, discipline, idiosyncratic rearing practices, and changes in parental values. Her examination brings light to some of the dim concepts commonly held about socialization, while the blurring of sex-typed roles in family tasks and child-caring of both parents and children is mentioned. There have been changes in parental values of those who are upwardly mobile or who prepare their children for mobility through "anticipatory socialization." The differences that do exist in Black lifestyles are presented within the context of the family's attempt to shield the child from a hostile environment as long as possible.

John McAdoo describes the limited literature available on the father's involvement in his child's development. An extensive review is given of father stereotypes, the differential role he plays, his influence on the mother, his involvement in child-related decision making, and the interaction patterns and expectations he holds for his children. The earlier, exclusive reliance on his instrumental role has changed to one of greater involvement. Fathers themselves rate the companionship of the child as primary and not their instrumental role. As fathers gain more economic security, they tend to become more involved with their children. Decision making has moved from dominance to a greater egalitarian sharing between father and mother. The chapter gives a delineation between authoritarian and authoritative fathering, and shows that the father-child interactions of Blacks have tended to be more supportive for the achievement and independence of girls rather than boys. The parent-child interaction is not unidirectional but circular. The Black father's role is still not clearly understood. Fathers of all races have similar expectations for their children, but may use different approaches. Few ethnic differences have been found in actual parenting style. The reciprocal relationship between father and child has yet to be researched adequately.

Wilhelmina Manns discusses the roles played by significant others in the lives of Black families. These are the persons who one would like to hold one in high esteem and are influential in one's life. These significant others are those persons who have been found to be the components of the extended family support networks, both kin and nonkin, who enable families to survive under continuing adversity. Nonrelatives were often found to be as influential as relatives, highlighting the elasticity of the extended family. Those of lower status and with few financial resources have been found to have more people who are significant kin. Blacks of lower incomes have been found to have a greater number of significant others, to offset their negative life experiences. Black parents were important in relation to achievement. Lower-income parents mandated achievement, and middle-income parents provided an achievement-oriented atmosphere. However, neither group was extensively involved in teaching as a component of their support. The parental influence lasted throughout the life cycle, with more Blacks having parents who were significant in these dimensions well into adulthood. The other relatives who were supportive tended to do this by providing models, while the nonrelative supporters tended to be members of structured institutions such as the church or community center.

James Jackson, Wayne McCullough, and Gerald Gurin have presented a new chapter on the role of the family in the formation of identity and socialization in Black American society. They examine the roles the family plays in the development of the child's group identity and consciousness. The family forms a buffer within the home that protects the child and then gradually introduces him or her into the heterogeneous, often hostile society, and remains a refuge for the child, as pointed out by Peters. An extensive review is given of the differences found in the pre- and post-civil rights literature. The earlier studies related a negative effect of Black identification, and all accepted the premise of self-hatred, yet they did not measure the racial attitude and self-concept variables separately. The post-civil rights research looked at the positive psychological effect of a strong Black identification and went beyond simple measures of association. The racial homogeneity of the home is felt to aid in the personal identification of race, to assist the child in the compartmentalization of their private and public selves, and to filter the impact of the nonsupportive environment. The child then is able to go out in the heterogeneous environment and be successful. The family is seen as the mediating link between the individual's self-concept and the individual's racial group. The call is made for the refinement of group identity theories.

15

PARENTING IN BLACK FAMILIES WITH YOUNG CHILDREN
A Historical Perspective

MARIE FERGUSON PETERS

Most Black parents, as do most parents in every society, socialize their children to become self-sufficient, competent adults as defined by the society in which they live. For Black families in the United States, socialization occurs within the ambiguities of a cultural heritage that is both Afro-American and Euro-American and a social system that espouses both democratic equality for all citizens and caste-like status for its Black citizens. Although social scientists have appreciated the uniqueness of Blacks, research on Black children and their families has generally been simplistic and often pejorative in approach (Allen, 1978; Mathis, 1978).

Today, many social scientists are moving beyond the comparative, pathological approach of much of the research of the sixties and early seventies and are beginning to study Black families from a perspective that recognizes the cultural variations, functionality, and validity of Black family lifestyles. This research has begun to provide basic information about parenting in Black families. The purpose of this chapter is to describe briefly the history of research on the behaviors and attitudes of Black parents and to summarize the major findings concerning child rearing and the parent-child relationships that many families with young Black children share.

Because the topics social scientists choose to research and the scientific research methodologies they use reflect the prevailing philosophies and concerns of the time, research which has focused on Black mothers and fathers has changed through the years. Early research was descriptive. It was generally replaced by comparative deficit-oriented research. Currently, much research on Black parenting and parent-child interaction employs ecologically oriented and culturally relevant approaches.

CRITIQUE OF RESEARCH APPROACHES

For those interested in parent-child relationships in Black or other minority families, a search of the literature reveals many methodological weaknesses and problems in many of the available studies. The most prevalent shortcomings include the following: (1) Many studies do not specify the race of the participants. Culture-specific influences are thus ignored. (2) Research is often unidirectional: The focus is typically on mother's influence on child and does not observe child's influence on mother. (3) When the research population involves both Black and white parents, the research design, typically, compares Blacks to whites and comparative statistics are used. Rarely is the research ethnomethodological and descriptive. (4) Simplistic correlations often exclude the possible influences of other environmental forces. For example, in the Radin and Kamii study (1965), it was assumed that if a child identified with a warm mother, the child's intellectual development would be positive. Yet teacher warmth was not measured, nor was the child's relationship with other adults in the family considered. The influence of kin in the lives of Black children has been well documented (McAdoo, 1978; Nobles, 1977; Stack, 1974). (5) Researchers tend to view Black families as monolithic. Few studies incorporate both lower-class and middle-class Black families in the study population. Consequently, the accessibility of lower-class families in welfare agencies or urban schools (and their concomitant absence in college communities) generally influences researchers to use the all-inclusive category of race as a monolithic variable. (6) When Blacks are studied, so-called problem populations are often the focus of research—single parents; parents of emotionally disturbed, mentally retarded, or academically nonachieving or delinquent children, and/or youths; or low-income families. The majority of Blacks are ordinary American citizens not in special trouble categories, but are typically not included in these research studies. (7) The research design used to study an all-Black population often differs from that used to study whites. When a white population is used, an investigation may be concerned with process, examining how various influences affect the subjects in the study. This central concern shifts subtly to one of intervention when a Black population is involved. The focus of research becomes *changing* the target subject to conform to the abilities and behaviors of white parents and children, and investigators are concerned with the achievement or nonachievement of this goal. (8) Studies that examine parent-child interaction and include Blacks in their sample are often conducted in an unfamiliar, intimidating experiment room. Data are often correlated with IQ or SES and are typically based on but one or two observations. We know parent-child interaction is much higher in a laboratory setting than in the natural setting of the home. (9) The presence of an outside "expert" is often an unmeasured influence. Studies have shown that when the research study or intervention program requires visiting homes with a bag of toys and books and observing or recording parent-child interaction with these special toys/books only, mothers talk to their child more than they normally do every day. (10) The research methodology may incorporate subjective measures of the quality of home environments—based on the researcher's personal unarticulated values, such as organization versus disorganization or "quiet" home environment believed to be conducive to study versus high noise level and activity, presumed to be distracting and confusing to a child.

DESCRIPTIVE APPROACHES

Systematic research on Black families was first approached within a descriptive framework which recognized the pressures, demands, and extreme constraints of the environment in which Blacks lived. This research essentially provided facts about Blacks and described aspects of the lives of Black families. Publishing the first sociological study of Black families in America in 1908, W. E. B. Du Bois described the social conditions of Afro-American families living in Philadelphia at the beginning of this century. He accounted for the influences of Africa and of slavery on the development of Black people. However, Du Bois said little about child rearing. Some years later, social scientists such as Charles S. Johnson, in his books *Shadow of the Plantation* and *Growing Up in the Black Belt,* provided insightful descriptions of family life among Blacks in the South, including child rearing and socialization practices. The publications of social scientists before World War II, such as historian Carter G. Woodson, together with the slave narratives collected during the thirties have provided a rich source of descriptive data essential to understanding Black family life today. However, during and after World War II, descriptive approaches to research on the Black family began to be eclipsed by more sophisticated research methodologies patterned after the physical sciences (see Lewin, 1935). This approach reflected changing perspectives in this country regarding race.

COMPARATIVE DEFICIT APPROACHES

During the forties and fifties research was highly stimulated by the assimilation theories of two outstanding sociologists, Robert Park of the University of Chicago and Gunnar Myrdal, author of *An American Dilemma*. The theories of Park and the writings of Myrdal, in assuming that assimilation of Blacks into American society was possible and probable, helped to provide a scientific basis for research which investigated why Blacks were not assimilating into American society (Lyman, 1972). They articulated a rationale for comparative deficit approaches which assume Blacks are culturally deprived and view differences found between white mainstream Americans and Black Americans as deficits. Behaviors, abilities, or attitudes observed in Black mothers, it was assumed, "needed to be changed" (see Mathis, 1978).

The perspectives of sociologists studying Black families, in shifting from descriptive research to comparative deficit approaches, reported findings about Black families within a Black/white comparative framework. For example, Davis and Dollard (1940), two of the first researchers to describe in detail the socialization of Black children, analyzed Black families according to class, structure, and parental roles. Comparing Black families to white families, they reported Black mothers were more restrictive than white mothers in toilet training and more likely to employ physical punishment in disciplining their young children. Twenty-five years later, Radin and Kamii (1965), whose innovative methodology has served as a model for much parent-child observational research, similarly provides an example of this approach. In the Radin and Kamii study a small group (45) of "culturally deprived" Black mothers, over half of whom received public assistance, and a small group (50) of middle-class white mothers were observed in a laboratory play room. Their behaviors in interacting with their preschool child were compared. The finding that Black mothers often shield children from problems was interpreted by these researchers as "overprotective." Neither the importance of varying influences of environmental differences in the home situations nor the differential effects of the laboratory observations on the mothers was acknowledged in this interpretation of the research findings.

In many similar studies, if white mothers participated, Black mothers were compared to whites directly; if white mothers were not part of the study, the Black mothers were compared to whites indirectly and by assumption. In either case, the Black mothers were viewed negatively, as generally inferior and as unable to fulfill their responsibilities adequately.

Frazier's classic study, *The Negro Family in the United States,* a major source of information about Black families, provides a dramatic illustration of the comparative deficit approach. In this and other works (Frazier, 1933, 1950) Frazier accurately reported findings, descriptive of Black families, but interpreted the behaviors of Blacks pejoratively. He supplied a model for the study of Blacks which emphasized family disorganization and dysfunction—an approach that directly influenced subsequent research of the sixties and early seventies. The influential government-sponsored Moynihan report (1965) viewed differences between Blacks and whites as deficits and identified Black "matriarchal" mothers as responsible for the "breakdown" and "pathology" of Black families (who, he claimed, were responsible for high rates of illegitimacy, delinquency, and unemployment). The deficit perspective of Moynihan spawned more than a decade of research that focused on improving the child-rearing practices of Black mothers, and it influenced many of the programs and policies subsequently developed for Black children and their parents.

In response to the government's "war on poverty" efforts, a number of sociologists and psychologists turned their research interests to low-income Black families who received public assistance and who lived in public housing or in inner-city ghettoes. These findings on low-income families, although about a minority of the Black population, became generally accepted as descriptive of the family life of all Blacks in America (Hannerz, 1969; Liebow, 1966; Rainwater, 1966; Schulz, 1969). In much research Black families were viewed as monolithic and were conceptually linked to data regarding low-income families. Socioeconomic differences were often assumed to be the same as Black/white differences. This methodological weakness made it difficult, if not impossible, to unravel the "packaged variable" of class and race in much of this research (Whiting, 1973). The comparative deficit perspective of most Black parent-Black child studies of this period influenced family sociology textbooks which similarly incorporated the cultural deprivation deficit approach (Peters, 1974).

ECOLOGICAL APPROACHES

Perhaps in reaction to the negativism of the comparative deficit approach and the criticisms of many social scientists of this research emphasis (Richardson, 1980), in the past decade much research on parenting in Black families shifted to an ecological approach. Similar to the earlier descriptive research, but incorporating the more sophisticated social science theories, methodologies, and techniques of the present, the ecological approach observes parental and child behavior within the environment in which it occurs and analyzes behavior according to the value system of a family's indigenous culture or subculture.

By providing a theoretical framework for ecologically oriented research, the writings of Lewin (1935) and Kuhn (1963) had an important influence on many researchers concerned with understanding the sociological and psychological factors involved. Black families and parent-child interaction were now examined from a culture-specific or functional perspective, and the Black family's socialization of its children was considered in terms of the values and realities of its Afro-American culture.

Research findings of ecologically oriented studies have dramatically changed the picture of parenting and child behaviors of Blacks and are providing interesting, myth-destroying information. It is assumed that Black families encourage the development of the skills, abilities, and behaviors necessary to survive as competent adults in a racially oppressive society (Willie, 1976), and a number of studies have investigated the characteristic, often culture-specific, child-rearing behaviors and survival mechanisms which enable Black parents to cope with everyday exigencies or with crisis situations (Gutman, 1976; Hill, 1971; Stack, 1974).

In general, Black families are reported to be strong, functional, and flexible (Aschenbrenner, 1973; Billingsley, 1968; Hill, 1972; Martin and Martin, 1978; Scanzoni, 1971, 1975; Stack, 1974). They provide a home environment that is culturally different from that of Euro-American families in a number of ways (Abrahams, 1970; Gay, 1975; Ladner, 1971; D. Lewis, 1975; Nobles, 1974a; Young, 1970). The environment of Black children is described as including not only the special stress of poverty or of discrimination but the ambiguity and marginality of living simultaneously in two worlds—the world of the Black community and the world of mainstream society, a phenomenon unique to Blacks (Willie, 1976). This perspective views Black children as socialized into a dual but normal existence of being both Afro-American and Euro-American, and many ambiguities and inconsistencies are reconciled without surprise or conflict (Dixon, 1971).

APPROACH TO DISCIPLINE

Discipline techniques of Black parents have often been noted by observers of Black parent-child interaction. Although definitive studies of discipline in Black families have yet to be done, many researchers have described the Black parent's more direct, physical form of discipline that differs from the psychologically oriented approach preferred by mainstream families, such as withdrawal of love or making approval or affection contingent on the child's behavior or accomplishment. The strict, no-nonsense discipline of Black parents—often characterized as "harsh" or "rigid" or "egocentrically motivated" by mainstream-oriented observers (Chilman, 1966)—has been shown to be functional, appropriate discipline of caring parents (Peters, 1976; Young, 1970).

A recent study of discipline techniques in a sample of working-class Black families reported that mothers became more dynamic in their disciplining as their young children began to understand the appropriate behavior parents expected. Most parents emphasized obedience. However, obedience was not viewed negatively; it was an important issue, often of special significance to a parent. Parents said that they believed obedience "will make life easier for my child," "means respect," "is equated with my love," or "is necessary if my child is to achieve in school" (Peters, 1981).

SOCIALIZATION TOWARD ENCOURAGEMENT OF NONCOMPETITIVE INDIVIDUALISM

A number of researchers have commented on the high value placed on personal uniqueness in Afro-American culture. Young (1970), who studied parental behavior and child-rearing practices of Black families in a southern community during the late sixties, noted the highly idiosyncratic interactions of mothers in the preparation of food, feeding, and toilet training of young children. Others (such as D. Lewis, 1975; H. Lewis, 1955) have described individualism within great interpersonal involvement of infants, children, and adults with one another. This individualism is often expressed in the way Black men and women as well as young Black boys and girls have been observed to interact with and respond to the infants and young children in the family (D. Lewis, 1975; Young, 1970).

SEX/AGE ROLES

Within many Black families more importance is attached to getting a job done than to the sex of the child for a task. Children's behaviors are viewed more in terms of the child's competency and age than the child's gender. The first-born, for example, whether boy or girl, is expected to become nurse-child to a younger child in many Black families (Young, 1970), and a high positive valuation is placed on "mothering," whether the person is male or female (D. Lewis, 1975).

COMPARATIVE RELEVANT APPROACHES

Concomitant with ecologically oriented research, comparative relevant studies have examined the child-rearing patterns of both Black and white parents with young children. This research perspective espouses cultural pluralism and uses the nonevaluative cultural variant model (Allen, 1978). The comparative relevant approach observes differences in behaviors but attempts to avoid enthnocentric judgments by focusing on process and through empirical research which attempts to link parental behaviors with child outcomes. Ethnicity, race, education, and social class indicators are typically controlled.

PARENT-CHILD COMMUNICATION

There have been many studies of parent-child communication patterns of Black and white parents and of differences in the verbalization of Black children compared to white children. Investigators have analyzed the grammar and language patterns of Black and white parents and their children. Although it has been found that Black parents talk to young children less than do white parents, the significance placed on race may be misleading. Schacter's (1979) review of this literature emphasizes the importance of social class. Studies show verbal stimulation to be a major factor in distinguishing between the environments of young children from economically advantaged and from economically disadvantaged homes. However, Schacter's research reported that "differences in total verbal production are related to maternal educational level and not to race. . . . Black mothers with educational and economic advantages speak just as much to their toddlers as do whites with similar advantages" (p. 155).

PARENTAL TEACHING STYLES

Black mothers, according to Hess et al. (1968), appear to prefer two types of teaching styles, both of which have an influence on the cognitive competence of four-year-old Black children. One style, which Hess et al. describe as the "personal-subjective" style, is responsive to the child—its needs, preferences, interests, moods, stage of development. The mothers who employ this style are concerned about the orientation and preparation a child needs in a new situation and try to make a task rewarding to their child. A second style is identified by Hess et al. as the "status-normative" teaching style. Mothers using this style tend to teach their child a task or insist on a certain behavior because it is the "correct" way or because it conforms to a rule or regulation. They do not generally consider the child's preferences. The differences between these two parenting behaviors appear to be quite similar to the differences between authoritative and authoritarian parenting styles identified by Baumrind (1972).

Hess's findings have been supported by other studies. For example, Schacter (1979: 65) reported that educated mothers "appear to adopt a responsive communication style." Similarly, Carew et al. (1976) found that the intellectual quality of the play activities created or encouraged by the mothers of toddlers correlated with their children's IQ at age three. Clarke-Stewart's (1973) study of Black/white working-class children age nine to eighteen months also reported that a relationship existed between parental behaviors and their child's academic abilities. The quantity of a mother's verbalization, the responsiveness, warmth, and stimulation of her interactions with her young child, significantly affected the child's intellectual development and linguistic performance.

A study of Black infants and preschool children by Andrews et al. (1975) reported that parents differed in their interactions with their children and that their children's subsequent social and cognitive behaviors reflected this difference. A series of studies conducted by Bradley and Caldwell (1976a, 1976b, 1978) and Elardo et al. (1975, 1977) found that measures of the child's home learning environment predicted IQ scores significantly better than did socioeconomic status (SES) variables typically used in studies of achievement or IQ. Slaughter (1978) examined linkages between parental teachings styles and children's cognitive development and play behaviors. Her findings, supporting the observations of Hess, Carew, Clarke-Stewart, and others, also show a relationship between specific maternal behaviors and children's abilities and behavioral styles. Mothers in Slaughter's study were supportive and nondirective with their children. White et al. (1977) reported that one- and two-year-old children whose caregivers talked to them a lot were developing better than children raised in a less verbal environment. Zegiob and Forehand (1975) investigated interactions of mothers and their children, ages four to six, in an experimental room equipped with toys. They found that the most significant factor in determining maternal interactive behavior was the socioeconomic status of the family. Other studies have reported similar findings.

PARENTAL ATTITUDES

Zegiob and Forehand (1975) observed that many Black parents were in the process of changing their values and attitudes. As they became upwardly mobile, many began to adopt middle-class values concerning child rearing. Scanzoni (1971) described how lower-class Black families prepare their children to be upwardly mobile via "anticipatory socialization." Thus parenting behavioral styles among Blacks may be in a state of flux. Many identify with middle-class value systems, especially when their own family is upwardly mobile.

These studies of parent-child interactions in their natural home environment provide the most reliable information available about childhood socialization. Although this research can only involve small samples, the rich descriptive data, often facilitated by audiovisual recordings, can enable us to view socialization processes in families with young children—to see what parents do, to understand why they do it, and to see the behavioral outcomes of their children.

THE IMPACT OF RACE ON PARENTING

An inescapable aspect of the socialization of Black children is that it prepares them for survival in an environment that is hostile, racist, and discriminatory against Blacks (Bernard, 1966). According to Harvard psychiatrist Pierce (1969), Black Americans live in a unique but mundane extreme environment of subtle to overt racism. Oppressive environmental forces influence how Black families live and raise their children (Peters, 1980). Research on the socialization of Black children supports these observations.

Daniel (1975) in a study of 25 Black fathers of preschool sons reported that 19 of the fathers mentioned specifically that race had an impact on their fathering. Renne (1970: 62) found that in Black families of all income levels, racial identity had a strong impact on the amount of protection a Black parent could provide a child. Even families with adequate income, wrote Renne, cannot protect their children completely from the "irrational restrictions, insults, and degradation black people encounter in this society." Renne further suggests that rearing children in a white-dominated society places special pressures on the black parent. However, as Harrison-Ross (Harrison-Ross and Wyden, 1973: xx-xxi) wrote in her manual on child rearing for Black parents, Black parents want "to bring their children up to be comfortable with their blackness, to be secure, to be proud, to be able to love. . . . [They] want their children to grow up being and feeling equal, comfortable, responsible, effective, and at home in the world they live in."

Peters and Massey (in press) describe how Black families have developed coping behaviors that enable them to deal with the racism they and their children may encounter. Black parents recognize that their children must be accepted in the Black community in order to have friends, and they must be accepted in the white community in order to survive. Parents understand the stress placed on their children when forced to perform better than whites in order to be recognized. Black parents, Peters and Massey summarized, "have internally developed patterns of coping with racial oppression, strategies proven to be effective in the past that are incorporated into their own socialization process" (p. 3).

In her study of Black mothers of young children, Richardson (1981: 154-164) reported that most parents believed "this society places more limitations on Blacks' life chances and opportunities than on any other group of people within the society" because of racism. They agreed that "being black in this country full of anti-black feelings and/or actions (racism) presents real problems." Their own experiences influence their decisions about how they will raise their children. In preparation for expected encounters with racism, the mothers in Richardson's study felt that it was necessary to develop high self-esteem and self-confidence in their children. Other studies of Black parenting have also reported the high priority Black parents give to developing self-esteem in their children (Peters, 1976; Peters and Massey, in press).

A number of parents decide not to discuss racism or discrimination with their children because they do not want them to feel bitter, resentful, or prejudiced against others (H. Lewis, 1955). These protective parents expect that their children will discover institutional or individual racism some day, and they are prepared to help children cope with this reality as necessary (Peters, 1976, 1981). Black parents provide a buffer for the negative messages that may be transmitted to their children by a society which perpetuates stereotypic images of Black people (Ogbu, 1978; Scanzoni, 1971).

SUMMARY

Researchers are beginning to learn about the socialization of young Black children and to explore how they grow and develop to become self-sufficient, competent adults in the face of the real constraints American society places on Black Americans. The lives of Black parents and their child-rearing approaches are embedded in the racial, cultural, and economic situations of Blacks in America. Research on parenting in Black families must reflect this reality.

Research on Black families overwhelmingly shows that the behaviors and lifestyles of Black people are different from those of whites. Their child-rearing priorities, attitudes, and patterns of behavior have developed out of the exigencies of the unique economic, cultural, and racial circumstances in which they have lived. However, because of the pervasive belief that Blacks can and should eventually assimilate into mainstream society once they learn the "ways" of white mainstream Americans, social scientists often have not recognized or been interested in the validity and functionality of the parenting behaviors Black families have developed based on the realities of survival in a continuing, hostile environment. Instead, social scientists have frequently viewed the adaptations of Black families to the circumstances of poverty and discrimination and the subtle behavioral aspects that reflect their African heritage, where they differed from the behaviors and living patterns of whites, as the source of "their problem." Research priorities, therefore, have often emphasized educating Blacks to conform to the values and behaviors of mainstream white Americans.

Recently, however, researchers are describing the child-rearing patterns and socialization practices of Black parents from the perspective of their effectiveness as relevant, supportive, or practical strategies appropriate to the social realities Black people face. Mainstream America and its social scientists are becoming aware of a reality in American life that Blacks cannot, for long, forget—that this is a cultural pluralistic country and the historical roots of its multiethnic peoples are varying, valuable, and strong. As Richardson has observed (1981: 100-101), the cultural styles and child-rearing approaches unique to Black families have enabled them "to provide supportive and effective environments for the development of black children." Research into the parenting and socialization of Black children promises to provide rich data essential for developing social and educational policies by local, state, or federal governing agencies which determine and support programs directed at Black families and Black children.

REFERENCES

ABRAHAMS, R. D. (1970) Deep Down in the Jungle. Chicago: AVC.

ALLEN, W. R. (1978) "The search for applicable theories in Black family life." Journal of Marriage and the Family 40 (February): 117-129.

ANDREWS, S., J. BLUMENTHAL, W. BACHE, and G. WIENER (1975) "Parents as early childhood educators: the New Orleans model." Paper presented at the Society for Research for Child Development, Denver, Colorado.

ASCHENBRENNER, J. (1973) Lifelines: Black Families in Chicago. New York: Holt, Rinehart & Winston.

BAUMRIND, D. (1972) "An exploratory study of socialization effects on Black children: some Black-White comparisons." Child Development 43: 261-267.

BERNARD, J. (1966) Marriage and Family Among Negroes. Englewood Cliffs, NJ: Prentice-Hall.

BILLINGSLEY, A. (1968) Black Families in White America. Englewood Cliffs, NJ: Prentice-Hall.

BRADLEY, R. and B. CALDWELL (1976a) "Early home environment and changes in mental test performance in children from 6 to 36 months." Developmental Psychology 12: 93-97.

——— (1976b) "The relation of infants' home environments to mental test performance at 54 months: a follow-up study." Child Development 47: 1172-1174.

——— (1978) Home Environment, Social Status, and Mental Test Performance. (unpublished)

CAREW, J. V. with I. CHAN and C. HALFAR (1976) Observing Intelligence in Young Children. Englewood Cliffs, NJ: Prentice-Hall.

CHILMAN, C. S. (1966) Growing Up Poor. Dept. of H.E.W. Welfare Administration Publication, No. 13. Washington, DC: Government Printing Office.

CLARKE-STEWART, K. A. (1973) "Interactions between mothers and their young children: characteristics and consequences." Monographs of the Society for Research in Child Development 38 (6-7, Serial No. 153).

DANIEL, J. (1975) "A definition of fatherhood as expressed by Black fathers." Ph.D. dissertation, University of Pittsburgh.

DAVIS, A. and J. DOLLARD (1940) Children of Bondage. New York: Harper & Row.

DIXON, V. (1971) "Two approaches to Black-White relations," in V. J. Dixon and B. G. Foster (eds.) Beyond Black or White: An Alternate America. Boston: Little, Brown.

DU BOIS, W. E. B. (1908) The Negro American Family. Atlanta: Atlanta University Press.

ELARDO, R., R. BRADLEY, and B. CALDWELL (1975) "The relations of infants' home environments to mental test performance from six to thirty-six months: a longitudinal analysis." Child Development 46: 68-74.

——— (1977) "A longitudinal study of the relation of infants' home environments to language development at age three." Child Development 48: 595-603.

FRAZIER, E. F. (1933) "Children in black and mulatto families." American Journal of Sociology 39: 12-29.

_____ (1939) The Negro Family in the United States. Chicago: University of Chicago Press.

_____ (1950) "Problems and needs of Negro children and youth resulting from family disorganization." Journal of Negro Education 19: 269-277.

GAY, G. (1975) "Cultural differences important in education of Black children." Momentum (October): 30-33.

GUTMAN, H.G. (1976) The Black Family in Slavery and Freedom: 1750-1925. New York: Random House.

HANNERZ, U. (1969) Soulside: Inquires into Ghetto Culture and Community. New York: Columbia University Press.

HARRISON-ROSS, P. and B. WYDEN (1973) The Black Child—A Parents' Guide. New York: Peter H. Wyden.

HESS, R.D. (1970) "Social class and ethnic influences on socialization," in P. Mussen (ed.) Carmichael's Manual of Child Psychology. New York: John Wiley.

_____ et al. (1968) The Cognitive Environments of Urban Preschool Children. Report to the Children's Bureau, U.S. Department of Health, Education, and Welfare. Washington, DC: Government Printing Office.

HILL, R. (1971) The Strengths of Black Families. New York: National Urban League.

JOHNSON, C.S. (1934) Shadow of the Plantation. Chicago: University of Chicago Press.

_____ (1941) Growing Up in the Black Belt. Washington, DC: American Council on Education.

KUHN, T. (1963) The Structure of Scientific Revolutions. Chicago: University of Chicago Press.

LADNER, J. (1971) Tomorrow's Tomorrow: The Black Woman. Garden City, Doubleday.

LEWIN, K. (1935) A Dynamic Theory of Personality. New York: McGraw-Hill.

LEWIS, D. (1975) "The Black family: socialization and sex roles." Phylon 26 (Fall): 471-480.

LEWIS, H. (1955) Blackways of Kent. Chapel Hill: University of North Carolina Press.

LIEBOW, E. (1966) Tally's Corner. Boston: Little, Brown.

LYMAN, S.M. (1972) The Black American in Sociological Thought. New York: Capricorn Books.

McADOO, H.P. (1978) "Factors related to stability in upwardly mobile Black families." Journal of Marriage and the Family 40 (November): 761-778.

MARTIN, E.P. and J.M. MARTIN (1978) The Black Extended Family. Chicago: University of Chicago Press.

MATHIS, A. (1978) "Contrasting approaches to the study of Black families." Journal of Marriage and the Family 40 (November): 667-678.

MOYNIHAN, D.P. (1965) The Negro Family: A Case for National Action. Washington, DC: Government Printing Office.

MYRDAL, G. (1944) An American Dilemma. New York: Harper & Row.

NOBLES, W.W. (1974a) "African root and American fruit: the Black family." Journal of Social and Behavioral Sciences 20 (Spring): 66-77.

_____ (1974b) "Africanity: its role in Black families." The Black Scholar (June): 10-17.

_____ (1978) "Toward an empirical and theoretical framework for defining Black families." Journal of Marriage and the Family 40 (November): 679-690.

OGBU, J. (1978) Minority Education and Caste: The American System in Cross-Cultural Perspective. New York: Academic Press.

PETERS, M.F. (1974) "The black family: perpetuating the myths: an analysis of family sociology textbook treatment of black families." Family Coordinator 23 (October): 349-357.

_____ (1976) "Nine Black families: a study of household management and childrearing in Black families with working mothers." Ph.D. dissertation, Harvard University.

_____ (1980) "Childrearing in Black families: potential continuities and discontinuities between home and school." Paper presented at annual meeting of National Council on Family Relations, Portland, Oregon, October.

_____ (1981) "Childrearing patterns in a sample of Black parents of children age 1 to 3." Paper presented at Annual Meeting of Society for Research in Child Development.

———— and G. C. MASSEY (in press) "Chronic vs. mundane stress in family stress theories: the case of Black families in White America."

PIERCE, C. (1969) "The effects of racism." Paper presented at the American Medical Association AMA 15th Annual Conference of State Mental Health Representatives, Chicago, Illinois.

RADIN, N. and C. KAMII (1965) "The child-rearing attitudes of disadvantaged Negro mothers and some educational implications." Journal of Negro Education 34 (2): 138-146.

RAINWATER, L. (1966) "Crucible of identity: the Negro lower-class family," pp. 160-204 in The Negro American. Boston: Beacon Press.

RENNE, K. R. (1970) "Correlates of dissatisfaction in marriage." Journal of Marriage and the Family 32: 54-67.

RICHARDSON, B. B. (1981) "Racism and child-rearing: a study of Black mothers." Ph.D. dissertation, Claremont Graduate School.

SCANZONI, J. (1971) The Black Family in Modern Society. Boston: Allyn & Bacon.

———— (1975) "Sex roles, economic factors, and marital solidarity in Black and white marriages." Journal of Marriage and the Family 37 (February): 130-144.

SCHACTER, F. F. (1979) Everyday Mother Talk to Toddlers: Early Intervention. New York: Academic Press.

SCHULZ, D. (1969) Coming Up Black. Englewood Cliffs, NJ: Prentice-Hall.

SLAUGHTER, D. (1978) "Modernization through education of mother-child dyads." Final Report I to the National Institute of Child Health and Human Development. Evanston, IL: Northwestern University.

STACK, C. B. (1974) All Our Kin: Strategies for Survival in a Black Community. New York: Harper & Row.

WHITE, B. L., B. KABAN, B. SHAPIRO, and J. ATTANMUCCI (1977) "Competence and experience," in I. C. Uzgiris and F. Weizman (eds.) The Structuring of Experience. New York: Plenum Press.

WHITING, B. (1973) "The problem of the packaged variable." Paper presented at the Biennial International Conference on Behavioral Development, Ann Arbor, Michigan, August.

WILLIE, C. V. (1976) A New Look at Black Families. New Bayside, NY: General Hall.

YOUNG, V. (1970) "Family and childhood in a southern Negro community." American Anthropologist 72 (April): 269-288.

ZEGIOB, L. and R. FOREHAND (1975) "Maternal interactive behavior as a function of race: socioeconomic status and sex of the child." Child Development 46: 564-568.

16

FAMILY, SOCIALIZATION ENVIRONMENT, AND
IDENTITY DEVELOPMENT IN BLACK AMERICANS

JAMES S. JACKSON
WAYNE R. McCULLOUGH
GERALD GURIN

Family and environmental influences have been largely ignored in previous empirical work on personal and group identity development in blacks. The major research on group identification and self- and group attitudes is reviewed in the current chapter. The important role of the family and socialization environment is stressed and the possible nature of their effects on the development of group identification in black Americans is discussed. Explanations for the lack of an observed relationship between group and personal identity are presented. It is suggested that a negative or neutral relationship between black group identification and traditional measures of self-esteem may be the result of the pivotal role of the family in inculcating a strong and positive sense of black identity. Family socialization themes that emphasize the importance of racial group history and togetherness are

AUTHORS' NOTE: We wish to particularly acknowledge Phillip Bowman, Clifford Broman, Ronald Brown, Patricia Gurin, Shirley Hatchett, Harold Neighbors, and M. Belinda Tucker, collaborators on our previous and ongoing research. They helped us to formulate our ideas on group identity and consciousness, and made major contributions to other substantive and theoretical areas as well. We appreciate the research support of the Ford and Rockefeller Foundations, Carnegie Corporation, National Institute of Mental Health and National Institute on Aging. This chapter was revised while the first author was a Ford Foundation Senior Postdoctoral Fellow at Groupe D'Etdudes Et De Recherches Sur La Science, Ecole Des Hautes Etudes En Sciences Sociales, Paris, France.

antithetical to Western-oriented conceptualizations and measures of self-esteem. Analyses on data from the National Survey of Black Americans revealed that personal identity is weakly related to racial group identity and not related to group consciousness. Possible reasons for why a strong sense of black group identity is not strongly related to measures of self that stress individual striving and a sense of personal achievement are discussed.

Over the last 40 years, much of the social and psychological literature on black Americans has addressed, directly or indirectly, issues of group identification and consciousness. This interest in group identity derives largely from the minority status of blacks in this society. In any group experiencing discrimination, a central issue becomes how individual members relate to the group, to its history of discrimination, and, in the case of black Americans, to the current active collective struggle to overcome a racist system. Furthermore, how black Americans deal with their minority status has been viewed as a critical determinant of their general psychic health and functioning. Writers have differed on whether they focused on the pathological consequences of discrimination or the strength of coping in the face of it. But all have agreed on the central significance of this psychological relationship to the group, the individual's group identity.

Despite the universal unquestioned assumption of the link between group identity and psychological health, it is surprising that the actual documentation of this relationship is ambiguous, overly simplistic, and ill-defined (Cross, 1985). Recent reviews have noted that there is no consistent empirical support for the assumption that there is a simple positive relationship between group and personal identity (Cross, 1985; Spencer, 1985). Most studies in this area have had serious conceptual and measurement limitations (Banks, 1976; Semaj, 1985). There has also been conceptual confusion in the definition of personal and group identity and consciousness, as well as inadequate formulation of the conceptual links between the two sets of concepts (Harrison, 1985). Measurement problems have followed largely, although not entirely, from these conceptual confusions.

As a result of the empirical findings and the conceptual and measurement limitations of earlier literature, much of the current work (see McAdoo, 1985 for an exception) in this area has focused on the conceptual independence of self- and group identity, rather than on the relationship between the two concepts (Cross, 1985, Harrison, 1985; Peters, 1985; Rosenberg, 1985; Semaj, 1985). This emphasis on the conceptual independence of the two concepts is consistent with the position that we presented in the previous edition of this book.

ᴧis current chapter attempts to clarify the distinction between personal and group identity, and discusses some of the conceptual and measurement issues that remain unresolved. Also, although the literature continues to be sparse, we present some speculations on the role of the family and other socialization influences in the development of personal and group identity.

GROUP AND PERSONAL IDENTITY

BLACK FAMILY AND BLACK IDENTITY

Within our conceptualization, the rudiments of the self are conceived as emerging initially in infancy and early childhood. This evolving self is influenced primarily, but not exclusively, by the socialization practices of the family and insulated local community (Alejandro-Wright, 1985; Peters, 1985; Semaj, 1985; Spencer, 1985; Young, 1970). Similarly, social group identity is conceived to be developed through the persons' perceptions, filtered by the family and other primary groups, of the relationships and cleavages that exist in the larger society between and among various social, economic, and political groups (Tajfel, 1980; Turner, 1982). Both personal and group identity are viewed as essentially cognitive phenomena—one as the self-placement of the individual in relationship to the primary group and local community (Who am I?); and the other, as the recognition by the individual of the societal placement of the group(s) to which he or she belongs within the stratification system that characterizes a particular society (Who are we? Who are they?). Related to these essential cognitive processes are the affective loadings that become attached to one's individuality and to one's group belongingness.

There is little systematic evidence regarding the buffering and insulating functions and the identity nurturant roles served by the black family in fostering a functional group or personal identity (Lipscomb, 1975; Taylor, 1976). Similarly, the coping strategies and situational adaptations derived from this identity and fostered in the familial context only recently have begun to receive theoretical and empirical attention (Bowman and Howard, 1985; McCullough, 1982; Peters, 1985; Spencer, 1985).

The minority family is the important agent of socialization, for it is within the family context that the individual first becomes aware of and begins to grapple with the significance of racism and discrimination (Alejandro-Wright, 1985; Washington, 1976). The intrafamilial socialization of group and personal identity has considerable bearing upon personal functioning in a society that cultivates negative conceptions of minority group members through direct interaction, the media, and institutional barriers (Allen and Hatchett, 1986). An important social structural factor discussed in this chapter is racial homogeneity or heterogeneity of the socialization environment. How do such environments differentially affect the development and compartmentalization of group and personal identity? Our focus is not only on the degree of racial homogeneity of the socialization environment, but also the timing of socialization and the elements of group and personal identity that are transmitted across generations.

GROUP AND PERSONAL IDENTITY

The literature on black identification and personal functioning can be divided into two distinct periods demarcated by the Civil Rights Movement of the 1960s. The studies antedating the Civil Rights Movement focused almost exclusively on the supposedly negative effects of black identification. Identifying as black was seen as a "problem," because it meant identifying with an oppressed group and internalizing the negative group image from the dominant white society. Two types of studies predominated in this period: those based on intensive clinical material (Kardiner and Ovesey, 1951), and the empirical studies with young children, mostly around their choices and reactions to black and white dolls. These latter studies were particularly influential in promoting the view that black identity implied self-hatred. Following the early work of the Clarks, a number of these studies showed that, given one choice, a majority of black children tended to choose a white rather than a black doll, saw the white doll as "nice" and the black doll as "bad" (Clark and Clark, 1947; Goodman, 1952; Landreth and Johnson, 1953; Radke and Trager, 1950; Stevenson and Steward, 1958; Moreland, 1962). These choices were viewed as reflecting rejection of the group and self-hatred.

A critical characterization of these doll studies should be noted: they did not measure group identification and self-feeling as *separate* sets of variables. Rather, the choice of the white doll was seen as both group rejection and self-rejection. The relationship between group rejection and self-rejection was an unquestioned assumption, rather than a hypothesis to be empirically tested. This assumption was not peculiar to views of the psychic consequences of black identification; it was applied to the supposed internalization of negative group images held by the majority of individuals belonging to any minority group that was discriminated against. Many of the writers on black identification and self-rejection referred to Lewin's (1948) classic statement about Jewish identification. Rejection of one's Jewishness was seen as automatically implying "self-hatred."

Literature on black identification published during the period after the Civil Rights Movement differs from the earlier writings in two major ways. First, although some writers still stress negative black identity (e.g., Gitter, Mastophy, and Satow, 1972), the majority of studies focus upon the positive psychic effects of black identification. This emphasis predominates in the speculative writings on the psychological impact of the movement, as well as in the empirical research (Barnes, 1972; Cross, 1985; Hall, Cross, and Freedle, 1972; Hraba and Grant, 1970; McAdoo, 1985; Spencer, 1985; Thomas, 1971; Ward and Braun, 1972; Wyne, White, and Coop, 1974). While obviously different in tone, this literature nonetheless shares important conceptual similarities with the work conducted prior to the Civil Rights Movement. Akin to the studies that tied negative group identity to self-rejection and other negative psychological consequences, much of the newer theorizing and empirical studies have tied positive identity to high self-esteem and other positive psychological consequences. Both perspectives assume, however, a simple, direct relationship between group identification and psychological outcomes.

Recently some writers, in a further departure from premovement thinking, have directly attacked the assumption of any simple relationship between personal and group identity (Cross, 1985; McAdoo, 1985). For example, both Barnes (1972) and Peters (1985) indicated that earlier work, projecting a negative identity and a negative self-image as almost automatic consequences of a powerless minority status, neglects the role of family and community in mitigating the affects of the wider society on the developing child. The assumption that discrimination is internalized as self-hatred (rather than as hatred of the oppressing group, for example) represents the majority group's perspective (and wish). Zavalloni (1973) suggests that the relationship between a particular group identification and self-attitudes cannot be automatically assumed since any given group identification is only one aspect of a person's social identity.

McAdoo (1985) has also made this point, noting that very few studies have actually separately measured racial identification and self-feelings. When measured separately, the two have not consistently been related to each other. Whereas some empirical studies suggest that there is a positive relationship between black identification and positive self-concepts (Mobley, 1973; Ward and Braun, 1972), other empirical studies have found no such consistent relationships (McAdoo, 1970, 1985; Sacks, 1973). This lack of support in the empirical findings has been noted in recent reviews of this issue (Cross, 1979, 1985; Porter and Washington, 1979).[1]

These inconsistencies in the empirical findings are reflected in some results from a recent national study of 2,107 black adults (Jackson, Tucker, and Bowman, 1982; Jackson and Hatchett, 1986) that investigated the relationships among self- and group identity, and group consciousness. Self-identity was conceptualized and measured as self-esteem and personal efficacy. Group identity was conceptualized and measured as feelings of closeness to the ideas and feelings of a variety of black groups (Broman, Neighbors, and Jackson, 1986). Group consciousness was assessed as the willingness to take action on behalf of the group (Gurin, Miller, and Gurin, 1980; McCullough, 1982; Pitts, 1974).

As expected, both self-esteem and feelings of personal efficaciousness (personal efficacy) were positively related (r = .26). Group identity and group consciousness showed a moderate positive relationship (r = .16). Self-esteem and personal efficacy, however, were found to be differentially related to group identity and group consciousness. Self-esteem was moderately related to group identity (r = .14) and weakly related (r = .05) to group consciousness. Personal efficacy was not related at all to either group identity or group consciousness. The pattern of results were not affected by any background or socioeconomic status factors. These findings suggest that certain aspects of self may be tied to feelings held toward the group; specifically, affective feelings about the self (self-esteem) are related to affective feelings about the group (group identity). This is consistent with some previous literature (Cross, 1985). Group consciousness on the other hand, is apparently not strongly related to feelings of self-esteem or self-worth. The feelings of personal efficaciousness, the belief that one has personal control over one's life, has absolutely no relationship to either group identity or group consciousness. This is in spite of the fact that self-esteem and personal efficacy are related to each other in an expected, positive manner. In short, the relationship between orientations toward the self and orientations toward the group depends on the particular self and group attitudes being measured.

These analyses highlight a major limitation in existing conceptualizations of group identification and consciousness; the simplistic "either-or" perspective, a person identifies or does not identify, feels pride in or rejects the group. This has been true in the writings on group identification and consciousness generally, not just in the literature specific to blacks. With few exceptions (e.g., Zavalloni, 1971; 1973), the empirical literature has not dealt with the fact that the feelings toward the group are usually a complicated mixture of positive and negative, and the process of identification usually involves identifying with some aspects of the group and attempting to disassociate oneself from others (McAdoo, 1985). This is particularly true for minority group members who, no matter the degree of their positive identification, have to psychologically confront the negative images of their group found in the majority culture (Tajfel, 1982; Turner, 1982).

In summary the relationships among group and self-orientations have been viewed as self-evident. It has seemed an obvious assumption, not requiring testing, that disassociating oneself from one's blackness implied some rejection of the self, that feeling pride about black people implied feeling pride in the self, that blaming blacks for their life conditions implied inappropriate blaming of the self. The literature has taken for granted a high degree of permeability between the boundaries of the group and the boundaries of the self, so that the view of the group automatically fuses with the view of the self. But, as we have already indicated, the empirical evidence to support this seemingly self-evident assumption is lacking (Cross, 1985; McAdoo, 1985). Cross (1985), in a recent review of this literature, is particularly eloquent on this issue: "An entire people have been burdened with images of their children's self-hatred even though no empirical link between racial preference behavior and direct measures of low self-esteem has been demonstrated" (p. 165). The review by Porter and Washington (1979) also emphasizes this discrepancy.

Why hasn't consistent empirical support been found for assumptions that to so many have seemed self-evident and obvious? As we have indicated, the major problem is a conceptual one. The thinking in this area has been overly simplistic.[2] A more complex view of the nature of an individual's relationship to the group, and of processes, such as the family and other major socialization influences, that make this relationship to the group relevant to an individual's self-concepts and personal functioning, is needed. In the following pages, we turn to a discussion of some of these possible family and socialization processes.

THE FAMILY AND SOCIALIZATION ENVIRONMENT
FUNCTIONAL SEPARATION OF
SELF FROM GROUP MEMBERSHIP

The compartmentalization of group and personal identity is viewed as psychically functional (Cross, 1985; Turner, 1982), permitting adaptations to the variety of environmental situations confronting the individual. Simmons (1978) describes the possible psychological separation of self from minority group status:

> It is very possible that an individual may rate the black race less good in general than whites without feeling that he, himself, is less deserving as a total human being. While other minority members may be seen as deserving of societal prejudice, one may view oneself as an exception . . . at some fantasy level, a person might prefer to be white or lighter skinned without feeling dissatisfied with himself as a total human being. Such fantasies may assume

> less significance than the fact that he is well-regarded by parents, teachers, and peers (most of whom are also black), or that he is skilled at highly valued activities [Simmons, 1978, p.55].

Simmons' statement suggests several things. First, there is a distinction between personal identity and esteem and group identity that has important implications for psychological functioning. Second, the individual can actually identify with the outgroup while still maintaining highly valued self-worth. And third, self-worth (personal identity) evolves out of the interaction with the primary group, family, peers, and teachers. If these conditions are likely, as much of the evidence leads us to believe, how is it possible that the compartmentalized identities develop and foster such development?

The suggestion that the socialization environment may have a bearing upon the development of identity has some empirical grounding. The optimal environments that foster independent identity development are suggested by the findings of several studies (Bowman and Howard, 1985; McAdoo, 1985; McCullough, 1982; Porter and Washington, 1979; Wellman, 1970). Hare (1977), in delineating general self-esteem from area-specific self-esteem (school, peer, and home) analyzed data collected from fifth grade black and white students for the effects of socioeconomic status, race, and sex. He found that home and peer self-esteem were not significantly different by racial group; however, school self-esteem was significantly higher among whites. These findings indicate that the typical racially homogeneous settings (home and peer group) have nurturing effects upon self-esteem development. For blacks, only home area-specific esteem accounted for a significant amount of variance in general self-esteem. These data suggest both differences in racial groups and the influence of the socialization environment in the development of group and personal identity.

FAMILY AND SOCIALIZATION ENVIRONMENT

As intimated earlier, self-esteem and other aspects of personal functioning are developed mainly in the context of an individual's immediate personal relationships, particularly those involved in early socialization in the family, but also peer relationships and those in the immediate community (Young, 1970). For most blacks in our society this has meant an all-black setting for these formative personal relationships. Self-evaluations develop almost totally with other blacks as the comparative reference group. In contrast, group identification and consciousness develop out of the relationships of blacks to a broader set of influences and referents, specifically blacks' relationships and experiences in white-dominated environments. These differences in influences and reference points lead to different and possibly unrelated consequences in self- and group orientations. Porter and Washington (1979) point out that this may explain the suggestive findings in the literature antedating the Civil Rights Movement that middle-class blacks were higher in personal self-esteem (for which they were comparing themselves predominantly with blacks as a group) but lower in racial esteem (for which they were using the majority world as their comparative referent). Cross (1985) also draws upon this difference to explain the findings that the Civil Rights Movement seems to have wrought a great increase in black identification and consciousness but no apparent change in the personal self-esteem of black Americans.

The evidence previously cited suggests that the racial composition and degree and quality of intergroup contacts may affect the positiveness of personal identity development and its compartmentalization from group identity. If we presume that personal identity development (Who am I?) temporally precedes the internalization of group identity, the family serves at least two important functions in this early development. First, there is the development of self-worth and the personal frame of reference for achievement and other behaviors in this society. Second, the insulating function of the family serves to lessen the negative and often deleterious consequences of minority group status—for both personal and group membership.

It has been suggested that the racially homogeneous home environment may also serve an insulating or buffering role with regard to personal identity development (Hare, 1977; Lipscomb, 1975; McAdoo, 1985; Peters, 1985; Lipscomb, 1975; Porter and Washington, 1979; Simmons, 1978). Self-worth and self-conceptions are formed under the auspices of the family/primary group. In the homogeneous racial environment there are fewer occasions than in the heterogeneous environment for negative messages regarding group membership to impinge directly upon personal identity development. Thus, the homogeneous environment can help to foster a high degree of individual compartmentalization. Once the development of self is established, integrating conceptions of one's relationship to the group and understanding the group's status in society can be achieved through exposure to images such as art, stories, history, and culture.

Introduction to more racially heterogeneous environments (e.g., school, camp) consequently leads to a reduction of the buffering or insulating role played by the family. The family's filtering of input from the larger society is reduced as a broader range of experiences is encountered. As the minority individual gains more inter-group experience, however, the family has an increasing interpretative function. This translation role is critical for maintaining the integrity of the already developed early personal identity as well as the evolving conceptions of group identity (Bowman and Howard, 1985; Peters, 1985).

In comparison to the homogeneous environment, the racially heterogeneous environment may serve to hasten the development of the individual's group identity (McCullough, 1982; McCullough, Gurin, and Jackson, 1981; Porter and Washington, 1979; Simmons, 1978; Tajfel, 1982). The categorical treatment that minority individuals receive (as distinct from interpersonal treatment based upon individual traits or characteristics) helps to place them within the bounds of the minority group and to discern their group's status with regard to the dominant group (Who are we? Who are they?). Other intragroup and intergroup comparisons help to further define boundaries, commonalities, and other discrepancies between groups. It should also be pointed out that in a nonhostile, nonsegregated, and nondiscriminatory intergroup environment, the development of even a meager sense of belonging to a minority group would undoubtedly be difficult to foster.

Little has been mentioned to this point relative to the role that family ideology about the society serves in identity development. We believe that it is through the enactment of parental ideologies that the external world is buffered and filtered through to the developing individual (Lipscomb, 1975; Peters, 1985). It is not very likely that individuals socialized to a strong sense of compartmentalized personal identity and a thorough understanding of their minority group status, in addition to the historical cultural underpinnings of their group, will hate themselves because they are black. For example, Bowman and Howard (1985) in an analysis of the Three-Generation Family Study data (Jackson and Hatchett, 1986) found positive effects on personal efficacy and academic achievement in black youth who reported receiving strong black socialization messages. The possibility also exists that significant influences outside the family (e.g. peer group) affect the relative valences of personal and group identities (Hare, 1977). This is most plausible in those circumstances in which parental ideologies are neither communicated nor grounded in the socialization that transpires.

It is also conceivable that minority group members, regardless of the racial homogeneity or heterogeneity of the environment, evolve with an incorporation of group and personal identities that are undifferentiated. Individuals reared in family and environmental settings devoid of an emphasis on separateness may develop an orientation in which their fate is inextricably linked to that of the group. The individual internalizes all images, characteristics, and treatments of the group as statements of his or her individual nature. This fatalism entails a total dependence upon the group for "individual definition." The lack of differentiating socialization by the primary group in the racial homogeneous setting or the unbuffered press (categorical treatment and characterizations) by the dominant majority may accentuate this effect.

It is possible that the strong inculcation of black pride and a sense of common fate with other blacks may negate any possible relationships among group identification and consciousness with frequently used measures of self-esteem. Some work suggests that negative relationships are most often demonstrated when group identity is related to highly individualistic, achievement oriented, and Western value dominated measures of self-esteem (Adams, 1978; Gordon, 1976; Nobles, 1973; Taylor and Walsh, 1979). Rasheed (1981) found in a study of black third graders that the highly positively identified youngsters demonstrated negative levels of self-esteem, and that the most negative relationships existed in those youngsters socialized in the highest black-consciousness home situations. This relationship was also found following experimental manipulations designed to increase group identification. If socialization attempts of parents to inculcate a strong sense of black group identity and consciousness are successful, then either negative or null relationships may be found with traditional measures of self-esteem, particularly those that are the most individually achievement-oriented.

CONCLUSIONS

In this chapter we have reviewed some of the basic literature regarding the meaning, definition, and complexity of group and personal identity. In so doing we directed our attention to the observed relationships between group identification and personal functioning, most often operationalized as self-identity or self-esteem. Some of the problems in the relationships between these concepts were noted, most notably conceptual and methodological difficulties, and the failure of researchers to consider other major factors that may have an important role in the development of both personal and group identity in blacks. We suggested that the family and community racial environment may be two important structural factors that mediate the link between self- and racial/social group conceptions. The role of the racial environment in buffering, insulating, or confronting group membership was briefly reviewed and the functions of the family as a filtering and supportive agent were also noted.

Finally, a possible reason why current conceptualizations and measures of group and personal identity might consistently demonstrate a negative relationship with one another was briefly discussed. Though speculative, some literature supports the view that parental inculcation of black pride and strongly held group images of survival might be antithetical to Western-dominated conceptions and measures of self-esteem that are commonly used in empirical studies. Under these circumstances, blacks who hold the strongest group identification might be less likely to endorse self-esteem items that stress highly individually oriented conceptions of self.

In conclusion, we believe that more empirical research is needed on those conditions that affect both group and individual orientations, and that make the group a salient element in the formation of personal identity. Special emphasis should be placed on the study of family relationships and socialization patterns since, as we have suggested, the black family is the purveyor of both group and personal identity. Because of the simplistic nature of conceptualization in this area, there is a need for more refined and specified theory, rather than the testing of existing notions. Despite over 40 years of studies and speculations on the relationship between black personal and social group identity, the complexities are only beginning to be recognized and conceptualized.

NOTES

1. In addition to these two theoretical reformulations, some recent writings have also raised methodological questions about the earlier work on negative black identity and self-concept. In a review of the studies on preference behavior in blacks, Banks (1976) points out that most of the studies indicate that preferences do not depart from chance; he also questions whether they have demonstrated self-rejection and indicates the need to appreciate the complexity of the issues. In a similar vein, Brand, Ruiz, and Padilla (1974), in their extensive review of studies of ethnic identification and preference, point up the questionable state of our knowledge in this area. They note that results vary according to method and nine other situational, contextual, and individual variables.

2. An engagement of personal values may also provide some explanation of this simplistic view. Cross makes an interesting comment on how difficult it is to challenge the assumption that there is a direct relationship between group identity and psychological functioning. After noting that we have not been able to empirically demonstrate a direct relationship between RGO (reference group orientations) and PI (personal identity), Cross (1979) comments: "During several recent lectures, this observer has found it difficult to even present the idea that RGO and PI may not be related, so emotional was the response of students and faculty in the audience" (p.30).

REFERENCES

ADAMS, B. A. (1978) "Inferiorization and self-esteem." Social Psychology 41: 47-53.
ALEJANDRO-WRIGHT, M. (1985) "The child's conception of racial classification: a social-

cognitive developmental model," in M. B. Spencer, G. K. Brookins, and W. R. Allen (eds.) Beginnings: The Social and Affective Development of Black Children. Hillsdale, NJ: Lawrence Erlbaum.

ALLEN, R. L. and S. J. Hatchett (1986) "The media and social reality effects: self and system orientations of blacks." Communications Research 13: 97-123.

BANKS, W. C. (1976) "White preference in blacks: a paradigm in search of a phenomenon." Psychological Bulletin 83: 1179-1186.

BARNES, E. J. (1972) "The black community as the source of positive self-concept for black children: a theoretical perspective," in R. L. Jones (ed.) Black Psychology. New York: Harper & Row.

BOWMAN, P. J. and C. HOWARD (1985) "Race related socialization, motivation, and academic achievement: a study of black youths in three-generation families." Journal of the American Academy of Child Psychiatry 24: 134-141.

BRAND, E. S., R. A. RUIZ, and A. M. PADILLA (1974) "Ethnic identification and preference: a review." Psychological Review 81: 860-890

BROMAN, C. L., H. W. NEIGHBORS, and J. S. JACKSON (1986) "Racial group-identification among black adults." (unpublished manuscript, Institute for Social Research, University of Michigan, Ann Arbor)

CLARK, M. L. (1985) "Racial stereotypes and self-esteem in black Americans." (unpublished manuscript, Department of Psychology, Wake Forest University, Winston Salem, NC)

CLARK, K. B., and M. P. CLARK (1947) "Racial identification and preference in Negro children," in T. M. Newcomb and E. L. Hartley (eds.) Readings in Social Psychology. New York: Holt, Rinehart & Winston.

CROSS, W. E. (1979) "Black families and black identity development: rediscovering the distinctions between self-esteem and reference group orientations." Presented at the International Seminar on The Child and the Family (August). Gustavus Adolphus College, St. Peter, MN.

———— (1985) "Black identity: rediscovering the distinction between personal identity and reference group orientation," in M. B. Spencer, G. K. Brookins, and W. R. Allen (eds.) Beginnings: The Social and Affective Development of Black Children. Hillsdale, NJ: Lawrence Erlbaum.

GITTER, A. G., D. J. MASTOPHY, and Y. SATOW (1972) "The effect of skin color and physiognomy on racial misidentification." Journal of Social Psychology 88: 139-143.

GOODMAN, M. E. (1952) Race Awareness in Young Children. Reading, Massachusetts: Addison-Wesley.

GORDON, V. V. (1976) "Methodologies of black self-concept research: a critique." Journal of Afro-American Issues 4: 73-81.

GURIN, P., A. H. MILLER, and G. GURIN (1980) "Stratum identification and consciousness." Social Psychology Quarterly 43: 30-47.

HALL, W. S., W. E. CROSS, and R. FREEDLE (1972) "Stages in the development of black awareness: an exploratory investigation," in R. L. Jones (ed.) Black Psychology. New York: Harper & Row.

HARE, B. R. (1977) "Racial and socioeconomic variations in preadolescent area-specific and general self-esteem." International Journal of Intercultural Relations, 1: 1-59.

HARRISON, A. O. (1985) "The black family's socializing environment: self-esteem and ethnic attitude among black children," in H. P. McAdoo and J. L. McAdoo (eds.) Black Children. Beverly Hills, CA: Sage.

HRABA, J. and G. GRANT (1970) "Black is beautiful: a reexamination of racial preference and identification." Journal of Personality and Social Psychology 16: 398-402.

JACKSON, J. S. and S. J. HATCHETT (1986) "Intergenerational research: methodological considerations," in N. Datan, A. L. Greene, and H. W. Reese (eds.) Intergenerational Relations. Hillsdale, NJ: Lawrence Erlbaum.

JACKSON, J. S., M. B. TUCKER, and P. J. BOWMAN (1982) "Conceptual and methodological problems in survey research on black Americans," in W. Liu (ed.) Methodological Problems in Minority Research. Chicago: Pacific/Asian American Mental Health Center.

KARDINER, A. and L. OVESEY (1951) The Mark of Oppression. Cleveland: World.

LANDRETH, C. and B. C. JOHNSON (1953) "Young children's responses to a picture and inset test designed to reveal reactions to persons of different skin color." Child Development 24: 63-79.

LEWIN, K. (1948) Resolving Social Conflicts. New York: Harper & Row.

LIPSCOMB, L. (1975) "Socialization factors in the development of black children's racial self-esteem." Presented at the annual meeting of the American Sociological Association.

McADOO, H. P. (1970) "Racial attitudes and self-concepts of black preschool children." Doctoral Dissertation, University of Michigan, Ann Arbor. University Microfilms No. 71-4677.

———(1985) "Racial attitude and self-concept of young black children over time," in H. P. McAdoo and J. L. McAdoo (eds.) Black Children. Beverly Hills, CA: Sage.

McCULLOUGH, W. R. (1982) "The development of group identification in black Americans." Doctoral dissertation, University of Michigan, Ann Arbor.

McCULLOUGH, W. R., G. GURIN, and J. S. JACKSON (1981) "Racial identity and consciousness: the socialization of ingroup and outgroup orientations." Presented at the annual meeting of the American Psychological Association. Los Angeles. ERIC Document Reproduction Service No. ED 212 687.

MOBLEY, B. (1973) "Self concept and conceptualization of ethnic identity: the black experience." Doctoral dissertation, Purdue University, West Lafayette, IN.

MORELAND, J. K. (1962) "Racial acceptance and preference of nursery school children in a southern city." Merrill Palmer Quarterly 8: 271-280.

NOBLES, W. W. (1973) "Psychological research and the black self-concept: a critical review." Journal of Social Issues 29: 11-31.

PETERS, M. F. (1985) "Racial socialization of young black children" in H. P. McAdoo and J. L. McAdoo (eds.) Black Children. Beverly Hills, CA: Sage.

PITTS, J. P. (1974) "The study of race consciousness: comments on new directions." American Journal of Sociology 80: 665-687.

PORTER, J. R. and R. E. WASHINGTON (1979) "Black identity and self-esteem: a review of studies of black self-concept." Annual Review of Sociology 5: 53-74.

RADKE, M. J. and H. G. TRAGER (1950) "Children's perceptions of the social roles of Negroes and whites." Journal of Psychology 29: 3-33.

RASHEED, S. (1981) "The development of ethnic identity and self-esteem in Bilalian (black) children." Doctoral dissertation, University of Michigan, Ann Arbor.

ROSENBERG, M. (1985) "Summary," in M. B. Spencer, G. K. Brookins, and W. R. Allen (eds.) Beginnings: The Social and Affective Development of Black Children. Hillsdale, NJ: Lawrence Erlbaum.

SACKS, S. (1973) "Self-identity and academic achievement of black adolescent males: a study of racial identification, locus of control, self-attitudes, and academic performance." Doctoral dissertation, Columbia University, New York.

SEMAJ, L. T. (1985) "Afrikanity, cognition and extended self-identity," in M. B. Spencer, G. K. Brookins, and W. R. Allen (eds.) Beginnings: The Social and Affective Development of Black Children. Hillsdale, NJ: Lawrence Erlbaum.

SIMMONS, R. B. (1978) "Blacks and high self-esteem." Social Psychology 41: 54-57.

SPENCER, M. B. (1985) "Cultural cognition and social cognition as identity correlates of black children's personal-social development" in M. B. Spencer, G. K. Brookins, and W. R. Allen (eds.) Beginnings: The Social and Affective Development of Black Children. Hillsdale, NJ: Lawrence Erlbaum.

STEVENSON, H. W. and E. C. STEWARD (1958) "A developmental study of race awareness in young children." Child Development 29: 399-410.

TAJFEL, H. [ed.] (1982) Social Identity and Intergroup Relations. Cambridge, England: Cambridge University Press.

TAYLOR, M. C. and E. J. WALSH (1979) "Explanations of black self-esteem: some empirical tests." Social Psychology Quarterly 42: 253-261.

TAYLOR, R. L. (1976) "Black youth and psychosocial development: a conceptual framework." Journal of Black Studies 6: 35-72.

THOMAS, C. (1971) Boys No More: A Black Psychologist's View of Community. Beverly Hills, CA: Glencoe.

TURNER, J. C. (1982) "Towards a cognitive redefinition of the social group," in H. Tajfel (ed.) Social Identity and Intergroup Relations. Cambridge: Cambridge University Press.

WARD, S. and J. BRAUN (1972) "Self-esteem and racial preference." American Journal of Orthopsychiatry 42: 644-647.

WASHINGTON, V. (1976) "Learning racial identity," in R. C. Granger and J. C. Young (eds.) Demythologizing the Inner-City Child. Silver Springs, MD: National Association for the Education of Young Children.

WELLMAN, B. (1970) "Social identities in black and white." Sociological Inquiry 41: 57-66.

WYNE, M. D., K. P. WHITE, and R. H. COOP (1974) The Black Self. Englewood Cliffs, NJ: Prentice-Hall.

YOUNG, V. H. (1970) "Family and childhood in a southern Negro community." American Anthropologist 72: 269-288.

ZAVALLONI, M. (1971) "Cognitive processes and social identity through focused introspection." European Journal of Social Psychology, 1: 235-260.

——— (1973) "Social identity: perspectives and prospects." Social Science Information 12: 65-91.

17

THE ROLES OF BLACK FATHERS IN THE SOCIALIZATION OF BLACK CHILDREN

JOHN L. McADOO

Sociological and psychological research related to the socialization of the child has been described as matricentric in character (Lamb, 1976; Rapaport et al., 1977). Rapaport et al. (1977) have even suggested that the matrifocal parenting paradigm for parenting in our society is in need of revision, while most researchers feel that the role of the father in the socialization of their children is only beginning to be understood (Lamb, 1976; Biller, 1974). We find that the exploration of the Black father's role in the socialization of his children is almost nonexistent in social science literature. From the matricentric researcher's point of view, the Black father is usually seen as an invisible man who is not active in and has no power, control, or interest in the socialization of his children (McAdoo, 1979). There is a need, then, to describe some of the research findings related to Black fatherhood.

The objectives of this chapter are to present some of the literature related to the parenting styles of Black fathers in the socialization of their children, to examine some of the trends in father-child research, and to indicate some of the implications of these trends to the stereotyping of the Black father's role in the socialization of his children. We will be examining a variety of roles: that of provider; the father's influence in decisions related to child rearing, nurturing, and control functions; the father's expectations of his children; and interaction patterns between father and child.

PROVIDER ROLE

Most of the sociological literature relating to the provider role of the father follows Parsons and Bales's (1955) description of the instrumental and expressive modes of family process. The father was described as playing only an instrumental role. That is, he was seen as being primarily a provider who both protected the family from the outside world and was the conduit of information and resources between the family and the outside world. The mother-child relationship was the key expressive relationship until the child had passed the preschool stage. While Parsons and Bales's theories have served as a theoretical model in early family socialization literature, the literature does not provide clear-cut support for their thesis. At least one researcher has provided evidence suggesting that fathers are engaged in expressive socialization functions (Cazenave, 1979).

Price-Bonham and Skeen (1979) noted that the effectiveness of the Black father in his role as a provider is viewed as dependent on his ability to aid in supporting his family and to share the provider role with his wife, thus legitimizing his authority within the family and allowing him to serve as a model of responsible behavior to his children. Tausch (1952) noted that Black fathers and fathers of other racial and ethnic groups saw themselves as more than just economic providers to their families, and they valued companionship with their children more than the provider role. The role of provider for these fathers may have presented a dilemma for them, since the amount of time fathers spent with their children was partially controlled by employment pressures.

In analyzing the research of Maxwell (1976) and others (Cafritz, 1974; Fasteneau, 1976), Cazenave (1979) found that they overemphasized the provider role as a parenting style in focusing exclusively on the lack of paternal participation, involvement, and expressiveness in white middle- and upper-middle-income classes. In his research with middle-income Black fathers, Cazenave notes that the greater the economic security, the more active the father becomes in the child-rearing function. His findings on 54 mailmen seem to support this conclusion, as these fathers were found to be more active in child-rearing activities than their fathers had been.

In summary, while many researchers appear to use Parsons's theory as a guide, it now appears evident from Cazenave's and others' data relating to paternal nurturance (McAdoo, 1979; Radin, 1972; Radin and Epstein, 1975) that Parsons may have overemphasized the instrumental or provider role of the father. It is safe to assume that the American father plays many roles in the family—that of provider, decision maker, nurturer, husband, and father. Research that isolates or focuses on any of these roles may provide misinformation about his role in the nurturing of his children. While this evaluation analyzes each of the roles of fathers separately, it is important to recognize the interrelationship of the roles the father plays and the reciprocity of father/mother, sibling/child roles in the socialization process.

DECISION MAKING

Several authors have described the Black family as equalitarian in their decision-making patterns (Dietrich, 1975; Hill, 1971; Lewis, 1975; Reuben, 1978; Staples, 1976; Tenhouten, 1970; Willie and Greenblatt, 1978). Much of this literature was in reaction to social scientists' assertions that the Black family was matriarchal in structure (Moynihan, 1965). Willie and Greenblatt (1978), in reviewing the power relationship literature, found that Black families appear to be more equalitarian than white families, with the middle-class Black family being more equalitarian than any other type. McDonald (1980), in an extensive review of the family power literature, suggests that because of theoretical and methodological problems inherent in family power research, we have not moved much beyond the original finding of Blood and Wolfe (1960) on this issue.

Blood and Wolfe (1960) and others have demonstrated that American fathers are moving toward an egalitarian relationship in the decision-making and power relationship in the home. Jackson (1978) reported that lower-class Black fathers tended to be more patriarchal in their decision-making patterns than lower-class white fathers and Black and white middle-income fathers. Her review of selected literature on Black and white families noted that wife-dominant families (matriarchal) were more characteristic of white professional families with unemployed wives. Mack (1978) found that regardless of race or class, fathers perceived themselves as the dominant decision makers.

The studies related to child-rearing decision making in Black and white families indicate that the predominant pattern is egalitarian. That is, fathers share equally in the decisions about the child's needs (McAdoo, 1980). McAdoo (1979) had previously found that middle-income Black fathers shared equally with their wives in decisions on child-rearing activities. However, the Cromwells' (1978) analysis of husbands' and wives' reports of dominance on child-rearing decision making revealed conflicts in Black and Chicano homes on this issue. This points up the need to develop theoretical and methodological frameworks that allow researchers to look at both process and outcomes of decision making in child-rearing practices. The reports by either father, mother, or both about the father's role in this process may be limited without some actual observational data in conflictual and nonconflictual situations (McDonald, 1980).

Our conclusions, given the previous assertions, are that both Black and white middle-income fathers' involvement in decision making regarding child-rearing practices appears to be changing in the same general pattern found by Bronfenbrenner's (1958) analysis of the literature 23 years ago. He found the predominant child-rearing decision-making pattern to be equalitarian and attributed the change to the influence of professional child development practitioners. These changes perhaps were also due to the addition of mothers to the work force and the use of television in getting child development practitioners' message to more people.

More systematic study is needed on the impact sharing of the provider's role has on child-rearing decision making within Black and other families. While the sharing of the provider's role has led in most cases to greater economic and educational resources in Black families, there is some need to understand what this change has meant for other family processes and functioning in addition to decision-making processes. A question may be raised as to the impact on paternal attitudes and parenting style.

PARENTING STYLE

Very few studies related to father's expectations and parenting style were found. In a review of the literature, Bartz and Levine (1978), in a study of 455 parents of different ethnic groups, noted that fathers of all socioeconomic classes shared similar expectations of their children's behavior. Ethnic differences in fathers' expectations of their children's behavior were a matter of degree and not kind. Working-class fathers of all ethnic groups and races believed that children should help formulate rules and have the right to express their own ideas within the family. Black fathers and fathers belonging to other ethnic groups think parents earn the respect of their children by being fair, not by imposing parental will or authority.

While Bartz's data seem to suggest that lower socioeconomic Black fathers may be changing their traditional values to meet the new demands for socialization in society, it is clear from other literature (Staples, 1978; Taylor, 1978; Coles, 1978; Schulz, 1978) that many of them retain and support the values of their socioeconomic status. These men see themselves as the head of the family, and they believe they are expected to provide punishment to their children for transgressing externally imposed rules and regulations. They describe themselves as strict, using physical as opposed to verbal punishment liberally. The child's punishment is related to the transgression's consequence rather than the intent of the child's actions.

Cazenave (1979), reviewing the changes in child-rearing activities in two generations of Black fathers, found that middle-income fathers reported being more actively involved than their fathers in child-caring activities. This sample was more actively involved in changing their children's diapers, in babysitting, and in playing with their children than their fathers had been. They reported spending more time with their children and claimed to punish their children physically less often than their fathers had punished them.

Black middle-income fathers in McAdoo's (1979) study resembled those in Cazenave's study, in that they were equally involved in making child-rearing decisions. Most of these fathers could be described as traditional (Duvall, 1946) in their values toward child rearing. They expected their child to respond immediately to their commands, would almost never allow angry temper tantrums from their child, and perceived themselves and their attitudes toward child rearing as moderate to very strict. These fathers expected good behavior from their children as opposed to assertive and independent behavior. They were more likely to tell the child that they approved of his good behavior as opposed to hugging and kissing him. Their attitudes appeared to be like Baumrind's (1968) authoritarian fathers.

Baumrind (1966, 1967, 1973), in a series of research studies, has described three parenting styles that cut across all ethnic groups. The permissive, authoritarian, and authoritative parents have different child-rearing values and different expectations for their own role behaviors. The permissive father was described as the father who responds to his child's impulses, desires, and actions in a nonpunitive, accepting, and affirmative manner. This father made very few demands on his child for orderly behavior or doing household chores. He sees himself as a consultant to be used as the child desires and not as an agent responsible for shaping the child's ongoing or future behavior.

In contrast, the authoritarian father attempts to shape, control and evaluate his child's behavior and attitudes in accordance with a set standard of conduct. He values and expects obedience as a virtue and believes in punitive, forceful measures to control the child's behavior when it is in conflict with what the father believes is right. There are few give-and-take discussions, and the child is expected to accept the father's view of what is right.

The authoritative father seems to be a composite of the best points of the authoritarian and permissive fathers. This parent, according to Baumrind's findings, also attempts to direct the child's activities but in a more rational, issue-oriented manner. The authoritative father is able to encourage give-and-take discussions and gives reasons for his rules and expectations. The authoritative father tends to value both expressive and instrumental attributes, both autonomous self-will and disciplined authority. The father provides firm control with explanations when the child violates family policy. He believes in the use of reasoning as well as power in achieving his objectives with the child.

Baumrind's (1971) series of observational studies demonstrated that authoritative fathers promoted purposive and dominant behavior in boys and girls. Authoritative paternal control was associated with the development of social responsibility in boys and with achievement (but not friendly, cooperative behavior) in girls. Fathers who were either authoritarian or permissive in their child-rearing styles had children who were either markedly high or markedly low on overall competence (Baumrind, 1971).

In a comparative exploratory study observing Black and white fathers and their preschool children, Baumrind (1973) found sex differences in the fathers' expectations and the behavior of the children. There were few significant differences in Black and white fathers' expectations of their sons' behavior. Black sons were expected to behave in a more mature fashion, and the fathers were likely to encourage independent behavior. While no significant differences were observed in the behavior of the children, Black boys appeared to be less achievement oriented and more aggressive than white boys. Fathers of Black girls appeared to be significantly different from fathers of white girls in their parenting styles and child-rearing practices. The Black fathers did not encourage individuality and independence or provide enrichment of their daughter's environment. Black fathers did not promote nonconformity and were authoritarian in their practices.

The conclusion drawn by Baumrind was that socialization practices which would characterize Black families as authoritarian by white social science standards, and therefore in need of change, actually benefit Black daughters. In comparing Black and white girls Baumrind found that Black daughters of authoritarian parents were exceptionally independent and at ease in the nursery school setting where the observations took place. The study provides us with an interesting observation which needs to be verified and clarified in future research. Black authoritarian fathers and families differ significantly from white authoritarian families in the degree to which they adhere to rigid standards. White fathers who were found to be authoritarian in Baumrind's studies were more likely to be seen as having an authoritarian personality syndrome (Adorno et al., 1950)—that is, dogmatic and intolerant attitudes being motivated by repressed anger, emotional coldness, and a sense of impotence.

In summary to this section on parenting styles, it would appear that Black fathers socialize their children differently than white fathers, and the impact of that process may lead to the development of high competence in girls. There appears to be a need for more research related to the Black father's attitude toward child rearing, some observational validation of his behavior in relationship to his expressed values, and some validation through data gathering from significant others in the family. There is a need to evaluate the three types of parenting styles in more depth to determine whether cultural, ethnic, or racial differences influence our particular parenting style and its relationship to child outcome variables. Finally, there is a need to determine how the particular parenting style a father adopts influences his relationship to his son and/or daughter.

PARENT-CHILD RELATIONSHIPS

Walters and his associates (Walters and Stinnett, 1971; Walters and Walters, 1980) have done the most consistent reviews of the research related to parent-child relationship issues. Their latest work focused on the emerging research trends of physiological influences, parent-infant relationships, divorce, fathering, stepparenting, child abuse and neglect, values of the child, methodological issues, and intervention strategies.

Some of their conclusions were that patterns of parent-child relationships are influenced by parenting models which fathers and mothers provide to each other. To understand the concurrent contributions of parents to each other and to their children, research studies should focus on the mother-father-child relationship and on the mother-father-sibling-child relationship rather than on the father-child, mother-child relationship.

Walters believes that a clearer picture or conceptualization is emerging from the research literature on the reciprocal effects of relationships between parents and children. Family researchers are moving away from a unidirectional model, which sees the relationship going from parent to child, toward one which emphasizes a reciprocal model of relationships between parent and child. Children not only influence their parents' behavior but are also important determiners of their own behavior patterns (Walters and Walters, 1980).

While Walters's review emphasizes the need for research on parent-child interactions and reciprocal relationships, it is also clear from his review and that of others (Lamb, 1977; Price-Bonham and Skeen, 1979) that the role of the father in the parent-child relationship studies is not clearly understood. Studies of father-child relationships tend to emphasize the relationship between fathers and sons and leave the impact on daughters virtually unexplored (Walters and Stinnett, 1971). Further, as Staples (1970) notes, the role of the Black father in these studies is not explored very well. He concludes that the Black male may be more difficult to reach, the implication being that social science researchers select other sources for their information on Black fathers.

Price-Bonham and Skeen, (1979), in their review of the literature, agree with Staples's assessment and suggest that studies of Black father-child relationships suffer from the same deficiencies as do studies of other ethnic groups. Most researchers doing family relationship studies generally collect data on fathers from mothers and/or wives (Walters and Stinnett, 1971; McAdoo, 1979), neglect to control for social class (Busse and Busse, 1972), and focus on the impact of absent fathers.

In summary to this section on father-child relationships, what seems lacking from the various literature reviews is a theory which describes how these relationships differ over the life span of the child's development within the family. This theory should address racial, ethnic, and social class differences within the father-child relationship. More descriptive research methodologies need to be developed using both questionnaire and observational techniques to generate data bases related to the general concept of parent-child relationships and to particular aspects of that relationship. For Black father-child relationships, given socioeconomic class and other variables, there is a need to develop the boundaries, quality, and quantity of the parent-child relationship over time.

Once the relationships between fathers and children are identified, more sophisticated research designs can be used to determine the impact of mothers, siblings, and the kin network system on the development and changes in the parent-child relationship process. This would suggest the use of multitraits and multimethod approaches with more complex research designs (Walters and Walters, 1980). Using such approaches, researchers could begin to measure the impact of the child on the relationship and move away from linear models to curvilinear or other models that are appropriate.

FATHER-CHILD INTERACTION

The observations of father-child interaction patterns and their effect on the preschool child's social and cognitive growth are relatively new phenomena for social science researchers. The two most studied interaction patterns are nurturance and control. Nurturance may be defined as the expression of warmth and positive feelings of the father toward the attitudes and behaviors of his child.

Several researchers (Radin, 1972; Radin and Epstein, 1975; Baumrind, 1971) have suggested that maternal warmth (nurturance) facilitates the child's identification with the mother, particularly the female child. Radin (1972) has suggested that paternal nurturance facilitates the male child's identification with the father. Identification with either parent should lead to an incorporation by the child of the parent's ideas, attitudes, beliefs, and feelings about the child. The parent communicates to the child a positive acceptance of the child as a person. Nurturance is one of the patterns of interaction that is important in the development of social competence in preschool children.

Nurturance (warmth) is used most by parents who recognize and respond to their child's needs, who communicate acceptance, and who are available for interaction than by parents who are inaccessible and insensitive. Warmth is seen as a characteristic of both parent roles (Newman and Newman, 1978). Newman notes that warmth is usually expressed in praise or approval in nonverbal interactions including patting, touching, stroking, hugging, kissing, and in playful activities. Rodman (in Newman and Newman, 1978) suggests evidence that warmth and rejection can be observed across a variety of cultural groups.

Parental control is another dimension of father-child interaction patterns. Control refers to the parent's insistence that the child carry out important directions and adhere to rules that the parent feels are important. Control and nurturance are seen as necessary ingredients in authoritative parents' socialization patterns (Baumrind, 1973). Authoritarian fathers usually use restrictive control interaction patterns in socializing their children. These fathers' verbal interaction patterns with their preschool children are described in the literature as being restrictive, rather cold, unfeeling and aloof, and therefore represent an expression of the authoritarian father's negative feelings toward his child's attitudes and behavior within the family (Radin, 1972).

Parental restrictiveness does not facilitate positive communication and identification (Radin, 1972) between the child and his parent. Restrictive behaviors are those behaviors that are not warm, loving, and supportive of the child. Nonsupporting behaviors are usually in criticism or expressed disapproval and may also include grabbing, pushing, or restraining the child from some event or activity without explanation. It may be viewed as a negative reaction by the parent to the child's attitude, behavior, and beliefs. Nonsupport may also lead the parent to handle the symptoms of the problem and not the needs of the child, or to control behavior and cut off the usual patterns of identification and communication of the child. Restrictiveness in the parents could lead the child to develop a negative image of himself and his worth as a human being, as well as having negative feelings about those around him.

Radin and her associates (Radin, 1972; Radin and Epstein, 1975; Jordan et al., 1975) observed white lower- and middle-income fathers interacting with their preschool children. She found the predominant pattern of interaction to be nurturance. The fathers were warm and loving toward their children. She hypothesized that children of nurturant fathers would do well on cognitive tasks in kindergarten. They were able to support the hypothesis for boys of middle income fathers but not for boys of lower-class fathers. Her studies also found that the relationship between paternal nurturance and the child's intellectual functioning was higher for boys than for girls. It was suggested that the fathers of girls may be sending mixed messages to their daughters and this may lead to a reduction in intellectual performance (Radin and Epstein, 1975).

McAdoo (1979) partially replicated Radin's work with Black middle-income fathers. He hypothesized that the predominant pattern of verbal interaction between Black fathers and their sons and daughters would be nurturance. He was able to support the hypothesis: 75 percent of the Black middle-income fathers were found to be nurturant toward their children. Fathers were equally nurturant toward their sons and daughters. One unanticipated finding was that children of restrictive parents initiated the interaction between them and their fathers significantly more often than children of nurturant parents. This finding supports the Walterses' (1980) suggestion that there needs to be an examination of the impact of the reciprocal nature of the pattern of interaction between parent and child.

McAdoo was not able to find any relationship between a father's interaction patterns and his sons' and daughters' self-esteem. The children's positive self-esteem led McAdoo to suggest that the relationship between father-child interaction and self-esteem may be indirect. Walters and Stinnett (1971), in their decade review of parent-child relationships, noted that the research results converge in suggesting that parental acceptance, warmth, and support are positively related to favorable emotional, social, and intellectual development of children. They further found that extreme restrictiveness, authoritarianism, and punitiveness without acceptance, warmth, and love tend to be negatively related to a child's positive self-concept and emotional and social development. The studies they reviewed also indicate that parental attitudes and behaviors vary according to sex and behavior of the child.

Mackey and Day (1979), in one of the most comprehensive cross-cultural observational studies involving father figures in the United States, Ireland, Spain, Japan, and Mexico, found that American father figures did not interact much differently than father figures of other nations. They noted that father figures interacted more nonverbally with younger children and were closer to them. American men were as nurturant to their children as were American women. No differences in intensity of interaction level between men and women were observed in American families.

SUMMARY

Selected literature related to the roles Black fathers play in the socialization of their children were reviewed. It was noted that when economic sufficiency rises within Black families, an increase in the active participation of the Black fathers in the socialization of his children was observed. Black fathers, like fathers of all ethnic groups, take an equal part in the child-rearing decisions in the family. Their expectations for their child's behavior in the home also appear to be similar given socioeconomic status patterns. Unlike other fathers who are authoritarian, Black fathers appear to be socializing their daughters to be more competent and independent at an early age. His predominant relationship and interaction pattern appears to be nurturant, warm, and loving toward his children. Finally, as Lamb (1976) has suggested, the father's socialization role is defined by his position within the family system.

The implications of these findings appear to be that research should now move beyond the ethnocentric studies of the past that focus on the most problematic, economically devastated Black families, sometimes inappropriately comparing them to families of college professors, and study the various roles the Black father plays in the socialization of his children. More studies are needed which describe the father's attitudes, expectations, values, and beliefs about the roles he plays in both problematic and nonproblematic or both stressful and nonstressful situations. There needs to be more observational research related to the kinds of socialization activities and interaction patterns that take place between the father and his child in the home and community.

Theoretical frameworks and methodologies are needed that examine all the reciprocal socialization relationships of the total family system. We need to describe and evaluate reciprocal interaction and relationship patterns between father, mother, child, siblings, and kin. There is a need to go beyond the dyadic models and linear relationships to a more dynamic interaction model which looks at the family interaction processes in a developmental way and evaluate these processes in terms of social, emotional, and cognitive development of the child and his family members over time.

REFERENCES

ADORNO, T. W., E. FENKEL-BRUNSWICK, D. J. LEVINSON, and R. N. SANFORD (1950) The Authoritarian Personality. New York: Harper & Row.

BARTZ, K. W. and B. S. LEVINE (1978) "Child rearing by Black parents: a description and comparison to Anglo and Chicano parents." Journal of Marriage and the Family 40 (4): 709-720.

BAUMRIND, D. (1966) "Effects of authoritative parental control on child behavior." Child Development 37 (4): 887-907.

―――― (1967) "Child care practices anteceding three patterns of preschool behavior." Genetic Psychology Monographs 75: 43-88.

―――― (1968) "An exploratory study of socialization effects on Black children: some black-white comparisons." Child Development 43: 261-267.

―――― (1971) "Current patterns of paternal authority." Developmental Psychology Monographs 4 (1) Part 2.

―――― (1973) "Authoritarian vs authoritative parental control," in M. Scarr-Salapatek and P. Salapatek (eds.) Socialization. Columbus, OH: Charles Merrill.

―――― and A. E. BLOCK (1967) "Socialization practices associated with dimensions of competence in preschool boys and girls." Child Development 38 (2): 291-327.

BILLER, H. B. (1972) Parental Deprivation. Lexington, MA: Heath.

BLOOD, R. and D. WOLFE (1960) Husbands and Wives. New York: Free Press.

BRONFENBRENNER, U. (1958) "Socialization through time and space," in E. E. Maccoby, T. M. Newcomb, and E. L. Hartley (eds.) Readings in Social Psychology. New York: Holt, Rinehart & Winston.

BUSSE, T. and P. BUSSE (1972) "Negro parental behavior and social class variables." Journal of Genetic Psychology 120: 289-291.

CAFRITZ, J. S. (1974) Masculine/Feminine or Human? Itasca, IL: F. E. Peacock.

CAZENAVE, N. (1979) "Middle income Black fathers: an analysis of the provider's role." Family Coordinator 28 (November).

COLES, R. (1978) "Black fathers," in D. Wilkerson and R. Taylor (eds.) The Black Male in America. Chicago: Nelson-Hall.

CROMWELL, V. L. and R. E. CROMWELL (1978) "Perceived dominance and conflict resolution among Anglo, Black and Chicano couples." Journal of Marriage and the Family 42 (4): 749-759.

DIETRICH, K. T. (1975) "A reexamination of the myth of Black matriarchy." Journal of Marriage and the Family 37 (May): 367-374.

DUVALL, E. (1946) "Conceptions of parenthood." Journal of Sociology 52 (November): 193-203.

FASTENEAU, M. (1976) The Male Machine. New York: Macmillan.

JACKSON, J. (1978) "Ordinary Black husbands: the truly hidden men," pp. 139-144 in M. E. Lamb (ed.) The Role of the Father in Child Development. New York: John Wiley.

JORDAN, B. E., N. RADIN, and A. EPSTEIN (1975) "Paternal behavior and intellectual functioning in preschool boys and girls." Developmental Psychology 11: 407-408.

LAMB, M. E. (1976) "Interactions between eight-month old children and their fathers and mothers," in M. E. Lamb (ed.) The Role of the Father in Child Development. New York: John Wiley.

_____ (1977) "The role of the father: an overview," in M. E. Lamb (ed.) The Role of the Father in Child Development. New York: John Wiley.

LEWIS, D. K. (1975) "The Black family: socialization and sex roles." Phylon 36 (Fall): 221-237.

McADOO, J. (1979) "A study of father-child interaction patterns and self-esteem in Black preschool children." Young Children 34 (1): 46-53.

_____ (1980) "Socializing the preschool child." Government grant funded by the National Institutes of Mental Health, Contract No. 1 R01 MH25838-01.

McDONALD, G. W. (1980) "Family power: the assessment of a decade of theory and research 1970-1979." Journal of Marriage and the Family 42 (4): 881-854.

MACK, D. E. (1978) "Power relationships in Black families." Journal of Personality and Social Psychology 30 (September): 409-413.

MACKEY, C. W. and R. O. DAY (1979) "Some indicators of fathering behaviors in the United States: a cross-cultural examination of the adult male interactions." Journal of Marriage and the Family 41 (2): 287-298.

MAXWELL, J. (1976) "The keeping of fathers in America." The Family Coordinator 25: 387-392.

MOYNIHAN, D. (1965) The Negro Family: The Case for National Action. Washington, DC: Department of Labor, Office of Planning and Research.

NEWMAN, B. M. and P. R. NEWMAN (1978) Infancy and Childhood Development and its Contents. New York: John Wiley.

PARSONS, T. and R. F. BALES (1955) Family Socialization and Interaction Process. New York: Free Press.

PRICE-BONHAM, S. and P. SKEEN (1979) "A comparison of Black and white fathers with implications for parents' education." The Family Coordinator 28 (1): 53-59.

RADIN, N. (1972) "Father-child interaction and the intellectual functioning of four-year old boys." Developmental Psychology 8: 369-376.

_____ (1973) "Observed paternal behaviors as antecedents of intellectual functioning in young boys." Developmental Psychology 6: 353-361.

_____ and A. EPSTEIN (1975) "Observed paternal behavior and intellectual functioning of preschool boys and girls." Paper presented at the Society for Research in Child Development, Denver.

RAPAPORT, R., R. N. RAPAPORT, and Z. STRELITZ (1977) Fathers, Mothers and Society. New York: Basic Books.

REUBEN, R. H. (1978) "Matriarchal themes in Black literature: implications for family life education." Family Coordinator 27 (January): 33-41.

SCHULZ, D. A. (1978) "Coming up as a boy in the ghetto," pp. 7-32 in D. Y. Wilkerson and R. L. Taylor (eds.) The Black Male in America. Chicago: Nelson-Hall.

STAPLES, R. (1970) "Educating the Black male at various class levels for marital roles." The Family Coordinator 20: 164-167.

_____ (1976) "The Black American family," in C. H. Mindell and R. W. Haberstein (eds.) Ethnic Families in America. New York: Elsevier.

_____ (1978) "The myth of the Black matriarchy," in D. Y. Wilkerson and R. L. Taylor (eds.) The Black Male in America. Chicago: Nelson-Hall.

TAYLOR, R. L. (1978) "Socialization to the Black male role," pp. 1-7 in D. Y. Wilkerson and R. L. Taylor (eds.) The Black Male in America. Chicago: Nelson-Hall.

TAUSCH, R. J. (1952) "The role of the father in the family." Journal of Experimental Education 20: 319-361.

TENHOUTEN, W. (1970) "The Black family: myth or reality." Psychiatry 2 (May): 145-173.

WALTERS, J. and N. STINNETT (1971) "Parent-child relationships: a decade of research," in C. B. Broderick (ed.) A Decade of Family Research and Action. Minneapolis: National Council on Family Relations.

WALTERS, J. and L. H. WALTERS (1980) "Parent-child relationships: a review 1970-1979." Journal of Marriage and the Family 42 (4) November: 807-824.

WILLIE, C. V. and S. L. GREENBLATT (1978) "Four classic studies of power relationships in Black families: a review and look to the future." Journal of Marriage and the Family 40 (4): 691-696.

18

SUPPORTIVE ROLES OF
SIGNIFICANT OTHERS IN BLACK FAMILIES

WILHELMINA MANNS

Many persons, performing a variety of roles and functions within individual lives, contribute to the socialization process of members of the family. Moreover, such persons are often significant others. Examining the influence of the significant other in the life of individual blacks, therefore, increases knowledge about selected aspects of the socialization process of the black family.

The concept of the significant other developed from the formulations of Cooley (1902/1964) and later Mead (1934/1962), who suggested that the self-concept develops out of social interaction and that the individual assumed the viewpoint (reflected appraisal) of the "other" and "generalized other" of the general society of which he is a member. Expanding on these earlier formulations, Sullivan (as cited by Kuhn, 1972) described a specific "significant other" later defined by Denzin (1970) as a person "whose evaluations of his behavior and attitudes, the individual, holds in high esteem." These evaluations and/or reflected appraisals from both the "generalized other" (the community) and a specific significant other can be either positive or negative and thus may influence the individual's self-concept accordingly.

For the past 25 years, investigators have examined various factors in the sphere of the significant other influence. Among these studies is the work of

Haller and Woelfel (1972), who concentrated on developing an instrument that would identify significant others and measure their influence, simultaneously examining the influence of the significant other on the educational and occupational aspirations of high school students. They concluded that their findings supported earlier formulations by Mead and Sullivan that stressed the role of the expectation of other persons in determining the goal orientations of the individual, and that "significant other" is a precise and flexible concept currently available "for use in assessing interpersonal influence on orientation variables" (p. 591).

The significant other as a factor in the lives of black people has received attention in both theoretical formulations and empirical research. In suggesting reasons for his finding that black people, despite minority racial status, managed to achieve stability and social status, Billingsley (1968) included reference to the influence of the significant others—from not only the individual's family but also all segments of the wider community, the latter of whom functioned primarily as social supports. Whereas Billingsley's sample for the most part concentrated on blacks from established achieving families, Manns (1974) examined the autobiographies of blacks from low socioeconomic background and found that parents, other relatives, and nonrelatives were identified as significant others and that they influenced the individual in several ways. Other empirical research included the work of Shade (1978), who examined the significant other influence of "disadvantaged Afro-American freshmen" and found that although both family and nonfamily members were identified, the nonfamily significant others were more prevalent. There were questions, nevertheless, that persisted about the influence of the significant other. Accordingly, this chapter will share selected findings from an intensive study that focused on two areas: (1) identification of the type of significant other, and (2) delineation of the manner of the influence of the significant other.

The study participants included 20 black adult respondents, purposively selected according to: education, minimum master's degree in social work; socioeconomic status of the family of origin as determined by a modified version of the Hollingshead-Redlich SES scale; age between 40 and 65; and sex. The influence of the significant other was examined in terms of the respondent's educational and occupational achievement in order to anchor the influence to an observable event. In addition, because the perceived response of others is more important than the actual response (Quarantelli and Cooper, 1966/1972), the perception of the influenced individual was a perspective selected for identifying the significant other.

NUMBER OF SIGNIFICANT OTHERS

The respondents identified a large number of significant others—212, approximately ten per person. A persistent pattern in the data suggested that there is an association between the respondent's societal status, as determined by race and socioeconomic background, and the number of significant others. In a larger comparative study that examined race and socioeconomic status as variables, it was found that there was a tendency for blacks to have more significant others than whites, and also for the lower class to have more than the middle class (Table 18.1). In addition, the low variability of the black middle class indicated group stability that supports the notion that minority racial status accounts for the difference between blacks and whites (Table 18.1). Finally, an accumulative effect was observed in the black lower class, which, confronted with both minority racial status and low socioeconomic status, tended to have more significant others than the black middle class (Table 18.1).

The observed pattern implies that groups which are viewed as low status (blacks and the lower class) by the larger society tend to have more significant others than higher-status groups (whites and the middle class). In order for low-status groups to achieve, they may require more specific significant others than high-status groups.

Black people, as a minority group, experience negative appraisals from the overall society (the "generalized other"). When individuals experience negative appraisals from the "generalized other," the specific significant other may take on special meaning. It is suggested that a sizable number of specific significant others compensate, in part, for the negative aspects of the minority experience. However, in order to achieve, lower-class blacks may require even more significant others than middle-class blacks, because they are confronted with negative life experiences from both minority racial status and low socioeconomic status.

TYPE OF SIGNIFICANT OTHER
AND MODE OF INFLUENCE

An initial grouping of the type of significant other as caretaker or parent, relative and nonrelative was followed up with a more precise specification of both the relative and the nonrelative.

TABLE 18.1   Frequency, Mean and Standard Deviation of the Number of Significant Others by the Race and Socioeconomic Status of the Respondents (N = 20 black, 20 white)

Respondent Groups				
Race	SES	f	M	S.D.
White	middle	84	8.4	5.31
White	lower	93	9.3	6.37
Black	middle	98	9.8	3.32
Black	lower	114	11.4	6.43

As a result of analyzing the manner in which almost 400 significant others influenced, eight modes of influence categories were established: modeling, validation of self, emotional support, achievement socialization, learning elicitation, providing, disconfirmation of self, and negative modeling.

The pattern in which individual significant others used these modes varied. A specific significant other, for instance, may have influenced through validation, or through validation and modeling—in other words, through two or more modes.

CARETAKING SIGNIFICANT OTHER

Of 212 significant others identified by the black respondents, 15 percent were caretakers or parents. This percentage must be considered within the context of the parent pool generally limited to two parents per individual. Actually, parent significant others were prominent among the respondents, especially the middle class. Eighty percent of the middle-class respondents designated both parents as significant others, as opposed to only 50 percent reported by lower class respondents.

The majority of the parents influenced respondents through the mode of achievement socialization (Table 18.2), in which the significant other inculcates an achievement orientation in the individual, either by establishing an achievement atmosphere or by mandating achievement. The former was described by a middle-class male whose parents were both college graduates: "It was just something I grew up with. There was always the idea that I was to go to college and achieve something. I cannot break it down, further. It was just a way of life."

In contrast, a mandate to achieve is a clear and explicit requirement. Directives of this nature sometimes were attributed to the family reputation. A middle-class mother told her son that "you have come from a family who has

TABLE 18.2 Percentage Distributions of Type of Significant Other of Black Respondents by Mode of Influence (N = 20)

Mode of Influence	Type of Significant Other %		
	Parent	Relative	Nonrelative
Modeling	39	52	35
Validation of self	6	13	33
Emotional support	23	17	12
Achievement socialization	71	22	13
Providing	19	17	21
Learning elicitation	6	15	18
Disconfirmation of self	0	7	15
Negative modeling	3	2	7
	N = 31	46	135

achieved . . . and you will be expected to achieve also." Another rationale was attributed to racism in society and can be seen through the statement of a female respondent who was an only child in a middle-class home. The mother had three years of college but added to the family income by taking in sewing. She "always said that 'as a black person, you really have to go to college and get an education in order to get a job.' I grew up with the idea." Although mandates to achieve appeared in both classes, the middle-class parents were more likely to establish an achievement atmosphere, while the lower-class parents were inclined to mandate achievement.

Historically, both middle-class and lower-class black parents have extolled achievement as the means of combating the negative aspects of minority status. The class difference found in the achievement socialization mode, however, is probably a function of the difference between the interpersonal environments. Middle-class parents are able to establish achievement atmospheres (even casual ones) because of the inherent support from the interpersonal environment: parents and other significant persons are more likely to be educated than significant persons in the interpersonal world of the lower class. Therefore, lower-class parents, who may be achievement-oriented but are usually uneducated and lack support from the interpersonal environment, rely to a greater extent on mandating achievement. Irrespective of this class distinction, the parental emphasis on achievement was persistent and relenting.

Almost 40 percent of the parents influenced respondents through the mode of modeling (Table 18.2), in which the significant other projects a quality and/or performs in a manner that inspires the individual to emulate and/or to adopt the said quality and/or performance. A middle-class female described the exemplary life of her father, a physician:

> My father was extremely committed to anything he did; to his family, to the community, and to the institution that he served for many, many years. There was always the expectation that you would go to school, that you would develop a skill and thus prepare to be of service to others.

Accordingly, she selected social work as her life's work.

Parents exerted influence through the other modes of influence, to a lesser extent (Table 18.2). Through emotional support, significant others sustained, supported, and/or nurtured. Interestingly, the parent significant others were described as sustaining and supportive but they were not described as nurturing, a usual caretaking or parental function. (Since the sample consisted of achievers only, it is assumed that a foundation of self had been established in early life and thus it is probable that nurturing on the part of the parents was either "lost in the unconscious" of the respondent or taken for granted (and consequently not designated as significant). The fact, however, that parents were not described as nurturing merits further study.

Through providing, the significant other gives or makes available to the individual a concrete item, a service, and/or an opportunity. Of those using this mode, the lower-class parents were more prevalent than the middle class. A lower-class male offers a clue to the reason for this class difference. He described his father as a significant other because he "worked hard in a dirty job at the steel mill, but he always stuck with us and provided food, clothing, and a roof over our heads. He wanted me not to give up or quit." Lower-class respondents credited their parents for items that the middle-class parents, undoubtedly, also provided their offspring. It is surmised that in the middle-class these items—basic to life—were taken for granted and hence were not designated as significant.

Learning elicitation involves a couple of subcategories, one of which is teaching—the significant other facilitates the acquisition of specific knowledge and skills. Very few of the parents influenced through teaching, although this finding is not supported by Jones (1981), who, in a study on a current group of low-income black mothers, identified a "range of teaching styles as characterizing [their] interaction with their children."

None of the respondents described his or her parents as influencing through disconfirmation of self, a mode in which the significant other manifests disapproval and/or a rejection of the individual. More than likely, already confronted with minority racial status, blacks who also experience a disconfirmation by a parent find the dual stress an intolerable trauma and tend to disappear from the achievement structure. Other findings indicated that this notion may be especially applicable to the black lower class, which faces both minority and low socioeconomic status.

Almost all of the parents exerted influence during the respondents' early childhood and adolescent years, but a majority continued to influence during a large part of the respondents' adult life cycle. (In fact, in the larger study it was found that black parents were more likely than white parents to influence during the respondents' adult years of 18 to 40, at a significant level.) In this group of achievers, black parents remained an important factor in their offsprings' transition to adulthood and during many of the years that followed.

RELATIVE SIGNIFICANT OTHER

Twenty-one percent of the significant others were relatives. As with the percentage of parents designated significant others, this finding must be considered along with the recognition that there is a limit to the number of relatives one can have. Other findings, nonetheless, clarify the extent of relative involvement. Eighty percent of the respondents mentioned at least one relative as a significant other. From another perspective, some of the respondents (30 percent), who did not mention a specific significant other, referred to a number of their relatives as a group influence. Thus, although the majority of the respondents mentioned at least one relative significant other, only a few mentioned a number of them.

The array of relative significant other types that were found is extensive: aunt/uncle, sibling, grandparent, spouse, cousin, great-relative and even the in-law. The sibling, aunt/uncle, and grandparent were more likely to be named a significant other than the latter four types. Thus, although most relatives had the potential for being a significant other, those who were close in blood relationship were more likely to be viewed as a significant other.

The majority of the relative significant others influenced by serving as models (Table 18.2). There were various aspects to the manner of the influence of the modeling, but whether the influence was through a projected quality and/or a performance on the part of the significant other, almost all incidents of modeling (irrespective of the type of the significant other) reflected one major theme; the effort, planning, personal quality and/or lifestyle which culminated in achievement (as measured by education and occupation). This proneness can be observed in the following description of an older brother.

> He was a kind of great guy; I really admired his ability to lead. When I was eleven, I became a tenderfoot because he was the scout master. He managed to pass the civil service exam in 1939 and get a job in the postal service. He could have been a doctor, but it was during the Depression. Still, he did manage two years of junior college. Quite a feat for a poor black then.

There were a few instances of what might be called structural kinds of modeling such as pairing. This occurred when cousins of the same age paired up and formulated mutual achievement goals and/or agreed to follow family expectations, as with two cousins who "went off to college together." The family "expected it because she was my pair." Pairing is characterized by friendly competition, reciprocal modeling, and a prolonged relationship. Also observed was a pairing that was not mutual (one-sided pairing) and, in fact, the significant other was unaware of its existence. Such cousins were not intimately close, and usually the significant other cousin "came from the side of the family that was better off financially." These respondents were often from the lower class and used the opportunity to observe that "it was possible within the family" to achieve and were inspired "to keep up."

The family ghost model was another instance of special modeling. These were family members who had achieved—sometimes a first for the family, or even the race. They related peripherally, if at all, to the respondents. Their deeds were known through family lore passed around to extended family members and down to succeeding generations. "Aunt _____ was important in my life. She always worked into every conversation that Poppa (her father and my grandfather) had gone to _____ College; had not graduated but had just 'gone.' But his children were all so proud." Hearing the story "reinforced my desire to get an education." No one had ever clarified how long "Poppa" had attended the college; it didn't matter, it was enough that he had "gone."

Although relatives influenced the respondents primarily through modeling, to some extent, they also influenced through other modes of influence (Table 18.2).

A wise and persistent grandmother exerted influence through validation of self as she set forth her expectations.

> My grandmother . . . conveyed to me that she had high expectations, and she saw me fulfilling aspirations for the family that other members of the family, like my father, had not been able to achieve. She talked to me about the importance of an education, the importance of staying in school. I was devoted to her.

And through her efforts, family "dreams deferred" were finally realized. This illustration calls attention also to the "grandparent factor" in black life (Manns, 1977) which has been sensitively depicted in autobiographies (for example, Waters, 1978; Angelou, 1969) and fiction (for example, Walker, 1970).

Older siblings sometimes influenced younger brothers and sisters through emotional support; some often really parented. A middle-class male whose father was dead and whose mother took a second teaching job in the evening spoke of his brother.

> My oldest brother was wonderful, just the end of the world for me; he was responsible for getting my sister and me our evening meal. At dinner, and after dinner while doing the dishes, he had a game of whistling. He would whistle songs and my sister and I had to guess the name. He read everything and retained everything; but in those hours together, we read everything, too. I still love to read and cannot go into a store without buying a book.

How nourishing this must have been during crucial growth and development years. And what a beautiful way in which to learn to appreciate a basic achievement tool—the book. The older sibling has been more critical to black family life than has been recognized in either research or literature, and merits study.

The majority of the relative significant others influenced the respondents when they were between the ages of six and seventeen. Some, however, continued their influence during the youth and adult years that followed, although at a decreasing rate. Nevertheless, 22 percent of the relatives influenced respondents when they (the respondents) were in their forties.

Occasionally, a "great significant other factor" manifested itself. These were relatives who were described in superlatives, served as models in several ways (in contrast to the usual one-dimensional modeling of most significant others), and profoundly influenced the lives of the respondents. Thus, the relative significant other, through modeling, represented sources of inspiration for other family members in their quest for achievement.

The black family, for some time, has been described as a vital force in its members' overall efforts to survive and cope, as well as in their efforts toward achievement (Billingsley, 1968; Hill, 1971). Recent studies, whether reporting on the middle-class family (McAdoo, 1977) or perhaps less solvent families (Martin and Martin, 1978), also delineated the support by the black family's kinship network.

The findings in this study generally support the notion of a black family support system, but further clarify specific dynamics of the system. Relative significant others who influenced the achievement of the respondents were not as prevalent as the large, extensive kinship network that has been described as supporting overall survival and coping efforts. (However, in comparison to whites, the black relative significant other was more prevalent, at a significant level.) In addition, it was found that although almost all relative types were identified as being significant others, those closest in blood relationship were more likely to be so designated; and that although relative significant others influenced the respondents through a variety of modes of influence, they tended to influence through modeling.

NONRELATIVE SIGNIFICANT OTHER

More than half (64 percent) of the significant others were nonrelatives, suggesting that, in addition to the parent and the relative, the nonrelative is greatly involved in the achievement of black family members. Furthermore, these nonrelatives were found in almost every segment of the respondents' lives.

The largest group of nonrelatives was the education significant other (47 percent), of which the majority were teachers and professors from grade school through graduate school. Other institutional personnel responsible for different aspects of the educational experience (counselors, administrators, and others) were described, pointing out that the source of the education significant other extended beyond that of the teacher-learner configuration.

The work significant other included administrators, supervisors, and work colleagues from the respondents' job. The appearance of this significant other (18 percent) focuses attention on the role of the work environment in its influence on the individual. It also indicates that the influence occurs during the adult years—a part of the life cycle frequently overlooked in discussions of the significant other—and has implications for adult development theory that is emerging.

Mental health significant others included a playground instructor and a boy scout leader. Characterized as professionals and other helpers who relate to individuals around life coping efforts, these significant others were not prevalent (2 percent) among the respondents.

The religion significant others (8 percent) were ministers for the most part, but included persons outside the church leadership, such as the minister's wife. Half of the respondents also mentioned that black ministers, as a group, influenced their achievement.

Thus, 75 percent of the nonrelatives were from education, work, mental health, and religion—which underscores the importance of the structured institutional environment in the socialization process. Outside the family, such institutional arrangements reflect most of the areas of living. In addition, and particularly germane to black life, is the fact that many of these institutions are white dominated. Thus, their potentiality as a source for significant others is a critical issue.

Close nonkin (11 percent) included peers, family friends, and sweethearts who shared a relationship qualitatively near to that intimacy usually ascribed to caretakers and close relatives. The majority were family friends and were found primarily in the middle class.

Three other types of significant others were categorized: the neighborhood (4 percent), community (4 percent), and the world-at-large (6 percent) significant other. Although only representing 14 percent of all nonrelatives, these types are noteworthy because, along with the significant others from the institutional settings, their presence speaks to the extensiveness of the sources of possible significant others. The neighborhood and one of the subtypes of the world-at-large (the chance encounter) were found only in the lower class, indicating that lower-class respondents "required" significant others from a broader base than the middle class.

Unlike the parent and the relative, the nonrelative significant other did not tend to influence primarily through one mode (Table 18.2). Nonetheless, more than one-third influenced through modeling and/or validation (Table 18.2). Pairing and one-sided pairing, special kinds of modeling described earlier as being characteristic of some cousins, also appeared with a nonrelative—the peer. Pioneering was another instance of modeling in which the significant other penetrated educational and occupational areas previously closed to blacks and "showed that it could be done." After overcoming many obstacles, a lower-class male entered college but worried about job possibilities. One day he heard a black male social worker address a public forum. "He became a role model for job possibilities and opportunities open to blacks. So I switched to social work." A necessary condition for pioneering is a situation in which the significant other—a member of one's own group—can be observed achieving.

The cultural or lofty hero was another instance of modeling and were persons of renown—gracious Marian Anderson of the concert stage and Joe Louis beloved by his people for both his skill and his integrity. The element of pioneering was present also, because the lofty hero was often one of the first blacks to achieve distinction in his or her field and thus opened up a new possibility for other blacks.

There were several nuances of the validation of self mode. The most frequently observed was that of positive defining, in which the significant other articulated a direct positive definition of the respondent. A teacher told a respondent's mother that "'she was very bright and that she should attend college'; it reaffirmed that I was somebody." Along class lines an interesting difference was noted in the manifestations of positive defining. In the middle class there was a tendency for the positive definition, although appreciated, to serve as reinforcement of information already known to the respondent. In the lower class the significant other, in contrast, often offered information that was either unknown and/or not quite believed by the respondent. In the following episode, the respondent's father was dead and the mother, burdened with a large family, worked long, hard hours as a farm laborer. An interested high school teacher "raked me over for considering giving up a scholarship to college. It finally got through to me that I was getting information about myself, and it made me feel important. Maybe, I was worth something."

Another nuance of validation was heritage-reminding, in which the significant other advised the respondent of his or her racial background. One respondent recalled the first time a teacher who happened to be black "taught us black history. It inspired all of us. We really got a sense of what it was like really being black." Although heritage-reminding appeared infrequently as a nuance of validation of self, it was observed as an aspect of other modes. For example, modeling significant others, in demonstrating achievement, sometimes projected a sense of pride in black roots and the need to appreciate it.

More than a third of the nonrelatives influenced through validation of self, indicating that the nonrelative (Table 2) was important in meeting a human need—the need for positive appraisals (Rogers in Maddi, 1968).

It is recalled that the parent exerted influence through the achievement socialization mode either by *establishing* an achievement atmosphere or by *mandating* it. In contrast, the nonrelative influenced through achievement socialization by *stipulating* educational and occupational goals. Such incidents occurred primarily in the lower class, which indicates that they may have required information on the options available to them from others outside the family.

Nonrelatives also influenced through one of the subcategories of learning elicitation: teaching. A respondent recalled her first boss, who "taught me administrative skills and how to handle budgets, committees, and boards." In addition to knowledge and skills, teaching sometimes emphasized the rudiments of everyday living. For example, a significant other articulated thoughts on living in the form of a proverb, such as the one provided by a librarian who employed a respondent as teenager, after school. "'If anything is worth doing, it is worth doing well.' It helped me to incorporate a certain thoroughness in my work." The black elderly was found to use a similar teaching tool the "maxim" in interactions with younger family members (Martin and Martin, 1978).

Most of the family friends (close nonkin) performed supplemental parenting roles—nurturing—through the mode of emotional support. A middle-class female, though loved by her two busy and task-oriented partners, remembered a close family friend who was uneducated but

> who saw me as a child always. She was one of those very good people who always give tender, loving care. She had the capacity to give and the capacity to love. She nurtured me; my mother did not. She gave me something to fall back on; somebody who was always there.

However, the respondent also described her mother as important in her life and as a significant other, but for mandating achievement. This combined input of parent and nonrelative significant other illustrates a kind of partnership in parenting that may characterize some black families.

Numerous nonrelatives, persons outside the family system, influenced the respondents' achievement. Thus, these findings support earlier references to the influence of the nonrelative significant other in the achievement of various groups of black individuals (Billingsley, 1968; Manns, 1974; Shade, 1978). However, the findings additionally indicated that the nonrelative was proportionally more prevalent than the relative and parent, combined, irrespective of class; that although nonrelative significant others were from almost all of the life areas, they were most likely to be from the instructured institutional environment, especially education and to some extent the work arena; and that although they concentrated in influencing through modeling and validation of self, they were more inclined than the parent and the relative to influence in all of the categories of the mode of influence. It is concluded that the nonrelative significant other was an important and necessary presence in the achievement of the respondents.

A profile of the nonrelative significant other was developed. For the most part, the nonrelative significant other tended to be like the respondent on ascribed characteristics, race and sex. Although nonrelative significant others were of both races—black and white—they tended to be black. Since relative and parent significant others were also black, the majority of all significant others who influenced the achievement of the respondents were black. For influence on achievement, members of these black families were dependent primarily, but not exclusively, on their own race.

On achieved characteristics, nonrelative significant others were at a higher educational, income, and community level than the respondents. In a sense, this finding supports an accepted definition of significant other as "someone the individual holds in esteem." Yet is also raises a question. To what extent are potential significant others who influence achievement available to the black lower socioeconomic class, often surrounded by people who are of the *same* or *lower* educational, income, and community levels? This question is particularly relevant to growing attention to the locked-in plight of a special group of the black lower class, the *underclass* (Glasgow, 1980; Wilson, 1980).

Nonrelative significant others were older in age than the respondents. Although nonrelative significant others appeared throughout a large part of the respondents' life cycle, they concentrated during the respondents' childhood, adolescence, and young adulthood, which underscores the importance of the black adult in black life.

This concentration on the influence of the significant other is not intended to negate the role of the black individual's inner resources or self-directiveness, which is also a factor in achievement. Rather, the discussion focused on examining the influence of the many persons who contributed to that achievement and thereby participated in the socialization process of these black families.

REFERENCES

ANGELOU, M. (1969) I Know Why the Caged Bird Sings. New York: Random House.

BILLINGSLEY, A. (1968) Black Families in White America. Englewood Cliffs, NJ: Prentice-Hall.

COOLEY, C. H. (1964) Human Nature and the Social Order. New York: Schocken. (Originally published, 1902)

DENZIN, N. K. (1970) The Research Act. Chicago: AVC.

GLASGOW, D. G. (1980) The Black Underclass. San Francisco: Jossey-Bass.

HALLER, A. O. and J. WOELFEL (1972) "Significant others and their expectations, concepts and instruments to measure interpersonal influence on status aspirations." Rural Sociology 35 (December): 591-621.

HILL, R. B. (1971) The Strengths of Black Families. New York: Emerson Hall.

JONES, R. L. (1981) "The effects of person-environment fit, locus of control and the mother's perception of the teaching behaviors of the significant other on the teaching behaviors of low income Black mothers." Ph.D. dissertation, Case Western University.

KUHN, M. H. (1972) "Major trends in symbolic interaction theory in the past twenty-five years," in J. Manis and B. N. Meltzer (eds.) Symbolic Interaction: A Reader in Social Psychology. Boston: Allyn & Bacon.

McADOO, H. P. (1977) "The impact of extended family variables upon the upward mobility of black families." Final report to Department of Health, Education and Welfare. Washington, DC: Office of Child Development.

MADDI, S. R. (1972) Personality Theories: A Comparative Analysis. Homewood, IL: Dorsey Press.

MANNS, W. (1974) "Significant others in black autobiographies: an exploration." (unpublished)
———— (1977) "Significant others in black autobiographies." Paper presented at conference on

Black Families: A Source of National Strength, sponsored by National Urban League's Project Thrive. Chicago, November.

MARTIN, E. P. and J. M. MARTIN (1978) The Black Extended Family. Chicago: University of Chicago Press.

MEAD, G. H. (1962) Mind, Self and Society, vol. 1 (C. W. Morris, ed.). Chicago: University of Chicago Press. (Originally published, 1934)

QUARANTELLI, E. L. and J. COOPER (1966) "Self-conceptions and others: a further test of Meadian hypotheses." Sociological Quarterly 7 (Summer). Reprinted in J. G. Manis and B. N. Meltzer (eds.) Symbolic Interaction: A Reader in Social Psychology. Boston: Allyn & Bacon, 1972.

SHADE, O. (1978) "Significant other influences on the educational and occupational goals of disadvantaged Afro-American college freshmen." Dissertation Abstracts International, Vol. 38 7200-A.

WALKER, A. (1970) The Third Life of Grange Copeland. New York: Harcourt Brace Jovanovich.

WATERS. E. (1978) His Eye is on the Sparrow: An Autobiography. Westport, CT: Greenwood Press. (Originally published, 1951)

WILSON, W. J. (1980) The Declining Significance of Race. Chicago: University of Chicago Press.

PART V

FAMILY POLICIES AND ADVOCACY
FOR BLACK FAMILIES

Marion Wright Edelman of the Children's Defense Fund begins this section with positive steps that can and should be taken. Whenever one makes lists of all that ails the Black family, the tendency is to become depressed and to feel powerless. Instead, this section gives positive, manageable, but definitive actions that are within the ability of all families. The premises for effective advocacy are presented in a form that could be disseminated to local parent and community groups. The major premise is that nothing will be done for Black families except what they do for themselves. Edelman outlines the ground rules of each institution that must be mastered and then used to advantage, with an effective focus of energy. Family members should not expect rapid change, for they must be prepared to fight a long battle for what they want. The need for unity and focus on real enemies is emphasized.

Joyce Ladner presents a serious problem that affects all races and economic groups and that has caused increasing difficulty for children of Black and poor families. Norms have changed; girls are no longer expected to marry when pregnant and extended family arrangements of informal adoption are too often unavailable to care for these children. American attitudes and sexual behavior have changed and have affected the actions of Blacks. Ladner takes us through all the relevant statistics that reinforce this problem and discusses them in terms of the present structural arrangements of families. The Black family is seen as a barometer for all families in the future.

Robert Hill ends the section with a discussion of cash and noncash benefits that have been given to poor Black families. This is a good ending for this book, because the provision of government aid is the only way that many families will be able to survive and move themselves into a more self-sufficient stance. Although families and communities will need to begin to offer more help to themselves, the basic necessities of life must first be provided. This chapter is an invaluable one, for it gives the history and the census data on this problem. The Urban League's Black Pulse study is used to illustrate how the help is being translated into the reality of the homes. It reveals that over half of all low-income Black households are *not* on welfare in any form. Therefore, the provision of jobs, training, and eventual employment is going to be necessary as we move into a society that is composed of service workers on the one hand and high-technology workers on the other.

19

AN ADVOCACY AGENDA FOR BLACK FAMILIES AND CHILDREN

MARIAN WRIGHT EDELMAN

A PORTRAIT OF INEQUALITY

A Black child still lacks a fair chance to live, learn, thrive, and contribute in America.

A Black baby is three times as likely as a white baby to have a mother who dies in childbirth and is twice as likely to be born to a mother who has had no prenatal care at all. A Black infant is twice as likely as a white infant to die during the first year of life. The Black infant mortality rate in 1978 was about the same as the white infant mortality rate in 1950.

Black teenagers die from heart and congenital defects at twice the rate of white teenagers, and Black teenage girls die from heart disease at three times the rate of white teenage girls. There are five times as many newly detected tuberculosis cases among Black as among white children.

Black children are more likely to be sick because they are more likely to be poor. They are twice as likely as white children to have no regular source of health care, are likely to be more seriously ill when they finally do see a doctor,

AUTHOR'S NOTE: Sections reprinted from *Portrait of Inequality: Black and White Children in America* by permission of the Children's Defense Fund, 122 C. Street, N.W., Washington, D.C. 20036.

and are five times as likely to have to rely on hospital emergency rooms or outpatient clinics.

A Black baby today has nearly one chance in two of being born into poverty and faces a losing struggle to escape poverty throughout childhood. A Black child is more than two and one-half times as likely as a white child to live in dilapidated housing and is twice as likely to be on welfare. A Black child's mother is more likely to go out to work sooner, to work longer hours, and to make less money than a white child's mother. As a result, young Black children are far more dependent on full-time day care arrangements than are white children.

A Black child's father is 70 percent more likely than a white child's father to be unemployed, and when Black fathers find work, they bring home $70 a week less than white fathers. When both parents work, they earn only half what a white father earns.

A Black child is twice as likely as a white child to live with neither parent, three times as likely to be born to a teenage mother, seven times as likely to have parents who separate, and three times as likely to see his or her father die.

A Black child is three times as likely as a white child to live in a single-parent home. A Black preschool child is three times as likely to depend solely on a mother's earnings. Because the Black woman still faces discrimination as a Black and as a woman, she is the lowest paid among workers and the family she heads alone is the poorest in the nation.

A Black child is twice as likely as a white child to grow up in a family whose head did not finish high school and is four times less likely than a white child to grow up in a family whose head graduated from college.

In school, a Black child faces one chance in three of being in a racially isolated school and is twice as likely as a white child to be suspended, expelled, or given corporal punishment. A Black child is twice as likely as a white child to drop out of school, almost twice as likely to be behind grade level, three times as likely to be labeled educable mentally retarded, but only half as likely to be labeled gifted. The longer a Black child is in school, the farther behind he or she falls.

A Black youth is three times as likely as a white youth to be unemployed. A Black student who graduates from high school has a greater chance of being unemployed than a white student who dropped out of elementary school. A Black college graduate faces about the same odds of unemployment as a white high school dropout.

Between the ages of 11 and 17, a Black teenager has a better than one in ten chance of getting into trouble, is seven times as likely as a white youth to be arrested for violent crimes, and is twice as likely to be arrested for serious property crimes. A Black male teenager is five times as likely as a white male teenager to be a victim of homicide and is twice as likely to be detained in a juvenile or adult correctional facility—the conclusion of a winding, uphill struggle to beat the odds against success.

ELEVEN PREMISES FOR EFFECTIVE ADVOCACY

Become an active and effective advocate for Black and poor children. We all must take a stronger, more systematic, and more programmatic interest in alleviating the problems that affect Black children. No one has a greater stake than we do in whether our children read, write, think, survive, and grow up healthy. If the widespread nutrition, health, child care, education, and employment needs described are to be met, Black parents and leaders must constantly raise them in public, organize to challenge them, and vote for leaders who will do something about them.[1]

Become well informed about the needs of Black children and families in your area and nationally. We will not help Black children if we are uninformed. We must argue with facts as well as with emotion. We must teach as well as preach. Homework is a key to effective change. We must take the time to define specifically the problems facing children in our communities. We must then analyze and seek a range of appropriate remedies within our own families and institutions and through appropriate policy changes in other institutions. Those who care about Black children and families should hold study groups in churches and in women's, civic, and social clubs; invite speakers knowledgeable about and active on behalf of children; and find out how to achieve specific positive policies for children.[2]

Don't give or accept excuses for doing nothing. Too many of us hide behind excuses:

> "Whatever I do won't make a difference anyway."
>
> "I've already done my bit or paid my dues. Now I'm going to get mine."
>
> "It'll just get me and my child into trouble."

These and other do-nothing excuses are an abnegation of personal responsibility for one another and for our children. We are not out of the woods because some of us have two cars, a big mortgage, and several charge accounts. Any Black person who thinks this way is courting danger and jeopardizing our children's future.

The Black community today stands poised between progress and regression. We should heed Frederick Douglass's warning about how fragile change is:

> I know that from the acorn evolves the oak, but I know also that the commonest accident may destroy its potential character and defeat its natural destiny. One wave brings its treasure from the briny deep, but another sweeps it back to its

primal depths. The saying that revolutions never go back must be taken with limitations [1972: 284].

The hard-earned progress of the 1950s and 1960s is not a keepsake that can be taken for granted. Indeed, it is threatened daily. There is a growing resistance to affirmative action, programs targeted for the poor, increased government spending, and strong federal regulations. There is a defense budget that is regarded by many as a tradeoff for children's futures. And there is a national impatience that resents the fact that the effects of centuries of segregation and discrimination did not disappear quietly and cheaply in a decade or two. The revival of Ku Klux Klan activity, increasing clashes between the police and Black communities, and threatened retrenchment of Black political power through restrictive judicial interpretation of the Voting Rights Act of 1965 are all causes for concern.

The Black community must be constantly vigilant lest our rights and our children's futures are undermined by subtle and not-so-subtle means. Today's atmosphere, against the end of the Reconstruction era and the backsliding on equal opportunity during the Nixon and Ford administrations, should be adequate warning.

Understand clearly that nobody is going to give us or our children anything. Frederick Douglass put it bluntly: "Men may not get all they pay for in this world, but they must certainly pay for all they get" (1972: 200). Whatever we achieve for Black children and families will depend more on what we do with our votes and political power than on what those in power do on their own. We must vote strategically and intelligently and, through our example and leadership, encourage Black youths to participate in the political process.[3]

Even as we seek additional resources and laws, we must constantly monitor the enforcement of laws already on the books, help weed out those that do not work, and see how existing money can be used better to reach the children intended to be served. For example, only one-sixth of the children eligible for Medicaid get the Early and Periodic Screening, Diagnosis and Treatment (EPSDT) services to which they are entitled (U.S. Department of Health, Education and Welfare, 1979). These children are disproportionately Black. Tens of thousands more children could receive needed health services *now* if their families knew of the program's availability and if Black organizations demanded better enforcement of that law by states and the federal government.

Recognize that the ground rules for achieving change are different now than they were five or ten years ago. The resource pie is contracting. The burden of proof and the level of competency required of groups seeking social change have increased. We cannot represent the interests of children and families effectively simply by asserting that what we want is morally right. We cannot look at children's or poor people's or civil rights programs and simply ask for more money.

We must gain greater technical proficiency in how bureaucracies work; how programs are administered; how services are delivered; and how budget decisions are made at the federal, state, and local levels. We must be aware of and learn to influence the complicated tradeoffs that are made by those in power. "Whoever controls the budget controls policy and will have a critical impact on jobs and services for Black families in the decade to come" (Children's Defense Fund, 1981).

Focus attention and energies. We should always maintain our vision and work toward longer-range goals for Black children and the Black community. But we must break down our big goals into manageable, practical pieces for action. Too much of our current effort is diluted by our failure to set priorities and stick with them until they are accomplished. Too many possible, incremental gains are overlooked while we focus on long-term agendas we cannot accomplish in the foreseeable future. We must act now to deal with our children's immediate needs for adequate nutrition, education, child care, health care, and family stability. They only grow up once. Another generation should not be sacrificed while we work toward ideal solutions. A child health bill that we can help pass now, for instance, is worth a lot more than a national health insurance program that may or may not pass in the next five years or at all.[4] We must set specific immediate, intermediate, and long-range goals and go systematically, step by step, until we achieve them.

Expend energy on real issues, not symbolic ones. We must not be bought off by appeals to vanity or status. We must avoid a treadmill of endless consultations and meetings that result in little or no action. Consultations, conferences, and commissions are not substitutes for programs and money. We must set substantive goals, think about how to achieve them, and choose the means that get us there.

There is another, more important dimension to this substance versus symbolism issue for the Black community. Nannie Burroughs, a leading Black churchwoman, spoke of the need for Black people to organize "inside" and to teach our children

> the internals and eternals rather than the externals. Be more concerned with putting in than getting on. We have been too bothered about the externals—clothes or money. What we need are mental and spiritual giants who are aflame with a purpose [1972: 522-553].

In the 1980s, we must focus more on what is in our children's heads and hearts and less on what is on their backs and feet. Black people have always brought a special dimension to our nation because of our struggle for freedom and equality. We must not squander it by buying into the materialistic values of the culture and abandoning the commitment to serve others that our past has dictated. We have not come so far to seize so little.

Persist and dig in for a long fight. Recognize that a major agenda for Black children and families is possible and essential—but will not be achieved overnight. There are no miracles on the horizon to make the dream of equal opportunity a reality for Black children. There are no Moseses or Kings in the wings to lead us to light. We must each take the responsibility for lifting ourselves and bringing along others. Everything we have earned as a people—even that which is our own by right—has come out of long struggle. The latest civil rights movement did not start in the 1950s. It started in the 1930s with a small band of brave parents and lawyers plotting to challenge legal segregation. As in past decades, nothing is more likely to bring about change now for our children than determination and persistence.

Use what you have to do what you must. Don't hide behind lack of education or wealth as a reason for inactivity or despair. To do so is to betray a central quality of our history and key to our futures. Our attitude must be like the father on a plantation in Issaquena County, Mississippi, when his child's Head Start center did not appear to have any chance of being refunded: "If there is no way, we'll find a way anyway" (Greenberg, 1969: 1). And they did.

Sojourner Truth, a woman who could neither read nor write, pointed the way for us. She never gave up talking or fighting against slavery and the mistreatment of women, not even against odds far worse than those we and our children face today. Once a heckler told Sojourner that he cared no more for her talk "than for a fleabite." "Maybe not," was her answer, "but the Lord willing, I'll keep you scratching" (Lerner, 1972: 524).

Her retort should be ours today and tomorrow to a nation that keeps turning its back on our children. Although many politicians, voters, schoolteachers, corporations, and unions do not really want to hear or act on the problems of our families and children, Black parents and leaders have got to "make them scratch" all over the nation. Every single person can be a flea and can bite. However poor, however unlearned, everybody can stand up for a child who is mistreated. Enough fleas for children can make even the biggest dogs mighty uncomfortable. If they flick some of us off and others of us keep coming back, we will begin to get our children's needs heard and attended to.

Attack the right enemy. Stand united. We remain our own worst enemies. Some Black people spend more time fighting and picking at each other than at the real opponents of Black children and families. Too many of us are forever looking over our shoulders to see who else is doing something. People who always look over their shoulders are not looking ahead. The facts make plain that there is plenty for all of us to do without stepping on each other's toes. Let us pull together. It is Black children who lose from our ego-tripping and fragmentation. How can we expect other people to place our children's needs higher than their own interests if we ourselves do not? And how can we ask others to invest more time, energy, and service than we do? Our ideas will not work unless we do.

Teach our children our history so that they can gain confidence, self-reliance, and courage. I recall hearing Mary McLeod Bethune, who founded Bethune-Cookman College, talking about the need to arm ourselves with the facts of our past so that we and our children could face the future with clear eyes and sure vision. Yet there are some Black youngsters in our urban schools who have never heard of Martin Luther King, Jr. There are talented Black students in Ivy League universities who complain about how tough it is to get an education. There are Black youths who neither know who Benjamin Mays is nor what he went through to get from the town of Ninety Six, South Carolina, to Bates College, to become the president of Morehouse College (see Mays, 1971). Too many Black students in Black colleges today do not know the debt they owe John Lewis or that Andrew Young earned his way to fame by way of the jailhouse and billyclub. They have not basked in the eloquence of Frederick Douglass, Countee Cullen, or James Weldon Johnson or escaped slavery and death with Harriet Tubman. They do not know the Negro national anthem, "Lift Every Voice and Sing," that many Black adults learned before "The Star Spangled Banner." They have not flared up indignantly against discrimination with Sojourner Truth or laughed with Langston Hughes's "Simple" or raged with Claude McKay (see, for example, Hughes, 1965). They are unaware of the contributions Charles Drew and Ralph Bunche made to world health and peace. Too many of our children are not anchored in the faith of a Bethune, who could envision and start a college on a dump heap and promised down payment of $5.00 that she did not have. They do not sense or share deeply enough the sorrowful despair channeled into song and sermon that allowed our grandparents, fathers, and mothers to keep going when times were so tough. They are missing the pride, confidence, and purpose of a Nanny Burroughs, who boasted about specializing "in the wholly impossible" (Lerner, 1972: 132).

More critically, too many of our middle-class children do not know the dangers of taking anything for granted in America or what remains to be done to achieve justice because we adults are not sufficiently teaching them and leading the way. That is the task before us now if the portrait of inequality drawn here is to develop into a portrait of hope.

The 1980s may look complex and bleak. But not as complex and bleak as what the Tubmans, Truths, Douglasses, Bethunes, DuBoises, Everses, Parkses, and Kings faced when they began to stand up for our children and for the justice to which the Black community is entitled. That is what each of us must do now: Find the ways to help those of our Black—and white and brown and red—children still left behind and to guide the nation away from the moral shame, the ongoing toll of dependency, lost talent, foregone productivity, and unrealized promise that ignoring our children brings.

AN ACTION AGENDA FOR
BLACK CHILDREN AND FAMILIES

This agenda is by no means all-inclusive. It focuses on specific goals to help Black children that are critically important and that can be accomplished immediately or in the near future. It calls not only for new legislation and more resources, but also for better enforcement of laws and more efficient administration of programs already on the books. It calls for improving some programs, like the EPSDT program, that are not working well. It calls for expanding others, like Head Start, that are successful. It also calls for the enforcement of new laws—such as the Adoption Assistance and Child Welfare Act of 1980, which holds promise of getting Black and other children out of costly, long-term, and discontinuous foster and institutional care. In sum, we must analyze what we have, eliminate practices and programs that do not work, build on those that do, and improve or redirect those that could be made to work better.

In looking at specific problems of and programs for children, we do not ignore the overarching importance of adequate jobs and income to Black family stability and to Black children's well-being. We will continue to lend our support to civil rights, labor, and other proponents addressing these important issues.[5] But jobs and income alone are not enough to meet children's needs. We must, in addition, find specific remedies to alleviate the education, health, child welfare, child care, and housing problems daily facing millions of Black children and families. Equally important, we must change the negative attitudes and expectations that so many who teach and come into contact with Black children hold and transmit to them.

No one institution—the family, Black churches, corporations, the government—has all of the power and responsibility to meet all the needs of Black children and families. To blame or place responsibility on government or business alone would be as much a mistake as blaming parents or communities for all the problems their children face in schools, health clinics, and a range of other institutions over which they can exercise little or no control (see, for example, Keniston, 1977; National Academy of Sciences, 1976; U.S. Department of Health and Human Services, 1985). Rather, we call for the primacy of Black parents in making decisions affecting their children. They can and must exercise responsibility for their children. But public and private officials and institutions must be more sensitive to Black children and families.[6] They must ensure that their policies and practices are fairly administered and implemented and help rather than hurt, strengthen rather than undercut, parental roles and children's well-being.

Included in this agenda are two kinds of activities: those that can be undertaken by local organizations (often using existing resources) and those that require changing the policies and practices of other institutions. Both are critically important.

Do not be overwhelmed by all that needs to be done. Take one issue or set of problems that are most pressing in your community or that most concerns your church or organization. Make a plan and begin to learn who can help you. Reach out to friends, neighbors, and local groups for support. Call CDF for assistance.

NOTES

1. For more discussion, see Edelman (1987). For a step-by-step description of how parents and others can become more effective child advocates, see Children's Defense Fund (1979).

2. For sources and pointers to help you do research on the needs of children in your community see Children's Defense Fund (1980). In addition, facts about children's needs and strategies fo addressing them appear in other CDF publications and in our monthly newsletter, *CDF Reports* for information, call our toll-free number: (800) 424-9002.

3. Only 27.7 percent of Black youths aged 18-20 are registered to vote. Black voter participa tion rates for this age group are 30 percent below white voter participation rates. Current efforts by number of Black organizations to register young voters and get them to vote must be continued and strengthened (see U.S. Department of Commerce, 1979).

4. Therefore, one of CDF's top 1980 legislative priorities was passage of the Child Health Assurance Program (CHAP, S. 1204 and H.R. 4962), even as we work toward national health insurance.

5. For discussion of the effects of structural unemployment and inflation on children and families, see Keniston and Carnegie Council on Children (1977). For a series of recommendations pertaining to jobs, inflation, and economic policy, see Joint Center for Political Studies (1980).

6. For information on the current federal government policies, see *A Children's Defense Budget: An Analysis of the President's FY 1988 Budget and Children* (Children's Defense Fund, 1987).

REFERENCES

BURROUGHS, N. H. (1972) "Unload your Uncle Toms," in G. Lerner (ed.) Black Women in White America: A Documentary History. New York: Vintage.

Children's Defense Fund (1979) It's Time to Stand Up for Your Children: A Parent's Guide to Child Advocacy. Washington, DC: Children's Defense Fund.

———— (1980) Where Do You Look? Whom Do You Ask? How Do You Know? Information Resources for Child Advocates. Washington, DC: Children's Defense Fund.

———— (1985) Black and White Children in America: Key Facts. Washington, DC: Children's Defense Fund.

———— (1987) A Children's Defense Budget: An Analysis of the President's FY 1988 Budget and Children. Washington, DC: Children's Defense Fund.

DOUGLASS, F. (1972) "The mission of war" and "If there is no struggle, there is no progress," in The Voice of Black America (P. Foner, ed.). New York: Simon & Schuster.

GREENBERG, P. (1969) The Devil Has Slippery Shoes. Toronto: Macmillan.

HUGHES, L. (1965) Simple's Uncle Sam. New York: Hill and Whang.

Joint Center for Political Studies (1980) The National Black Agenda for the 80's: Richmond Conference Recommendations. Washington, DC: Joint Center for Political Studies.

KENISTON, K. and Carnegie Council on Children (1977) All Our Children: The American Family under Pressure. New York: Harcourt Brace Jovanovich.

LERNER, G. (1972) Black Women in White America: A Documentary History. New York: Vintage.

MAYS, B. E. (1971) Born to Rebel: An Autobiography. New York: Scribners.

National Academy of Sciences (1976) Toward a National Policy for Children and Families. Washington, DC: National Academy of Sciences.

U.S. Department of Commerce, Bureau of the Census (1979) "Voting and registration in the election of November 1978." Current Population Reports, Series P-20, No. 344. Washington, DC: Government Printing Office.

U.S. Department of Health, Education and Welfare (1979) Data on the Medicaid Program: Eligibility/Services/Expenditures. Baltimore, MD: Health Care Financing Administration.

U.S. Department of Health and Human Services (1985) Report of the Secretary's Task Force on Black and Minority Health. Washington, DC: Government Printing Office.

20

THE IMPACT OF TEENAGE PREGNANCY ON THE BLACK FAMILY
Policy Directions

JOYCE A. LADNER

In recent years an enormous amount of attention has been focused on Black teen pregnancy. Over the past year major newspapers, magazines, and television networks have highlighted the subject. Although the problem has only recently been recognized by the media, it has long been researched by scholars. Unfortunately, the singular focus on *Black* teen pregnancy obscures the larger problem—teen pregnancy does not confine itself to the Black community—it transcends racial, economic, geographic, and subcultural boundaries. In recent years, teen pregnancy rates have increased at a faster rate for youngest white teens than for Blacks as a group. However, unlike whites, the special problems posed by Black teen pregnancy emerge from the fact that most girls remain poor, unmarried, and dependent on welfare (60 percent).

Teen pregnancy disproportionately affects poor minority youths. The consequences of long-term poverty have a corrosive effect on many of these youths, some of whom suffer from low self-esteem, and do not envision that they can become successful adults. Many come from single-parent families in which their parents experience great amounts of stress. Lack of opportunity, and lack of training and education will often produce a person with no conceptualization of the future. Babies become fantasized partners expected to provide love and affection. Having children may be the only way of establishing "masculinity" and "femininity," or achieving an adult role (District of Columbia Department of Human Services, 1985). Far too often they become members of the underclass with little opportunity or hope of ever achieving upward mobility.

Teen pregnancy is not a recent occurrence in the Black family. It has existed since slavery, but only in recent years has it become such a serious threat to the stability of the Black family. It was a problem that began in slavery when, in a legal or technical sense, all births occurred outside the boundaries of marriage since slaves could not legally marry. The illegality of marriage did not prevent slaves from placing a high value on the sanctity of marriage, because they found ways to maneuver around these barriers. As a solution, slaves wishing to marry would "jump the broom," a ceremonial tradition undoubtedly imported from Africa. The couple held hands as they jumped over the handle of a broom while in the presence of others (Guttman, 1976). Immediately following emancipation, many slaves living together in common law marriages, or who had become separated during slavery reunited and legally married. This demonstrated their strong affinity for having children in wedlock.

The Black community's norms dictated that if a girl became pregnant she must marry. The so-called shotgun marriage took place and the couple's families and community gave them material assistance to start their family. The community bestowed respectability on persons willing to legitimize their child's birth. However, the Black family has, because of its peculiar history of oppression, always been a fragile family structure in many respects at the same time that it has exhibited tremendous strengths. The cumulative effects of economic, racial, and political hardships over time did little to guarantee that all the children conceived would be born to married parents. Economic hardships have always had a disproportionately greater negative impact on Black male household heads. Under more ideal circumstances, legal marriage may have occurred in far greater numbers, but the long-term effects of Black men being unable to support families caused many children to be born to single mothers and others to eventually grow up in homes where fathers were no longer present. Historically, the single most important factor contributing to unwed parenthood has undoubtedly been the inability of Black males to support a family.

The Black race, like other races in America, has also had its share of out-of-wedlock births resulting from couples being involved in unstable relationships in which at least one partner neither expected nor desired marriage. The white and Black community has usually resolved the problem of teen pregnancy by forced marriage or adoption, leaving relatively few children in out-of-wedlock status. However, a significant part of the Black community has always considered it to be a gross violation of its norms to place the child for legal adoption. The Black community has viewed this as tantamount to "giving the child away to strangers," never to be seen again.

Moreover, it has been only within the past two decades that adoption agencies have made any significant attempts to serve a clientele that reaches beyond the Black middle class. Historically, when Black children became wards of the courts, the parents placed them in foster care and institutions rather than in adoptive homes. The Black community's perceptions of the adoption agency as a white, unsympathetic, almost alien institution was not without foundation. Blacks viewed adoption agencies, therefore, with suspicion, rather than as a viable alternative to solve a family problem (Billingsley and Giovanonni, 1972).

The practices of adoption agencies also alienated many Blacks who saw the practice of paying fees for a service as reminiscent of slavery. Children, they reasoned, should not be bartered and bargained for lest it remind Blacks of one of the darker sides of their history. This attitude still exists among some Blacks.

There is a historical precedent for Blacks informally adopting and caring for the homeless children within their midst. During slavery, countless children were separated from their parents by slave owners mainly concerned with maximizing their profits instead of maintaining intact families. The tradition of informal adoption continued after slavery. Johnson noted that the practice of informal adoption among poor Blacks in the South continued into the early part of the twentieth century (Johnson, 1934). Oftentimes, informally adopted children were granted a special place in their new families, perhaps as a way of compensating for their birth parents' absence. Such children were "pitied" in a manner that evoked tender feelings from others, since a prevailing religious value among these southern rural people regarded orphaned children as "special," and adults felt duty bound to provide for them. Again, Johnson (1934) notes that "'the sentiment' sometimes carried itself to the point of surrounding the child with an importance which many children in normal families lack" (p. 71).

Because these children were informally adopted within the communities into which they were born, they were often reared to know and respect their birth parents. The prevailing attitude was that every individual has a right to know his roots, a practice that has aided the close extended families into which many of the children were adopted. It was regarded as shameful for parents to give a child to a complete stranger. According to Lewis, regardless of how difficult the family conditions were, one was expected to "stick to your own, take care of your own, and never turn them away"

(Lewis, 1965). Rarely did Black families banish their children from their homes for some transgression.

Not all Black children were informally adopted or taken care of by extended families, or wider communities. Some became wards of the court that entrusted them to the care of public welfare agencies, while others took care of themselves at early ages. The Black community used its scarce resources to care for its own past the mid-twentieth century. But as the economy took a downward turn, the Black unemployment rate increased and families found themselves faced with a severe shortage of resources to share. The scarcity of resources to share and urbanization proved to be instrumental in fracturing formerly close-knit communities.

Urbanization proved to be a factor in rupturing extended families as well (Martin and Martin, 1978). The Black family has always relied heavily on the extended family to meet its obligations, particularly in child rearing. When Black families migrate to an urban area, they find themselves faced with two major problems—unemployment and inadequate housing for multigenerational households. Thus, urbanization removes an important source of support for maintaining a cohesive family.

There were an estimated 1.1 million pregnancies to teens in 1983 resulting in about 500,000 births. Blacks accounted for 142,105 or 24.2 percent of all teen births with 27.7 percent being a repeat birth. Between 1978 and 1983 the rate of Black teen pregnancy declined slightly (5 percent), while the rate of white teen pregnancy increased slightly (2 percent) (Moore, 1985). Today a majority of births to teens of all races are out of wedlock. Moreover, the overall rate of out-of-wedlock births to teens has dramatically increased over the past 20 years, from 15 percent in 1960 to 30 percent in 1970 to 51 percent in 1982.

Black teen pregnancy poses difficult problems because of its magnitude and because it occurs most frequently among teens least able to provide for the child because of a crippling economic situation. Furthermore, almost all of them (90-94 percent) keep the child rather than place it for adoption (Alan Guttmacher Institute, 1981). This often sets them on the path of long-term poverty and the assumption of adult responsibilities long before they can handle them.

Over the past two decades vast changes have occurred in Americans' sexual attitudes and practices. Blacks have been deeply influenced by this shift in the wider society's different world view. Both Black and white teens experience the residual effects of a sexual revolution that brought about a decline in the double standard of sexual conduct, an increase in premarital sexual activity, a lessening of the stigma of having an out-of-wedlock birth, the legalization of abortion, and the widespread availability of contraceptives. In fact, the availability of contraceptives and abortions made it possible for American females to separate sexual relations from procreation.

By the early 1970s an estimated five million teen females and seven million teen males were sexually active. Yet of this figure, only about 8.5 percent were married. The number of sexually active teenagers increased by two-thirds during the 1970s (Alan Guttmacher Institute, 1981). However, the proportion of teen females having premarital sex seems to have leveled off. In 1982, 30 percent of females aged 15-17 and 57 percent of females aged 18-19 reported they had had sex (Moore, 1985).

Unprotected intercourse often results in early pregnancy. Adolescents seeking information on contraception do so on an average of approximately 14 months *after* their initial sexual experience (Alan Guttmacher Institute, 1981). However, half of all first pregnancies occur to young women who have first had intercourse within the previous six months (Moore, 1985). Younger teens, though, prove to be especially ineffective avoiding conception. A major reason is that teenagers often do not have the maturity to adhere to the routine practices of contraception now on the market. All present forms of contraceptives require a degree of planning and consistency in performance that teenagers, as a group, do not practice as well as do adults.

Among teens younger than 15 at first intercourse, only 3 in 10 used contraception, compared to 5 in 10 at ages 15-17 and 6 in 10 at ages 18 or older (Moore, 1985). Of today's teens, sources indicate that 4 out of 10 who are 14 years old and younger will become pregnant, 2 out of 10 will give birth, and 3 out of 20 will have an abortion (Alan Guttmacher Institute, 1981).

There are many problems associated with teen pregnancy. These include high rates of infant mortality, underweight infants, restriction of educational and employment opportunities, welfare dependency, low achievement among the children born to teens, and a high divorce rate. One in six Black mothers under age 15 deliver underweight infant boys. In the 15 to 19 age group, young Black women have a 25 percent higher chance of giving birth to an underweight infant than do Black women in their twenties (Children's Defense Fund, 1985).

Overall, 1 in 8 Black newborns is underweight, compared to 1 in 18 white newborns. Babies born to teenage mothers are more likely to be underweight than those born to 20-29-year-old mothers (Children's Defense Fund, 1985). Infant mortality rates have declined since 1940 for the nation as a whole. However, Black rates have remained about twice those of whites. The infant mortality rate for Blacks remains about the same as it was for whites 20 years ago (Children's Defense Fund, 1985).

Black infants are twice as likely as white infants to be born to mothers who received late prenatal care or delivered their babies without ever having had a prenatal examination. Almost 1 Black baby out of 10 is born to a mother who received minimal or no care. Among Black teenage mothers under age 15, the proportion increases to 2 in 10 (Children's Defense Fund, 1985). Teen mothers are more likely to give birth to a premature and low-birth-weight baby (less than 5.5 pounds). Low birth weight is a major cause of infant mortality, as well as a host of serious childhood illnesses, birth injuries, and neurological defects, including mental retardation (Alan Guttmacher Institute, 1981). The average medical care in neonatal units for a low-birth-weight baby costs between $10,000 and $15,000, whereas the average complete prenatal care package costs $600 (Pittman, 1986).

The severe restriction of educational and job opportunities are especially characteristic of teen parents. Blacks must also suffer the consequences of racial discrimination as well. Their parents often live in poverty and thus cannot provide the necessary support for them to remain in school.

Becoming a teen parent most often means that the young mother will fail to complete her education. A study based on a national sample found that mothers who had given birth before they reached 18 were half as likely to have graduated from high school as those who postponed childbearing until after they turned 20 (Card and Wise, 1978). This study also found that adolescent males who became fathers before age 18 were two-fifths less likely to have graduated from high school than those who waited.

Women who had their first baby as teenagers can expect to have lower status jobs, accumulate less work experience, receive lower hourly wages, and earn less per year (Moore and Burt, 1982). Most teen parents regard welfare as a short-term stop-gap method to provide for themselves and their children. However, their inability to complete high school, find an adequate job, and find child care encourage long-term welfare dependency. The estimate of 1985 public costs attributed to teenage childbearing was $16.65 billion including AFDC, food stamps, and Medicaid (Burt, 1986).

Like their parents, children of teen parents usually suffer educational and cognitive deficits. They tend to have lower IQ and achievement scores than the children of older parents. They also tend to repeat at least one grade in school (Baldwin and Cain, 1980).

These children are also more vulnerable to abuse and neglect, and to eventually being placed in foster care because of the inability of their parents to provide adequate care. Stress and frustration caused by an inadequate education, an inability to obtain a job, and being placed in adult roles before achieving the necessary maturity cause mounting frustration that can lead to abuse.

The once-preferred tradition of marrying to legitimate a child's birth no longer exists for whites or Blacks. Social norms and mores no longer function to require that a couple marry if a child has been conceived. An additional factor is the inability of the teen father to provide for a family. Many teen girls' welfare dependency, though not an ideal option, is preferable to marrying an unemployed male whose prospects for long-term economic stability remain bleak. Finally, there are few if any negative sanctions exercised against those who choose not to marry.

Since about 1970, more than two-thirds of the first-born children of teen mothers have been conceived outside of marriage. Over a 20-year period, since the late 1950s, the marriage rate for young Black women dropped 71.1 percent for 15- to 17-year-olds and 61.6 percent for 18- and 19-year-olds. White rates have decreased about one-third (Children's Defense Fund, 1985). Among women aged 19, the proportion of singles rose from 60 percent in 1960 to 69 percent in 1970 to 83 percent in 1983 (Moore, 1985).

In no area can the consequences for becoming a teen parent glare more dramatically than in the newly emergent phenomenon of intergenerational teen pregnancy. An alarming number of teen parents had been born to teen mothers. This has led to a growing population of young grandmothers as early as their mid-twenties and popularly referred to by social welfare experts as YGMs. This occurrence poses serious problems for already-fragile families in which the mother is often still in her childbearing years; she may be employed and she usually is deeply saddened and disappointed that her daughter (or son) has repeated a pattern that interrupts adolescent development and contributes to poverty and an inability to develop fully (Ladner and Gordine, 1984).

From the foregoing, it can be inferred that teen pregnancy has an adverse effect not only on the teen parents and child(ren) but also threatens the fragile stability of low-income Black families. Such families are already more vulnerable to the consequence of poverty, and a teen pregnancy places added strains that are manifest economically, socially, and educationally.

Controversy exists over whether the high rate of teen pregnancy and single parent households are a *cause* or a *consequence* of a so-called new Black family structure.

This new Black family structure was cast within the public policy framework by the Reagan Administration. Members of the Reagan Administration became embroiled in the "fairness issue" when they tried to justify domestic spending cuts. They argued that the plight of poor female-headed families derives from family structure and may be beyond the scope of government intervention. The Reagan Administration attributes poverty to family composition, and not to social structural factors such as income and education. Their position is that despite the economic gains they assume Blacks have made relative to whites, substantial cultural differences exist between Blacks and whites that manifest themselves within the family structures. Hence, the alarming increase in female-headed households and teen pregnancy emerge as symptoms of a more serious alleged malaise.

The family structure rationale acts as a two-edged sword. On the one hand, it would encourage social and political conservatives, especially in the Reagan Administration, to practice a form of "benign neglect," because it could be argued that this so-called fundamental family structure is resistant to change. Cultural and historical imperatives would make it resistant to social intervention. It provides a rationale for those working in the government and policy arena to steer clear of the problem and, of equal importance, to rationalize why the federal budget cuts in social programs become necessary. Thus they may argue that the funds and programs directed toward the poor in general, and more specifically toward teenage parents, would have little effect on changing the conditions under which they live.

The alternative view is that the government must provide more support than it has in the past. The argument can be made that, contrary to popular opinion, the welfare population is a less permanent, fixed one, and that poor women, given the opportunities in the employment and educational sectors, will become self-sufficient and independent. Unfortunately, the government has not been willing to make the substantive and long-term investment in training, education, and job placement. The notable exception is the Massachusetts state funded employment and training program that has had remarkable results in moving females who head their households off AFDC and into permanent employment.

The conservatives now argue that the changing Black family composition is an indictment of the social engineering of the 1960s' Great Society Program of President Lyndon B. Johnson. The massive intervention of the state into the internal affairs of poor families leads the conservative analysts to blame the state for the present conditions of the Black family structure. They argue that liberal federal programs and policies encourage teenage girls to engage in sexually permissive behavior, have children outside of marriage, and depend on welfare. The conservative columnist and White House staffer Patrick Buchanan wrote, "In interfering with, impeding the process by which children in America become men and women, the welfare state has created a permanent subclass of angry, dependent children-perpetual adolescents who prey upon the society that denied them the chance to grow up" (*New York Post*, July 23, 1983).

The proponents of this position advocate a return to traditional "moral" values, noninterference from government, and an increase in individual self-reliance as methods to curb teen pregnancy and the rise of female-headed families. A need does exist for more emphasis on traditional values, which include teaching teens to exercise restraint in premarital sex. Families and communities should encourage an increase in self-reliance whenever possible. However, the poor have few choices and options to enhance their futures. Only when American society has made an investment to provide greater opportunities for Black youths will it be easier for Black youths to become productive workers rather than teen parents. Very few teens would choose babies, welfare, and a lifetime of poverty at the subsistence level if they had more realistic choices.

A recent study by the National Research Council of the National Academy of Sciences found that despite the high rate of teen pregnancy in the United States, there is no coherent policy to deal with the problem. Noting that early, regular, and effective use of contraceptives results in fewer unintended pregnancies, the panel recommended as remedies, support for school-based clinics, more effective sex education with information on contraceptives and access to abortions for teenagers who want and need them.[1] Although the panel's authoritative study has high merits, it was immediately met with controversy by conservative right-to-life opposition groups. The implementation of these recommendations will be difficult, given the strong opposition that has already been waged.

It is very easy to focus entirely upon the weaknesses in Black families, emphasizing the increase in single-parent families and teenage pregnancy. The American family is undergoing a tremendous period of transition, as it moves away from the norm of the ideal type of nuclear family to a family that increasingly experiences divorce and a range of other social problems. Largely because of displacement in the labor force, the Black family is more severely affected by problems that are confronting a broad cross-section of families throughout the society.

The Black family should serve as a barometer for what lurks in the future for the American family. A proper investment in the Black family today will strengthen the American family and the society at large in the future. Adolescent pregnancy is but one of the many problems facing Black families; however, its prevention is integrally related to the long-term outcome of families. It is critical that public policies and programs be oriented toward prevention of adolescent pregnancy within a family context (Ladner, 1986; Ladner, 1987).

REFERENCES

Alan Guttmacher Institute (1981) Teenage Pregnancy: The Problem that Hasn't Gone Away." New York: Author.
BALDWIN, W. H. and V. S. CAIN (1980) "The children of teenage parents." Family Planning Perspectives 12.

BILLINGSLEY, A. and J. GIOVANONNI (1972) Children of the Storm: Black Children and American Child Welfare. New York: Macmillan.

BURT, M. (1986) Estimates of Public Costs for Teenage Childbearing. Washington, DC: Center for Population Options.

CARD, J. J. and L. L. WISE (1978) "Teenage mothers and teenage fathers: the impact of early childbearing on the parents' personal and professional lives." Family Planning Perspectives 10: 199-205.

Children's Defense Fund (1985) Black and White Children: Key Facts. Washington, DC: Author.

District of Columbia Department of Human Services (1985) Preventing Childen from Having Children. Washington, DC: Author.

HAYES, C. D. [Ed.] (1987) Risking the Future: Adolescent Sexuality, Pregnancy and Child Bearing. (National Research Council) Washington, DC: National Academy Press.

GUTTMAN, H. (1976) The Black Family in Slavery and Freedom. New York: Vintage.

JOHNSON, C. S. (1934) Shadow of the Plantation. Chicago: University of Chicago Press.

LADNER, J. A. (1986) "Black women face the 21st century: major issues and problems. Black Scholar (September-October): 12-18.

———— (1987) "Black teenage pregnancy: a challenge for educators." Journal of Negro Education 56(1): 53-63.

LADNER, J. A. and R. N. GORDINE (1984) Intergenerational Teenage Motherhood: Some Preliminary Findings, Vol. 1. Beverly Hills, CA: Sage.

LEWIS, H. (1965) Agenda Paper No. V: The Family—Resources for Change. Washington, DC: Government Printing Office.

MARTIN, E. and J. MARTIN (1978) The Black Extended Family. Chicago: University of Chicago Press.

MOORE, K. (1985) Fact Sheet (on Teenage Pregnancy). Washington, DC: Child Trends.

MOORE, K. A. and M. R. BURT (1982) Private Crisis, Public Cost—Political Perspectives on Teenage Childbearing. Washington, DC: Urban Institute.

PITTMAN, K. (1986) Model Programs Preventing Adolescent Pregnancy and Building Youth Self-Sufficiency. Washington, DC: Children's Defense Fund.

21

CASH AND NONCASH BENEFITS
AMONG POOR BLACK FAMILIES

ROBERT B. HILL

Millions of Americans experienced extreme social and economic hardships during the Great Depression of the 1930s because of the lack of adequate economic supports to "cushion" its impact. In order to prevent such widespread suffering in the future, a broad range of programs were instituted to provide individuals with some social and economic security against unemployment, poverty, old age, or physical disability. Thus, the Social Security Act of 1935 was passed and has continued to serve as the cornerstone of social welfare policies and programs in this nation for over half a century.

Two kinds of income support programs were established by this legislation—public assistance and social insurance. Public assistance (or "welfare") programs were designed to aid the poor and needy, while social insurance programs were designed to provide benefits to individuals, regardless of economic need, based partly on their own financial contributions to the system. Thus programs for the poor, such as Aid to Families with Dependent Children (AFDC) and Old Age Assistance (OAA) were instituted at the same time as key social insurance programs, such as Social Security and Unemployment Compensation. The public assistance programs expanded sharply during the "War on Poverty" era of the 1960s, resulting in a greater mix of *in-kind* (Medicaid, food stamps, day care) and *direct cash* benefits. At the same time, with Americans living longer and longer, social insurance income transfer programs also expanded.

Between 1960 and 1983, social welfare expenditures went from $52 billion to $642 billion. Payments from public assistance programs for the poor rose from $4 billion to $86 billion, while payments for social insurance programs spiraled from $19 billion to $331 billion from 1960 to 1983. By 1983, expenditures for all types of income transfer programs comprised about one-fifth of the U.S. Gross National Product (GNP) (U.S. Social Security Administration, 1985).

Because of the wide range of economic support programs, many observers began to claim that poverty had been virtually "abolished" in the U.S., since anyone who was hungry, sick, or jobless could "easily" avail him- or herself of the benefits of some program to reduce the hardship. However, although these observers "felt" that poverty had been abolished, the official government figures on poverty continued to reveal that the poor were still very much with us. According to the Census Bureau's figures, the proportion of all persons who were poor in the U.S. remained virtually unchanged (at about 12 percent) between 1968 and 1975. Moreover, these figures also revealed that there were 500,000 *more* poor people in 1975 than there were in 1968 (Anderson, 1980).

Such official poverty figures were especially distressing to proponents of "balanced budgets" and "fiscal austerity," who could not understand how the number of poor people could be increasing at the same time that expenditures for the poor were at record levels. It never occurred to many of them that one reason why there were more poor people in 1975 than in 1968 was because this nation was in the depths of the most devastating recession since the Great Depression of the 1930s. And this recession occurred only about five years after another serious economic downturn (during 1969-71). Consequently, two recessions took place during that interval and resulted in a doubling of the number of unemployed persons between 1968 and 1975. Many of the "poverty has been abolished" proponents find it hard to believe that poverty actually increases when unemployment soars! Furthermore, they fail to take account of the fact that, concurrently, double-digit inflation of the 1970s outstripped the rate of increase in governmental expenditures for the poor. Many recent analyses have revealed that the "real" benefits to the poor (in constant dollars) are less today than they were a decade ago (Center on Budget and Policy Priorities, 1985).

But to such proponents, the real villain is not recession or inflation, but the inaccurate statistics of the U.S. Census Bureau. They argue, correctly, that the official poverty statistics are based primarily on *cash* income (from earnings, social security, welfare, interest, dividends, pensions, rents, and so on) and do not take account of *in-kind* benefits to the poor (such as Medicaid, food stamps, free school lunches, day care, public housing). But they argue, incorrectly, that since these in-kind benefits are "universally" available to the poor, when they are "cashed out" in dollar value, the "real" incomes of the poor take most of them far above the official poverty level.

The U.S. Census Bureau has experimented with alternative estimates of poverty rates based on three methods of placing a cash value on various in-kind benefits for the poor—without raising the official poverty threshold. Depending on the valuation method used—market value, recipient value, or poverty budget share—the rate of poverty in the U.S. was reduced from its official level of 14.4 percent in 1984, to between 9.7 percent and 13.9 percent. However, no experiments have yet been conducted to "cash out" the wide range of in-kind benefits available to the nonpoor—such as employer-paid health insurance, sick leave, paid vacations, maternity leave, free college tuition for children of alumni, free or sharply reduced air or rail travel, perquisites as a result of private club memberships, fraternal associations, as well as noncash assets and liberal tax loopholes and benefits. It is invalid to "cash out" only the in-kind benefits of the poor and attempt to depict the poor relative to the nonpoor in this nation. An accurate description of the economic well-being of the poor relative to the nonpoor requires the "cashing out" of in-kind benefits, noncash assets, and tax payments as well as tax benefits among *both* groups (U.S. General Accounting Office, 1986).

Furthermore, such across-the-board "cashing out" of in-kind benefits for the poor are based on the unproven assumption that most of the poor actually receive most of these benefits. In fact, studies that were based on the "actual" benefits received by the poor, rather than on simulations of "potential" benefits, have found that most of the poor do not in fact receive most of these in-kind benefits. In addition, certain in-kind benefits (such as Medicaid, which is paid to the vendor and not to the poor recipient) are much more difficult to "cash out" than other kinds of in-kind benefits (such as food stamps). Based on the "cashing out" mentality, the sicker the poor get, the richer they become. And, as Mollie Orshansky has often chided, the poor who die in the hospital after an extended period of hospitalization are the "wealthiest" of all! For they have, clearly, benefited the most from their Medicaid entitlements (Orshansky et al., 1978).

Yet the issue of the actual extent of poverty in this nation is not merely a debate among statisticians and economists. Major cutbacks in expenditures to the poor are occurring daily throughout this nation because of the widespread belief that severe economic hardships are not extensive in the United States today because:

(a) Existing economic support programs, such as unemployment insurance, welfare, and food stamps, provide adequate levels of benefits to the poor, jobless, helpless, and infirm; and

(b) These income cushions are easily available to virtually all who are in acute economic distress.

Consequently, many policymakers sincerely believe that (1) most unemployed persons are receiving unemployment compensation, (2) almost all poor families are receiving either AFDC, SSI, or General Assistance (GA), and (3) all AFDC recipients are benefiting from Medicaid and food stamps. They find it difficult to concede the possibility that most of these programs and benefits may not in fact be reaching most of those who need them, especially among blacks and other minorities.

Unfortunately, few studies have been conducted to determine the actual extent to which the minority poor have in fact benefited from the *broad* range of governmental economic support programs. Most studies have usually focused on the participation of minorities in only one income transfer program at a time; they have not systematically assessed the extent to which multiple benefit participation actually occurs among the minority poor and jobless. The primary purpose of this chapter will be to make such an assessment. It is vital that policymakers and social action groups be provided with empirical data in place of speculations concerning the "universality" of income cushions for the poor, especially among minorities.

The NUL Black Pulse Survey will provide the primary data base for this report. The Black Pulse is a nationwide survey of 3,000 black households that was conducted by the National Urban League and its affiliates in the fall and winter of 1979. It was designed to: (a) assess the needs and status of blacks in such areas as employment, housing, child care, education, health, crime, political participation, family patterns, and discrimination, and (b) attempt to determine the extent to which major governmental policies, programs, and services were in fact reaching blacks and meeting their needs. Thus it provides a unique opportunity to determine systematically the extent to which major government economic support programs are indeed "cushions" for blacks who are poor and jobless (Hill, 1981).

IMPACT OF INCOME CUSHIONS ON BLACKS

Because of the sharp increase in the level of spending for both social insurance and public assistance programs over the past decade, many commentators, such as Martin Anderson, are declaring that the "war on poverty has been won" and that "poverty has been virtually eliminated in the U.S.":

The key criteria by which to judge the efficacy of welfare programs are two: the extent of coverage and the adequacy of support.

Coverage of the eligible welfare population is now almost universal—if one is sick, or is hungry, or cannot work, or is blind, or has small children to care for, or is physically disabled, or is old—then there are dozens of welfare programs whose sole purpose is to provide help.

And the level of help is substantial . . . Virtually all people who are eligible qualify for government checks and government-provided services that automatically left them out of the official ranks of poverty . . .

There will be isolated instances where a person in unaware of being eligible, or is unjustly denied aid by a welfare bureaucrat or simply chooses not to accept the social stigma of being on welfare. But these cases are the exceptions. In fact, just the opposite concern—those getting welfare who have no right to it—is the one that seems to be growing [Anderson, 1980].

Several studies of income transfer programs strongly challenge Anderson's assumption about the "universality" of coverage of the eligible poor population. Moreover, we contend that among certain segments of the poor, especially blacks and other minorities, the unjust denials of aid are not "isolated instances" or "exceptions."

Unfortunately, although there appears to be widespread consensus concerning the easy availability of public assistance benefits to minorities, there have been few systematic studies of the actual extent of participation of minorities in the various income transfer programs—both cash and in-kind. Moreover, surprisingly, there have been even fewer studies of the actual extent of multiple benefit participation of the poor—whether black or white. Most observers merely assume that all welfare families *automatically* receive Medicaid, food stamps, free lunches, housing subsidies, and so on without systematically verifying the extent to which this is in fact the case.

Perhaps the most comprehensive attempt to determine the incidence of multiple benefits in income transfer programs on a nationwide basis was undertaken in the early 1970s by the U.S. Congress Joint Economic Committee's Subcommittee on Fiscal Policy under the chairmanship of Martha Griffiths. Based primarily on samples drawn from administrative case records in selected areas across the nation, estimates were derived concerning the extent of program overlap by beneficiaries of cash and in-kind income transfers. Attempts were also made to estimate the value of in-kind benefits to participants (U.S. Congress, Joint Economic Committee, 1974).

This Congressional committee study revealed that sizable proportions of the poor did not receive most of the multiple benefits for which they were "automatically" eligible. For example, although almost all AFDC recipients were supposed to be covered by food stamps or food distribution programs, it estimated that only about two-thirds of them participated in either one of those food programs. Moreover, it estimated that only 50% of AFDC children benefited from free or reduced-price school lunches, while only 13% of AFDC benefited from publicly subsidized housing. Since this analysis did not present its data by race, it was not possible to determine whether or not there were racial differences regarding participation in multiple income transfer programs.

Government agencies tend to conduct special studies and surveys to determine the extent of participation in only the income transfer programs funded by those agencies. For example, the Agriculture Department periodically conducts studies of characteristics of food stamps households; HUD's Annual Housing Survey obtains data on extent of participation in public housing units; HEW conducts a survey every two years on the characteristics of AFDC families; and the Labor Department conducts its own studies of the characteristics of participants in employment and training programs.

Since 1979, however, the U.S. Census Bureau has obtained data annually on the extent of recipiency of selected in-kind benefits by race from special Current Population Survey supplements. Those surveys reveal that about two-fifths of poor households among blacks and whites do not receive benefits from any of the four key in-kind programs for the poor: Medicaid, food stamps, school lunches and subsidized housing (U.S. Bureau of the Census, 1984). And, since 1983, the Survey of Income and Program Participation (SIPP) has significantly enhanced this nation's knowledge of the extent of wealth and asset ownership in the U.S. According to the 1984 SIPP Survey, for example, the median net worth of white households ($39,135) was 12 times greater than that of black households ($3,397) and eight times greater than the net worth of Hispanic households ($4,913) (U.S. Bureau of the Census, 1986).

However, because of the lack of any national data on the extent of participation of blacks in various cash and noncash programs at that time, the National Urban League included questions related to this area in its nationwide survey (Black Pulse) of 3,000 black households conducted during the fall and winter of 1979.

The Black Pulse asked *only* the heads of household (i.e., either a husband or wife or an unmarried adult head) about the extent to which members of that household had received income or other benefits from the following "means-tested" sources over the past year:

(1) public assistance or welfare
(2) Supplemental Security Income (SSI)

    (3) Medicaid
    (4) food stamps
    (5) free school lunches
    (6) public housing
    (7) rent subsidy

Information was also obtained concerning receipt of income or benefits from non-income-based social insurance programs, such as Social Security, Medicare, workmen's compensation, government pensions, and veterans benefits. In order to keep the face-to-face interviews within a manageable length of time, no information was sought concerning the amount of income that households received from these various sources.

In order to determine the extent of multiple participation of blacks in income transfer programs for the poor, an index was developed consisting of the seven income-based benefits listed above. This was scaled from 0-7 and indicated only the *number* of different income benefits received. In later studies, we intend to examine these multiple benefits patterns according to the various types of combinations (for example, welfare and SSI; food stamps, SSI, and welfare; public housing, welfare, free lunches, and Medicaid).

UNEMPLOYMENT INSURANCE

The Black Pulse survey revealed that the overwhelming majority (70%) of unemployed black household heads received no income from unemployment compensation. Only one-tenth (11%) of the unemployed black household heads were currently receiving jobless benefits, while 18% had exhausted their benefits because of their extended periods of unemployment.

But these findings are not too surprising, since it was noted in previous studies that the majority of the unemployed are not eligible for unemployment insurance—since they have not been laid off. Therefore, we examined the extent to which blacks who had been laid off received jobless benefits. Once again, the Black Pulse Survey revealed that even the majority (56%) of laid-off unemployed black household heads had not received any jobless benefits. Only 20% were currently receiving benefits, while one-fourth (24%) had used up their benefits.

Although only a small fraction of the unemployed received unemployment benefits, one should not conclude that they did not receive any income support. In fact, about half (52%) of all the unemployed black household heads were on welfare. Dependence on public assistance was especially significant among the unemployed who had used up their jobless benefits (58%) or who had never had any unemployment benefits (53%). Only one-fourth (26%) of the unemployed who were currently receiving unemployment compensation also received public assistance. Thus, since unemployment insurance is less available to jobless blacks, there is a greater need for them to rely on public assistance to meet their family needs during extended periods of unemployment, especially in times of recession.

PUBLIC ASSISTANCE

Although about half of unemployed blacks receive public assistance, one should not infer that a similar proportion of *all* black households are on welfare. On the contrary, only about one-fourth (24%) of all black households received some public assistance. The Current Population Surveys conducted by the U.S. Census Bureau have also regularly revealed that about one-fourth of all black families are on welfare.

Interestingly, however, over half of all low-income black households are *not* on welfare. The Black Pulse Survey revealed that 56% of all black households with income under $6,000 receive no income from public assistance. Moreover, 60% of all black households with no income from wages also did not receive any income from welfare benefits. Thus, contrary to popular belief, over half of all poor black households receive no income from welfare.

MULTIPLE BENEFITS

Since it is widely believed that welfare families are automatically eligible for virtually all of the other income transfer programs for the poor, we decided to determine the extent to which this was the case among blacks. In the Black Pulse Survey, except for food stamps, a significant majority of black households on welfare did not receive most of the other benefits. For example, although all welfare households are supposed to be eligible for Medicaid, only half (51%) of black welfare families reported that they had Medicaid coverage. Moreover, only one-third (32%) of welfare families were in public housing units and only one-fourth (25%) received rent subsidies. And, only 45% of black welfare households received free school lunch benefits, while 72% of them participated in the food stamp program.

The extent of participation of low-income black households in general in income assistance programs for the poor was lower than that of households on welfare. For example, among black households with income under $6,000: only 51% received food stamps; 39% were covered by Medicaid; 33% were in public housing; one-fourth had rent subsidies (25%) and free school lunches (25%); and only 22% had Supplemental Security Income (SSI). Thus, it is apparent that large segments of the "eligible" poor black population are not in fact receiving most of the so-called universal benefits for the poor.

These findings further underscore the need to distinguish "potential" and "actual" benefits from income transfer programs. Two past studies that made significant contributions in this area were a later study by the Joint Economic Committee, "How Public Welfare Benefits are Distributed in Low-Income Areas," which used actual case records from various administrative agencies of recipients in six poverty areas across the nation and a Rand Corporation 1976 Study, *Multiple Welfare Benefits in New York City*. The Rand study used agency records in New York City to examine the actual multiple benefit participation of 42,250 AFDC recipients. Both studies found that actual participation of low-income groups in various income transfer programs was much lower than revealed by simulation research studies of "potential" participation based on categorical eligibility. In addition, both studies revealed quite a wide range of combinations of benefits received by the poor—depending on their individual circumstances. The findings from these and related studies of actual participation patterns were reinforced by results from the Black Pulse Survey when key means-tested income transfer were combined into an Index of Economic Benefits for the Poor (U.S. Congress, Joint Economic Committee, 1974; Rand Corporation, 1976).

INDEX OF ECONOMIC BENEFITS FOR THE POOR

As we observed previously, an Index of Economic Benefits for the Poor was developed by combining seven income-based public assistance programs—welfare, SSI, Medicaid, public housing, rent subsidy, food stamps, and free school lunches. Although the index was scored from 0-7, none of the 3,000 Black Pulse households received all seven of the benefits. Therefore, the results actually ranged from 0-6.

First of all, contrary to the popular image of most black families being dependent on public assistance programs, the Black Pulse Survey revealed that almost half (45%) of all black households did not receive benefits from any of the seven best-known income support programs for low-income persons. And only 20% benefited from one of the seven low-income programs. In other words, about two-thirds (65%) of all black households participated in only one or none of these seven programs for low-income persons.

However, these results may not be too surprising for those who believe that the majority of black families are already "middle class" and have no need to participate in income support programs for the poor. But, one would expect the overwhelming majority of *low-income* black households to receive most of these governmental benefits for the poor.

On the contrary, the Black Pulse Survey also revealed that the majority of low-income black households are also *not* recipients of most of these "universal" income cushions for the poor. In fact, one-fifth (20%) of all black households with incomes under $6,000 participated in none of the seven income programs for the poor, and another 20% received benefits from only one of the seven programs. Similarly, one-fourth (24%) of the black households with no income from wages also received no benefits from any of the seven programs, while 18% benefited from only one of the seven programs. In short, about two-fifths of all poor black households received benefits from only one or none of the seven most popular and heavily funded income transfer programs for the poor. Clearly, these results suggest that the billions of dollars in expenditures for those programs are not being effectively targeted to the black poor across the nation.

But what about multiple participation among black households that are already receiving at least one of these benefits? Certainly, there should be a high level of multiple use among low-income families that have been reached by one of these programs for the poor.

Results from the Black Pulse Survey do reveal, as might be expected, that recipients of one of these benefit programs are more likely than low-income persons who are not recipients to also participate in other income transfer programs for the poor. But not to the extent that simulation studies of potential benefit participation suggest.

For example, only 7% of the welfare recipients benefit from none of the other six programs. But 19% benefit from only one of the remaining six programs for the poor, while one-third (32%) benefit from only two additional income support programs. In other words, about one-fourth (26%) of all black welfare recipients benefit from either one or none of the other six programs, while 58% benefit from two or less of the six remaining programs. These findings are quite startling since most policymakers (as well as the general public) believe that welfare recipients are "automatically" eligible for Medicaid, food stamps, free school lunches, rent subsidies, and public housing.

But eligibility should not be equated with participation. Although further in-depth analysis will be made of the Black Pulse data in order to be more definitive about the "eligibility" of households based specifically on their household size and other attributes, these preliminary findings strongly suggest that even the majority of black welfare households are not benefiting from most of the major government income programs for the poor.

If the majority of welfare households are not receiving benefits from most of these economic support programs, it is not surprising to note that multiple participation is even lower among recipients of other programs. For example, one-fifth (18%) of SSI recipients receive benefits from only that program, while 27% benefit from only one additional program. Similarly, 16% of Medicaid recipients benefit from none of the remaining six programs, while 19% benefit from only one additional program. One-fourth (23%) of public housing recipients receive no benefits from any of the other six programs, while 19% benefit from only one additional program. Likewise, 47% of free school lunch recipients either get no benefits (29%) from any of the remaining six programs or only one (18%) additional benefit. But while 22% of food stamps recipients benefit from only one of the remaining six programs, 11% receive benefits only from the food stamps program. In short, excluding welfare recipients, between one-third to half of the recipients of other public assistance programs receive only one or no benefits from the remaining six income transfer programs for the poor.

In sum, these preliminary findings from the Black Pulse Survey revealed that:

(1) Only one-fifth of all unemployed blacks who have been laid off their jobs currently receive unemployment benefits.
(2) About two-fifths of all low-income black households received benefits from only one or none of the seven most popular income support programs for the poor.
(3) About one-fourth (26%) of all blacks on welfare benefited from only one or none of the other six income transfer programs for the poor.
(4) Between one-third to half of the non-welfare/public assistance recipients received benefits from only one or none of the other six income support programs.
(5) Two-thirds (65%) of all black households received benefits from only one or none of the seven income support programs for the poor.

CONCLUSIONS

These findings strongly suggest that large segments of the low-income black population in this nation are not being reached by most of the major government income transfer programs for the poor and jobless. Why these "universal" income cushions are not readily available to most low-income blacks has not been revealed by this study. Some of the black poor may be unaware of these programs; some may be aware, but because of pride may refuse to apply for their benefits; some may be unjustly denied benefits for both racial and nonracial reasons; and many may not be "eligible" based on unique regulations of their states. And, most significantly, many of them may have been former recipients in one or more of these programs, but were removed from the rolls as a result of more stringent eligibility criteria resulting from "budget-cutting" and "budget balancing" efforts at the federal, state, and local levels.

Moreover, these results also indicate that it is erroneous to "cash out" all the *potential* benefits to the poor, since they do not receive most of them. And if the benefits they actually received were cashed out, most of them would still probably remain *below* the official poverty level!

Furthermore, these data indicate that the black community was already in a state of economic depression before the onset of the official recession during the first half of 1980. Thus this recession, which was deliberately induced by the government as a primary means of fighting inflation, clearly was borne disproportionately by blacks across this nation. This fact was especially highlighted in an earlier Black Pulse report that revealed that one-fourth of all black heads of households were unemployed during the last quarter of 1979.

Based on these results, we feel that some of the following actions should be taken by major policymakers:

(1) Efforts to ensure full employment for *all* groups in this nation should be mounted as a number one priority.
(2) More effective targeting of economic support programs to the poor and jobless in the black community.
(3) Insensitive and punitive eligibility criteria for economic support employment and income programs should be removed.
(4) Intensive efforts should be made to eliminate or reduce racially discriminatory practices in the administration of economic support programs at the federal, state, county, and city levels.
(5) Surveys of the needs of minority and low-income groups should be conducted periodically in order to systematically determine the extent to which government programs are in fact reaching those most in need of them.

REFERENCES

ANDERSON, M. (1980) "How to think about welfare for the 1980's." Testimony before the U.S. Senate Committee on Finance, Subcommittee on Public Assistance, Washington, DC (Senior Fellow, Hoover Institution, Stanford University).
Center on Budget and Policy Priorities (1985) Smaller Pieces of the Pie. Washington, DC: Government Printing Office.
HILL, R. (1981) Economic Policies and Black Progress. Washington, D.C.: National Urban League Research Department.

ORSHANSKY, M., H. WATTS, B. SCHILLER, and J. KORKEL (1978) "Measuring poverty: a debate," Public Welfare (spring): 46-55.

Rand Corporation (1976) Multiple Welfare Benefits in New York City. New York: Author.

U.S. Bureau of the Census (1984) Characteristics of Households and Persons Receiving Selected Noncash Benefits: 1982. Washington, DC: Government Printing Office.

―――― (1986) Household Wealth and Asset Ownership: 1984. Washington, DC: Government Printing Office.

U.S. Congress, Joint Economic Committee Subcommittee on Fiscal Policy (1974) National Survey of Food Stamp and Food Distribution Program Recipients; A Summary of Findings on Income Sources and Amounts and Incidence of Multiple Benefits. Studies in Public Welfare, Paper No. 17. Washington, DC: Government Printing Office.

U.S. General Accounting Office (1986) Noncash Benefits: Initial Results Show Valuation Methods Differentially Affect the Poor. Washington, DC: Government Printing Office.

U.S. Social Security Administration (1985) Social Security Bulletin, Annual Statistical Supplement, 1984-85. Washington, DC: Government Printing Office.

CONTRIBUTORS

AUDREY B. CHAPMAN, an active family therapist in the Howard University Counseling Center, has been active in running training workshops on male-female relations and support groups. Her B.A. was from Goddard College, her M.A. from the University of Bridgeport, and she is working on her Ph.D. in clinical psychology. She has appeared on several national talk shows and has been widely quoted in major magazines and papers on the recent book, *Mansharing: Dilemma or Choice?*

JUALYNNE DODSON received her Ph.D. from the University of California, Berkeley. She has been on the faculty of the Atlantic University School of Social Work, where she was founder and director of the Research Center. She has served as the Dean of Student Life at the Union Theological Seminary. She has been active in developing training multimedia materials and lecturing on child welfare. She has completed extensive research on the roles of women in historically Black churches. She is married and the mother of a daughter and a son.

MARIAN WRIGHT EDELMAN, President and Founder of the Children's Defense Fund, received her B.A. from Spelman College and her LL.D. from Yale. She directed the Harvard Center for Law and Education and the Legal Defense and Education Fund of the NAACP. She wrote *Portrait of Inequality: Black and White Children in America* and most recently, *Families in Peril: An Agenda for Social Change.* She is Chair of the Spelman College Board and a MacArthur Foundation Prize Fellow. She is married and the mother of three sons.

JOHN HOPE FRANKLIN graduated from Fisk University and received his master's and doctorate in history from Harvard University. He now holds the James B. Duke Chair Emeritus at Duke University. He was John Matthews Manly Distinguished Service Professor and Chair of the Department of History at the University of Chicago. He was on the faculties of Fisk, St. Augustine's, North Carolina at Durham, Howard University, and Brooklyn College. He was the Visiting Professor at Harvard, University of Wisconsin, University of California, and Cambridge University in England. He has just completed 52 years of teaching. He was a Fulbright Professor in Australia, and held both a Rosenwald Fellowship and a Guggenheim Fellowship. He has been President of the American Historical Studies Association, the Southern Historical Association, and the Organization of American Historians, and of Phi Beta Kappa. Among his books are: *From Slavery to Freedom, A History of Negro Americans* (1987, 6th edition, Knopf); *The Free Negro in North Carolina; The Militant South, 1800-1860; Reconstruction After the Civil War; The Emancipation Proclamation; Southern Odyssey*; and *Racial Equality in America.* He is married and has one son.

PAUL C. GLICK served with the U.S. Census Bureau from 1939-1981 and was Senior Demographer for 10 years. He is an Adjunct Professor of Sociology at Arizona State University, where he works closely with graduate students. He received his Ph.D. and M.A. in

Sociology from the University of Wisconsin at Madison and his A.B. from DePauw University. DePauw established an annual award in his name and he presented the first award in 1988. He was the President of the National Council of Family Relations and Population Association of America. He is a coauthor of *Marriage and Divorce* and is renown for his many published works on family demography. He was married for many happy years to Joy, who recently passed, and is the father of Paul, Jr. and David.

GERALD GURIN received his Ph.D. from the University of Michigan in 1958. He is currently a research scientist at the Institute for Social Research and Professor of Higher Education. He has worked and published extensively in the area of group identity and consciousness. He is married and has three children.

ALGEA O. HARRISON received her Ph.D. from the University of Michigan. She is Professor of Psychology at Oakland University in Rochester, Michigan. She was a Visiting Professor at the University of the Virgin Islands in 1986-87. Harrison's research interests center on interrole conflict among Black women and the socialization process among Black families. She is the mother of two children.

JEROLD HEISS received his Ph.D. from Indiana University and is currently Professor of Sociology at the University of Connecticut. His books include *The Case of the Black Family: Sociological Inquiry* and *The Social Psychology of Interaction*. He is the father of two daughters.

ROBERT B. HILL, formerly Research Director, National Urban League, received his B.A. from the City College of the City University of New York and his Ph.D. from Columbia University. He is the author of *Strengths of Black Families* and *Informal Adoption Among Black Families*. He is the father of two children.

JAMES S. JACKSON received his Ph.D. in social psychology from Wayne State University in 1972. He is Professor in the Department of Psychology and Faculty Associate at the Institute for Social Research at the University of Michigan. He is Director of a nationwide, three-generation study on Black families and is an Associate Dean in the Rackham Graduate School at Michigan. He was a Ford Foundation Senior Postdoctoral Fellow in 1986-1987 at Groups D'Etudes En Science Sociales in Paris. He is married and has two daughters.

LEANOR BOULIN JOHNSON received her Ph.D. in Sociology from Purdue University and taught at Florida State and Howard Universities. She was a senior research associate at the Urban Institute in Washington, D.C. and Westat, Inc. in Maryland. She was a 1985-1986 Senior Postdoctoral Ford Foundation Fellow and is currently completing a major work-family stress study, funded by the National Institute of Mental Health. She is a Research Faculty Associate in the Department of Psychology at Arizona State University. Her publications focus on marriage and family and human sexuality. She lives in Scottsdale, Arizona with her husband, mother-in-law, and two sons.

JOYCE A. LADNER is a sociologist and a Professor in the Howard University School of Social Work. She received her Ph.D. from Washington University in St. Louis. She has taught at Southern Illinois University and Hunter College. She has been a senior research fellow at the Institute of the Black World and at the University of Dar-es-Salaam in Tanzania. She is known for her publications in the field of adolescent pregnancy and Black women. She is the author of *Tomorrow's Tomorrow, The Black Woman; The Death of White Sociology* and *Mixed Families: Adopting Across Racial Boundaries.* She is the mother of one son.

JULIANNE MALVEAUX received her Ph.D. in Economics from Massachusetts Institute of Technology. She has been on the Faculty at San Francisco State University and was a visiting research associate at the University of California, Berkeley. She was a research associate at Radcliffe College, where she continued her research on Black women, an area in which she is widely published. She has been active in California politics and recently ran for office in San Francisco.

WILHELMINA MANNS, a Professor in the School of Social Work at Howard University, has taught at Case Western Reserve and Cleveland State University. She received a B.A. from Ohio State University, an M.S.W. from Case Western Reserve University, and her Ph.D. from the University of Chicago in the Human Development program. She maintains an active clinical social work practice and has been active in the development of national test for accredited social workers. She has four grown children and four grandchildren.

HARRIETTE PIPES McADOO is a Professor at Howard University in the School of Social Work and a Visiting Lecturer at the Smith College School for Social Work. She received her B.A. and M.A. from Michigan State University, her Ph.D. from the University of Michigan and has done postdoctoral studies at Harvard University. She is Director of the Groves Conference on Marriage and the Family and was formerly a National Adviser to the White House Conference on Families, a Director of the National Council on Family Relations (NCFR), and a member of the Governing Council of the Society for Research in Child Development. She was the first person honored by NCFR with the Marie Peters Award for Outstanding Scholarship, Leadership, and Service in the Area of Ethnic Minority Families. She has published on racial attitudes and self-esteem in young children, Black mobility patterns, coping strategies of single mothers, and professional Kenyan women. She coedited *Services to Young Families, Program Review and Policy Recommendations* and *Black Children: Social, Educational, and Parental Environments* (Sage Focus Edition) and is a coauthor of *Women and Children, Alone and in Poverty.* She is married to John Lewis McAdoo and is the mother of four children and one grandchild.

JOHN L. McADOO is on the faculty of the University of Maryland School of Social Work and Community Planning. He received his B.A. from Eastern Michigan University and his M.S.W. and Ph.D. from the University of Michigan. He did postdoctoral studies at Harvard University, was a Postdoctoral Fellow in the Johns Hopkins University School of Public Health, and was a summer Fellow at the Institute of Survey Research at the University of Michigan. He has published in the area of parent-child interactions, parenting by Black fathers, and fear of crime among the elderly. He and his wife, Harriette Pipes McAdoo, coedited *Black Children: Social, Educational and Parental Environments.* They have four children and one grandchild.

WAYNE R. McCULLOUGH received his Ph.D. from the University of Michigan in social psychology. He works for IBM, where he has worked in personnel research, management development, and employee relations, and is presently manager of market research. He was an adjunct faculty member at New York University. He is presently conducting research in group identity and consciousness and organizational commitment. He and his wife, Michele, a Michigan University Ph.D. in linguistics, currently live in Florida. They are expecting their first child.

WADE W. NOBLES received his Ph.D. from Stanford University. He has been President of the Urban Institute for Human Services and Director of the Black Family Research Project at Westside Community Mental Health Center and has written widely on the Black family and African-American continuities. He is married and the father of five children.

JOHN U. OGBU, a native of Nigeria, is Professor of Anthropology at the University of California, Berkeley, where he received his Ph.D. in anthropology. He was a research associate with the Carnegie Council on Children and a distinguished Visiting Professor at the University of Delaware. His major publications include *The Next Generation: An Ethnography of Education in an Urban Neighborhood* and *Minority Education and Caste: The American System in Cross-Cultural Perspective.* He has published widely on the cultural contexts of the educational achievement of African-American children. He is married and has four children.

MARIE FERGUSON PETERS was a former member of the faculty of Human Development and Family Relations at the University of Connecticut and P.I. Toddler and Infant Experiences Studies. She received her Ed.D. from Harvard University and her undergraduate degree from Fisk University. She was Secretary of the National Council on Family Relations, Director of Groves Conference on Marriage and the Family, and edited the Black family issue of *Journal of Marriage and the Family* in 1978. She conducted research on socialization, stress, and development of children in Black families, and was honored by the National Council on Family Relations when they named a major award in her honor, the Marie Peters Award. She was named, posthumously, a member of the Academy of the Groves Conference on Marriage and the Family. She had a strong influence on the socialization of Blacks and other ethnic minorities into the professional organizations and existing networks of the family and child development fields. She was married to James Peters, Ph.D. and had three children and three grandchildren. She died on January 8, 1984.

WILLIAM HARRISON PIPES, Professor Emeritus, American Thought and Language, Michigan State University, was the author of *Say Amen, Brother: Is God Dead?* and *Death of an Uncle Tom.* He earned his B.A. at Tuskegee Institute, his M.A. at Atlanta University, and his Ph.D. at the University of Michigan, the first U.S. Black to attain this degree in speech. He was formerly President of Alcorn State University and Dean of Philander Smith College. He was on the faculties of Southern University, Fort Valley State College, and Wayne State University. He was active in directing college theater productions and debate teams. His recordings of rural Georgia old-time Negro preachers, made during World War II, are considered to be some of the few existing remnants of this unique preaching style. They have been archived at the University of California, Berkeley. He married Anna Howard Russell and was the father of three: Harriette Ann, Willetta Ada, and William Howard; and had six grandchildren: Michael, John, Julia, David, Kahmara, and Paul Russell. He died on August 10, 1981.

ROBERT STAPLES, a Professor, has been on the faculty of Howard and Fisk Universities, California State University at Hayward, and Bethune-Cookman College. He received his Ph.D. from the University of Minnesota. He is the author of the *Black Woman in America, Introduction to Black Sociology, The Lower Income Negro Family in St. Paul, The World of Black Singles,* and *The Black Family: Essays and Studies* (3rd edition). He was a Director of the National Council of Family Relations and received their second Marie Peters Award for Outstanding Scholarship, Leadership, and Service in the Area of Ethnic Minority Families.

NIARA SUDARKASA (formerly Gloria A. Marshall) is President of Lincoln University in Pennsylvania. She was formerly the Professor of Anthropology and Director for Afroamerican (which is the way they spelled it) and African Studies at The University of Michigan, where she also served as the Associate Vice President for Academic Affairs. Sudarkasa received her Ph.D. from Columbia University and her B.S. from Fisk University. She has published widely on the migration of Africans around the world and on women, trade, and family organization among the Yoruba of Nigeria and other West African countries. She is married and the mother of one son.

NOTES

NOTES

NOTES

NOTES

NOTES